The Power of
God
Against the
Guns
of Government

The battle of Tomochic as depicted by José Guadalupe Posada.
(Author's collection)

The Power of
God
Against the
Guns
of Government

Religious Upheaval in Mexico at
the Turn of the Nineteenth Century

Paul J. Vanderwood

STANFORD UNIVERSITY PRESS
Stanford, California

Stanford University Press, Stanford, California
© 1998 by the Board of Trustees of the Leland Stanford Junior University
Printed in the United States of America

CIP data appear at the end of the book

For Rosalie and Eric, Carolyn and Glenn,
and other fine friends

Acknowledgments

MY JOURNEY TOWARD this book has taken more than a decade (too long, say some, even good friends), but it has taken me that long not only to gather the data but to ponder it, to decide what it means and how I feel about it. Along the way I have received the encouragement and assistance of so many, from long, probing conversations with concerned colleagues to quick flashes of insight from unexpected sources, like the folk healer casually encountered in a splendidly ornate Catholic church in Oaxaca, Mexico. I do not even know her full name, nor do I know the complete names of many others who generously assisted me along the way. This does not mean that I have forgotten them—though unidentified, their words are in this book, a tribute to their wisdom.

Many other names do come to mind, however, perhaps because of their persistent forcefulness or remarkable generosity (not that the two are necessarily incompatible). Some, such as William Christian, Jr., and Ramón Gutiérrez, guided me out of frustrating cul-de-sacs at especially troublesome junctures. Others, including my longtime compadres Bill Beezley, John Hart, Gil Joseph, Tom Langham, Colin MacLachlan, John Mraz, Jaime Rodríguez, and Anne Staples-Pérez stubbornly nudged me along with genuine cariño. Several who did not even know me—and they are thanked at appropriate places in my footnotes—graciously allowed me to plunder by telephone and mail their expertise on points like Spiritism, the political nature of baptism, the rationality behind mystical practices, and other specifics that befuddle the uninitiated.

Three very knowledgeable caballeros from Chihuahua City bolstered me throughout: Dr. Rubén Osorio, an anesthesiologist and local historian who himself has written a fine book on Tomochic; Ing. Victor Mendoza, an agronomist and also a historian who has done splendid original work on the Apaches; and Lic. Zacarías Márquez Terrazas, professor, historian, Cronista of Chihuahua City, who has published well and widely on the region of our interest. These three men helped me to locate and to plow my way through the local archives that are at the heart of this book. Just as important, they taught me about Chihuahua and what it is to be a Chihuahuense, which is more about spirit than place. Nor do I owe any less gratitude to Roberto Beristáin Rocha and Liborio Villagómez Guzmán, who unlocked the secrets of Mexico's National Archive for me. Without these sources, the story of how a religiously inspired uprising in a small pueblo reverberated through all levels of Mexican government could not be told. I should add that all translations of Spanish-language documents that appear in the text are my own.

For both concrete and intangible contributions, I thank my sorely missed buddy, the late Tom Gillooly, an exemplary mathematics teacher who solved many mysteries of computer calculations for me; and finally, but certainly not least, my loyal research assistant, Glenn L. Syktich, who literally carried the weight of this project in some truly improbable places.

In the concluding stages, William Taylor offered invaluable recommendations on an earlier draft of this book, as did Carolyn Sexton Roy and Charles Roy, Alice Marquis, and Cheryl Martin. Brianda Domecq, who has written lovingly of Teresa Urrea, provided important biographical details on the Santa. The talented Bardy Anderson, who directs the graphics division of Media Technology Services at San Diego State University, prepared the maps included here, and Ellen F. Smith gave the manuscript a careful final editing. My genuine gratitude goes to all the above, but I have always depended for my toughest criticism and greatest encouragement on my two great San Diego friends, Rosalie Schwartz and Eric Van Young, both renowned historians in their own right and wonderful human beings to boot, who somehow found the time in their own clogged schedules to help me through the toughest moments in preparing this book. They, among others, joked (more than half seriously) that this book would never see its last punctuation mark.

Well, here it is, and I thank you all.

P.J.V.

Contents

Illustration section follows page 198

Maps

The Power of
God
Against the
Guns
of Government

1

"The Sons of Satan Are Upon Us!"

ON A CRAGGY MOUNTAIN RIDGE high above the small pueblo of Tomochic, edgy soldiers fidgeted with their rifles, checked and rechecked their cartridges, and pondered the temper of their enemy below. On this morning of December 7, 1891, the men knew little of their mission, only that some villagers had publicly vowed to obey no one but Almighty God, an oath that rejected the usual authorities. In response, the soldiers had been dispatched to restore normalcy, but having been in service for only a few months, they were both unseasoned and anxious. This was their first real duty outside of garrison, a sudden unexpected local crisis.[1]

Such flare-ups were not uncommon in this region of northwestern Mexico, but they normally erupted over political differences, often long-standing and predictable. By contrast, this outburst had religious overtones and required caution, for religious movements can spontaneously arouse multitudes and generate a fervor that knows no bounds. Fueled by an unbridled faith and a strong sense of justice, this sort of enthusiasm sorely frightens officials because it seems to defy reason. With this in mind, the military commander in charge of the expedition ordered two spies, posing as itinerant merchants, to ease themselves down the main road into the pueblo in order to gauge the mood of its inhabitants.[2]

Viewed from the surrounding heights, the pueblo of Tomochic was especially picturesque, nestled in a lovely valley nourished by a good-sized river flowing along the length of its western flank. Rugged, flat-topped mountains bordering the eastern side where the soldiers hovered rose sharply from the pueblo and to the south culminated in several spectacular weather-carved rocky profiles. This terrain of porous volcanic rock is cave country. Centuries of rainfall had etched out an especially large cave in the face of a cliff overlooking the pueblo—the Cerro de la Cueva—quite near an outpost of the military contingent. On the other side of the valley, gentler mountains rippled westward. And in the center of the valley itself a formidable hill—the Cerro Medrano—rose abruptly, dominating the scene and offering spectators (not to speak of military strategists) an unobstructed close-up of the pueblo at its foot— a modest clutch of dwellings, their surrounding farm fields, and the impressive church standing alone at the fringe of the settlement.[3]

A cacophony of vigorously sung hymns and shouted incantations to the Divine resounded from the church and drew the attention of the two spies sent to reconnoiter Tomochic on that chilly morning. Otherwise, to the military observers the village seemed at peace with itself. Drab adobe homes, perhaps three or four dozen of them, of varying dimensions but all squat and solid, one story high, lay scattered in no evident pattern by the main roadway that cut through the valley, east to west. Most of the home builders had taken advantage of the higher ground south of the road and away from the river's flood plain. Water rushing from the nearby mountains had cut a deep arroyo right through the center of the settlement, but the inconvenience that the crevice created for transit was more than compensated for by the water it supplied for daily life. The church had been constructed on the highest ground, really just a rise in the terrain, on the southern edge of the pueblo.[4] In comparison with other churches of the region Tomochic's was an immense structure, distinguished by its massive bell tower and adjoined by a two-room *curato*, the office and quarters for a priest, which doubled as the village hall for public business. But as the military spies soon learned, no parish priest was conducting the ceremonies that drew them to the church.

Leading the mystical rites from a small wooden table set in front of the main altar of the church was a tall, wiry, relatively light-skinned man in his mid-thirties named Cruz Chávez. Some thirty men listened intently to their leader, reciting prayers and other invocations at his urgings. As an assistant called each of their names from a written list, the disciples came forward to face the piercing stare of their minister and receive his benediction. Each knelt down and proffered his rifle to

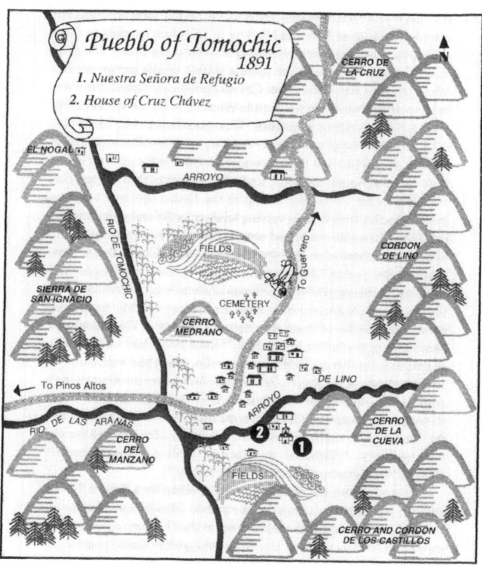

Map 1. The Pueblo of Tomochic, 1891

Chávez, who blessed it with a sign of the cross. Then the weapon was passed to another assistant standing at their leader's right, who pressed brass tacks in the form of a cross into the wooden stock.[5]

Throughout the ceremony, Chávez seemed possessed by a mystical force; the spies later described him as divinely driven. Perhaps it was a role that the leader deliberately fostered, but his followers obviously felt comfortable with and even uplifted by it. (As often happens in these affairs, they may have even pressed such a role upon Cruz.) The spies surely recognized some of the prayers recited by the group—an Ave María and the Pater Noster—but Chávez periodically lapsed into a verbal staccato unfamiliar to the outside listeners; today we would probably describe it as talking in tongues.[6] We cannot be sure why he did this, but such a tactic is not unknown to those trying to mobilize and firm up belief in themselves and their message. Unfathomable utterances can raise the religious stature of the leader in the eyes of the congregation and indicate his closer relationship to the Divine. Because religious people practice their faith at varying levels of belief and with differing intensity, Chávez no doubt had some convincing to do among his followers as he prepared to lead them against the "forces of Satan" now watching the pueblo.[7] He needed to shore up their confidence, and therefore, in that commonplace dictum of divinely insured invincibility that so frequently accompanies these groups into combat, he assured them, "The bodies of those who fight for the law of God cannot be penetrated by the bullets of the devil."[8] Such words had undoubtedly accompanied earlier assemblies of the group, which had been at prayer for several days in the church. At any rate, for Chávez the moment had come. A boy, Agustín Mendías, had advised the group that the soldiers they expected had indeed arrived on the heights above the pueblo, and the congregation readied to leave the sanctuary of the church for the holy battlefield. "¡Vámonos, muchachos! [Let's go, boys]," shouted Chávez, "In the name of the Most Holy Trinity."[9]

The government was not particularly spoiling for a fight at Tomochic. In fact, Silviano González, the public official most directly responsible for overseeing domestic order in the Guerrero district of the state of Chihuahua to which Tomochic belonged, hesitated to act at all. González, *jefe político* (political chief—a powerful regional administrative position common in Mexico at the time), understood that quietly settling troublesome problems presented the opportunity to prove his competence to his superiors, one of the keys to tenure and longevity in the country's political system. But beyond that, Tomochic held fond remembrance for him. The González family at one time lived in the Tomochic valley, and as a child Silviano had played with many of those who were now accused of civil disturbance. Relying on these connections, as well as his political influence, he expected to cajole the disgruntled villagers into submission, predicting that he could get them to lay down their weapons and resubmit to accustomed authority without a struggle.[10] He and former jefes had done as much with previous outbursts of disorder in the municipality.

Under these circumstances, Silviano González determined to handle the problem himself. He was so confident of success that when the commander of the military contingent suggested that his infantry troop be reinforced by a squad or more of dragoons from the state capital, González played down the idea as an unnecessarily provocative show of strength.[11] That stance left the commander with only thirty men from the Eleventh Infantry Battalion for the campaign, ten to fifteen local volunteers spoiling for adventure and a little extra pay, and five Tarahumara Indians from the nearby village of Arisiachic, whose inhabitants had little fellow-feeling for the people of Tomochic.[12] From today's military point of view those numbers did not represent much of an expeditionary force in the face of an uncertain situation, now made even less predictable by the report of the spies who had witnessed the spectacle at the church.

With nightfall only a few hours off, the military geared up for action with the reluctant endorsement of the jefe político, who though he yearned for a settlement, began to fear the worst. The commander, Francisco Castro, had in a decade of service worked his way up through the ranks to captain but possessed only limited experience with this sort of combat. He had earned the majority of his promotions in the early 1880s, fighting the mobile Apaches in anti-guerrilla fashion further north. Now facing a fixed position, he followed the military handbook—two prongs forward, one held in reserve at the command post. He ordered a squad of ten soldiers and the Tarahumara scouts to occupy the Cerro Medrano, that distinctive topographical landmark which so dominated the pueblo. He sent a second squad of ten men to the village cemetery, which lay at the foot of the mountains where the main road entered the pueblo from the east. The stone wall surrounding the cemetery would give good protection. It was four o'clock in the afternoon. Castro waited for developments.[13]

"¡Viva el poder de Dios!" (Long live the power of God!) "¡Muera el mal gobierno!" (Death to bad government!) "¡Viva el poder de la Santísima Virgen y la Santa de Cabora!" (Long live the power of the Most

Saintly Virgin and the Saint of Cabora!)[14] Mexicans shout vivas to tell others what they stand for and who they stand with; it is, in other words, an oath of allegiance. There was no doubt now about these campesinos as they streamed from the church, formed a long skirmish line, and began their advance on the military positions. Captain Castro saw the enemy coming and hurried his command and reserve force to reinforce the contingent in the cemetery. There the battle was joined. In the official investigations that followed, considerable rhetoric muddied the question of who fired first—perhaps a religious zealot or a nervous soldier—but what does it matter? The adversaries exchanged shots, and soon bullets were peppering the cemetery and its surroundings.

Lieutenant Domingo Manzano fell with a light wound in his right arm. A bullet tore through the lips of the troop's bugler just as he sounded a call. One other federal soldier was slain. One of the faithful, his rifle ready for action, advanced against the army's position with the steadfastness of a farmer plowing his field. The soldiers fired at this phantom advancing toward them, but he was in that warrior state where a person can pass through a barrier of bullets and emerge to kill several of the enemy before succumbing to the odds. Puffs of dust right, left, and far beyond their target confirmed the soldiers' panic and lack of practice. Finally, a bullet to the head felled the warrior, Santiago Gallegos, at age 45 the first martyr to his faith.[15] Other Tomochitecos were wounded, including David, the younger brother of Cruz Chávez, shot in one knee. What the faithful lacked in cover from the terrain they partly made up for in firepower. A few fired magazine-loading Winchesters, so they could get off two or three shots for every one delivered by the soldiers from their single-shot Remingtons.[16] Yet the troops remained reasonably secure behind the stone fences. Rather than storm the stronghold, the faithful headed for the Cerro Medrano, trying to gain a topographical advantage over their enemy. As they started deliberately up the Cerro they were surprised by the soldiers and scouts stationed there and so turned westward around the base of the mountain and headed for the canyon at the northern end of the valley, which would carry them deep into the protective folds of the Sierra Madre. The inexperienced soldiers on Cerro Medrano failed to follow up aggressively their advantage. By the time Captain Castro had rallied his troops for a pursuit, the Tomochitecos had disappeared into the mountains. Night was falling, and Castro dared not follow for fear of ambush. He regrouped his forces and with Jefe Político González returned to secure the village.[17]

Mopping Up

Reyes Domínguez, one of the most prominent men of Tomochic, offered his house as command post for the army forces. Although he was the brother-in-law of Cruz Chávez, married to Chávez's sister, Consolación, he had not joined the religious movement. Neither had a number of other villagers, which hinted at some sharp differences of opinion in the community.[18] Visibly shaken by his failure to resolve peacefully the disturbances in Tomochic, Silviano González ordered care for the wounded on both sides. The village had no doctor, but a medical practitioner, Lorenzo Martín del Campo, who accompanied the expedition, was on the scene. At the same time González sent word by courier to the district center at Ciudad Guerrero, a good day's travel away, for Robert Nichol, the only licensed doctor in the municipality. Meanwhile, Captain Castro posted sentries at strategic points around the village and ordered a house-to-house search for any remaining rebels and weapons. Although they hardly welcomed a search of their premises by outsiders, and military ones to boot, most of the villagers submitted to the ordeal without more protest than verbal insult.[19]

When the soldiers reached the house of José Dolores Rodríguez, however, those inside refused to unbar the door, and the army men surmised (perhaps they were told) that families of several rebels cowered inside. After a brief consultation with Captain Castro and Jefe Político González, the lieutenant in charge borrowed an ax from Reyes Domínguez and hacked down the door. As it fell, those inside extinguished all candles, so that the soldiers faced an ominous darkened cavern. Suddenly one of the occupants, later described by the military as a corpulent Indian wielding a machete, hurled himself upon the second lieutenant who stood in the doorway. In self-defense the lieutenant fired his Remington, and a bullet caught the aggressor full in the stomach. "Oh, God!" he cried, dropped his weapon and clutched at his wound, his life ebbing from his gut. Three other men armed with knives and machetes threw themselves on the military patrol, killing two soldiers before they were themselves slain by the bayonets of others in the troop. Inside someone struck a light. Hugging the body of the fallen Tomochiteco who had originally assaulted the lieutenant was a young boy, Francisco Camacho, only twelve years old, himself horribly wounded in the throat by the same bullet that had felled his would-be protector. Resistance had ceased. No other men save those killed in defense of the place were found in the dwelling, only women and children, family members of those who had been driven into the Sierra.[20]

Concerned that the rebels might counterattack the village, later that evening Captain Castro had soldiers use iron bars (such as wagon axles) borrowed from the eagerly cooperative Reyes Domínguez, to poke holes in the adobe walls of the Domínguez dwelling, transforming the command post into a fort. Mexicans call such a place a *cuartel*, or combination military headquarters and ammunition and supply dump. Normally it is the most heavily buttressed point in a fortified position and meant to be the final point of defense. Domínguez also loaned the military a number of wooden barrels to store water in the cuartel in case of siege. When Castro inspected his troop, he found that a good many lacked ammunition—some had not even a single cartridge left. Such deficiency was not uncommon in the Mexican military. Before battles superiors issued each soldier very few cartridges, usually only five or six, in hopes that for fear of running out of ammunition they would fire their weapons with more discipline. But the system rarely worked; frightened soldiers everywhere tend to fire indiscriminately (if they are not hunkered down trying to save their hides), especially when an adversary threatens to overrun their position. This was the case around the cemetery at Tomochic. Now Captain Castro warned his men that with the limited ammunition on hand he could issue only five new cartridges to each soldier. In case of counterattack, he told them to use only four of their bullets. The fifth, he advised, should be reserved for a bayonet attack on the enemy should the situation require it. None of this made the inexperienced soldiers rest any more easily.[21]

Its encampment relatively secure, the military settled into its routine. Captain Castro prepared official reports—they never ceased—for his superiors about the conduct and results of his mission. He handwrote (or had a scribe write) the initial batch in quadruplicate, one each to General José María Rangel, who commanded the military zone;

Colonel José María Avalos, commander of the Eleventh Infantry Battalion; Lieutenant Colonel José María Ramírez, second in command of the Eleventh; and Major José Suray, the battalion's administrative officer.[22] They in turn forwarded those reports to civil authorities such as Jefe Político González and the state governor, who used them to compose their own accounts for the War Ministry and the president of the republic in Mexico City.

Such reports were normally formalistic and self-serving. Freely employing the flowery embellishments of the Spanish language, the signatories assured superiors that nasty disturbances were under control and that it was an honor to have fulfilled their duties. Field officers tended to tell superiors what they wanted to hear and frequently sacrificed truth to invention. For example: Silviano González assured Governor Carrillo that he was tenaciously pursuing the rebels and would soon have them in his power when in fact he was licking his wounds in Tomochic and hoping that the villagers would return on their own. For his part, Carrillo telegraphed President Porfirio Díaz on December 10 that "the matter was purely local, and we consider it ended" when he knew that the enemy had hardly been contained. Finally, one of the president's confidants in the state, Miguel Ahumada, wired Díaz (also on December 10) that a rebellion had erupted the previous day in Tomochic, which made him two days late with the news.[23]

Mendacity and obsequiousness permeated much of the official correspondence of the times, but superiors knew the game. More often than not they politely responded, and then fleshed out their knowledge with myriad communications and scuttlebutt that flooded in from other officials, friends, political sycophants, complainers, favor seekers, and a long list of others who furthered their ambitions with such paperwork. The conflicting perceptions of events developing around them remind us of the numerous and distinct points of view various participants normally bring to the same drama.

As Captain Castro attended to administrative duties, his soldiers arrested seven suspects while searching the pueblo for evidence of sedition. One of them, 60-year-old Julián Rodríguez had suffered a serious chest wound in the combat and lay all the night of December 7 on the battlefield, comforted only by his two grown and married sons, who refused to leave their stricken father for the safety of the Sierra. Another, the Tarahumara Indian Valentín Banda, returned to the village on his own, arguing that the faithful had forced him to join their movement, a common defense for those who may face heavy penalties in the aftermath of violent disturbances.[24] Felipe Acosta, also wounded, staggered back into the pueblo and gave authorities their first big break. He named names: the four Chávez brothers, Jesús and Carlos Medrano, and members of the Ruiz, Mendías, and Rodríguez clans. In all, Acosta identified 30 men as rebels, and stated there were four more whose names he could not remember. No women seem to have been with Chávez in the church just before the outbreak of hostilities; certainly none took part in the assault itself. The government circulated the roster of names over all of northwestern Mexico and even into the lower reaches of the United States. Authorities throughout the area were alerted to the ferocious and unrepentant religious fanatics of Tomochic.[25]

Tidbits, rumors, suspicions, and suppositions drifted into official hands: the Medrano brothers had furnished the weapons; Cruz Chávez had fired the first shot with a pistol; Francisco Ledesma had warned of the approaching soldiers. That alarm had led to the ceremonies at the church—but all along the faithful had been preparing to do battle with the forces of Lucifer, without any thought of parley or conciliation. It was said that Chávez expected to purchase weapons and ammunition in the mining town of Jesús María, higher up in the Sierra. But did he really have the money for such acquisitions? Who, if anyone, backed him? Were miners in the area ready to pitch in with help? Did the government have something more widespread and conspiratorial on its hands? And perhaps most intriguing for our reflection, did Cruz Chávez invite a conflict with the *federales*? Did he want it and welcome it as *his* means to a better world to come—a world still envisioned and promised, however imprecisely, in so many varieties of religiosity?[26]

Preliminary Findings

District Judge Manuel Rubio arrived on December 9 to officially investigate the disorder, in which blood had already been spilled and which was not yet concluded. Like most such authorities he concentrated narrowly on precipitating events and immediate explanation, as if fearful of what he might discover by more penetrating, thoughtful investigation. First, a detail of men exhumed the cadavers of the four men killed in combat. A commission of notables including the doctors on the scene and Tomochic's judicial authority, Jesús María Ortiz, who also had not joined the Chávez movement, identified the remains and confirmed the causes of the deaths. Then the investigation, conducted in the former priest's quarters attached to the church, turned to the episode at the house of José Dolores Rodríguez, now suspected of being (or conveniently labeled as) one of the main promoters of the uprising. The wife of Rodríguez testified that out of stark fear she had not opened the door of her home to the soldiers. She did not know who wanted to enter, and furthermore she knew nothing of the intentions of Cruz Chávez, her husband, or others involved in the affair. (In fact, she did, but she was not talking.) Others, however, shed some additional, if flickering, light on the circumstances leading to the actual confrontation between the faithful and the army. They focused their remarks on Cruz Chávez, his religious inclinations and associates.[27]

Before the explosive events of December 7, Chávez and a coterie of his followers had been seeing the *viejitos* (the little old ones) at a rancho called El Chopeque a good day's mule ride southeast of Tomochic, out of the Sierra proper and down in the more hospitable plains that stretched toward the great mining complex at Cusihuiriachic. The *viejitos*—a humble-looking man named Carmen María López, dressed in tattered, commonplace clothing, and a pregnant woman, María, possibly his wife, who traveled on a mule—had apparently impressed Chávez with their religiosity. He called them *santos* and thought the unassuming couple to be in special communication with the Divine. They could be Joseph and Mary, or perhaps even Christ Himself fulfilling His promise to return in order to reward the righteous and punish the wicked—in short, to set wrongs right. Furthermore, the *santos* had a ringing message to deliver: that the Tomochitecos who followed Chávez would be invulnerable in war, that the bullets of the enemy would not penetrate their bodies, that they would be victorious, that they should pursue their objectives (unspecified) without fear, for the *viejitos* would protect them.[28]

The testimony to authorities did not make clear who motivated whom in the exchange. Did Chávez seek confirmation for an undertaking he had already designed, or did "El Cristo del Chopeque" put those ideas in his head? Such exchanges are rarely clear-cut. If Cruz Chávez judged the Apocalypse to be upon him (and we shall see he believed he had abundant material and spiritual evidence to do so), then the timely presence and assurances of a prophet could only confirm his conviction about the duty to be done.

The witnesses in general agreed that on the evening of November 30 a riotous gathering of Chávez and his supporters took place at the dwelling of Tomochic's leading authority, Presidente Seccional Juan Ignacio Chávez (no relation to Cruz). Shouting resounded in the night: "Long live the Virgin!" "Death to Lucifer!" And then Cruz Chávez proclaimed to the pueblo's presidente: "We do not recognize your [meaning civil government's] authority; we will obey no one but God," or words to that effect. Whatever the precise language, it amounted to the outright rejection of all those in official positions throughout the regime.

Authorities may tolerate all sorts of deviance, even when it is well known to the community at large, until it is publicly proclaimed. Then it becomes a challenge, and the institutional response is all too often repressive. In this case the presidente later claimed to investigators that he warned Chávez of the consequences of his assertions and advised him to desist. Although he produced a signed document in which Cruz Chávez supposedly declared his "absolute independence" from all but God's authority, the text and signature appeared to have been forged, and the presidente's allegations seem more self-serving than plausible. Juan Ignacio Chávez was not a conciliatory man, and he had previously experienced sharp differences with Cruz Chávez. Fearful and vengeful, the presidente probably communicated to Jefe Político González that the pueblo was in rebellion against the government and asked for immediate help to restore order.[29]

The Chase Begins

The governor of Chihuahua, Lauro Carrillo, was anxious to settle the disturbance at Tomochic promptly. He was standing for reelection and already in deep political trouble. This disruption of public order could support the opposition's charges of his overall inadequacy. He was also suspicious that his adversaries, or even outside political radicals, might actually be behind the uprising at Tomochic. Better to quell it quickly and assert publicly that peace reigned in his state of Chihuahua. So Carrillo determined to smother the unwelcome occurrence his own way, that is, to minimize public attention and avoid entanglements with other governmental agencies. Rather than call on the military for additional assistance, or even the state militia, he asked an old friend and political compadre from the Guerrero district, Ramón E. Sáenz, to mount a posse and track down the rebels expeditiously and with no fanfare. The wealthy owner of Rosario, one of the region's largest and most prosperous haciendas (which also happened to border on El Chopeque), Sáenz relished the call. In fact, as he thought back, Sáenz remembered seeing not so long ago an armed band of campesinos leaving El Chopeque and heading toward Tomochic. At the time he had wondered about them and been suspicious of their intentions. Now handsomely dressed in his suede leather outfit and Tarahumara-woven palm leaf sombrero, Sáenz arrived at Tomochic on December 12 with his finely mounted and well-armed troop of 40 horsemen to begin the pursuit.[30]

Captain Castro welcomed his old friend to the campaign, and Reyes Domínguez ordered several of his cattle slaughtered and roasted to celebrate the occasion. They discussed the events unfolding around them. Jefe Político Silviano González had already returned to the municipality's hub at Ciudad Guerrero and through his brother Celso, himself an ex-governor, urged Carrillo to extend mercy to the malcontents at Tomochic, who he argued did not understand the consequences of their actions. Judge Rubio had just about completed his investigation and remanded seven prisoners, three of them wounded, to safekeeping in Guerrero. Meanwhile, military superiors ordered Captain Castro to stay put with his troop in Tomochic while General Rangel ordered 100 cavalrymen from the army's major garrison in the state capital to Guerrero as reinforcements, just in case.[31]

At some point the pair—Sáenz and Castro—must have recognized that they had little idea of the whereabouts of Cruz Chávez and his party. Reyes Domínguez told them that Cruz had sent word that should the army not immediately pull out he would attack the pueblo, but Domínguez probably made up that story so the army troops, which afforded him protection and paid him well for food and lodging, would not leave.[32] Castro said that he had seen some smoke signals to the

west, over toward the mining camp at Tutuaca, and presumed they had
come from elements of the Chávez group, whom he surmised to be
familiar with Apache tactics. Further west, authorities in the neighboring state of Sonora had been alerted to the possible approach of the
band toward their demarcation. They were to keep an especially sharp
eye on a rancho called Cabora in the southern part of the state, where a
"santa" named Teresa had for almost two years now been preaching to
increasing crowds of devoted admirers. During their shoot-out with the
military the faithful had shouted vivas to Teresita and "La Santa de
Cabora," so the government suspected a connection between this
"santa" and Cruz Chávez. But all that was speculation. The truth was
that the government had no idea where their quarry lay, only up there,
somewhere in the Sierra Madre. Still Captain Castro and Sáenz vowed
to find them.[33]

None of those given the responsibility to investigate and quell the
movement granted it much political importance, in keeping with the
usual official treatment of such matters. They insisted that it was unrelated to the current electoral upheaval in the state or to the intentions of
Mexican political radicals who had taken refuge just across the border
with the United States. Judge Rubio blamed the flare-up on religious
fanaticism inflamed by the *viejitos,* while the governor dismissed the
religious enthusiasm at Tomochic as simply a subterfuge to arm a gang
that planned to attack a mule train laden with silver bullion scheduled
to pass through the pueblo. In other words, the Tomochitecos were
little more than scheming bandits, much easier for the governor to
visualize and deal with than religiously inspired rebels. Carrillo assured
the president: "The incident is ended. Nothing remains but the severe
punishment I mean to apply." A wary Díaz responded that he celebrated the end to the matter, but he did not order the troops returned to
their barracks.[34] Much too much remained unresolved about this very
strange affair.

Reconstructing Tomochic

With the benefit of hindsight, detailed and provocative archival documentation, and a century of reflection we may now examine how a

small group of religiously inspired but otherwise quite ordinary farmers from the pueblo of Tomochic embarked upon a death struggle with the Mexican government—and how that story is remembered and has seeped into the public consciousness. In company with so many of today's tragic human sagas, this is the chronicle of a people trying to make sense of a rapidly changing world that both seduces and repels them, forcing them to weigh their time-proven customary ways of life and belief against novel, exceedingly dynamic, and attractive forces labeled "modern."

Many have come to think of modernization as an inexorable, overwhelming historical current, but people from all segments of society have always influenced its content, pace, and direction. Its advocates have labored mightily to mold the new project to their advantage, but the rest of humanity has not just stood passively by and accepted the direction of others. Individuals, clusters, and masses who felt themselves disadvantaged and engulfed by the gathering tide of change have demanded dialogue both on shaping the process and on their share of the benefits. Occasionally a group simply digs in its heels and shouts, "No more!"

The Tomochitecos were just such dissenters, magnificent in their anger, as they weighed Mexico's modernization program called The Reform against the bedrock of their own morality—their sense of what was right for them—and rejected the offer because it did not mesh with their idea of how things ought to be. They gave up on government and its modernizing ways and proclaimed for all to hear: "We will obey no one but God!" At the same time they made plain their intentions to seek the blessings and counsel of a teen-aged girl named Teresa Urrea, revered by thousands of fervent followers as a *santa*, a folk saint, who lived on the Rancho Cabora in the adjoining state of Sonora. Teresa was said to be "muy milagrosa"; God had given her special powers to perform miracles, and the Tomochitecos soon battled ferociously against the "Sons of Lucifer" (the Porfirian army) in her holy name: "Viva La Santa de Cabora!"

The drama unfolding here begins, in Part I, with the Tomochitecos in their pueblo, immersed in their material and spiritual worlds—not that they ever separated the two. Then they are seen in a somewhat larger cosmos as people of the Papigochic region of Chihuahua, active in politics and social life, linked to the economy beyond, who liked to

think of themselves as blue bloods, much to the amusement of outsiders. Finally, the Tomochitecos are considered as Norteños (Northerners), outside the pale of the official Church and the pull of central
government, independent-minded, outspoken, fast with fists and a
gun, honed by centuries of warfare against the Apaches. The initial
response of state and federal authorities to the outburst of troubles at
Tomochic is also examined. In Part II, as Cruz Chávez and his followers cross the Sierra Madre to embrace Santa Teresa, we review the
early life and teachings of this remarkable young woman. With all the
major characters now in place, their setting and context secure, we
return to the main focus of the narrative in Part III—the power of God
against the guns of government—and follow it through to its denouement. The aftermath and remembrance described in Part IV bring the
story up to date.

One hundred years ago, the pious of Tomochic swore, "None but
the justice of God!" Only yesterday, a 24-year-old peasant rebel in
Mexico's southern state of Chiapas avowed, "I seek a decent life—
liberation—just as God says." Indeed, in our own times, if we dare to
look around us, we find almost everywhere the same sort of heightened,
expectant religiosity that permeated the world of those we are about to
visit. It seems to me that the Tomochitecos had determined to stand
their ground in the name of all humanity, then and now.

Part I

The People of the Papigochic

2

A Sundered
Spiritual World

JUST OFF THE NARROW, rock-studded wagon trail that dipped and twisted its way westward through the scrub oaks and pines from Tomochic higher up into the Sierra, Cruz Chávez and his followers paused to ponder their next move. It was December 8, the day after the shoot-out, and they were still in familiar territory, not far from their home village; many of them had prospected for silver and worked as employees in the mines that dotted the area. But now they needed to determine where to go from here—both geographically and spiritually.

Among this wary group were the relatively well-to-do Carlos Medrano (who may well have become involved more for economic reasons than anything else), along with several members of the dirt-poor Rodríguez family, who only recently had been on village charity; the educated Jorge Ortiz as well as the illiterate Calderóns; men who over the years had been local authorities, and others who had never held official positions. All were in their late teens or older, and they tended to cluster in family groups, although here and there a member was missing. Only three or four Tarahumaras were present, quite likely coerced by Cruz to join the cause.[1]

Chávez knew where *he* wanted to seek solace and advice; he invited the group to go with him to visit La Santa de Cabora, the teen-aged girl Teresa, who professed to be in communication with the Virgin Mary. But at this point Chávez only "invited." He must have suspected or known that some were less convinced than others of his own divine inspiration. Moreover, the hesitant allies had legitimate concerns about leaving family and property behind in the hands of outsiders and rivals while they traversed the Sierra to consult with a teen-aged girl who may or may not have been in contact with the Divine. Levels of doubt normally accompany these movements, especially at their onset. Who knows why people join a social movement—the flap of a flag, the beat of a drum, a perceived injustice, even respite from a nagging spouse or rambunctious children? Commitment, perhaps, or opportunity. Machismo, adventure, peer pressure. Some are simply swept into a movement by the moment itself; others, meaning only to test it, become engulfed in its momentum.[2] Once in, it is hard to get out; too many friends and family are also involved. Peer pressure makes strong glue.

It is a gigantic step from speaking out, no matter how vigorously, to picking up a rifle and pointing it at an agent of the law. Most people think twice about such a move, even if for a higher cause. At this point Cruz Chávez was trying to convince his followers to abandon at least part of their customary values and habits of thinking for a very different sort of total commitment. In other words, he sought to inspire his own kind of belief in others. Such change does not occur all at once, nor is it as complete for some as for others. Though his spiritual guidance was without doubt engaging and his rage compelling, material misfortunes surrounding Tomochic and the moral failure of civil authority also were critical factors in launching the pilgrimage to El Chopeque and forging the confrontation with the federales that propelled the faithful toward Cabora and their destiny. How might Chávez himself have developed such steadfast conviction and abiding faith? Let us turn to his heritage, background, and experience for clues.

The Chávez Family

Little is known of the parentage and childhood of Cruz Chávez. He descended from those blue-blooded (at least, that is how they thought of themselves) Spaniards of the Chávez lineage who in the seventeenth century pioneered in New Mexico and during the next century or so spread out along the Rio Grande to places like Isleta, now in Texas, and Janos. As a group they proudly counted themselves *norteños*, tough-minded, aspiring Northerners, honed by their hostile environment and protective of their independence from the institutional pretensions of

Church or State. By the early part of the nineteenth century the Chávez clan had spread through much of Chihuahua, a migration stimulated by Mexico's loss of its northern provinces to the United States after the War of 1846–48. In the wake of that debacle, Mexicans who chose to remain Mexican established entire communities south of the new international boundary, and it is altogether likely that Cruz's grandfather, Vicente Chávez, came about that time into the foothills of the Sierra and on the alluring Papigochic Valley, then as now the centerpiece of the region which encompasses Tomochic. Once there, he married into the well-known Orozco family of San Isidro, near Ciudad Guerrero, and presumably took up farming and ranching, as did many who moved into the area at that time, giving the area its distinctive personality. The fourth of Vicente Chávez's children was Jesús and the fifth and youngest José. It is not clear which of these sons was the Jesús José Chávez Orozco who settled in Tomochic about 1850, when he was in his early twenties. He seems to have brought with him his wife, Clara Beltrán, for the Beltráns are not shown to be among the early settlers of the pueblo itself, although there were Beltráns living in Santo Tomás, a village in the nearby Papigochic.[3]

Personal tragedy quickly struck young Jesús José. His infant son David died in April 1851, and four months later his wife was also dead. Chávez, however, remained in the village and eventually remarried, had children, and by 1854 had become a local public official. At that time—not long after the war with the United States—Mexico was passing through another of its political convulsions. The peripatetic and seemingly indomitable Antonio de Santa Anna had been returned to the presidency for the fifth time in 30 years of political turmoil and not unexpectedly had declared himself to be His Most Serene Highness—meaning absolute personal dictator—in defiant violation of the nation's constitution. During his regime the government appointed *intendants* (a title that later became "presidente") to head up village authority. Antonio Pedregón became intendant of Tomochic in 1854 and Jesús José Chávez his substitute, or vice intendant.[4] Chávez served many of the next thirteen years as Tomochic's presidente. So the family knew firsthand about state and federal law, as well as the region's politics.

By 1864 Chávez was again a widower. His second wife (we do not know her name) had died, quite possibly while giving birth to the couple's fourth son, another David, so named in remembrance of his de-

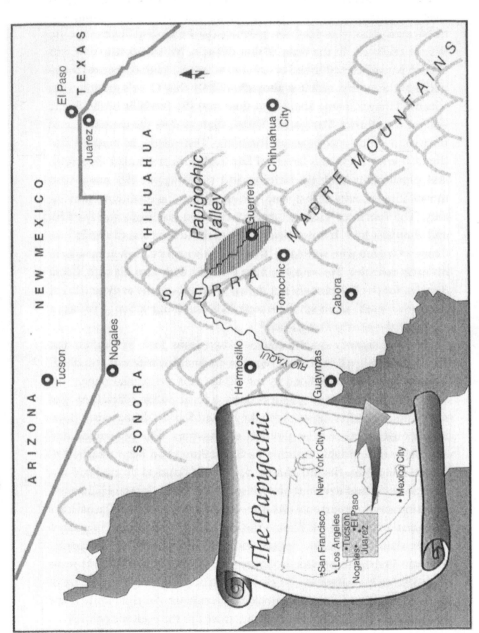

Map 2. The Papigochic Region

ceased half-brother. Among the surviving children was Cruz, no more than six years old.[5] Cruz does not appear to have been completely motherless, however. The census for the period indicates that an older widow, possibly one of his grandmothers, lived in the household along with his brothers Manuel, Jesús José, and David, as well as two other children, ages four and nine, whose different surnames indicate that they may have been the offspring of other deceased friends or family. (It was not unusual for families of the period to share child-rearing responsibilities, especially when husbands became widowed.) Therefore, Cruz spent his early years in a family of six children headed by a farming father, age 36 in 1864, and a 60-year-old woman who may have been a relative. His sister Consolación, three years his senior, lived outside the household with the Calderóns, at least at the time of the census. Why she was there is not certain, but the Calderóns seem to have been especially close friends, perhaps compadres, of the Chávez family. (Cruz's older brother, Manuel, later married a Calderón.) The family composition of the Chávez household was not uncommon in the region, and it is quite possible that Cruz soon had a stepmother too. Church records show Jesús José married to Teresa Mendoza in 1886, the year of his death, but without indication of when they married or of Teresa's age.[6]

Resources in the Chávez household must have been limited, although the family's material circumstances were far from unique in the pueblo. The patriarch of the family not only farmed but worked for additional income at the mines around Yoquivo. When he died at age 58, he left an estate worth a modest $250 pesos (or about $200 U.S. at the time) to be divided among his survivors.[7] What might this very small inheritance indicate? Perhaps over the years there was a decline in Chávez family status, with its subsequent implications for the personality development of the children. On several occasions Jesús José had been Tomochic's presidente, a position that normally yielded considerable personal revenue, for some, indeed, a relative fortune. Other village presidentes during this period ranked among the better-off in the community, but the sons of Jesús José never held high public posts and were hardly well-off. It is possible, of course, that the elder Chávez was an underachiever or that his opportunities for earning income have been overestimated here. The record suggests, however, a man who valued money less than justice, a stance buttressed by rigid honesty and high morality.

When authorities above Jesús José issued new decrees, unlike the presidentes of other pueblos, he pointedly read them out at a public forum so that no individual could later claim ignorance of the law. He was, however, frank with superiors about his inability to enforce some of their edicts, like the one issued on June 14, 1858, which restricted the drinking of tesgüino (beer made from fermented corn kernels) among the Tarahumaras.[8] Chávez could no more enforce that decree than can officials today, since tesgüino is intimately linked to the ceremonial and spiritual lives of the Tarahumaras; it is an indispensable part of their value system and family networks.[9]

Chávez did not seem to understand all that much about Tarahumara culture, nor did he concern himself about such matters, but he plainly worried about how much tesgüino the natives drank and how his fellow mestizos exploited the Tarahumara appetite for other kinds of alcohol. Official regulation prohibited mestizos from selling alcohol to the Indians on any days but Sundays, yet Chávez found them selling it anywhere, anytime. He noted that the Indians sold their labor in order to buy mescal and brandy. Moreover, to purchase the liquor they frequently mortgaged their oxen for from one to three pesos, which meant they had no draft animals to plow their fields. Chávez wrote the jefe político on July 3, 1858, that as presidente his repeated complaints about the illegal sales failed to quell the practice, which he labeled a *tumulto*—a commotion approaching turmoil. Chávez allowed that the situation weighed heavily on him and that he could not avoid his responsibilities as presidente of the pueblo; that he could not allow the practice to continue, "because it is against God, mankind, and prudence." And so he couched his frustration and disgust not only in legal, but also in moral terms. He then recommended that all sales of tesgüino and other liquors be prohibited in the village, even small amounts that cost no more than one peso. Chávez felt so strongly about his suggestion that should the jefe not accept it, he asserted that he would resign from public office.[10]

This did not mean his relations with the Tarahumaras were always smooth. On February 10, 1859, the priest in the pueblo, Felipe de Jesús Silva, complained to the jefe político in Ciudad Guerrero of Chávez's mistreatment of natives who had vociferously complained about a new regulation Chávez had read to them at one of the public gatherings.[11] Nothing is known of the particulars of the incident, but undoubtedly it was part of the ongoing friction between the clergy and local officials that centered on authority over the Indians. While investigating these charges, Juan Domínguez, the justice of the peace, discovered that the priest had himself whipped two Indians, a man and a woman, with a leather strap. The man bore eight welts and the woman two from the beatings, which had drawn blood from the calves of their legs. Domínguez questioned the legal authority of priests to administer corporal punishment to the Indians, but—though lacking official sanction— padres had done the same since colonial days.[12] On other occasions Padre Silva charged that Chávez treated the natives with scorn, that he punished them without pity, and that he disdained the priest who came to the assistance of the Indians. In official reports the truth and disposition of these disputes are rarely established, but they reflect the crass competition among colonizers for the land, labor, and souls of the natives.

Although the Chávez family was certainly known—like most others— to take direct action with gun in hand, their obvious knowledge of and reliance on the law as remedy for settling controversies is noteworthy. Jesús José took legal action to collect his debts. Manuel, in agreeing to arbitrate his father's will, trusted several prominent citizens from Ciudad Guerrero to administer justice, specifically to get his due from his father's debtors.[13] In fact, Manuel's insistence on legal accountability drew a complaint in 1883 from the village treasurer, Julián Rodríguez, who wrote the jefe político that Chávez as justice of the peace was abusing his office by demanding written reports from the treasurer, who insisted that he was under no obligation to render such accounts. Perhaps this was harassment—or Manuel Chávez may have been on the scent of some peccadillo. The archives do not tell us.[14]

The Mind of Cruz Chávez

Cruz Chávez displayed much the same pronounced moralistic and litigious bent as his father. At two o'clock in the afternoon of May 3, 1885, Cruz, now a man in his mid-twenties, had gone to the house of a Brigida Rosas on personal business. There he met various people, including the Tarahumara Pedro de la Cruz and his wife, who, he charged, had gravely insulted him—treating him like a thief (the worst sort of insult among these country people)—harsh words that stemmed from a controversy concerning a fine assessed against the Indians on the previous day for other invectives they had hurled at Chávez. One thing appears certain: Cruz Chávez wore his feelings on his sleeve; he seems to have been especially sensitive to accusations that he had in some way broken or evaded the law, especially when the aspersion was made public. One did not imply that Chávez was a thief and escape repercussion. In this instance, Chávez immediately levied charges of defamation or disrespect with the local police commissioner, who ordered the de la Cruzes arrested. But the de la Cruzes had their defenders in two well-known villagers, Julián Rodríguez and Santiago Gallegos, who openly mocked Cruz Chávez for his irate response, further attacking the man's reputation. Two weeks later a furious Chávez denounced his tormentors to the jefe político himself and went on to castigate village officials for their failure to uphold the law. In doing so Chávez cited articles from the penal code and gave the appropriate pages to document his argument: the officials who had declined to act in his behalf had violated Article 904 of the Penal Code, Book Three, page 211. Moreover, because they were relatives of the comisario, Gallegos and Rodríguez had not been fined the 4 reales each (about 50 cents U.S.) mandated for such offenses by Articles 906 and 922 in the Third Book of the Penal Code. Finally, the comisario had hesitated to arrest Pedro de la Cruz and ignored the complaints of Chávez, who charged the official with "bad faith" and negligence, especially in his failure to administer the protection of the law due a complainant. To put it mildly, Chávez (and whoever, if anyone, had assisted him, as one might question Cruz's level of literacy at this point) had assembled an extraordinary legal brief in his own behalf.[15]

A full-blown investigation followed. Depositions were taken and forwarded to higher authority, but these seem to have escaped the historian's net. Too bad; it would be gratifying to know how this fracas ended, and like so many other village feuds it must have left a discernible mark. But what is astonishing here is the manner in which Cruz utilized codified law to seek redress for perceived injustice. Something traumatic must have occurred within the next five years or so to have soured him so completely on the legal prescriptions and procedures of government and caused him to rely solely on folk saints and higher authority for guidance. By about 1890 he had given up on public law and sought redress only in the Divine: "We will obey no one but God!" Even then, however, Chávez hewed to civil law; he cloaked his declaration in his constitutional right to religious freedom.

Cruz's early life seems to have been quite ordinary. At age twenty, he counted among the eligible voters in the pueblo, almost all of them, including Cruz, listed on census sheets as illiterate.[16] He did become literate later on, but perhaps his earlier educational shortcomings prevented him from greater participation in official community business, such as in the roles of comisario or his substitute, or local civil judge. The Tomochitecos seem to have passed these jobs around among themselves, preferring that the holders be literate. To be sure, some names appear more than others as the signatories on official correspondence, names such as Ortiz, Domínguez, and Medrano. Even Manuel Chávez, the brother of Cruz, turns up every so often, albeit in minor positions, but rarely Cruz.[17] Cruz may have turned down such public positions because he was primarily involved with issues pertaining to the church. Certainly, when problems arose concerning such matters as the loss of church property, Cruz Chávez stepped to the fore. It is also quite possible the villagers considered him either too thin-skinned about criticism or too authoritarian to allow him a position of civil authority. Without doubt, Cruz possessed a strong streak of authoritarianism, which we might speculate was founded in the aforementioned decline of local status experienced by the entire Chávez family since the village presidencies of its patriarch, Jesús José. Cruz Chávez could have been angry at much more than just some public officials and how they practiced the law.

Like Manuel, two years his senior, Cruz married somewhat later than other men in the pueblo. He was already 26 when he married María Trinidad Mendías, who was four years his junior. The Mendías family had lived in Tomochic for decades and had intermarried with a number of families there, including the Rodríguezes and the Villareals. By April 1890, Cruz and María Trinidad had three children: Cruz, Jr., age six; Rafael, five; and María Manuela, one year old. Chávez's youngest brother, David, still single at age 22, also lived in the household.[18]

The Chávezes farmed relatively small plots of land in the valley, growing corn and beans along with a few chilies and perhaps some squash. They also possessed some animals—chickens and pigs close by the house, and five or six head of cattle that grazed the low growth above the pueblo. Like other villagers they intermittently supplemented their income. They may have sold some corn to the mining communities or worked as muleteers or security guards for the convoys plying the Sierra. Cruz once sold a horse to an itinerant priest; like his father, Manuel worked for a mining outfit in Yoquivo, probably the same one.[19] Cruz certainly recognized the potential of a new mining discovery. In October 1887 a Tarahumara, Martín de la Cruz, complained to a judge in Guerrero City (did he not trust the judicial authorities in Tomochic?) that Cruz Chávez and Jorge Ortiz had forcibly taken him from his house at about seven in the morning, bound him, and locked him up all day long without food in the dwelling of Reyes Domínguez. About midnight they led him into the Sierra and demanded that he reveal to them the location of a mine he had supposedly discovered in the area. When de la Cruz protested that he knew of no such mine, they stripped him bare and whipped him while prodding him through the surrounding Sierra in search of the alleged mine. De la Cruz produced no details, so they lashed him some more, and he showed the judge the welts and bruises as proof. Now de la Cruz (perhaps related to the de la Cruzes whom Cruz Chávez had accused of defamation two years earlier) wanted justice: Chávez and Ortiz should be arrested and made to pay him civil damages. Moreover, the incident was not the first of its kind; the accused had done the same to the Tarahumaras Santiago Toribio and Enrique Herrera. Other natives testified that on various occasions they also had been forced to hunt for mines and suffered the accompanying abuses, although it is not clear that they specifically blamed all of the outrages on Chávez and Ortiz. The practice seems to have been reasonably widespread in Tomochic, where the hope of discovering an El Dorado "up there" in the mystique of the Sierra above the pueblo still runs high today.[20]

By the time of Cruz Chávez, indigenous Mexicans like the Tarahumaras had already been relegated to the lowest levels of the social hierarchy. Many thought the natives had no place in national society at all. Chávez may not have gone that far, but he treated Tarahumaras as if they were *meant* to do his bidding. He saw the slur of himself by a Tarahumara as profound disrespect punishable by law—or punishable by his own hand. To him Martín de la Cruz was duty-bound to provide him information about the possible location of a mine.

Like many others among the dominant mestizos who ran the pueblo, Chávez also unabashedly exploited the Tarahumaras through a practice called *amo/sirviente* (master/servant), which was rooted in Mexico's colonial past and sanctioned by state constitutions during the nineteenth century. Amo/sirviente, patrón/peón: however such labor arrangements were labeled, they amounted to contract peonage and social degradation.[21] However, this relationship carried no high moral concerns for Cruz Chávez and the others. Instead, they considered it a codified cultural practice. To them amo/sirviente concerned civil, not religious, authority; servants did not worship masters like people worshipped God. Competition developed between amos for the best working and most loyal sirvientes, so if one amo coveted another's sirviente, he might encourage that sirviente to claim mistreatment and thereby gain his legal release. Or if bad blood developed between two amos, one might publicly charge his adversary with abusing his sirviente. Local judges who heard such complaints were normally amos themselves, so they might be expected to find for their kind. On the other hand, they could just as likely use the grievance of a sirviente as a weapon against an amo with whom they were in contention. The natives, taking a lesson from their mestizo "teachers," also learned to use the law for their purposes, as a way to escape debts, change amos, settle scores. They understood amo/sirviente as a contract, an agreement, far different from slavery, which to them was the final degradation.[22] Sirvientes were frequently at the center of village disputes, even when they were merely the pretext for airing other, more deeply etched differences. Cruz Chávez became embroiled in just such a fracas in June of 1887. Carlos Medrano was tending to some hogs in front of his house on the third of June when he stepped inside for a moment. On his return, he found two of the hogs missing. Subsequently he received a citation from the police commissioner, Bartolo Ledesma, saying the official had impounded the hogs because they were the comisario's property and that Medrano was under arrest, presumably for theft. Furthermore, he fined Medrano 5 reales for the five Medrano cattle found running loose in the village and now being held in the village corral reserved for stray animals, which owners could identify and reclaim for a fee. In his complaint to the jefe político, Medrano professed that Ledesma had jailed him for two days without explanation, then had also confined Carlos' brother, Jesús Medrano, saying that the latter had held the commissioner's authority in contempt. Actually, Ledesma and the Medranos had been feuding for quite some time.

This latest trouble between the Medranos and Ledesmas had begun to brew on April 10, at a dance in the house of Domingo López. Francisco Ledesma, the 32-year-old brother of Comisario Bartolo, evidently got roaring drunk, cursing people and insulting Manuel Chávez, who was being paid to maintain public order at the festivity. Tired of Francisco's insolence, Chávez asked Bartolo to arrest his own brother. Nothing happened, of course, and Francisco went on to another dance, this one at the dwelling of José Dolores Rodríguez, where he continued his wild antics and accusations. This time the culprit was taken to the local jail, but his jailers (perhaps deliberately) left the door ajar so that he could walk out, which he did, swearing to take revenge on the brothers Manuel and Cruz Chávez. Most expected Francisco to be punished for his drunken misdeeds, but the next day the commissioner simply pulled his brother aside and had a few words with him; no arrest ensued.

Obviously family favoritism was in play, and it infuriated onlookers like the Medranos. According to Carlos Medrano, the comisario was always stirring up trouble in the village and was guilty of numerous infractions of the law. In early June Ledesma had counseled the Tarahumara sirviente Benigno Montáñez to make a formal complaint against his amo, Cruz Chávez, alleging that Chávez had beaten him. However, under questioning by the local justice of the peace, Montáñez admitted that he had been put up to the accusation by his father, who was the sirviente of Ledesma. Had the charge stood, Montáñez could have legally broken his contract with Chávez and gone to work for Ledesma, who earlier had utilized the same tactic trying to lure a sirviente away from Medrano's brother, Jesús.

Now Bartolo Ledesma claimed that as police commissioner, he was only trying to control stray animals because they ruined agricultural plots, and. . . . But alas, here this human drama must end for us; the remainder of the document recording it has simply crumbled to dust.[23] On the surface, the scuffling between the Medranos and the Ledesmas over these issues seems rather petty; village squabbles frequently are. But beneath the trivialness may lurk strongly felt hatreds that are the products of a festering power struggle. Suffice it to say that some four and one-half years after these personal feuds erupted, the Medranos and the Ledesmas found themselves at even greater odds: the Medranos huddled against the cold in the Sierra with Cruz Chávez and his followers, while the Ledesmas, secure in Tomochic, searched for personal advantage in the unexpected occurrences unfolding around them.

Over the years Manuel and Cruz Chávez certainly had had their ins and outs with village controversy and local authority. Manuel Chávez was justice of the peace in April 1877 (he was only 22 years old at the time) when he became involved in a drunken brawl between "whites" and Tarahumaras, probably at some fiesta. Because Chávez opposed the arrest of the "whites," the police commissioner, Dolores Mendías, suspended Chávez from office.[24] Three years later Cruz tangled with the pueblo's justice of the peace, Domingo López, when the official tried to shortchange him. While López ran an errand, Chávez agreed to watch two burros for a couple of reales (25 cents U.S.), one of the ways Tomochitecos picked up some spare change. But when the official returned, he refused to pay up in full. Harsh words followed, and Chávez complained to the assistant comisario, not that López had refused him his due, but that López had insulted him. Here we get another glimpse of Cruz Chávez's priorities: honor before money. It is a trait, along with his contentiousness, that we will see much more of in the man. In this instance, he won his point; the policeman sentenced López to five days' custody.[25]

An incident in 1882 shows more of what could be expected from Cruz Chávez. On September 2, he had a run-in with Reyes Domínguez, then acting comisario. As a result Cruz refused to recognize the official's authority—the same position he took toward the village presidente, albeit in a more aggressive and fateful way, nine years later. Revealingly, Cruz detailed in writing (but not likely by his own hand) his reasons for refusing to respect the official's jurisdiction. Domínguez read them and then punished Chávez for disrespect. Perhaps the contention between the two men at this point was embryonic. Minds change and anger passes, but we should remember that nearly a decade later Domínguez not only did not join the Chávez movement, but provided vital intelligence, lodging, and food to government forces bent on suppressing it.[26]

Was Cruz Chávez involved in an inordinate amount of village strife or more part of the norm in an extremely fractious pueblo? Documentation on the question is incomplete, but what we have puts Cruz in more than his share of local conflict. Another illustrative example occurred in 1885 when Cruz and five others were convicted of cattle rustling in a case that the accused appealed to the state supreme court. At one point while the prisoners awaited transfer under escort to the jail in Guerrero City, Chávez rose from his sickbed and started for Guerrero on his own. He was not trying to escape; he apparently only intended to protest his innocence before regional authorities and could not wait to do so; when it came to defending his reputation, Cruz Chávez was a very adamant man. In January 1886 Cruz and the others were remanded to their homes pending a hearing of their case before the court, but the judges either dismissed it or could not resolve it for lack of evidence. In what could well be a corollary to the same matter, the state judge sitting in Guerrero fined Cruz and Jorge Ortiz 50 pesos each for failing to comply with his orders—a hefty fine. Because they considered the fine unfair, the pair refused to pay it, and Ortiz threatened to appeal this second case to the state supreme court.[27] Chávez was now heavily engaged with the law—perhaps becoming somewhat disillusioned by the process—only four years before his proclamation: "We will obey no one but God!" All along Cruz, in keeping with common religious practice, may have been seeking explanation for his misfortunes from the Divine, so when beset by a series of especially ferocious setbacks around 1890, he deliberately sought the special counsel of the viejitos and Santa Teresa.

God's Revenge or the Devil's Ploy?

Drought hit much of northern Mexico and the southwestern United States in 1887 and deepened over the next four years. Planting normally depended on the summer rains, which fell from June through August, and for those four years, there was barely enough to eke out a subsistence, let alone make a living. When rain did come, it cascaded down in brief, damaging deluges that ripped away topsoil, dug arroyos through the fields, and flooded areas so that plantings rotted away. In the late fall, vicious hailstorms thrashed to tatters whatever crops had survived. Drought stunted trees, killed cattle by the thousands, plunged substantial numbers of people into misery, threatening famine and death. By 1891 prices of farm goods had risen sharply; the price of black beans, for example, nearly tripled in a year. Famine riots erupted in the north-central state of Zacatecas. President Díaz was asked to eliminate national tariffs on beans and corn so that imports from the United States could help to fight the price rise of those staples, and Governor Carrillo ordered 100,000 bushels of U.S. grain to be distributed to the needy. This drought ranked among the worst climatological disasters ever to hit this region.[28]

Not that this was the first such catastrophe to strike the area. People still remembered the suffering caused by drought only a decade earlier. Inextricably bound to fluctuations in weather, the area's farmers were resigned to ups and downs, and their cultural traditions and memory as well as their religion persistently reminded them that some downs slide into disaster. They regularly prayed for sacred protection and then for relief when catastrophe occurred. Under the stress of such crisis, individuals may naturally ask, "Why me? Why us?" Then, "Why do I—or we—deserve what is happening here?" And finally, "Is the Almighty unhappy with me? Is He punishing us?" By his actions, Cruz Chávez indicated he was pondering just such questions.

Rain comes only in the one short summer season each year and never falls uniformly over this semiarid, subtropical region. Droughts, like most disasters, fall even more unevenly on the populace. Some may ride out a drought because they have deep water wells or because they have the material resources and foresight to store a surplus against a harvest failure. Or they have the money, despite inflated prices caused by shortages, to buy relief. When a well-off commercial farmer loses part, even a good part, of his herd and much of his crop to drought, he sinks into hard times, but when a petty rancher or small-time farmer does so, he faces dearth, even death. Such differences are notable even in small pueblos like Tomochic, where in the drought of 1878 only half the families needed special relief from the state.[29] In 1888, 44 households—nearly two-thirds of the town—needed assistance, but only 5 were absolutely destitute and required outright charity. The rest received grain at a reduced price but still paid for it.[30]

Crises such as these seem to bring out both the best and the worst in human behavior. Some of the more fortunate willingly share with those less well-off. Others choose to exploit the misery and desperation of the stricken. The scarcity of 1878 found fifty or more families in the largely Tarahumara village of Pachera, in the Papigochic Valley, literally starving to death. A nearby hacendado, José Armijo, had a hefty surplus to sell, but preferred doing business with the more profitable mining centers. The Tarahumaras offered their labor and some of their animals as payment for corn, but Armijo remained intransigent. The natives pleaded with the jefe político to stop Armijo from selling grain to the mines and to force him to offer it to them at any price, but it is doubtful that they received any relief.[31]

Tomochic was under the same sort of stress. In January 1878 it appeared that Dolores Mendías and Diego López, each of whom possessed substantial grain reserves, would voluntarily help to see the pueblo through the shortage, but over the next few months they proved to be uncompromising: no gifts, loans, or sales to their fellow villagers. In April, when grumbling about such selfishness escalated into anger and then demands for relief, the village presidente, Reyes Domínguez, asked of the jefe político, "How is it possible that the families of the protesters should starve, when two families in the village have enough to help them?"[32] By May the pueblo had set up an emergency relief board headed by Domínguez to coordinate subsidized assistance organized by the state out of Ciudad Guerrero. The presidente immediately asked for authorization to distribute the corn being sent by the government in order to avoid further turmoil. By June 8 corn had arrived in Tomochic to alleviate the crisis. Recipients paid a discounted price for the grain, all except the five individuals who had been reduced to begging and judged unable to pay anything at all.[33] In this manner Tomochic saw its way through the emergency, but at what expense to its sense of community?

The drought of 1887–90 was even more damaging to the social fabric of the community. In January 1888 the jefe político warned Guerrero's municipal council that it had better store up corn, because the price was going to go up. The next month brought an urgent message to the jefe from José Dolores Rodríguez, Tomochic's police commissioner: "Shortage of grain in Tomochic. Very scarce. Need help; if we do not get it, people will die."[34] The jefe reported the grim situation in Tomochic to Guerrero's municipal council: some residents of the pueblo had grain, but none of them were willing to sell any of it. By the first of April Jesús Medrano, now the pueblo's presidente, had forwarded a list of "those with the right to purchase corn [at the reduced price]" to the municipal council in Guerrero.[35] It included 49 names;

four individuals were said to be sick, two of them women, all four without income. Six other families were also listed as too poor to buy grain even at a reduced price. The rest could pay something for their corn, among them Manuel, Cruz (not yet rejecting government relief), and David Chávez; Bartolo Ledesma; the village schoolteacher, Santiago Simonet; Nepomuseno Acosta, with a family of eleven; and Josefa Morales, a woman apparently living alone. When the families of Tomochic's needy are included, fully 45 percent of the pueblo's 352 residents were due to receive assistance.[36] How the names for the list were selected is not known, but there were soon complaints from some of those left off. By the end of March the Medrano brothers, Carlos and Jesús, had distributed grain to those approved for aid, but within a week four others (all Tarahumaras) complained that they had received no ration, because they were sirvientes, a situation that if not redressed would reduce them to slavery. Jesús Medrano responded that his critics had received no help because they were not eligible—that they were not on the approved list, which apparently excluded sirvientes. Medrano added that the distribution was not going well, because some "undeserving" people had received handouts.[37] Unfortunately, we can only speculate on what he meant by "undeserving": Tarahumaras, outsiders, people with corn reserves, those better off who could afford to pay the full price of grain, those not held in official favor, perhaps even personal enemies.

In the midst of deepening drought other calamities assailed Tomochic. For some time now, in the absence of a permanent priest, the village had depended on Cruz Chávez to safeguard the church building along with its holdings. In June 1889 burglars robbed the church of precious ornaments and vessels. The thieves entered through the bell tower and, along with other religious artifacts, took from the altar a large crucifix and heavy candelabrum, the latter containing 34 kilograms of gold and silver plating. Cruz headed the posse of seven men charged with running down the culprits, and within three days they made their first arrest, Ramón Velázquez, a resident of the mining camp at Yoquivo, where the Chávezes worked from time to time. Although there was some question about Velázquez's complicity, Cruz sent him to the custody of the state judge in Guerrero City—a sign that he still considered institutions of government to be legitimate.[38] It is not known whether further arrests followed or even if the religious articles were ever recovered, but Cruz and his group soon had a much more formidable looter to deal with.

And Now the Governor

In November 1890 Governor Lauro Carrillo, accompanied by his administrative entourage, the president of the Supreme Court, and a military guard of 25 soldiers, visited Tomochic as he neared completion of what the Mexicans call a *gira* (a political campaign trek) through the Sierra. This gira marked the first time that any Chihuahuan governor had bothered to campaign in the Sierra. Carrillo ordered a telegraph line strung between the mining centers at Jesús María and Morís, and at the pueblo of Chínipas, another mining complex, he promised money for a new school. Better still, he would contribute one day's pay of his monthly salary toward that school, and he kept his word. Carrillo also meant to introduce the currency of the Banco de Chihuahua, a new bank in which he owned a substantial stake. By doing so he planned to drive out bills and coins issued by the rival Banco Minero, owned by his powerful and aggressive political adversaries, the Luis Terrazas clan, which hoped to recapture the state house in the gubernatorial elections of 1892. Carrillo was well aware that the political fight was already on and currency control was a big part of it.

Over the previous week or so the entourage had visited the major mining centers at Pinos Altos, Jesús María, Morís, Yoquivo, and was now wending its way on horseback through Tomochic, heading for a night's rest in Ciudad Guerrero. The following morning they would be off to the capital city by stagecoach. Carrillo was in a buoyant mood as he briefly toured the pueblo, admired the church—which despite the theft still held impressive ecclesiastical furnishings, especially the lovely oil paintings on the walls—and ate a hearty rural meal of *carne asada*; now he needed a siesta. Before he dozed off, the governor asked his captain of the state guard, Major Manuel Cárdenas, if he might not arrange with village authorities for the purchase of two of those most attractive religious paintings he had seen in the church, that of San Joaquín, the father of the Virgin Mary, and the other of Saint Anne, the Virgin's mother, portrayed gently combing the hair of her holy child. The paintings were truly extraordinary, perhaps even the work of a Spanish master such as Miguel Angel, Murillo, or even Ribera; they had been brought by Jesuits, who had headed a renowned mission in the village during the seventeenth and early eighteenth centuries. The governor was quite certain that Tomochic's rustics did not appreciate such fine art; perhaps they would even make a gift of the paintings to him. While Carrillo rested Major Cárdenas looked into the possibilities.

First he approached the village presidente, Juan Ignacio Chávez, certain of success; here was the opportunity for the pueblo to please the governor and most probably receive a favor in return. This was one way Mexican politics worked. In fact, Carrillo had indicated a willingness to pay 200 pesos (most likely from the state treasury) for the paintings, money which he suggested the villagers could use to improve their school. Therefore, the major was more than a little surprised when the presidente told him that, while he himself wished to accommodate the governor, all matters concerning church property lay solely in the hands of Cruz Chávez and his followers, who he admitted were antagonistic toward the presidente. Thus we see that Cruz Chávez and his devotees were already at odds with the village presidente for at least a year—quite possibly a good deal longer—before blood was shed in Tomochic.

Despite this apparent rift in the pueblo, Major Cárdenas remained confident in his mission. He made his proposal to Cruz Chávez, who agreed to consult with his associates about the alternatives and have an answer to Cárdenas by that afternoon. Undoubtedly Cruz himself already knew how he personally stood on the issue, yet he felt the necessity to seek confirmation from his followers. Within a few hours Cárdenas had his reply: the group unanimously and emphatically rejected any proposal to surrender the paintings. To give them up, they said, would be akin to the betrayal of Christ by Judas.

Tomochic's religious paintings were not precious to the faithful for their aesthetics or monetary value. Instead, the pious in the pueblo regularly prayed to these images to intercede with the Almighty in their behalf, especially in times of crisis, both communal and personal. The icons provided the villagers with security and hope and represented their lifeline to God. The grace that the pious received through these interceding figures guided them through painful loss and brought them success in love. Nor was the relationship between icon and petitioner always serene. The gaze of the images could change, sometimes warm and maternal, but at other times, harsh and unpredictable. If Tomochi-tecos were like most other Mexicans, they probably told stories and joked to one another about—perhaps even became angry with—these icons, which seemed to have such fickle minds. Then and today these religious images and the people who address them are best thought of as family, and the icons gave the people an important sense of participation in their own religion; they were not about to surrender them to anyone.

The uncompromising refusal of Tomochic's faithful to hand over the paintings stunned Major Cárdenas; he could not believe such a rebuff to the governor's solicitation. Yet he was not through. Cárdenas went to the sundries store of Presidente Chávez and purchased some wrapping paper. Then he sneaked into the church and with his personal razor cut the venerated paintings from their frames, which were embedded in the adobe walls of the structure. He rolled them up in the paper so that no one could see what he carried and, when the governor arose from his nap, presented him with the paintings as a gift from the village. Juan Ignacio Chávez must have been there at that moment but offered no protest, and so the governor rode off toward his next stop delighted with his new possessions. When he got to Chihuahua, he gave the paintings to his wife, Adelaidita Gutiérrez, urging her to have them framed so that they could be displayed as precious jewels in the family chapel.

Soon after the governor's departure from the village, Cruz Chávez and followers discovered the theft from the church and were outraged, but curiously restrained. They wrote Carrillo a note demanding the return of the paintings within two weeks or they would take "other actions." One of their number carried the message to Chihuahua City, handed it to a governor's aide, and retired to a local guest house to await a reply. Carrillo was dumbstruck. He summoned Major Cárdenas and angrily denounced him. Trying to exculpate himself, Cárdenas argued that the oils should not be returned to those ignorant country people who had gone so far as to threaten the governor; to return them would be a sign of weakness and later create even more difficulties. But the governor would have none of this and ordered him out. He then had the paintings returned to the courier with a note to Chávez, disclaiming any responsibility for their removal.

Cruz and his congregation received the paintings with jubilation. He read the governor's letter aloud to the crowd, and they paraded to the church where the paintings were sewn back into their frames. However, the discredited Major Cárdenas was not done; he felt his promotions, if not his career, threatened. So early in the spring of 1891 he welcomed a tip from an employee at the state judicial archive that a judgment against Cruz Chávez for cattle rustling remained unresolved. Although no new facts surrounding the matter seem to have appeared, Cárdenas conspired to resurrect the 1885 case that had gone to the State Supreme Court. He carried the Chávez file to the governor, urged that the case be reopened and Cruz arrested. Carillo hesitated; he suspected that any such maneuver would be cast by his political enemies as crass reprisal against innocent country people. Cárdenas pushed harder: the Tomochitecos had displayed overt disrespect for Carrillo and his regime. Moreover, they may have been motivated by Terrazas people, the governor's political enemies. Carrillo cocked an ear and then asked "his" Supreme Court to issue an arrest warrant against Cruz Chávez and have the prisoner brought to the capital.

News of these proceedings reached Chávez before the warrant. Either he had sympathizers within the governor's circles or Terrazas people sensed the opportunity to fan some political flames. Whatever the source of his information, Cruz told a tense gathering of his followers about the governor's intentions. His supporters exploded in anger, grabbing their weapons and vowing to defend their leader against his accusers. If it proceeded with its designs now, the government was in for a fight. But the uproar petered out. Either Carrillo backed off, or his original intentions were misread or exaggerated by those who have brought them to our attention.[39] Even so, the details of this entire affair must have made an indelible imprint on the spiritual and moral perceptions of Cruz Chávez. Governments may have the right to tax and legislate, but what right had the government to interfere with the pueblo's religious *patrones*, who belonged to *their* community and to no one else? For most if not all Tomochitecos, this had been their first direct contact with any state governor and his entourage. They must have asked themselves: Are these the sorts of things that governors do? And by what authority do governors even have the right to ask for our paintings? Most fundamentally, how do we really relate to these officials called "governor"? One can scarcely imagine the anguish, then the fear and fury, when the devoted discovered that someone meant to disrupt their religious belief and practice. The role of that "someone" is usually reserved for Satan.

Accusations of Banditry

Soon after the drama surrounding the paintings, sixteen bandits held up a mule train carrying a hefty payroll meant for mining centers not far from Tomochic. The raid occurred on January 28, 1891, at a narrow mountain pass called Puerto de las Manzanillas, about twelve miles out from Ciudad Guerrero. The bandits must have seen the mule train laden with some 45,000 pesos in bills and coin arrive in Guerrero from the banking center at Chihuahua City, and planned to bushwhack it on its way through the pass. A tough Scot named Cornelius Callahan was directing the transit with a security force of fifteen men when the brigands struck. Almost immediately the armed escort splintered in terror (or were they accomplices of the bandits?). But five of them, with Callahan, held their own, killed one of the marauders in a lively firefight, and drove off the others. The convoy then proceeded to the closest village, the Tarahumara pueblo of Arisiachic, where the crew waited for an official investigation to begin.

The jefe político, Silviano González, his aides, and a judge from Guerrero soon arrived. They quickly identified the body of the dead bandit as Emiliano Caraveo, a resident of Basúchil, very near Guerrero. So they took the body back to Guerrero, where it was publicly displayed for two days as an object lesson, while some of the runaway guardsmen returned to town and began to identify their assailants; members of Caraveo's family, his friends, and associates became prime suspects. The state judge soon ordered the arrest of five alleged accomplices. Posses ran them down, and on March 9 Manuel Cárdenas—likely the same Cárdenas involved with the paintings—started to escort the accused, along with other prisoners from Guerrero's jail, back to Chihuahua for further investigation and trial. They did not get very far. At a spot called La Mesa de Miñaca, just outside Guerrero, guards applied the Ley Fuga (the law of flight) to the five suspects—that is, they later told investigating authorities that the five had been slain in an escape attempt, but everyone knew Mexico's version of lynch law when they heard it. None of the other prisoners being escorted to Chihuahua were shot, only the five allegedly involved in the holdup of the mule train. Of the other ten raiders involved in the robbery, nine seem to have escaped, three of them apparently to the safety of the United States, and do not again appear in the historical record. The tenth, Manuel Jáquez, was captured and consigned to military service. Though all sixteen are believed to have come from the immediate area of Guerrero, the people of Tomochic suffered undeserved calumnies in the wake of the affair.[40]

Rumors circulated that Tomochitecos had been in on the mule train attack. Maybe the villagers did not actually participate, it was said, but they knew about it, and other convoys traveling to and from the mines should be wary in and around Tomochic. The gossip successfully diverted the mule trains around the village, and some went well out of their way to avoid the Tomochic region altogether.[41] Naturally, that detour affected the pueblo's economy, since villagers had regularly provided a variety of services to those mule trains. Nor did new security forces stationed on nearby haciendas such as La Generala or the arrival of federal army reinforcements in Guerrero lessen tensions any. Cruz Chávez was beside himself. It was not any material loss that concerned him, but rather the reputation of himself and his people. How dare anyone impugn their integrity? How dare they put him and his fellow villagers in league with bandits? Chávez, of course, was not reacting out of character. Remember his response when Pedro de la Cruz insulted him and when the state accused him of cattle rustling. Now he displayed the same sort of outrage.

We cannot be sure who was spreading these rumors, but some evidence suggests Joaquín Chávez—strangely enough a distant relative of Cruz—who for some time had speculated in real estate and mining in the region. Joaquín was a prominent local politician and one of the region's principal guarantors of public peace, whose security forces regularly accompanied the transport of silver and other valuable goods in the Sierra. (It was Joaquín Chávez who told the governor in December 1891 that the religious uprising at Tomochic was merely a pretext to muster an armed band bent on robbing a silver-laden convoy headed through Tomochic, an opinion the governor passed on to President Porfirio Díaz himself.)[42] Cruz Chávez had categorically denied the accusation and even offered to head up a security patrol of his own people that would guarantee the safe passage of any Joaquín Chávez convoy, but this offer was never accepted. When in the spring of 1892 the government tried to negotiate with Cruz to accept civil authority, Cruz made it clear that one of his greatest grievances was the smears Joaquín Chávez had spread on his honor.[43]

So we see the pressure building: drought ruining crops and causing Cruz and his family hardship; criminal accusations and judicial proceedings that he considered unjust; thefts from the church, first by ordinary robbers and then by agents of the government; accusations that he and fellow villagers had turned to banditry and intended more of the same. And beyond these very direct, personal calamities the country's announced program to modernize itself through a strong and secularized central government was gathering momentum and its vibrations had begun to rattle the pueblo's everyday life. Now one further personal rebuke was still to come, perhaps the one that finally caused Cruz to swear his allegiance only to God.

The Last Straw

Drought-related conditions worsened over the next three years. From Sonora in the spring of 1890 came the news that the lack of summer rains, after hailstorms in April, had cost the entire grain crop. People began to migrate from the worst-hit areas, not yet in waves, but a handful here, half a village there. Where they sought relief is not known; they simply wandered away, most likely to relatives elsewhere. In parts of Chihuahua cattle died at an alarming rate; in other parts too much rain destroyed crops. Silviano González, the jefe político at Guerrero City, reported no rain at all for 1890. Much of the mining in the Sierra had shut down for lack of water. And in 1891 González wrote: "Also, no rain for this year. The proletarian class will soon feel the hunger."[44] Governor Carrillo noted that as commerce slackened so did tax revenues, further depleting the state treasury. As far south as the state of Jalisco protest mounted, as those who held grain in storage deliberately withheld it from distribution so they could exacerbate the shortage and eventually get a better price for their product. Sonorans hired a U.S. rainmaker named Morley, but refused to pay his $2,500 fee when his magic failed to work.[45] Hard times everywhere, and threatening to get worse—and more socially explosive.

When the summer of 1891 failed to yield rain, it marked the fourth consecutive year of drought for Tomochic. Humans have long combated drought with prayer, and processions to shrines are one of the more common manifestations of appeals to the Divine for relief. It is normally the local priest's duty to lead the community in the procession, but Tomochic had not had a regular priest since the early 1870s, and in the absence of the region's itinerant priest, who only irregularly visited the pueblo, religious matters fell to a lay person—in this case, it seems, Cruz Chávez. We cannot be certain whether in the absence of a priest Chávez actually conducted religious services in the church itself, but by the late 1880s, at least, he was doing so in his home and it fell to him to organize a holy procession.

Processions to allay drought and other natural disasters are pensive and solemn. The faithful often parade the cross from the main altar of the church and display a banner emblazoned with the image of the local saint or perhaps the Virgin Mary. Relics, statues, paintings, and candles are carried through the pueblo and on to the local shrine or back to the church. Villages usually turn out en masse for these communal events, in which unquestioning believers mingle with those much less convinced of the possibility of heavenly relief, even those who are openly anticlerical. Such processions may be petitionary—they may ask a Divinity for a favor—but more likely they are penitential. The participants fear that disaster has befallen them because the Almighty is for some reason displeased with their behavior. A specific reason for God's anger is rarely evident, but the faithful have little difficulty coming up with possibilities. So they repent and ask forgiveness. In many places, certainly in Mexico, the majority of these processions are Marian; that is, the faithful pray to the Virgin Mary for Her intercession on their behalf. Almost certainly this would have been the case for the Tomochitecos, whose patron saint was Nuestra Señora del Refugio—the Virgin Herself—in a nation already remarkable for its Marian devotion.[46]

At the time Mexico's anticlerical laws, embedded since mid-century in the nation's constitution, required that church-sponsored religious activities be confined to the temple itself. Priests were not to wear their religious garb on the streets. No outdoor processions were to be allowed without the permission of local lay authorities—in the case of Tomochic, the presidente. But civil authorities rarely invoked the rules. In fact, they figured out ways to get around them. For example, in 1877 the jefe político for Guerrero district informed the governor that, because of drought, plague threatened the region. As a consequence, devotees wanted to parade a statue of the Virgin Mary outside the church as a sign of repentance and as a plea for divine redress. Under the circumstances, would the governor waive the law prohibiting such spiritual processions? The answer was "No, but . . ." The governor could not sanction such religious activities because they violated the law, but he suggested a compromise: let the procession proceed, and the governor would cover his responsibilities by levying a symbolic fine against the practitioners.

In fact, civil authorities rarely invoked the law against religious activities outside the church, but there was always the threat that they would do so. There is no evidence that previous Tomochic officials ever frustrated Cruz Chávez in his religious intentions within the community—just the opposite. However, in the latter part of 1891, Juan Ignacio Chávez was the pueblo's new presidente. The animosity that already existed between the two unrelated Chávezes was revealed during the fracas over the paintings. And this is the same Juan Ignacio who, as we have seen, accused Cruz of rebelling against the state and who forged a document to that effect.[47] So it is perhaps not surprising that he forbade Cruz to hold the procession that devotees had come to see as necessary to placate the Lord and break the drought.

Actually, Cruz had not asked permission to stage the religious manifestation. He just intended to do it in accordance with his beliefs, but Juan Ignacio learned of the plan and simply canceled the event.[48] Yet within this incident we sense something of the nests of contention that existed in the pueblo. After all, holy processions are not only manifestations of religiosity; they are also demonstrations of solidarity and power. Cruz and Juan Ignacio had been adversaries for a couple of years, and each had his allies among the villagers. And the dispute was not, in fact, so petty, for it symbolized—better, exemplified—that rift in the nation's soul: civil versus religious authority; rationality opposed to spirituality; modern practices in conflict with long-established and cherished cultural traditions. A few days after the procession had been canceled, the presidente summoned a follower of Cruz to discuss a minor complaint that had been levied against him. Framing his repugnance in spiritual terms, Cruz advised his associate not to appear before the "heretic" and insisted that exclusively divine law should be obeyed.[49] A battle line was being drawn.

In Search of Divine Guidance

Chávez's world was falling apart, his material life as well as his moral orientation. Like his father, Cruz paid more attention to justice than to pesos. He focused on honor, integrity, and spirituality, not wealth. These were not mere "feelings," but the organizing principles of his life. Unlike the governor's sycophant who stole the religious paintings, Chávez did not attempt to get ahead by bending the rules, and he could not reconcile his own view of what is morally correct with those who did. The truth is that Cruz may well have been overly moralistic in his judgments. Some people probably did not appreciate what they saw as his "holier than thou" bearing, his authoritarianism and intolerance, but no one could doubt his steadfastness and sincerity. Nor did anyone in the pueblo call him "loco" or openly question his rationality. Indeed, the historical documentation suggests pronounced personality traits, some of them quite disagreeable, but no hint of irrationality.[50] His concerns and beliefs were consistent with his time. Like his father, Cruz did not abhor official authority and even saw a need for government. But it very much mattered to him how such authority was exercised, and his trust had been shattered. In the face of the failures of the polluted state, he turned to a higher authority for guidance and explanation.

Pious figures, such as the viejitos of El Chopeque, were not strange to the Sierra. Indeed visions, weeping holy images, heralds of the Apocalypse, dancing crosses, bleeding Christs, apparitions, "signs" in the skies, spiritual mediums, wandering santos, and the like appear in a variety of cultural configurations. We need not move forward or backward in time, or even out of Mexico, to discover similar manifestations: an image of the Virgin Mary, for example, perched in 1891 on a maguey cactus conversing with campesinos in Jalisco, her second appearance at the site. At about the same time that year a new apparition of the Virgin occurred at Chalma, near the country's capital and home to one of its most revered shrines. Meanwhile, federal army officers assigned to quell an Indian rebellion in southern Sonora reported a virtual epidemic of folk saints among the Mayo.[51] But in most cases the lives of the faithful are not dramatically altered by these appearances, these santos. The viejitos of El Chopeque would not have generated such enthusiasm in Cruz Chávez and his followers unless something important in their lives had changed.

The viejitos had been wandering in the Sierra for some time. In many ways they resembled those strikingly ubiquitous beggars of Mexico's late colonial period who wandered the countryside as *religiosos* (some wore crowns of thorns), usually carrying a presumed relic in a small box, and beseeching alms, ostensibly to support the cult of their favorite santo. When people complained, rightly or wrongly, that these beggars kept the offerings for themselves, Spanish authorities endeavored to ban them, but with limited success. Now, near the end of the nineteenth century, the practice continued. An illiterate carpenter, Carmen María López y Valencia, well into his eighties, and María Carrasco, said to be his wife, had first arrived in the Chínipas district of the mountains from their home in Guadalajara. Despite Carmen María's advanced age he was said to be of medium, robust stature with expressive eyes, "brilliant, like those of a snake."[52] Begging as they wandered, they carried with them an icon, an image of La Virgen del Refugio in a niche of wood. (La Virgen del Refugio—the chosen protectress of Tomochic. What might Cruz Chávez and his cohorts have made of that "coincidence"?) In February 1891 they arrived at El Chopeque.

Why El Chopeque? The place lay on a secondary route from mining districts in the Sierra to the important center at Cusihuiriachic and did not seem to be imbued with any special sacred significance. The Rodríguezes were the best-known residents of the locale, descendants of those who came to Cusihuiriachic in the seventeenth century looking for mining fortunes, turning instead to ranching and farming when their luck failed to materialize or played out. There does not ever seem to have been a church or even a chapel at the site, although it is likely that in their home the Rodríguezes had a small personal chapel, or perhaps just a niche. At El Chopeque Carmen María and María were met by believers like Cruz Chávez and his group. People who came to visit the viejitos soon attributed miracles to the image they possessed. They called López "El Señor" and "El Santo Cristo del Chopeque," and referred to María as the Virgin.[53] To some—or perhaps just to Cruz—this scene may have seemed the return of Christ. Had the Lord returned, as promised—not just mentioned, but *promised* in Scripture—to inaugurate the Millennium: a thousand years of justice, bliss, and plenty prior to the Final Judgment? Were they already suffering through the Apocalypse that the Bible asserted would herald the blessed event? For many

Christians, all this is going to happen; it is just a matter of when, and so they remain on the lookout for signs of imminence. In this sense, El Santo del Chopeque must have given more than a few individuals a moment of pause.

Cruz Chávez was not the first Tomochiteco to visit El Santo Cristo. Before him, the Ledesma and López families investigated the credentials of the purportedly holy couple and decided they were frauds. When Carmen María suggested that they pray to the Virgin Mary and leave a donation behind, Timoteo Ledesma replied that Carmen and María were not saints but beggars of God. (How hearts can change; Timoteo later became a martyr to the cause of Cruz Chávez.)[54]

Although we can expect that some followers of Cruz Chávez had their doubts about the couple at El Chopeque, they still made their petitions and vows and despite shortages at home left offerings with the Santo according to their means: probably not much money, but chickens and corn, dried beef and some *pinole* (toasted corn meal). Cruz himself had any number of private conversations with the man.[55] Perhaps Carmen María reinforced what Cruz already knew of the miracles being performed over the mountains in Sonora by a Santa Teresa. We have already noted that he assured Chávez of divine protection for his holy mission—at least, that is what Chávez certified to his followers as they went forth to battle the soldiers of Satan. But we know nothing of the origins of this grand mission. Did Cruz already have an agenda in mind when he went to El Chopeque, or did the Santo put it in his head? Or did they design it together? To this point Cruz had not publicly announced his intention to obey no one but God. Perhaps the Santo encouraged Cruz to do so, but more likely Chávez needed no such encouragement. Whatever their interaction or their pact, Chávez and the Santo must have recognized that a public oath to obey no one but God could only provoke a sharp response from civil authorities. In fact, such a brazen proclamation would place them among the many other such spiritually motivated groups that eagerly anticipate a climactic struggle with the forces of the Devil in order to precipitate the Apocalypse that will be followed by the Millennium. Cruz and his associates may well have begun to prepare for the inevitable on their return to Tomochic. Perhaps the Santo only told Chávez what he had wanted to hear, but whatever passed between them, it unquestionably reinforced the leader's resolve.

As might be expected, Cruz Chávez was not the only one listening in on El Santo del Chopeque. Local civil authorities and the itinerant priest whose ecclesiastical responsibilities covered the district, Manuel Castelo, also paid him attention. The state was interested in possible sedition, the church in heresy. Both are traditionally suspicious of those who claim to know God's will. During a brief stopover at Tomochic on November 5, the priest learned of the single-minded devotion that Cruz and his followers were rendering to Los Santos del Chopeque. The priest's informant was Reyes Domínguez, who seemed especially anxious to discredit the believers. The news sorely pained Castelo, particularly so because it fit so snugly into a distressing pattern. Over in Sonora, not very far away, Santa Teresa's ministry had been building an assemblage for nearly two years and now this Santo del Chopeque had arrived on the scene. Padre Castelo decided that he must soon return to Tomochic and in no uncertain terms strip the congregation of these "false prophets." And so there he stood on November 15 in the plain pulpit of the church in Tomochic. Practically the entire pueblo had turned out to hear him. Cruz Chávez listened intently to the priest's thundering admonitions about obedience to Holy Mother Church, to the Law of God as learned only through Christian doctrine. Teresa Urrea was undoubtedly a virtuous young woman, but she must not be considered a saint. Only the Church can make such judgments; only the Church, if she merits it, can canonize her, and then only after her death. "Return from your errant ways, or suffer excommunication, and . . ."[56]

How far off, how starkly cold that powerful official institution with its threat of expulsion must have seemed to Cruz and the others at that moment. It was simply irrelevant to their everyday lives and had been so for some time. How dare this priest tell them what *their* religiosity meant to *them* and how it was to be practiced? *They*, not priests, decided what was important for *themselves*. Chávez became perturbed, stood up, and intemperately admonished the congregation: "Yes, they *are* saints," and as he stormed out of the church with his followers he very pointedly hurled a profanity at the bewildered, and yes, terrorized, priest.[57]

Within a few days, the faithful headed back to El Chopeque.

3

Religion as Practiced

PADRE MANUEL CASTELO had been apprehensive about the growing popularity of La Santa de Cabora for some time. Teresa's preachings and healings were attracting pilgrims by the thousands, some from the Papigochic region, where her reputation for making miracles ran especially high after Cayetano Parra, who had suffered from leprosy for more than two years, went to Cabora and returned home to the valley cured. Parra had written about the godsend. Teresa had applied hot compresses to his diseased body, and one day, in a high fever he drifted off into a delirium in which he dreamed he stood, nearly nude, in the presence of Teresa and others. He fled in embarrassment, but soon was calmed by the Almighty and returned from his spell to reason. From then on his leprosy began to heal. Testimony by other people from the Papigochic was equally astounding. Luis Bencomo, related to one of the area's elite clans, had gone mad, and in desperation his family took him to Cabora. Once there, he raved on, refused all food, and had to be locked up. Then Teresa gave him some broth "which the madness received with pleasure," and Bencomo regained his sanity. Even while retaining his doubts about her sanctity, one of the Papigochic's padres, Julio Irigoyen, recommended to her a parishioner pained by a long-festering sore on his heel that had puzzled medical doctors. But when the priest also suggested that Teresa make a formal doctrinal confession about her spiritual claims, she wrote a blistering reply, which ended their communications.[1]

At first La Santa's practices merely irked Padre Castelo and made him curious. Once he journeyed to Cabora to witness the goings-on for himself and, while there, encouraged two nuns to test Teresa's special powers. As La Santa lay in contemplation—a sort of trance—on her bed, he urged the nuns to stick a long hat pin through the calf of one of her legs. The nuns did what the priest bid, but when they tried to withdraw the pin, they could not dislodge it—it held firm. Then Teresa awoke and herself gently removed the pin from her own leg. No pain, not a drop of blood. The nuns fell to their knees, praised her miracle, and begged her forgiveness. Serenely, Teresa replied: "I do not perform miracles. Only God can do that."[2]

Whatever Castelo's reaction, he did not come away a believer. Most likely he simply belittled the commotion at Cabora and urged his congregations to do the same—that is, until he learned that Teresa had been advising her listeners to baptize and marry themselves; they did not need the Church, she counseled, to lead them to God. Not only was that heresy, plain and simple, but it put her in direct competition for power with the Church and its clergy. Still Sonora was in a separate ecclesiastical jurisdiction, with its own bishop; her preachings were that prelate's problem, even if Castelo considered it among his responsibilities to observe her. Besides, he had his own difficulties closer by with the Santo del Chopeque, who proselytized among his charges and was therefore a direct threat. Padre Castelo arrived in Tomochic on November 15, 1891, to set matters straight.

Itinerant priests such as Castelo tried to visit each pueblo within their jurisdiction on the day the village celebrated its patron saint. For Tomochitecos that normally festive and boisterous event occurred on July 4, with a special Mass and fiesta honoring Nuestra Señora del Refugio.[3] But because his parish encompassed such a vast expanse of the craggy Sierra—and because Castelo undoubtedly felt more comfortable at his parish house in the normally bustling mining community of Uruáchic (where the fees were steady and good) rather than riding horseback through hostile terrain to rather drab villages—he rarely made it to a pueblo on its designated feast day. The padre was no stranger to Tomochic, however; he had ministered to that congregation for at least six years.[4] Reyes Domínguez was his good friend, and he had bought a horse from Cruz Chávez in the spring of 1891.[5] That same year he had missed July fourth in the pueblo, but no matter; by celebrating the local saint's day on November 15, he assured himself a good turnout for the saying of the Mass and his special sermon, literally calculated to put the fear of God into his listeners. We already know the outcome. When Castelo vigorously chastised his listeners for their devotion to charlatans who posed as messengers of God, Cruz Chávez led his followers from the church—and into history.[6]

Padre Castelo was surprised and frightened—a large part of his congregation had walked out on him. The priest's personal friend, Reyes Domínguez, the pueblo's presidente, Juan Ignacio Chávez, and a couple of schoolteachers, Jesús J. Armenta and Santiago Simonet, had remained in the temple with their families, along with Sabino Ledesma and Domingo López and their families. Jesús Medrano had also stayed. Of these, only Medrano and young Timoteo Ledesma later joined Cruz Chávez, showing how the village had become factionalized. Padre Castelo declared that the church had been profaned and the Holy Eucharist violated; therefore, he could not continue with the Mass. When those present urged him to complete the service so that they could make amends (to the Almighty?) for the sinners who had left, the priest hurried through the remainder of the rite. Then fearful of physical harm—Cruz had seemed that threatening as he departed the church (some contend that he actually struck the priest with the flat of his hand)—Castelo opted for the safety of the Reyes Domínguez house. When tempers cooled, he would be off on horseback to continue his missionary rounds, but with a wary eye cast back over his shoulder for Cruz Chávez or any of his associates.[7]

Tomochic's Religious Heritage

Tomochic bore a special religious stamp, stemming from before colonial times. Because it occupied the largest, most habitable valley in the eastern part of the Sierra, it seems to have been an important center of indigenous religious activity well before Jesuit missionaries came to the region. The Jesuits were unable to establish a permanent outpost in Tomochic much before the eighteenth century because the rebellious Tarahumaras used it as a base for their forays against the Spaniards. Inspired Tarahumara holy leaders had promised the resurrection of Indians slain confronting the invaders, and many Spaniards—civil officials, ecclesiastics, soldiers, and settlers alike—were casualties to this belief.[8]

During the first quarter of the 1700s Tomochic became a fledgling Jesuit mission. Tarahumaras customarily did not live in villages or large settlements but instead on what were called rancherías, consisting of two to four families. Thus the missionaries had to scour the countryside for potential converts and struggle to pull them together into a settlement. Yet the Tarahumaras fell prey to their own curiosity. Perhaps attracted by the colorful ceremonies staged by the missionaries, they came to listen to doctrinal messages that, among other things, scolded them for their "barbarian" practices and rituals, especially those involving the unfettered consumption of tesgüino. In 1730 Padre Xavier de Estrada summed up the atmosphere at the mission this way: "To be brief, I say there is no vice or evil to which the Indians are not given. Foremost among these are theft, promiscuity, drunkenness and sloth . . . the root of all evil."[9] Actually, a good many Tarahumaras were not at all slothful, and they frequently ran off to work at the charcoal works, ranches, and mines of the colonizers in the region, switching from the diet of religious indoctrination and handouts at the missions to wages. In neither case did they give up their own culture.[10] But many Tarahumara resented being compelled by the priests to labor at the mission, and so they dragged their feet, got surly, and in a variety of ways resisted their exploitation. Sloth to some is protest to others.

Mass baptisms occurred, but mainly of children under seven years of age. Adult Indians persistently proved more reluctant to convert to the Holy Faith. When asked why they did not want to be baptized, they simply answered "Nagoche": "Because I do not want to be baptized," or more curtly, "Because I don't want to." That was that. The priests assured a native living near Tomochic that "Baptism is a sacrament which gives life and eternal grace," and urged that he not die without being baptized. The native replied, "I am a man and do not have to die." To him, men did not die. To priests such comments confirmed their failure: "The devil is still victorious."[11] The missionaries categorized the natives as either "gentiles" (non-Christian heathens) or "Cristianos," a distinction still used by many observers of Tarahumara life. Although it is always difficult to gauge the extent and profundity of conversion, priests toiling among the Tarahumara today doubt that nearly 300 years of proselytizing has in any meaningful way altered religious thought among any substantial number of the natives.[12]

In 1722 a German Jesuit, Herman Glandorff, took charge of To-

mochic's mission and over the forty years until his death has been credited with a benevolence toward the natives approaching saintliness.
Indeed, it is said that he performed miracles, including hands-on healings, that he could predict the future and penetrate one's consciousness, that he was, in fact, a saint. Some of his later admirers have advanced that possibility to the official Church, although the process of
beatification has not gone forward. It is said that Padre Glandorff regularly prayed to and communicated with the Divine in a cave located in
the broken terrain west of the pueblo in the Cañón de la Banderilla.[13]
The cave became known throughout the region and appeared on survey
maps for the period, the only point of reference identified in the countryside outside of roughly sketched-in settlements and large private
holdings. So the cave was an important point of regional orientation,
but whether it was a religious shrine or a pilgrimage site is not known.[14]
Villagers today still visit Glandorff's cave, though more for its pecuniary
possibilities than spiritual reasons, for it is murmured that the Jesuits,
when expelled by the Spanish king in 1767, buried some of Tomochic's
religious treasures there. If so, no one has yet discovered them.

Tomochic seems to have remained primarily native well into the
nineteenth century. A census taken there in 1765 just before the forced
departure of the Jesuits reports 368 inhabitants, all indigenous peoples.[15] Mexico's independence from Spain in 1821 seems to have
brought little change. Mines in the region fell quiet as investors waited
for politicians to sort out the nation's future, guarantee public order,
and provide other attractions for capital. Chihuahua's leaders staked
out their claims within the new federal republic, and much regional
attention focused on the increasing incursions of Apache raiding parties from the north. In 1831 the population consisted of 347 Tarahumaras, approaching the limit that the space and soil of the valley could
naturally support.[16] But within the next ten years the discovery of new
mines in the region drew whites and mestizos into Tomochic, and so
began the despoliation of the mission (now Franciscan) and its surroundings, a process that ran on throughout the century.

Tomochic had a priest in residence into the 1870s, far longer than
other similar pueblos in the Sierra.[17] What that meant for the religious
life of the village is difficult to assess, but it places a motherless Cruz
Chávez in close proximity to a priest all through his childhood and well
into his teens. (How the youth related to the priest and local religious

practices is not known, but later, as we have noted, in the absence of a priest Cruz became a leader in the pueblo's religious affairs.) While at Tomochic any priest would be more than 1,500 arduous miles away from his closest superior, the bishop at Durango City, so the official instructions of the Church only filtered up to the padre slowly by way of a *cordillera*, a kind of chain letter that took months to circulate from parish to parish in the geographically immense and relatively sparsely populated bishopric. Under the circumstances there was no way for the official church to know how, or even if, its edicts were being obeyed. Priests in places like Tomochic were pretty much on their own. Furthermore, they seem sometimes to have been capricious—or perhaps just human—so it is difficult to generalize about them. In 1853 Padre Silva complained to the jefe político that Tomochic's chief official, Antonio Pedregón, had illegally taken land from the Indians there, but hardly a year earlier the same priest had advised the jefe that the non-Indians in Tomochic had insufficient land to cultivate because the natives occupied more territory than they needed. "The greed of the Indians is very great," he wrote: for example, one native possessed seventeen and one-half acres but used only three for himself and his family. The remainder of the valuable land went untilled and wasted.[18]

Priests could also be in conflict with one another, as they were in 1869 when Tomochic's new padre, Ignacio Márquez, tried to grab the first fruits of the corn harvest away from his fellow priest at Yepachic, another village in the area. Even in more populated and accessible sites like the Papigochic, priests stole goods from each other's churches, altered the testaments of fellow padres to favor themselves, and could wear political stripes entirely different from one another. For instance, Padre Francisco de Paula Portillo, who had land and illegitimate children in Guerrero City, could hardly have been more aligned with the designs of government; he delivered the patriotic speeches on national holidays and served on the city's electoral board. At the same time Father Julio Irigoyen, in nearby Temósachic (the same priest who had earlier contacted Santa Teresa on behalf of a parishioner), proved to be a persistent political agitator and in the 1890s the state accused him of fomenting revolution.[19]

There are few details about the individual curates who worked in Tomochic. But judging by the recorded accusations they hurled at each other there was plenty of conflict between the priests and non-Indians in the village, with the natives frequently caught in between. We have already seen how in the late 1850s mestizos attacked the priest for his alleged mistreatment of the Tarahumaras and vice versa, and how the dominant groups utilized the same issue as pretext for the feuds among themselves. The right to flog natives was an issue for mestizos. When in the 1870s the bishopric decided no longer to staff what remained of its Tomochic mission, Ignacio Gallegos, the pueblo's comisario, asked the district's jefe político (in writing) whether or not civil authorities there could continue to whip the Indians as the padres used to do.[20]

Padres in the region seemed to live in a perpetual maelstrom, and their activities and altercations help us to focus on those things that most concerned local people and how politics became inextricably combined with spirituality. Indeed, for most people of the region religiosity meshed with daily living. They believed in a personal God who could make His plans, desires, and anger known to His adherents. They lived in a world full of temptation, one in which the Antichrist often successfully challenged the powers of Providence. Around Christmastime communities reenacted that eternal contest in elaborate pageants called *posadas*. Each drama had its local wrinkle; the one witnessed by American cavalry officer John Gregory Bourke in the 1890s along the Rio Grande carried a utopian theme with clear political overtones. In their songs the children, dressed as shepherds, said they were going to Bethlehem to witness a miracle: the birth of the Divine Redeemer who would set them free—although free from precisely what is not clear. En route they had to defeat the Devil, who had declared at the start of the posada, "War on Man, unending war, and death of all."[21] In pageants such as the Judas burnings during Holy Week, Mexicans frequently costumed their Judas or Devil to resemble a person they detested: a politician, for example, or a foreign entrepreneur. It distressed Bourke to learn that at the posada on the border the locals intended to put their Devil in the uniform of a U.S. cavalry officer.[22]

For Cruz Chávez, were the events that had befallen him—prolonged drought, canceled processions, stolen religious paintings, accusations of banditry—seen as irresistible and cataclysmic and therefore as a divine message? Was the Anti-Christ upon him and his people? Did the presence of the Devil herald the end of the world? Perhaps so: in attacking the federal soldiers, the believers did shout, "Death to the Sons of Lucifer!" (Of course, like all religiously responsive people, not every-

one who participated in the posadas carried the same degree of conviction. One could not be sure of God's plan. The American artist Frederick Remington, traveling by coach around Guerrero City about 1890,
inquired of a man why he thought it had not rained in eighteen months,
to which the campesino replied: "Because God wills it—I suppose."[23]
(That "I suppose" tells a lot.)

The Substance of Local Religion

In the absence of much guidance from the institutional Church, Tomochitecos probably sought ultimate meanings about life through tradition, experience, and culture, in effect believing in a God they had
fashioned for themselves. Most religious thought and practice, then
and now, is local, concrete, and practical (as opposed to official and abstract), reflecting everyday needs. These people generally understood
Christian doctrines but reworked them to correspond with their own
necessities, ambitions, and daydreams. The official Church (though
certainly not all priests) has traditionally been suspicious of local religion, especially in the ways that it subverts what the Church sees as its
sole authority to perform sacred rituals and to interpret the Word of
God, but that has rarely influenced the practice of local religion, especially in those locales where there are no, or only sporadic or lukewarm,
purveyors of official dogma around. This difference of opinion may be
seen as a power struggle, or at least an ongoing dialogue, but when the
official Church pushes its case too forcefully, it risks repercussions,
even rejection. Under such circumstances, local priests, if not the
Mother Church, customarily prefer compromise. The tenacious reliance of many common people on magic—the occult forces of nature,
both harmful and helpful—illustrates the sort of agreements that they
have negotiated with ecclesiastics over time and that cannot be easily
curbed by Church or State.

Though the populace in northern Mexico about the turn of the
century was largely illiterate, those who could read were likely to have a
copy of *Oráculo*, a dreambook to be consulted about the future. After
all, most believed the world would come to an end; it was just a matter
of when, and so they diligently looked for clues to the divinely promised

event. Witches, people in believed to be in contact with the devil, also abounded, as described by John Bourke. In fact, Rio Grande City, Texas, may have been the scene of the last witchcraft trial in America. In 1876 ten women (presumably all Hispanics, although we do not know their ethnicities) were convicted of being witches and fined $10.00 each with a month's prison sentence for their illegal practices.[24]

Bourke recorded the rich mixture of religiosity and magic that infused the lives of inhabitants in the north of Mexico, whose culture spilled over into the lower tier of the United States. According to one witch in Bourke's account: "You must never spit in a fire. Fire comes from *La providencia de Dios*. It is just like the law and represents God, who made it for our comfort. He who would spit in the fire would spit in the face of God." Or, "If a young lady wants to have soft skin and a clear, ruddy complexion, she must wait till the Eve of Saint John's Day, and then rub her face with a piece of the navel [umbilical cord] of a young male child." In search of the foundations of the spiritual practices of these people, Bourke visited a number of sacred shrines, in particular that of "La Virgen Sudanda" (the sweating virgin) at Agualeguas, somewhat south of the river in the state of Nuevo León. To him she resembled a French doll encased in glass, and attached to her skirt he noticed numerous votive offerings, gold and silver trinkets shaped like hearts, legs, arms, ears of corn, horses, feet, all witnesses to personal petitions and *milagros* (miracles received). In a nearby cave the faithful worshipped a stalactite that to them had become the Madonna swathed in flowing garments. Those who could not personally visit these sacred sites recited novenas from home dedicated to the appropriate image or venerated a bit of soil carried to them from the site by friends or relatives. There may even have been some professional pilgrims at work here being paid for their "delivery services." The area also featured its santos, such as an extremely popular healer at Los Olmos, in Cameron County, Texas, and a hermit who lived beneath a rocky overhang on the Rio Grande itself, where he carved statues from soft stone and sold them as grave-site ornaments.[25]

Witches, devils, saints, ghosts, rain dwarfs, and God Himself populated the universe of these Norteños. Supernatural beings explained sickness, bizarre personal behavior, even a criminal disposition. Demons with horns and long tails took possession of children and made them disobey their mothers. They made a pact with a girl to murder her parents, and tempted fathers to drink and adultery.[26] The persistence of this belief should not necessarily be attributed to an ignorance of science and technology. When the rare opportunity arose, some chanced more modern medicine, which seemed to carry a magic of its own. They sought out the leaders, often foreigners, of expeditions plying the Sierra and invested them with healing and spiritual powers. Carl Lumholtz, the Norwegian anthropologist, had just such an experience around Yepachic in 1892, when the local people hounded him for medicine and cures. "They were anxious to have me feel their pulse, whether there was anything the matter with them or not. They firmly believed that this mysterious touch enabled them to tell whether they were inflicted with any disease and how long they were going to live."[27] So it was the touch of the potential healer that mattered most. On the same journey but closer to the Papigochic Valley, Lumholtz learned that people ground up fossils of prehistoric bones—probably the tusks of mammoths known to have roamed the area—to make a concoction said to invigorate them. In their search for physical well-being, as well as explanation and meaning in life, these people liberally lumped magic with religiosity, and when available, seasoned the mix with a "mysterious touch" or even standard medicine.

The Tomochitecos knew few if any doctors. When the region's one licensed médico, Dr. Robert Nichol, came to the pueblo in the wake of the skirmishes of December 1891, it seemed to be his first visit to the community. For his participation in the exhumation of those killed and perhaps some attention to the few wounded, he submitted his bill to the state, the exorbitant fee of 510 pesos (some $400) for his rather meager services. A fuming Governor Carrillo rejected the bill and with the support of the state legislature ordered it to be resubmitted by Nichol in a more reasonable amount.[28] The following year, when the faithful had returned to Tomochic and were engaged in further confrontations with the military, Cruz Chávez and his followers declined all aid from military physicians. They themselves preferred the spirituality, magic, and herbs that had long served their hurts. In this instance we know they applied a mixture of soap, beef fat, and a fine, white powder to their injuries, but what that powder was—ground medicinal herbs and bones, a magic potion, soil from Cabora, or a substance blessed by Teresa—is not recorded.[29] Women around San Luis Potosí who wished to expedite delivery of their babies drank water in which they had dissolved a pinch from a small cake of white earth scraped from the local church and blessed by the padre.[30] Whatever Chávez and his coreligionists expected from the white powder, its presence confirms greater trust in the traditional and spiritual than in things modern and scientific.

Cruz and his associates did not hold others to their medical beliefs, however. In skirmishes during the early fall of 1892, they allowed an army doctor, Major Francisco Arrellano, to confer with and to treat wounded federal soldiers, and then politely dismissed the physician from their company. (Whatever Dr. Arrellano's medical skills, he was a useful spy and provided the military with valuable intelligence about the believers.)[31] In the next few days the serious leg injuries of a captured officer, Lieutenant Colonel José María Ramírez, began to fester, and now no doctor was available. Ramírez rejected the herbs and home-made remedies offered by Cruz and finally, in intense pain, begged Cruz Chávez to turn him loose to return to his accustomed medical care, or to amputate his badly wounded leg, or failing any such remedy to shoot him. Cruz chose the first option and set the officer free with an escort to guide him through the mountains to Guerrero. Chávez, in concert with so many Mexicans of the period, apparently had no faith in "modern" medicine. Like Teresa he probably saw its practitioners as evil or ineffectual, but in this case, at least, he granted the devil his due.[32]

The Stress of Becoming Modern

All during the second half of the nineteenth century Mexicans weighed doctors, technology, spirituality, priests, money, education, republicanism, individualism, progress—indeed the entire trajectory of their country and the balance of their lives between God and government—in the glare of the so-called Cuestión Juarista. The name *Juarista* derives from Benito Juárez, the full-blooded Zapotec Indian, who as president of Mexico in the 1860s began a great liberalizing and modernizing enterprise and became one of the country's great national heroes. His followers and successors made a pact labeled "The Reform" with the Mexican people: Trust us, follow us, and we will make you modern; that is, we will place you among the progressive peoples of the world. Regardless of the arguments on either side (and there were

many of them—both through intellectual persuasion and at gunpoint)
the government persisted in its intentions, aided by those who sensed
new opportunity for themselves. The Reformers offered Western-style
order and progress, and as those who accepted the invitation steadily
gained the reins of state, their insistence on *their* model grew more
strident. But humans do not ordinarily make decisions on how they
intend to lead their lives all at once, and once made, such judgments are
rarely clear-cut or irreversible. By no means did the changes occur
evenly across the landscape or all at once. Nor was the transition ever
complete. Tidbits, even large chunks, of traditional customs and beliefs
remained in place, many of them embedded in religious rituals and
practices that now came under criticism, even denunciation, by the
new regime and its supporters. The friction was bound to produce
sparks as the opportunities and drawbacks of The Reform rekindled
already smoldering animosities and disputes.[33]

In the case of religion, change forced Mexicans to contemplate the
relevance—or, if you please, the usefulness—of religion in their lives
and to reflect on the position and role of the official Church in the new
as well as the old society. Power struggles between priests and civil
authorities only amplified the stress in individual minds and caused
some to become harshly anticlerical, though still firm Christians. Religious newcomers such as Protestants and Spiritists took advantage of
the turmoil to offer alternatives to Catholicism. Each carved substantial inroads into the Sierra, down in the Papigochic, and over in Sonora
where La Santa de Cabora preached. Naturally, Catholic priests fought
to hold back the tide. When Augusta Lurris, representing the Evangelical Church, visited the Catholic Church in Batopilas in 1896, the local
priest rushed in after her "and by means of exorcisms and holy water
tossed out the devils from the church which had probably entered with
the dangerous visitor."[34] Perhaps the journalist reporting this incident
meant to be sarcastic, but still the comments accentuate the determination of the Catholic Church to deter religious dissidence.

The civil government's all-out assault at mid-nineteenth century on
the wealth, power, and influence of the official Church predictably
enraged that institution. Decades of outright civil war followed as ranking politicians and their military allies battled for supremacy over the
country's direction and affairs. Equally virulent power struggles seeped
into lower levels of society, especially in the countryside, where petty

officials battled priests for power. Higher civil authorities—governors, jefes políticos—advised consultation and compromise in these relatively insignificant local and regional disputes, but minor civil authorities anxious to exercise their newfound authority still frequently forced priests to toe the new legal line: no more processions during Holy Week, nothing resembling a political pronouncement from the pulpit. Priests even had to ask permission of the authorities to administer last rites to a parishioner dying at home.[35]

In 1858, the year of Cruz Chávez's birth and only a year after confirmation of the nation's new constitution, which sought to legitimize the new order, Tomochic's comisario wrote the governor that the priests in the pueblo (there were apparently two of them, Antonio Romero and Silva) openly opposed the new mandate. Here we learn something of the flavor and discourse of the new order: the priests are "enemies of enlightenment and progress": they treat the Indians "as beasts of burden and not as citizens with free use of their rights; they stop the Indians from achieving liberty."[36] Five years later the same two priests were still trying to skirt the new anti-Church laws. When the jefe político attempted to bring Padre Silva to heel, the priest claimed he did not understand the new law, yet asserted that "As a priest, I do not meddle in civil affairs." He also noted that the information provided by the local justice of the peace concerning the number of natives at the mission was incorrect and offered to pass on the proper statistics for the civil registry—but this concession should not be seen as any flag of truce.[37] Only the previous month, Padre Romero faced arrest because he declined to obey local officials, but when authorities attempted to detain him, the priest locked himself in the rectory of the church and refused to come out. Authorities finally arrested Romero (did they break into the church?) and hustled him off under a four-man guard to state judicial authorities in Guerrero City.[38] We can only wonder how this saga ended.

So Cruz Chávez grew up in an atmosphere in which priests not only refused flat out to obey the new civil regulations, but also developed strategies to get around them. In 1863 the Bishop of Durango advised the padres in his jurisdiction to obey the law prohibiting public religious display but, when it came to administering the Holy Sacrament outside the church, told them how to subvert the regulations: Wear regular clothes over your religious garb. Carry the Blessed Sacrament under your street clothes in some container that will not draw the attention of the authorities; it would be irreverent just to put the Host in your pocket. Do all this at night. Remember your obligation to administer the sacraments to priests near death, but should civil authorities consider this an offense, you must obey them. You must respect civil authority even if you go to jail carrying the sacraments.[39] But parish priests paid little heed to the advice from their ecclesiastical superiors. While the law prohibited them from making house-to-house solicitations, they organized lay societies from among their parishioners to do the task for them. When a santo made such collections in Morís, the presidente suspected that the local priest had put him up to it.[40] Bachíniva's parish in the 1880s devised an association to finance mortgages on land for its members as well as to pay for improvements to the church and other pious works. Powerful politicians in the town denounced the practice and urged the federal government to stop it, but investigation proved the fund to be legal.[41] Regardless of official cautions from the bishops, the battle between civil and church authorities raged on in the municipalities and villages.

Much of the controversy surrounded the Reform government's mandate that citizens register their vital statistics with the State rather than the Church. There was a lot at stake here: substantial fees and power over people's lives. Many priests certainly discouraged their parishioners from fulfilling these kinds of civil requirements and even held back the sacraments from those who did.[42] However, religious country people hardly needed the advice. Registering births was one thing, the removal of original sin something else, and a civil death certificate could not affect salvation. Birth, marriage, and death are the major markers of an individual's passage through life, and all churches sanctify them in sacraments. Some people fulfilled the conditions of both Church and State; some opted for one or the other—or even neither. But a very great number stuck with the Church and shamelessly ignored or even brazenly defied the State. In response the civil authorities could be understanding. At Tomochic in 1880 the Tarahumaras were relieved of a cattle-killing tax on those beasts slain for religious ceremonies and allowed to hold their traditional outdoor services on Christmas Eve. Nor was a native taxed like others for a tombstone he might carve. The poor, categorized as those who earned 50 centavos or less a day (itself a comment on wages of the period), did not have to pay fees connected with the civil registry in the Papigochic.[43] But for the most part authorities pressured people to adhere to the new practices, and many saw that as the intrusion of state politics on their religious sensibilities.

In Tomochic it was the job of the longtime civil judge Jesús María Ortiz to enforce the registry and collect the fees. Frequent discord developed. May 1880 found the local comisario, Jesús Medrano, complaining to the jefe político about the constant abuses by Ortiz couched in the name of duty. The feud simmered through much of the decade and finally boiled over early in the winter of 1888. According to Ortiz, the citizenry persistently ignored the registry, but he could not enforce the law because Jesús Medrano, now presidente, would intervene. A current example: Miguel Mendías, a widower who was literate, had not properly arranged for the marriage of his illiterate younger brother, Guillermo, through the office of the civil registrar. Specifically, he had not paid for a marriage certificate or the required copies—at a cost of 2 pesos ($1.60 U.S.). Right after the marriage ceremony, apparently just as the wedding party left the church, Ortiz confronted Miguel Mendías and demanded the payment. No such luck. Shortly thereafter the elder Mendías arrived with two friends, Santiago Gallegos and José Calderón, at the office of the judge, but only to declare that he did not recognize Ortiz's authority. Ortiz ordered Gallegos and Calderón to arrest Mendías, but of course they did not and Mendías left for his house. In response the judge sent a squad of men to the Mendías dwelling to arrest him. When they arrived, Mendías demanded a copy of the charges in writing. Then the village comisario (probably Jesús Medrano) merely issued Mendías a stay of arrest. Ortiz countered against Mendías with a 10 peso ($8) fine, as stipulated by law, a levy that the comisario promptly canceled. So now the beleaguered Ortiz appealed to the jefe político for advice and help. The jefe told him to forget the fine—but that hardly settled the acrimony. We should note that Mendías, Medrano, Gallegos, and Calderón all later joined the Cruz Chávez movement; Jesús María Ortiz did not—and perhaps we have a clue about why some folks rebel and others do not.[44]

The controversies of reform penetrated whatever ties bound Tomochic together as a community. Although nominally all Roman Catholic, as individuals Tomochitecos certainly differed in the substance, practice, and intensity of their beliefs. Reyes Domínguez, for example, owned books by the passionately liberal French historian and moralist Jules Michelet, who vehemently debunked traditional Catholicism and was especially hard on the Jesuit influence in his country's schools. Maybe that is why Domínguez became a major sponsor of primary education in Tomochic. In the margins of these books, and specifically at several places where Michelet excoriated religious fanaticism, Domínguez inked in a crucifix and the word "Cruz."[45] Was he thinking about Chávez as he read the diatribe? And pondering much more fundamental questions about being "modern" and blockades to "progress"? We have already seen in his cooperation with the military how anxious Domínguez was to bring Cruz Chávez's movement to bay. Was the religious fanaticism of the Chávez group his justification or simply a pretext?

Among the others who stayed put in the village church the day that Padre Castelo delivered his assertive sermon, and Chávez stormed out with his followers, were the primary schoolteachers, Jesús J. Armenta and Santiago Simonet, who most certainly taught the values of the new secular order. Also Juan Ignacio Chávez, a relative newcomer in town, the presidente who canceled the religious procession and did not object when the governor rode off with sacred paintings stolen from the temple.[46] Others, such as Sabino Ledesma and Domingo López and their families, had less obvious reasons for staying; we might remember that Sabino's son, Timoteo, had labeled El Santo del Chopeque a fraud— but the youngster himself later joined the movement.[47] No one was more concerned about the polarization in Tomochic than Padre Castelo, who had known ruptures in his congregations before, but nothing like this.

Countdown to Combat

Following the confrontation in the church, Castelo demanded that the village presidente use the law to punish Cruz and his group for their threats toward him, but Juan Ignacio Chávez wisely declined to act. He was not up to an open encounter with an angry Cruz Chávez. Reyes Domínguez offered the priest house protection, and Castelo appears to have stayed there for a couple of days. By November 17 it seems that tempers had calmed, so the priest left Tomochic to make the rounds of other relatively nearby pueblos in his jurisdiction: Yepachic, Temechic, Arisiachic, and finally Pachera, a largely Tarahumara community at the southern end of the Papigochic Valley.[48]

Not necessarily by coincidence, Castelo was present in Pachera on November 21 when Cruz Chávez and some thirty followers carrying weapons passed through the community on their way to visit with El Santo del Chopeque. Pachera's presidente wanted to arrest the participants as rebels against the state, but Castelo cautioned against it. Let them continue, he advised; they are only going to see their santo, a mistake to be sure, but still within the law (as long as the authorities chose to interpret it that way). More important, to stop them would threaten the public peace and (he might have added) risk his life and that of the presidente. So the band of faithful continued their trek to El Chopeque.[49]

A few days later, on November 25, a patrol from one of the security forces commanded by Joaquín Chávez made an unauthorized raid and weapons search at the dwelling of Jorge Ortiz at Rancho del Nogal, just outside Tomochic. Jorge was not at home at the time, and a rumor spread that the intruders had intended to forcibly draft him into the army. Or might they have had another object in mind? Since the bandit attack on the mule train at Puerto de Manzanillas earlier that year, Joaquín Chávez had been nervous about regional security. Remember that he had implicated Tomochitecos in that affair. He must have known about the armed group that Cruz Chávez led to convene with El Santo del Chopeque, and he may even have known more than we do about the exchange that occurred between them. Did Joaquín suspect that there was some stockpiling of guns and ammunition, no matter how minor, going on? On November 21 Cruz consulted with El Santo. Four days later the Ortiz home was raided. On November 30 some thirty to forty followers of Cruz gathered with their leader at the house of José Dolores Rodríguez, where they had often met to plan and pray. Orations followed; people got stirred up. Then the hot-tempered mob exploded into the cool evening air and stormed to the home of the village president. Angry shouts and vehement vows followed: "¡Viva la Virgen y muera Lucifer!" (Long live the Virgin and death to Lucifer!)[50] Here was the eternal conflict acted out in the posada come to life. The proclamation followed: "We will obey no one but God!" Now we are

only one week away from the confrontation with the army. In the mean-
time, Cruz summoned the faithful to the village church for prayer and
counsel, and he told them to come *armed*.[51] This sounds like a man
with a definite plan in mind.

In the first days of December Padre Castelo returned to Tomochic,
apparently in search of a resolution, and learned that he was already
much too late. Word was out about the vow of the Tomochitecos. Convoys already avoided the pueblo; military preparations to investigate
the uproar had begun. The schoolteacher Jesús Armenta and Reyes
Domínguez made one final attempt to dissuade the faithful from their
resolve, but with no success.[52] Cruz disdained the two men for their
lack of religious faith and moral understanding; the gulf between them
and the believers was unquestionably too great for any sort of compromise. The day that the troops began their march toward Tomochic,
December 6, 1891, the padre rode off on horseback for his residence in
Uruáchic. Castelo never returned to the pueblo, but Cruz Chávez was
not done with him yet.

4

Nests of Contention

IF, AS IS SAID, every village has its son of a bitch, Reyes Domínguez was it for Tomochic.[1] Domínguez was frequently at issue with others about land in and around the pueblo, and especially exploited the local Tarahumaras. As a pueblo official he enjoyed tossing his weight around. He kowtowed to jefes políticos and influential regional bosses called *caciques* (both titles could be held by one and the same person) to the detriment of fellow villagers; his instincts and interests lay as much outside as inside the village. He was pragmatic, opportunistic, and pretentious, and did not much like to share his wealth with less fortunate people. Domínguez became particularly truculent toward Cruz Chávez, his followers, and their families. He may have made a half-hearted attempt to mollify them at the start—to warn them of the error of their ways, as he saw it—but after the events of December 1891 he insisted that they be punished and eagerly prodded the military toward that end.

Nonetheless, Reyes Domínguez could also be a pretty good son of a bitch. He almost single-handedly promoted primary schooling in the village and even financed a local boys' band. He was also smart, practical, and literate, and could be socially engaging. Some might call him "modern." We have already spotted in his library the books written by the anticlerical Michelet. But if he was modern, it was not because the national reforms unfolding around him made him that way. His personal bent was his own, but it undoubtedly encouraged him to take advantage of the new opportunities.

Reyes Domínguez arrived in Tomochic around 1870. His family was part of the great Domínguez clan founded by Juan Mateo Domínguez de Mendoza in the Papigochic during the latter part of the seventeenth century. Domínguez de Mendoza was the son of a Spanish general, Tomás Domínguez de Mendoza, who had been assigned to the outpost garrison of New Mexico, and like so many scions of those early settlers on the fringe of New Spain's northern frontier, Juan Mateo migrated south into what became Chihuahua. He settled in Basúchil, just outside Guerrero City (then called La Villa de Aguilar), and had ten or twelve children who went on to make Domínguez one of the most common surnames in the region.[2] Reyes was in his early twenties when he wandered into Tomochic, perhaps attracted by the mining camps farther up in the Sierra, for he was not a well-to-do young man. We cannot say what decided him to settle in the pueblo, but it could have been romantic love, for he soon married—ironically as it came to be—into the family of Cruz Chávez.[3] His wife, Consolación Chávez, was at marriage only sixteen years old, seven years younger than he and three years older than her brother Cruz. The padrón of 1864 suggests that she was the first child in her father's second marriage, which like the first, had ended with the untimely death of his wife.[4] When she married Reyes, she was only two or three years younger than the pueblo's average age for brides, and within a year the couple had a son, Lisandro, who, like his father, became a longtime and powerful resident of the pueblo.

The Domínguez household consisted of just the parents and their children, as did about half those in the village. People tended toward such a household type, but the realities of high infant mortality, lack of medicine, bad luck, and personal choice led to a wide variety of household arrangements: families who took in old parents, orphaned children, friends, and the stricken. Then there were those who lived alone as bachelors, widows, and widowers. People also resided together in common-law unions, or with brothers, sisters, and friends. Those who lost a spouse frequently remarried, and if desirous and able continued to build a family. These family patterns remained fairly constant. For example, of the 26 mestizo families found in the pueblo in 1864, slightly under half included only parents and their children; the rest were in a variety of arrangements. Nearly thirty years later the distribution remained about the same for the then 43 mestizo families.[5] As these patterns suggest, kinship was strong in Tomochic, but hardly the only or even the main basis for crucial decision-making and bonding. When it came time to weigh one's fidelity to Cruz Chávez and to chance the uncertainties of his movement, several families, like those of Jesús María Ortiz, Nepomuceno Acosta, and Espiridón Ruiz, split apart.

Men tended to marry women who averaged four years or more their junior—as did Reyes Domínguez—and most men were well into their twenties before they married. Nor did they always marry local girls. New village surnames—Pérez, Montes, Torres, Muñoz—crop up often enough among wives to assure us that men found their marriage partners down in the Papigochic or in the mining camps of the Sierra. By 1890 family names like Almeida and Alvarez, Pedregón, and even Arriola disappear from census reports, which means that those families either died out or moved on. We know, for instance, that the ambitious and well-off González clan, prominent in Tomochic in the 1840s, departed to reestablish itself and thrive in the Papigochic. On the other hand, new families fairly steadily sifted into the village. The late 1800s brought among others the Porras merchant family, Jesús Armenta to teach, and Juan Ignacio Chávez, who figured so prominently in the disturbances of late 1891. The overall population of Tomochic stabilized during the 1880s at about 300 inhabitants. This must have been about all the resources the valley could bear, but within that total there was individual and family flux.[6]

For their dwellings the great majority of Tomochitecos built simple adobe structures, either along the main wagon route through town or a bit to the south, along both sides of the broad and deep arroyo called Lino that sliced through the village (today it measures 30 feet wide and 20 feet deep). They built on high ground, overlooking the Río Tomochic, as protection from flash floods, while the Arroyo de Lino handled drainage and sewage. Each dwelling undoubtedly expressed the personal tastes of its inhabitants, but the overall appearance of the pueblo was one of drab uniformity. Walls were constructed of sunbaked adobe bricks made of gravelly clay, water, and straw, 10 by 20 inches in size and at least 4 inches thick, tempered by the summer heat, which rose into the nineties, and the winter cold, which often dipped below freezing. The houses had virtually no windows, the better to protect against the elements and interlopers. For their entrances the residents hewed heavy front doors from local pines—rugged, practical doors bereft of artistic designs. Wooden beams supported a roof of

closely aligned wooden poles covered with a foot or more of earth and
stones as a kind of insulation, and then with pine planking held in place
against the elements by sizable rocks. Some roofs tilted slightly upward
along one side of the structure, allowing smoke from cooking and heat-
ing fires to escape. Adobe walls and earthen roofs made the structures
virtually fireproof. Wooden joints might be held together with rawhide
strips or by wooden pins, but normally not nails, which cost more than
30 cents a pound in the 1880s and were getting more expensive (the
silver-backed peso was in decline).[7] While almost all dwellings were
rectangular in shape, a few were L-shaped, to provide an enclosed area,
more a corral than anything else.

The dwellings did vary in size. One built according to one's means.
Reyes Domínguez had a comparatively large house where he could
entertain and lodge visitors, and the widowed mother of the Medrano
brothers ran a small sundries store from a corner of her ample home,
but most Tomochitecos lived in very modest one-room dwellings, with
hard-packed dirt floors and a slightly raised hearth positioned along
one of the walls. Some homeowners roughly plastered inside walls with
a clay mortar applied by hand. Saddles, leather straps and pouches,
sacks made from woven fibers, rifles, and straw sombreros hung from
the beams, along with some dried provisions like chilies. The remains
of a corn harvest might fill one corner and a box of beans another.
Decorative touches included plants and climbing vines outside, and
occasionally a rusty cage housing a big Sierra woodpecker. A picture of
the Virgin of Guadalupe and a homemade crucifix very likely adorned a
wall; religious icons and articles counted among a family's valuables
and were passed down through inheritance. And did any household not
have a dog or two?[8]

Pine and scrub oak from the surrounding mountainsides and pla-
teaus provided furniture, fuel, and perhaps fencing for a small corral
out back. Light was provided by candles fashioned from solidified lard
with a string run through it or by burning pine resin. A typical home
would have a homemade bedstead, a table, and a couple of chairs. A
good many inhabitants slept on straw mats on the ground or perhaps a
cured hide laid hairside up. The Tarahumaras furnished magnificent—
and heavy—handmade woolen blankets and fired large earthenware
pots for carrying water and cooking food. However, the residents of
Tomochic were not limited to native goods and modest homemade

articles. Carl Lumholtz discovered the material fallout of mining enterprises in many villages: cheap factory-made clothing, foods, iron cooking utensils, tawdry jewelry, firearms, farming implements, and the rest.[9] The shops in the pueblo probably offered coffee, panocha sugar (cakes of brown sugar), along with a few stalks of sugar cane, dried garlic, tobacco and cigarettes, lard in a tin can, and hidden to one side a pint bottle or two of mescal. Morris Parker, an American miner, even came across some dusty tins of Armour's corned beef at a small shop in the Sierra—no doubt traded by some miner for some more immediate necessity.[10]

Other, more unusual and intriguing products coursed through Tomochic on their way to the Sierra: Singer sewing machines and cook stoves, flywheels 30 feet in diameter, monstrous cylinders and engines, even some 15-gallon kegs of Scotch whiskey, packed on those hardy, dependable, and sometimes stubborn mules called "mountain schooners." (To avoid cutting and splicing cable, teamsters coiled the heavy wire on the backs of some ten mules, leaving the animals strung together by loops of cable, one behind the other.) Much carrying was also done by native porters, accustomed to long hauls but not heavy weight.[11] How much of this flow ended up in the pueblo itself is not known, but certainly the inhabitants were aware of what they saw passing through. Evidence of the upsurge in regional business activity lay everywhere, not only in the transport plodding down the main road of the village, but also among the hard-sell hawkers around the mining camps and in Guerrero's mercantile warehouses, stocked with tools, candle wax, and manufactured clothing, as well as in the array of shops and stalls around the city's plazas. Tomochitecos knew the excitement of new wealth in the Sierra, and no doubt some of them envied it.

Land: Crucible of Dispute

Although they supplemented their income and added diversity to their lives through mining, muleteering, and merchandising, Tomochitecos were at heart farmers. They called themselves *labradores*—small-time farmers who owned their land—even if they earned substantial amounts of money in other ways. *Labrador* seemed a badge of honor: up to 1890 census reports list all adult males as labradores, and only in that year do two newcomers called *comerciantes* (merchants) make their appearance among the solid block of farmers.[12] Land provided the basic subsistence and main security of Tomochitecos, and squabbles over land incited some of the fiercest feuds in village society. Yet property ownership was uncertain. In the seventeenth and eighteenth centuries the valley was mission land appropriated from the Tarahumaras (supposedly for their material and spiritual benefit), and villagers shared water rights, reserved large portions of common land for pasturage and woodcutting, while they also farmed (but did not own) individual family plots. Mexico's Reform laws of the mid-nineteenth century mandated that these largely communal properties, called *ejidos,* be split up and either deeded to those who had come to work them over time or sold as private property. In the Papigochic and the Sierra, however, the law was largely ignored; people were still defending their ejido lands as community property up to the Revolution of 1910.[13]

Mestizo newcomers to Tomochic in the 1840s hardly bothered about legal titles to the property on which they settled and farmed. They simply squeezed out the Tarahumaras who lived there, forcing the natives to reestablish themselves in clusters of three and four families on rancherías located on small and irregular pockets of land in crevices in the Sierra. In 1867 the federal government decreed that natives who worked properties for the maintenance of their families be given deeds to that land or a similar-sized plot nearby. In and around Tomochic these grants were exceedingly small, ranging only from a little more than an acre to five acres each.[14] Law prohibited Indians from selling such grants, but they did so anyway, both by volition and under coercion.

At the same time, Mexican politicians, even presidents, regularly handed out land titles in exchange for loyalty, especially in times of political crisis like the French Intervention of the 1860s. Some of the largest properties in the Papigochic can be traced to such origins,[15] but it is doubtful that any Tomochiteco received such largesse. The valley was too small, its inhabitants too ordinary. Instead, the mestizos who settled at Tomochic claimed the land they worked by right of occupancy, a custom honored in law. However, as additional settlers arrived and families grew and as heirs found the subdivided property left to them insufficient for their needs, land pressure intensified and land titles became more important. Deeds not only defended one's own rights but could be used as a tool to separate people from their untitled property.

The 1870s found villagers like Manuel Chávez buying land through the state bureaucracy. Chávez bought two irregularly shaped plots in 1873, one about 225 yards square, the other a bit smaller, not untypical parcels for the valley at the time. Each cost 8 pesos—not cheap—and was measured out in *cordeles*, a rope a little over 9 yards long stretched out between two poles (much like the markers used today in American football). Because property lines were imprecise, running from a pile of rocks to a marked tree, then from a hump in the ground to a gully, the possibilities for overlapping another's property—and creating caustic controversy—were very great.[16]

In the early 1880s the federal government announced a national land survey in order to identify public lands that could then be sold. The proposal created hysteria, among both those who saw it as a grand opportunity and others who felt weak and unprotected against official pressures. Tomochitecos seized the moment to survey their own village, probably the first time it had ever been done. If people were going to start grabbing land, they needed to know where to start. Manuel Chávez was put in charge of the survey, which suggests how much the villagers trusted and respected him. Actually Chávez did not have to deal with private plots; his task was to outline the boundaries of the settled core of the village itself, what the law termed its *fundo legal*. The legal size of such fundos was about 244 acres.[17] Within the fundo residents owned lots for their homes and gardens, and outside of it were the ranchos and ejidos, where they farmed and grazed cattle.

Whole villages turned out for such surveys, which turned into fiestas. Those particularly involved in the measurement pointed and gabbed along with the surveyor, turning up old stone markers and identifying creases in the terrain that supposedly defined old boundaries. In places like the Papigochic a priest normally went along to confirm findings and keep order.[18] There was no priest in Tomochic, however, when Manuel Chávez went to work in 1883. Typically, officials measured off the fundo legal in geographical quadrants, in four sight lines stretching outward from the front door of the village church. As Tomochic's church lay off center, almost all dwellings ended up in the northern quadrant, with a few spread east and west. But Chávez seems to have accomplished the measurement without friction. Natural objects like pine trees notched with a cross marked the outer limits of the fundo; then it was up to federal surveyors to define the perimeter of the surrounding ejido.

Two years later one of those survey teams reached Tomochic. Remarking on the poverty of the village, it recommended that the ejido be expanded to 1,539 acres by including some of the surrounding mountainsides.[19] The boundary survey thus gave the village further legal integrity by protecting the site against speculators and others buying up the heavily wooded public lands in the mountains. Within the ejido itself land steadily passed into private hands, although in late 1876 some common pasturage remained in the valley, and Tomochitecos officially complained to the pueblo's comisario that Jesús Medrano was charging individuals for the right to pasture on common land he claimed as private property. The jefe político ordered Medrano to bring in his titles so that his boundaries could be verified, but there is no further documentation concerning the case.[20]

Local authorities handled land surveys and acquisitions, and when it came to measuring parcels and allocating land, it was who you knew that really counted. As a village official, Reyes Domínguez pushed land laws to their limits—and frequently to his own advantage. Even though the natives had the same right as everyone else to petition the government for open land, Domínguez discouraged it, telling higher-ups in 1883: "If it's given to them, they'll just sell it." He also decried the way that Indians sold their corn crop to buy mescal, get drunk, and leave their families in want. Yet at the same time Domínguez was critiquing native morality, charges flew that he had deliberately plied the Indians with mescal from his own shop and then enticed the drunken Tarahumaras into illegally selling him their parcels.[21] On other occasions Domínguez complained that natives planted beyond their property lines, encroaching on public land available for purchase as private property. He wanted those plantings trimmed back to the legal holdings of the Indians.[22] Domínguez turned out to be a stickler for proper titles and appropriate taxes among illiterate people who had little or no expertise in such mestizo concerns.

Or did they? Natives also learned to play the land title game. For example, in 1884 two Tarahumaras complained that land adjudicated to Reyes Domínguez was really their old ranchería land and not public property up for sale. They admitted that they had not worked the property for years as required by law, but now they intended to do so and wanted it back. The jefe político reviewing the case was suspicious. It seemed probable that the natives had in fact abandoned the tract and now wanted to retrieve it so that they could sell it. He suspected that the Tarahumaras had already sold their titles granted under the law of 1863 and now sought new deeds to sell the same piece of property again. Though the truth remains uncertain, this demonstrates that natives knew the law, as well as how to manipulate it.[23]

Nor should we assume that aggressive land-grabbers like Reyes Domínguez always got their way. In 1885 the jefe político decided a land dispute between Domínguez and the Tarahumara Francisco de la Cruz in favor of the native.[24] Five years later, more of the same. Domínguez seems to have loaned money to a native, Jesús Lara, and taken the title to Lara's land as collateral. Then Domínguez suddenly took possession of the land itself along with that of two other Indians, Santiago Francisfortes and Jesús Benito. The natives complained to the village presidente that they had been bilked. There was some interesting background to this matter. Three years before, Francisfortes, who had been under contract as sirviente to Reyes Domínguez, had fled his master's charge, claiming that Domínguez owed him money and would not settle up. When he severed the relationship with his amo, he had intentionally taken cattle belonging to Domínguez in recompense for his missing pay. Now Domínguez sought revenge—but encountered frustration. Weighing the case, the jefe político agreed with Francisfortes and ordered the land returned to the Tarahumara owners. Moreover, he warned Domínguez in no uncertain terms to desist in his shady dealings with the Indians, to stop taking advantage of their presumed ignorance and bluntly reminded Domínguez that the Indians were protected by statutes. But Domínguez had some protectors of his own. When Lara received notice from the jefe político that his land would be returned to him, it meant that the property had to be resurveyed to set the proper boundaries. The local judge, Francisco Ledesma, handled the measurements in August 1891 and simply defined the boundaries to turn the disputed property back to his good friend Reyes Domínguez. The case lay in the hands of a state judge in Guerrero City when the troubles erupted in Tomochic that December.[25]

Despite the ambitions of a few like Reyes Domínguez, no one in

Tomochic seems to have been a truly large landholder. The Medranos owned considerable property, and Domínguez lusted after land, but no one piece could be termed a hacendado. The place simply was not large enough—only 747 acres in all on the valley floor, and chunks of that occupied by uninviting, but still majestic, rocky outcroppings, like the Cerro Medrano, leaving only 70 percent of the valley arable.[26] And land in the valley was chopped up into relatively small plots of an acre or two. An individual might own several such parcels, all separated from each other, and access to one's land, normally a public path along the boundaries of another's parcel, could ignite quarrels, especially when individuals began to fence off their holdings.

Besides the small farms devoted mainly to corn, beans, and potatoes, families normally worked a small plot near their dwelling for squash, chilies, and onions, and perhaps experimented with some other vegetables. Most kept a few pigs and chickens, or maybe some goats, and certainly pets, especially dogs and an occasional cat. It was a rare fence that could contain these scavenging animals from straying into another neighbor's patch, and if a victim wanted to make something of it, a nasty dispute could follow. Such controversies became so frequent one gets the impression that on occasion, at least, animals were willfully released to stray onto another's property, either in revenge for an alleged hurt or in order to create a pretext for confrontation.[27]

Tomochitecos allowed their larger animals—horses, cattle, and mules—to graze openly on the mountainsides around the village. Good grass was quite scarce in the immediate area, so the animals ranged widely in search of food. There seems to have been no formality to these pasturage practices; at least the documentation yields no disputes over who should pasture his cattle where. Large open spaces and natural forage eased competition for these kinds of resources but encouraged cattle rustling, considered one of the most heinous crimes—even compared to homicide—in a region where cattle meant food and transportation and were also a measure of wealth and social prestige. Steal a man's cow, or up to five of them, and you faced one to three years at public works in Guerrero City. For theft of six to ten beasts, the penalty increased to three to five years, and rustling ten or fifteen brought five to seven years of pounding rocks for road fill or sweeping streets of leaves, dirt, and garbage. Over fifteen beasts carried a sentence of ten years. So the law took rustling exceedingly seriously, even if first of-fenders normally had their terms cut in half.[28]

Loose animals naturally bred and gave birth in the out-of-doors, and law held that these newborn animals could be rounded up, branded, and retained as private property by the owners of the mature beasts. Frequently enough a cattleman protested that a calf claimed by another as "wild" had been born of his cow. Cruz Chávez ran into just such a controversy in 1887, the case already mentioned that went all the way to the State Supreme Court. In another example three years later, Municipal President Juan Ignacio Chávez charged Gertrudis Holguín with cattle rustling and assigned Manuel Chávez to escort Holguín to jail. Manuel tried to explain that he and Holguín had been paid by some Tarahumaras from the pueblo of Arisiachic to round up wild cattle and horses for them. He insisted that no theft was involved; the pair was only doing a hard day's work. (This defense hardly explains why Tara-humaras would pay for such services when they normally did their own roundups. Furthermore, the natives of Arisiachic openly disdained the mestizos of Tomochic and would not have been likely to hire them for any purposes.)[29] Although data on the case are incomplete, Manuel's explanation is suspect; he seemed bent on getting a friend (and perhaps himself) out of trouble. Nonetheless, as we have seen, such disputes punctuated ordinary life in the pueblo. They were not insignificant flaws in the social fabric of the village but, more aptly, a main thread.

Tomochic's village life, naturally grounded in its geographical en-vironment and cultural traditions, developed a certain routine. The valley receives a healthy 34–40 inches of rain a year, but this is concen-trated into one summer season and even then comes down in sporadic deluges that frequently do farms much more damage than good. In such heavy rainfall today's footpaths and animal trails become tomor-row's arroyos, and Lino was only the biggest of many arroyos traversing the village. Uncertain rainfall and fear of an early autumn frost rather tightly circumscribed the planting season. Farmers needed to get the crops in by mid-June, but certainly no later than the first couple of weeks of July. Corn needed three months to mature, and by early Octo-ber there lurked the danger of an early frost or killing freeze, which can blanket a deep valley like Tomochic with a punishing cold.[30]

At the same time, nature provided Tomochic with a generous quantity of good soil. Over centuries the Tomochic River meandered through the valley, cutting new paths here and forging fresh outlets there. In its wake it left abandoned riverbeds laden with rich soils and minerals washed down from the Sierra. The northern part of the valley contained spacious river overflow areas that over time had silted up and created fine farmland. Only toward the southern end of the valley was the terrain that rocky, balky soil that only grudgingly yields a crop, but this was not regularly farmed. (Rudimentary irrigation from the river could have made even that inhospitable portion productive, but the need or incentive to construct such works was not present.)

The farmers of Tomochic usually contracted one or two Tarahumaras as helpers through the practice of amo/sirviente. If we can assume as typical the farming practices observed by J. R. Flippin, an American who ranged the Sierra in the mid-1870s, Tomochitecos used wooden plows with only one handle and a shaped stone or hard oak as the tip, although surely by 1890 most could afford to buy an iron share. At times, plowing was a two-man operation: one held the plow upright while the other pulled the oxen with reins tied to a yoke lashed behind the horns of the beast.[31]

Three months after planting, the farmers harvested and turned their cattle loose to graze the remaining stubble. Resulting manure fertilized the tract. Annual yield naturally depended upon imponderables like weather, but a number of Tomochitecos had surplus grain to store and sell. This surplus was, of course, unevenly distributed; we have seen the disparities in the list of needy villagers prepared during the drought of the late 1880s. Witness this scene: It is the spring of 1888, the second or third year of a withering drought. Two widows, a single man, and the head of one family of four are sick and need immediate assistance. Six others—they all appear to be Tarahumaras—are too poor to pay even a minimal price for relief. Seventeen additional families, including those of the Chávez brothers, Cruz and Manuel, are in want and qualify for subsidized relief. While the number of needy is certainly impressive (roughly one-third to one-half of the villagers), so is the roster of those who, although afflicted by the same natural disaster, do not qualify for aid on the basis of daily income or grain reserve: among them, the Medranos, Reyes Domínguez, the Gallegos family with nine members, Domingo López with a family of eleven to support, the Calderóns, and José María Ortiz with a wife and six children at home.[32] The roster of those who were at this point at least able to ride out the drought is as noteworthy as the index of those who could not. Maybe they were better planners, had more income or luck—or even different values and ideas about the importance of material *things* in life.

Extra Income and a Broader Vision

Silver and gold mining operations in the Sierra offered Tomochitecos revenue to obtain some of those things, as well as entrance to a much wider world. Farming at one's own pace in open air, while not always idyllic, would seem to beat crawling down dark and dank tunnels on the orders of a section boss with time and money on his mind; but, beyond the obvious material bounty, mining also provided a respite from the old-fashioned clutches of village life. So when opportunity knocked Tomochitecos answered, knowing that miners could come and go pretty much as they wished. The state in 1856 requested the names of Tomochic's adult males eligible for national guard service, and received a list of 31 names of men ages 16 to 48, plus the comment that nearly 50 percent of them were then working in the mines.[33] In 1867 the pueblo could not raise volunteers to fight Apaches because all manpower was at the mines. (Or was this just an excuse to avoid hazardous duty?) The comisario himself, Jesús José Chávez, was reported at the Yoquivo complex. In 1889 and again in 1891 the village could not hold state elections because so many men were out of town at the mines.[34] Throughout the period public officials requested leave from the jefe político in order to attend to mining business. In 1863 Lucio Mendoza, comisario, and eleven years later Jesús María Ortiz, also comisario, headed for Yoquivo. The year 1886 found Carlos Medrano in Pinos Altos; two years later Jesús María Ortiz was back in Yoquivo. Manuel Chávez also worked at Yoquivo, though one suspects probably not at the same time as his antagonist Ortiz, or at least not at the same mine.[35]

These mining centers were really clusters of pits and tunnels, maybe fifteen or twenty of them, named in union for an ancient native site (Tutuaca, Urique, and Batopilas), a natural location (Pinos Altos), or a religious utterance (Jesús, María, José, locally shortened to Jesús María and then in 1893 changed to Ocampo), perhaps a national hero (José

María Morelos), or a combination of the sacred and profane (Guadalupe y Calvo—Guadalupe for the Virgin and Calvo commemorating a
former Chihuahuan governor, José Joaquín Calvo). By the late nineteenth century many of these mines had been worked and reworked, on
and off, since discovery three centuries earlier by truly audacious Spaniards addicted to golden visions and rumors, and crucially aided in
their search by local native guides. Mines slipped in and out of bonanza
following an unpredictable chronology linked to capital, perseverance,
and luck. Veins of silver ore located near the earth's surface were relatively easy to exploit, but by the 1880s they had largely played out, and
mining now required blasting and picking deep tunnels into sites often
unwilling to surrender their bounty without great expense in both
money and human toil. The vision of striking it rich persistently urged
men (and a few women) to accept the challenge. As one traveler put it:
"I challenge any American [or any person?] to pass the Sierra Madre
going to the interior of Mexico, without catching the 'silver fever.' " On
his journey through the Sierra in 1849, not far from Jesús María, James
Audubon met a Frenchman down on his luck but still resolute: "I asked
the Frenchman now so long a resident that he had almost forgotten his
own language, what induced him to live in such a country. His answer
was short and to the point: 'The love of gold.' Have you found it yet, I
asked? 'No,' came his reply, 'but I cannot return without it.' "[36]

Completion of the Mexican Central Railroad in 1884, linking Chihuahua City to the border at El Paso, encouraged New York City capitalists like Walter S. (Will) Logan and Bethnel Phelps, along with a
former U.S. senator from Colorado, Horace Tabor, to invest in Jesús
María. A year later they struck bonanza. (Mexicans use the splendid
word *opulencia*.) Laborers poured into the site, and the early boom
blossomed, although, as Tabor learned, it could just as quickly wilt into
bankruptcy.[37] At the same time, British capital injected new life in
Pinos Altos. Hubert Waitman, representing the Pinos Altos Bullion
Company out of London, signed a 20-year lease with the Mexican
government in 1886 to work the property with up-to-date equipment.[38]
As incentives the Mexicans had granted reduced export-import tariffs
and had exempted the enterprise from federal taxes. Still, it was no
sweetheart deal. The major mine at Pinos Altos was 873 feet deep,
down a precipitous 65 percent incline. About halfway down one encountered water, so pumping and hoisting equipment had to be im-

ported from San Francisco and Chicago. After arriving in Chihuahua
City by rail, the dismantled but still heavy and bulky machinery had to
be hauled 250 miles by wagon, and then the final 100 miles to Pinos
Altos on the backs of "mountain schooners." All this added up to very
expensive initial costs. But while the company spent a good 10 percent
of the value of its ore in transport costs, mint charges, export duties,
and insurance, profits still soared, and all this activity added up to
numerous jobs for locals from pueblos like Tomochic. In the summer of
1889 the population of Pinos Altos ranged between 1,500 and 1,800
individuals, and of them only 7 were British and 30 American. Mexicans held more than a thousand jobs in this one mining complex alone,
the nearest major mine to Tomochic.[39]

Records of the private mining companies, which so often changed
hands, went bankrupt, or were absorbed by larger corporations, are
hard to come by, so we have only a sketchy idea of which Tomochitecos
chose to work in the mines or exactly what they did there. We may
remember that Manuel Chávez and José María Ortiz both worked at
Yoquivo, and Carlos Medrano at Pinos Altos. These men were literate
and had served as public officials; chances are good that they worked in
mining administration. The summer of 1883 found Manuel Gallegos,
aged 23, married and illiterate, employed at Pinos Altos, while in early
1891 Isidro López, aged 25, literate, and married, was mining in Jesús
María. Three Tarahumara brothers, Cesario, aged 18, Higinio, 20, and
José Acosta, 29, all from Tomochic, labored there the following year,
while another native, Paulino Ruiz, 26, worked at Pinos Altos.[40] In
sum, it is safe to say that almost any Tomochiteco who wanted to work
in the mining districts could do so, since labor was chronically short,
forcing business agents to recruit workers in other Mexican states as
well as abroad. In the summer of 1884, mining company recruiters
journeyed to distant Paris, where they signed up 58 French immigrants, including wives and children. (Many of them backed out of
their commitment in Mexico City, because they felt that their contracts
had been violated—specifically, that the company had reneged on its
promise to provide them with rifles to fend off hostile Apaches.)[41]

Even if these French immigrants did not make it north, mining normally attracted a small but highly visible flock of foreigners. When
Tomochic's Isidro López was at Jesús María the winter of 1891, he
worked with Thomas Caine, a 29-year-old English bachelor, who was a

machinist; a 60-year-old married carpenter from the United States; Juan Ros, age 35, a single carpenter from Russia; and a single woman, Irene Frast, a 29-year-old machinery operator from Canada.[42] Perhaps such contacts did not make locals like Isidro López more cosmopolitan, but they must have pricked his curiosity, and we can only wonder at the tales about these foreigners that he carried home to friends and family and how the villagers soaked up these anecdotes.

The variety of mining labor specializations was enormous: drillers and blasters; carriers, separators, gang bosses, and administrators; mechanics, carpenters, smithies; metal cleaners, water pipers, shovelers, and winch turners; plus those who installed air and ventilation ducts, and caretakers for the drainage pumps. Add to this group those engaged in support services—food, transport, woodcutting, animal care, security, runners, office flunkies, general laborers, merchants—and we get some idea of the enormous assortment of employment in these centers. Put all these people in motion—quitting, hiring on, working hard, getting hurt, and getting drunk; add an international spice of laborers from China to Rome and the United States—and we can feel the quickened pulse of these sites at which Tomochitecos worked.[43]

For common laborers who descended into the tunnels, work was perilous. Down they would go hundreds of feet on crude ladders made of pine trees into which notches had been cut. Dim light from burning torches scarcely lit their way. Rocks fell and overhanging walls gave way, especially in the rainy season; timbers, ladders, and machinery broke; gases poisoned. On their backs in leather sacks supported by a strap across their foreheads they carried ore, water, and debris up those ladders six to seven hours a day; a slip meant horrible injury, often death. For such labor these peons averaged one peso (80 cents U.S.) to one and one half pesos a day, two or three times the money they got as day laborers on Chihuahuan haciendas. Furthermore, they supplemented their salaries by stashing the best ore they could find on their person and later selling it to petty merchants who infested the locations. At day's end bosses shook down the miners in search of stolen loot, but the miners countered with the ingeniousness of experienced smugglers, hiding their bounty in their huaraches (leather sandals), the folds of their clothing, and the orifices of their bodies. It was a game of cat and mouse that both sides seemed to enjoy. If they lost, laborers got fired but could find similar work nearby, for it was a worker's market. From time to time employers had to raise wages to attract employees.

Skilled miners—those who drilled into and picked at the veins, did the blasting, or otherwise had some mining expertise and experience—earned somewhat better: up to two pesos a day, perhaps two and one half pesos. Up top, ore sorters got a peso a day, and young boys who did odd jobs around the site, 37–45 centavos. This was the wage scale for Mexicans. Americans, usually employed only as skilled laborers, earned twice the amount, and administrators, of course, commanded the highest salaries.[44]

One can but imagine what Tomochitecos gleaned from their mining experiences. For one example, consider food. While their lives back home were never limited to just the plain staples of beans and tortillas (which themselves can be prepared and seasoned in a variety of savory ways), mining centers offered fresh fruit (peaches, oranges, lemons, watermelons) and river fish (a stick of dynamite tossed into a pool would kill and stun hundreds of them—suckers, catfish, and Gila trout up to three feet long) not often available at home. Recipes printed in mine town newspapers sounded quite tasty: *chuletas adobadas* (breaded, pan-fried pork or beef chops), seasoned with a spoonful of orange peel, plus oil, salt, pepper, and vinegar, served in an onion sauce spiced with more oil, vinegar, and oregano; or seasoned meatballs served in a spicy sauce. For a change, there was *camarones a lo marinero*, shrimp cooked in lard until golden, with fresh mashed tomatoes, a little good vinegar or red wine, and a touch of sugar. This was to be boiled until the broth had disappeared and served cold, or, if hot, on thin slices of bread dipped in the broth.[45] Whether such fine dishes even interested the Tomochitecos is not known. If they even dared taste them, they might have scoffed at them. After all, they had been reared on *atole* (corn gruel), *pinole* (roasted, ground corn), hog's head cheese, pork, and *carne seca* (beef jerky), and jolted by that common boiled coffee made from crushed green coffee beans. No doubt the smell of simmering lard in which they deep fried pig skin to make *chicharrón* (crackling) aroused their taste buds. They also knew village cheese, milk, and eggs, even occasional bacon, as well as a variety of natural fruits and vegetables that grew wild around them. At least these new dishes introduced them to the culinary delights of others, something new to ponder and probably laugh about.

The mining towns enjoyed an assortment of amusements that bypassed small villages, although Guerrero City had its full share of local and itinerant entertainment. The circus came to mining towns, and so did magicians with their tricks and photographers with their technically intriguing panorama shows. Carnivals meant gambling, hypnotists, flimflams, and fakers. Prostitution must have flourished. Of course, Tomochic knew its own diversions. It had a billiard hall, which must have encouraged gambling, already a Sierra pastime involving various card games (their favorite was *el monte*). The village had a band to play at patriotic celebrations, and such bands could usually be hired out by individuals for private serenades, which often developed into public festivities. People of the Sierra also played the egg shell game, filling empty egg shells with powdery confetti and breaking them over the heads of fellow partygoers at some celebration. We already have noted how much Tomochitecos enjoyed their alcoholic drinks and boisterous dances called *fandangos* or *bailes*, which often enough produced a brawl. Being typical Serranos, Tomochitecos also must have enjoyed their cock fights, horse racing, and bull-tail pulling, maybe not as organized as those marvelous competitions staged at the rodeos in Guerrero City but equally as spirited. Certainly strolling acrobats must have wandered into the pueblo with their gymnastic feats, and George Eastman's new little box camera, already loaded with its 100 shots, was reasonably well known in the Sierra. Guerrero's annual regional fair lasted eight days, December 8–15, and combined displays of the latest in farming equipment and animal husbandry with scientific innovations like the telephone and telegraph, all in an often raucous atmosphere of ranchero fiesta. Fairs meant Fiesta, most assuredly with a capital "F." Baseball, bicycles, and Italian opera did not arrive in the region until the turn of the century, but in the 1880s and 1890s much of the more riotous fun coalesced around the mining centers, and Tomochitecos took advantage of it. No doubt rubbing elbows and carousing with the rowdies and others in these uninhibited towns widened their world, which can be both an exhilarating and terrifying experience.[46]

On the more sober side, labor strife certainly must also have impressed Tomochitecos. On January 21, 1883, a riot over the way miners were being paid erupted at Pinos Altos. First of all, the company paid workers just half their due in cash and the other half in tokens that had to be redeemed in purchases of high-priced merchandise from the company store. In fact, state law prohibited any payment at all in such tokens, but administrators regularly ignored these statutes. Second, the workers demanded a return to their accustomed weekly pay schedule instead of the recently instituted fortnightly plan. Companies complained that drunkenness was endemic among workers, so they tried some moral engineering by lengthening pay periods. If workers were paid monthly instead of weekly, they would drink less, absenteeism from work would decline, and they would keep their minds on their labor. The tactic was never tested at Pinos Altos, because merchants who had set up shop there saw their daily profits reduced and retaliated by urging the miners to protest. A strike call followed; some joined, and as always, many did not. Local authorities armed twelve nonstrikers to control their fellow workers, but the strikers tried to disarm them, and a firefight broke out. In their fury, the strikers killed the manager of the mining operation, and the administrator, a British subject named John B. Hepburn, suffered a gunshot wound to the head. The following day a security force of 25 men under Carlos Conant, the municipal president of Jesús María, arrived to quell the disorder, declared martial law, arrested the reputed leaders, and formed a judicial proceeding with himself as president. Conant added the local judge and a company employee to the kangaroo court, and the presiding trio ordered five of the alleged ring leaders shot. Public executions followed. Continuing its hasty inquiry, the court then sentenced an additional dozen men to death, but other authorities, including the jefe político of the district, arrived in time to prevent the executions. Still, for the next several years the 12 accused men, along with 57 others, remained under indictment, accused of striking, murder, endangering foreign property, and resisting authority. The remaining miners returned to work with their conditions unchanged. The strike had been broken but not forgotten. In the summer of 1889 rumors circulated in the district that the miners at Pinos Altos had rebelled, but on July 9 an administrator at the mine assured Jefe Político Silviano González that the workers had not struck and that domestic order reigned. Nonetheless, rumors persisted like an explosion waiting to happen; it was only a matter of when. The government braced for the worst, and army units patrolled the place well into the 1890s.[47]

Women's Work

Mining did not greatly disrupt the rhythm of farming and family life in Tomochic. First of all, farming did not require the labor of entire fam-

ilies, especially those with plenty of hands, and Tarahumara sirvientes
did much of the dirty work anyway. And although many male heads of
households or their teen-aged sons regularly mined for a period, even
several months at a time, they then returned to the pueblo. No migra-
tions were involved; families were not split apart for very long periods of
time or permanently separated. Some miners brought their families
with them to the mining camps where they lived in makeshift huts,
but as far as we know, not the Tomochitecos. Still, with the men gone,
the full burden for the maintenance of family cohesiveness fell on the
women. The dominant role of women in organizing and sustaining
peasant households, normally the most vital and fundamental social
units in a village community, is well known, but in locales with males
frequently on the go and absent for quite long periods, their tasks and
responsibilities become both more onerous and more meaningful. Tomochic's women were undoubtedly a strong lot. Censuses show women
heading large households, living apart as widows, and raising the children of others.[48] The widowed mother of the Medrano brothers, for
example, ran a little sundries store by herself for many years. Nothing
was unusual about this: many women owned and operated shops and
stalls, cantinas, and boarding houses in and around Guerrero City.
Busy individuals like Señora Medrano were the center of attention. Not
only Tomochitecos gathered at her shop to gossip and discuss the day's
affairs, but also itinerants passing through town. So her little store
became a kind of information center. When troops came to quell the
disturbances of late 1891, their commanding officer, along with the
hacendado in charge of the voluntary security force that reinforced
the federales, visited Señora Medrano to buy a bit of her tasty homemade food—but also to sound out the attitudes of the villagers toward
the presence of the military in their midst. The outsiders later claimed
that at first the Señora thought of them as the agents of the anti-Christ,
but she soon warmed up to them. However, that is only their version of
the encounter.[49]

Wills, following traditional Spanish colonial patterns, tell us that
widows inherited much of the property of their deceased husbands or
at least what they had accumulated together as a married couple. Last
testaments naturally differed, but with children involved, half typically
went to the widow and the other half was divided among the children,
or virtually everything might be left to the widow to be divided among

the children upon her death. Where there were no children, the widow inherited the entire estate, which in many cases she then managed. But when it comes to telling us how women lived their lives, legally recorded wills only state that they "did the things that women do."[50] That stock phrase suggests a static formula that did not exist. Yes, they raised children, but so did some men. Yes, as part of their partnership with husbands and other males, they did domestic chores like the cooking (although men away from home made their own carnes asadas) and hauled water from the river in great clay pots perched upon their heads. But both sexes tended the chickens, goats, and pigs, and on numerous occasions women helped to prepare and bury the dead. Women also knew how to pack cartridges and if called upon, or mad enough, could even shoulder a rifle. Although there were no women among those followers of Cruz Chávez last seen crossing the Sierra toward La Santa de Cabora, the women of Tomochic later fought alongside their menfolk in their continuing conflicts with the military.

Women also knew the law, their rights, and how to speak their minds in public. Examples from Tomochic itself are limited, but remember it was a woman (as well as her husband) who in 1883 cursed out Cruz Chávez and sent him to the authorities for relief, and by all accounts women in the pueblo socialized on par with men.[51] Down in the Papigochic Valley we have records of women demanding that the jefe político punish abusive husbands and insisting on the official censure of philandering spouses. They also fought to keep their husbands out of the army and at home where they were needed to help support the family, and stood up—and right in public—against husbands who abused their children. At the same time, women like Javiera Acosta stood up for their right to earn a living. In 1882 Sra. Acosta passionately defended her right to continue making and selling tesgüino from her house in Guerrero City. Male customers had accused her of creating disorder at her establishment, and authorities had revoked her liquor license. But Sra. Acosta countered that she had been unjustly bad-mouthed by the drunks in her place, some of them among the so-called notables in town, and then pleaded that she was a poor woman, living alone, and promised that she would no longer permit those who might make trouble inside her house.[52] Sra. Acosta certainly was not cowed by the male bullies in town, some of them from ranking families.

Finally, ordinary women recognized, in some cases more so than males, the institutionalized inequalities and injustices of local society and forcefully spoke out against them. In 1870 María Concepción Sálazar was under contract as sirvienta to Abraham González, one of Guerrero's most respected minds and the father of a progressive son, also named Abraham, who became the state's governor during the Revolution of 1910. María Concepción was doing the dirty housework around the González home when she fell in love with one Juan José Pescador, of whose background nothing is known. They got married and recorded it as required by law with the civil authorities, but first her suitor was required to pay González 60 pesos to free his sweetheart from her contract. This probably was money that she owed González for a loan, but for some reason the payment seems to have gone sour and brought Sra. Pescador to the jefe político for relief. There she stated her abhorrence of that long-standing legalized social practice that bound sirvientes to their amos, calling it a "misfortune under which our society suffers," and declared how much she appreciated the endeavors of her husband, "who has always breathed the air of liberty," to remove her from the dependency in which she had lived and "to sanction her own freedom."[53] (Would Sra. Pescador have been that much different than the Tarahumara woman, herself most probably a sirviente, who Cruz Chávez charged had defamed him with her accusations?) These incidents—and the official record is replete with them—depict women of the Papigochic, some undoubtedly bolder than others, largely unfettered by the rhetoric and trappings of a purportedly man's world. What else can we say of all those women whom police discovered packed into a private home in Pachera, where they were having a dance, half of them dressed as men and "playing the role of caballero to perfection"?[54]

Public Education and Its Skeptics

Education was meant to be a pillar in Mexico's new modern state. As early as 1858 there was talk of a school in Tomochic for Tarahumaras in the vicinity, but the plan collapsed when natives from the nearby all-native village of Arisiachic refused to cooperate. Such schools were part of the federal government's plan to "civilize" the natives and "to make

them like us."[55] However, there seems not to have been any local initiative for a primary school for all youngsters in the pueblo until 1878
when Reyes Domínguez announced that a private teacher, Dolores
Hernández, wanted to establish a school in Tomochic, but his salary
was in dispute. Ultimately the venture collapsed because the villagers
could pay him only in corn and not in cash. Five years later Domínguez
collected 30 pesos from residents to start a school, but no teacher could
be found.[56] Then a godsend: the French-born Santiago Simonet, a
literate bachelor in his early forties, came to the pueblo about 1883 and
became its primary school teacher. Simonet had been in Mexico for
two decades, so he had probably arrived with the French Intervention
of the 1860s. Perhaps he became fascinated by the Tarahumara culture,
for 1882 found him teaching the largely native populace of Pachera.
The census of 1890 describes him as a single man living with a woman
and two teen-aged sons who carried his surname. Domínguez (who
might well have been introduced to Michelet by Simonet) moved his
sundries store from the curato at the church to provide classrooms, and
the school year 1887–88 saw 29 boys, ages nine to fourteen (six of them
Tarahumaras), attending school, among them Domínguez's fourteen-
year-old son Lisandro; Timoteo Ledesma, the teenager who denounced El Santo del Chopeque as a fraud; and Gregorio Ortiz, another of the civil registrar's sons, who later joined Cruz Chávez. The list
encompasses a good 85 percent of the pueblo's mestizo boys in that age
group, but not the sons of Cruz and Manuel Chávez, who were still too
young to attend.[57]

In harmony with its project to diminish the influence of the official
Church on the Mexican mind, the federal government's new program
of compulsory primary school education emphasized the values of the
new state: pupils were taught their civic duties, love of country, individual worth, trust in and obedience to civil authority, and the merits of
disciplined, hard work. The curriculum emphasized the "three Rs" but
also "moral practices," such as obedience, punctuality, self-denial, and
"other duties in the sphere of [social] action." Social engineering was
plainly at work here; the state admitted the link between schools and
social control, and authorities tied youthful laziness (grumbling about
work), obstreperousness (talking back to adults), and licentiousness
(carousing) to a lack of schools. In the state of Chihuahua (and undoubtedly elsewhere) the curriculum differed for boys and girls. While

the boys learned geometry, natural science, and the political organization of the nation, girls studied flower arranging, principles of hygiene,
and feminine duties, along with notions of history and geography. In
their second year girls read *The Angel of the Home* by Delfina G. Rodríguez, and in their fourth, *The Woman and the Home* by Correa Zapata.
Young girls were taught their place in society even if, as we have seen, as
adults they often refused to be cowed by it.[58]

Various sources financed education: state taxes, district and village
fees, parents of school children who paid according to ability, more-or-
less forced contributions from other individuals such as bachelors (who
along with others could pay in crops), and private donations from the
well-off, including the governor. Remember that Governor Carrillo offered money, his own or the state's, to be spent on community schools
in exchange for religious paintings. In fact, a number of private schools
emerged, paid for by the wealthy and socially conscious, places where
students learned French, world history, and astronomy. But the public
system remained under persistent financial stress.[59] In 1890 Bachíniva
closed its schools for lack of a budget, even though Governor Carrillo
forbade such closings. But two years later there was another closure at
Santo Tomás. A decade later, for lack of desks, Basúchil's pupils put
their inkwells on the floor, knelt down, and used their chairs as tables so
they could learn to write.[60] Paper, pens, pencils, and notebooks were
always in short supply. As the teacher at Pachera, Jesús Armenta, quite
eloquently stated, "Many talents are covered with the sad dust of ignorance," simply because parents could not afford to buy pencils and
paper for their children to use at school.

This financial shortfall most assuredly had an impact on teachers'
salaries. Some teachers were dedicated and many derelict, but very few
in either category got paid their due, which generally ranged from 30
to 50 pesos ($24–40) a month.[61] Tomochic's Santiago Simonet went
broke trying to keep the pueblo's school open during the drought of the
late 1880s. The villagers paid Santiago 200 pesos ($160) a year to teach
their children, but the drought eroded their ability to pay. In 1887 Reyes
Domínguez and Sabino Ledesma personally paid Simonet's salary—a
very generous commitment to local education—but two years later the
school was destitute; its teacher could not continue without financial
support, and the residents could no longer pay him. Simonet pleaded
with the jefe político for relief: "It's getting hard to live. If I am not paid,

I will have to close the school." Comisario Jesús Medrano warned the jefe político in April 1889 that the teacher had not been paid by the residents in four months, that he was poor and would have to close the school if not regularly remunerated. The jefe replied that the state would subsidize the teacher—a promise ill-kept. Four months later Simonet pleaded his own case to the jefe. Local support had altogether dried up. So far he had paid school costs out of his personal savings, but could not continue to do so; he was impoverished. A year later found Simonet demanding back pay of 110 pesos to cover his personal expenditures from December 1888 to October 1889. He made no claims for pay after that date, which suggests that the school closed down in Tomochic that October, a full two years before the disturbances erupted there.[62]

Degrees of Wealth

Both the position and frame of mind of women and the substance of education and the quality of schools were important clues to the nature of Papigochic society toward the turn of the century. Material wealth was another, and tax records reveal the distinct layers that existed there. At the top perched a substantial group of well-to-do real estate owners who had diversified into a great variety of business interests: mining, commerce, urban housing, sawmills, commercial crops, and cattle, even banking. Well below them but still decently set, were rancheros and business people, many of whom had received a consequential property inheritance which they worked to their advantage or leased out to others at a sizable profit. A third tier included those who had not fared as well by inheritance but did more than just manage, as well as others who had more recently come to the valley and begun to acquire significant holdings. These people farmed and sold cattle, and added income in a variety of other ways, including as subcontract muleteers, mill and dispensary owners, or professional practitioners. Then there was a large group of small farmers who also owned cattle and maybe a dwelling they rented out in one of the towns. Finally, we have the great mass of the population, who earned below the limits of taxable income; yet even they were layered from able artisans, who could demand a decent daily wage, and ambitious petty merchants, who found inventive outlets for their wares, to youthful peons and sirvientes, who were shamelessly exploited for their drudge labor.

In Tomochic itself these divisions were much less acute, the range more compressed. There were no enormously well-off Tomochitecos; nevertheless real differences existed. These can be seen in the lists of contributions for this cause or that charity, from which a pattern of sorts emerges. The first indication concerns contributions in 1840 to fight Apaches rampaging over much of the state. To direct self-defense and retribution, the state government hired an infamous American scalp hunter, James Kirker, to terrify or otherwise subdue the Indians (and Kirker did not always distinguish between peaceful and hostile natives) and solicited public contributions for the mission. In Tomochic, Rafael Estrada gave a very substantial 40 pesos, Pablo Hernández a noteworthy 16, and two others, Mónico Almeida and José María Arriola, 1 each. The rest of the village either could not afford to give or did not want to do so. Rafael Estrada owned the hacienda La Generala in the shadow of the Papigochic and did not stay long in Tomochic. Neither did Hernández. Their apparent wealth played no part in the future social structure of the village.[63]

By the early 1870s we find six Tomochitecos well enough off to pay business taxes: Dolores Mendías, Jesús Medrano and his mother, Patricio Arriola, Calisto González, and Rafael Orozco. The record does not indicate the types of businesses in which they were engaged, but with the exception of Jesús Medrano, who paid taxes for a professional license (probably that of notary), all were presumably merchants with connections to mining. We know that Medrano's mother had long been in such business, and in 1886 Domingo López hired a very influential lawyer from Guerrero to help him collect a substantial bill of 111 pesos owed him, likely for merchandise sold to Tarahumaras of Arisiachic. By far the biggest entrepreneur was Calisto González, who was taxed as a Tomochiteco although he did not live in the pueblo. Chances are he was part of the González clan, formerly of Tomochic, which was by then building its fortune in the Papigochic. Since the government taxed individuals mainly in accordance with the value of their property holdings, we can see that Calisto was far better off than the others being assessed. He paid 10½ pesos, all but one peso of it for his business; that lone peso went for his rural land holdings. Rafael Orozco paid 6 pesos for his commercial venture; Mendías, 4; the Medranos and Arriola, 3 each. The name Orozco does not reappear on the succeeding censuses for Tomochic, so he may be considered another "outsider" or someone who rather quickly moved on. But Mendías, Medrano, and Arriola all figured prominently in the future politics of the pueblo.[64]

In 1880 a state military expedition trapped and killed an elusive and vengeful Apache leader along with many of his followers. Chihuahua's government was overjoyed at the triumph and asked citizens to contribute to a gratuity for the victorious soldiers. Tomochic responded quite generously: 29 individuals, nine or ten of them Tarahumaras, donated a total of 42 ½ pesos. Dolores Mendías, along with the Medrano brothers, Jesús and Carlos, and Jesús Lara gave 4 pesos each, at least twice as much as anyone else. Again we have Mendías and the Medranos at the forefront of community contributions, whether taxes or charities. Jesús Lara is a mystery; his name appears on no other padrón, and he is certainly not the Tarahumara named Jesús Lara with whom Reyes Domínguez had a land dispute. But we do have four other villagers donating 2 pesos each: Reyes Domínguez, Domingo López, Jesús María Ortiz, and Julián Rodríguez. Manuel and Cruz Chávez are also mentioned: Manuel gave 1 peso and Cruz, 50 centavos, which placed the Chávezes with the majority, if lower echelon, of donors.[65]

When it came to paying monthly school fees, Domingo López and Reyes Domínguez headed the 1887 list with 2 pesos each, perhaps because they either had or subsidized more children in school.[66] Finally, in our search for clues about social structure based on material wealth, we return to the list of those qualified for drought assistance in 1888. The roster included only those earning less than the equivalent of one peso a day, among them Manuel, Cruz, and David Chávez, Julián Rodríguez, the schoolteacher Simonet, and Bartolo Ledesma. Among those not eligible for aid were people who had long possessed political and economic power in the community: the Medranos, the Domingo López family, Reyes Domínguez, the Mendías household, and Jesús María Ortiz. No doubt Tomochic had its upper crust of seven or eight families—not really wealthy people, but definitely better-off than others in the village. When seen as a group, most of their names appear over and over in positions of community leadership. At the same time, and even more consequential for local life, rivalries among the select spawned Tomochic's most vindictive disputes and led the villagers to choose sides.[67]

Tracing Tomochic's Rifts

Mexican campesinos are not often good neighbors, and complaining and backbiting, threats and reprisals were all part of daily life in Tomochic. We only have those examples of controversies that found their way into the official reports, but they are sufficient in number and vitriolic enough in substance to impress us with the fractious nature of village society and to point out those people of influence who led the way. Much of the pueblo's conflict swirled around Reyes Domínguez. We have a report about his use of liquor to pry land from the Tarahumaras, and in the 1880s he ran a mercantile outlet with partners (whose names are unfortunately unknown) from two rooms in the curato. Together these activities gave Domínguez a financial base, not large, but among the most solid in the pueblo, and linked him to important contacts in outside commerce. Because in 1875 he was one of the ten adult males in the village who could read and write—and because he craved the role—Domínguez quickly became immersed in the official business of the pueblo but controversy characterized much of his time in public office. As the village's civil judge in 1879 he married five Tarahumara couples at Arisiachic, charging the dirt-poor grooms 2 pesos each and the somewhat better-off ones 6 pesos. The natives complained to the jefe político that they had been overcharged, and the jefe agreed; by law people in poverty need not pay anything at all for such services. In response Domínguez pretended ignorance: "If I should not have charged anything, [at least] you [still] know I am obedient [to you]."[68] How obsequious this man could be, and also how arbitrary. Dolores Rodríguez charged in 1882 that Domínguez had shown a marked prejudice against him and had tossed him in jail without reason. Cruz Chávez rendered a similar complaint the same year. Domínguez had disdained Chávez and called him seditious and then, according to Chávez, had further slandered and punished him without cause. Chávez naturally presented the jefe político with documentation to support his allegation and suggested legal recourse to tame Domínguez.[69] Unfortunately, we can only wonder at the outcome of this particular dispute.

The Medranos caught the special wrath of Domínguez, quite possibly because they were in direct economic competition; each family owned a general store. The Medranos seem to have had a lock on such business in the community before Reyes Domínguez began to challenge them. Then the charges and countercharges flew. In 1880 the jefe político forced the resignation of Reyes Domínguez as comisario and placed Jesús Medrano in charge, with Manuel Chávez as vice comisario. The following year Medrano arrested the Tarahumara sirviente of Reyes Domínguez on an unspecified charge. Domínguez complained to the jefe político that Medrano had abused his authority. Two years later in 1883, Domínguez, once again comisario, got his revenge. He put out an arrest warrant against Jesús's brother, Carlos, for cattle rustling—but Carlos had left the district and apparently avoided arrest. A counterattack was bound to come. One such parry that is documented occurred six years later when Jesús Medrano, once again comisario, fined Domínguez for failing to keep his cattle penned up. The loose cows had wandered into fields farmed by Carlos Medrano and damaged the crops. Besides the fine, Carlos was due compensation. The comisario had put the animals in the village depository for strays, but Reyes Domínguez went to the corral, withdrew his cows, and simply ignored the charges against him. (Stray animals were a common problem in the pueblo, as we have seen, but villagers normally settled up damages among themselves.) Now the Medranos pressed the issue as part of their ongoing differences with Domínguez. This time the jefe político came down on the side of the Medranos. He fined Reyes Domínguez 5 pesos ($4.00) and made him pay the damages owed Carlos Medrano.[70] Domínguez probably paid up, but his rancor had undoubtedly only been fueled. The festering disputes between Domínguez and the Medranos highlight the split among those better off in Tomochic society. They were like scorpions in a bottle, fighting to the death.

Protagonists in this sort of village wrangling seek allies, while individuals in search of advancement hitch their futures to one of the adversaries in hope of a breakthrough. The result is frequently a marriage of convenience. Documentation suggests that one such clique had coalesced in Tomochic by the early 1870s with the Medranos and Dolores Mendías as its leaders, and Julián and Dolores Rodríguez, Patricio Arriola, and Ignacio Gallegos as likely associates, along with Regino Luna, José Puerto, and Alejandro Gaitán. Such cliques breathe; they expand and contract. So as we move into the 1880s Luna, Puerto, and Gaitán leave Tomochic, and Arriola dies, but Manuel Chávez joins up,

along with the Calveróns. Meanwhile, a rival group was crystallizing
around Reyes Domínguez, Domingo López, Jesús María Ortiz, and the
Ledesmas (Sabino and his son Bartolo). We can see the patterns embroidered in several marriages: Cruz Chávez married a Mendías, Manuel Chávez and Jesús Medrano each a Calderón, while on the other side
Sabino Ledesma was married to an Ortiz, and the Ledesmas and Jesús
María Ortiz went outside the village for marriage partners.[71]

Even more illuminating are the lines of conflict. As civil judge Jesús
María Ortiz, for example, broke up the Mendías wedding celebration
in 1888, earning the wrath not only of the wedding party but also of
friends of the Mendías family, including Santiago Gallegos and José
Calderón.[72] As far back as 1870, Carlos Medrano as comisario was
already at odds with Domingo López, his vice comisario. In planting
season of that year Medrano ordered residents to pen up their animals
or be fined; López simply refused to obey. Five years later, Jesús María
Ortiz, the village comisario, and Jesús Medrano, justice of the peace,
vigorously contested each other's boundaries of authority. Within two
years Domingo López, comisario, and Jesús Medrano were in dispute
over the sale of property. When Jesús María Ortiz sought property in
Tomochic the next year, Dolores Mendías and others headed the opposition. In 1882 the comisario of Tomochic (probably Jesús Medrano)
reported to the jefe político that the Ledesma boys, Francisco and
Bartolo, then in their twenties, were "brothers" of Reyes Domínguez.
He did not mean blood brothers, although they may have been cousins.
At any rate he stressed the closeness of the relationship.[73] Two years
later Francisco Ledesma, as comisario, complained that a native had
illegally sold land to the Medranos, and shortly thereafter Ledesma
protected Domínguez in the latter's ongoing land disputes with some
Tarahumaras. In 1887 Sabino Ledesma and Reyes Domínguez teamed
up to remedy the financial crisis at the pueblo's primary school. We
have witnessed many other examples of these alignments, or nests of
contention. To bring them into sharp focus, for some time it seems to
have been Jesús María Ortiz, Domingo Lopez, Reyes Domínguez, and
the Ledesmas pitted against the Medranos, the Medías family, and
their friends like Santiago Gallegos and José Calderón. Perhaps now it
is a good time to glance back at the village church in that November
1891 when Padre Castelo's sermon triggered the walkout of Cruz Chávez and his colleagues. Look at who stayed put: Juan Ignacio Chávez,

Reyes Domínguez, Sabino Ledesma, and Domingo López (along with the schoolteachers Simonet and Armenta).[74] Jesús María Ortiz may have been out of town at the time, but regardless of his whereabouts he certainly never joined up with Cruz Chávez.

As nearby mining boomed in 1890, commercial fever penetrated Tomochic. Goods passing through town were subjected to a municipal tax, as were local products transported by Tomochitecos from the village to the mines. Smuggling and fraud ran rampant, however; shippers lied about the contents of their cargoes and refused to pay their fees. In response the jefe político appointed a special agent to watchdog the transit of goods through Tomochic. As can be imagined, it was a position prized for its potential payoff, and in February, Domingo López, himself long active in trans-Sierra commerce and a sturdy ally of Reyes Domínguez and his group, got the job.[75] His adversary, Jesús Medrano, then comisario, protested to the jefe político that López was not collecting taxes on corn and paper products that Domínguez, Jesús María Ortiz, Sabino Ledesma, and his son, Bartolo, were shipping to the mines. There you have it—the Domínguez clique perfectly identified and opposed by the Medranos. On April 17, López lost his post to Carlos Medrano. The worm had turned. The month of May found Medrano frustrated by persistent smuggling, the reluctance of teamsters to detail the contents of their bulging loads, and the outright refusal of merchants to pay their taxes. Medrano did not name names (at least for the public record), but we can surmise whom he fingered.[76]

Mexicans call this competition between cliques *camarilla* politics, an interplay between sets of personal relationships. Loyalties develop between two or more individuals who with their followers and hangers-on form a camarilla. Rival camarillas then compete to advance through the system. In exchange for their loyalty the leader nurtures the career potential of his less potent collaborators. Heads of local camarillas make book with a regional camarilla, regional leaders with the state government, and so forth.[77] When in the spring of 1892 a state mediator visited Tomochic in a desperate attempt to lure Cruz and his people back into compliance with civil authority, he found the pueblo hopelessly divided among rival camarillas. He saw no hope of reassembling the village under its present leadership and recommended the appointment of an outsider who might be able to bridge the factions and earn the confidence of the entire populace. Although the mediator did not understand the motivation behind the religious movement and under-estimated the determination of its members, he certainly saw the polar-ization that rent the village.[78]

Even in small places like Tomochic there was a good deal for these camarillas to contest: the right to control taxes on tesgüino sales, on local goods sold at the mines, even on merchandise from elsewhere passing through town. Officials made arrests and collected fines for infractions of statutes, such as getting drunk and boisterous or allowing one's pigs to run loose. They identified land for sale and received fees for measuring it. For instance, Tarahumaras paid Reyes 6 pesos and two calves for surveying their property, which lay at quite a distance from Tomochic.[79] People paid for the right to erect a tombstone, for permission to slaughter their own cattle for meat, either for the home table or for export to the mining camps.[80] Dance permits cost money, along with those required to stage a serenade. People paid to register births, marriages, and deaths. Local officials raised and paid armed forces to maintain public order and arranged prisoner escorts; plenty of room for patronage there. Among other administrative duties they reg-istered branding irons and weapons, and organized the auction of stray animals. They conducted elections, shams though they were, for state and federal positions. In sum, they set and controlled the rhythm of life in the village and its environs.[81] In the process a lot of pesos exchanged hands, even if some of them were destined for the state treasury. How-ever, public positions not only meant money; they were also equated with the prestige that linked local influential groups to their kin in higher political places, in this instance Guerrero City, the real seat of regional power in the Papigochic, and on to the governor's palace in Chihuahua City.

Reyes Domínguez understood and played the camarilla system much better than did the Medranos. Not that the Medranos lacked contacts in mining and commerce, but Domínguez practiced better politics. When the jefe político, Silviano González, came to the pueblo, he stayed with Domínguez; so did the district priest, Manuel Castelo. Reyes Domínguez was also in league with another of the area's most powerful politicians and assertive businessmen, Joaquín Chávez, who had his eye on forest and farmland around Tomochic. This is the same Chávez who in December 1891 reported the outbreak of the violence in the pueblo to the governor. So it comes as no surprise that when a

newcomer with strong ties to the jefe político came to settle in Tomochic in late 1889, Domínguez sidled up to him.

The new man in town was Juan Ignacio Chávez, a bachelor in his
early forties. An ambitious and energetic merchant from Santo Tomás,
Juan Ignacio wanted to take advantage of an upswing in mining activity
throughout the zone. In July 1888 the jefe, González, had appointed
Juan Ignacio to be justice of the peace in Santo Tomás, but Chávez
declined, saying he was leaving shortly to establish the commercial
venture at Jesús María. He was only waiting for his business associate,
Pablo Porras, to return from Chihuahua City, the merchandising mart
and banking center of the state. Then they would be off together for the
Sierra. But if the jefe so wished, Chávez would take the appointment in
Santo Tomás for a month or so. Soon after, he left with his partner for
the mountains.[82]

We cannot be sure why he stopped and settled in Tomochic, but
perhaps he sensed a previously unforeseen commercial opportunity
there. After all, Tomochic was the largest mestizo-run pueblo in the
lower reaches of the Sierra, and a heavy flow of merchandise to and
from the mines regularly passed through. But something else more
likely influenced Juan Ignacio's decision to remain in Tomochic: he was
the client of the jefe político, and one suspects that his patrón sent
him there. González had mining interests of his own—or he may have
known of the factionalism that divided Tomochic and hoped to alleviate it. At the same time González also meant to further the aims of *his*
influential patrón, Governor Lauro Carrillo. These were uncertain and
troubled times in Chihuahuan politics. Only two years earlier the state
constitution had been altered by the legislature to permit the governor
to appoint jefes políticos, formerly an elective position in the districts.
In the wake of such political manipulation, potential rebellion bubbled
in the Papigochic, and domestic tranquillity was the jefe's major responsibility. González had a job to do for *his* governor and depended on
minions like Juan Ignacio Chávez for steadfast support. So now we
have yet another Chávez in Tomochic, a client of the jefe político and
actually related to the ubiquitous Joaquín.[83] Ironically, Juan Ignacio
might also have been a distant relative of Cruz and Manuel Chávez.

With a push from the jefe político, Juan Ignacio Chávez soon assumed official authority in the pueblo. In February 1889 the jefe named
Chávez justice of the peace, but Juan Ignacio declined, reminding the

jefe that in accordance with law he had not been a resident of the village long enough to qualify for the position—not that such technicalities were often honored in the region. Chávez also pleaded the need to nurture his fledgling business. Though he did not have much of his personal money in the enterprise, he had bought stock on credit, and those loans had to be repaid expeditiously, which meant that he and his partner Pablo Porras needed to act quickly to develop a substantial cash flow in a new community where they had few personal contacts and considerable competition.[84] Relatively little is known of Pablo Porras, just approaching 30 years of age at the time. The census of 1890 suggests a Porras connection to the Chávez network through his wife, the 26-year-old María Josefina Chávez. Equally intriguing, we find an Estanislao Domínguez, age 43, living in the Porras household.[85] Are we looking at a relative of Reyes Domínguez or just a tantalizing coincidence?

By the fall of that year the presence of the new merchant must have begun to show. Chávez was already in conflict with the widowed mother of the Medrano brothers, but her sons knew village politics. As presidente of the community in September 1889 Jesús Medrano began to apply pressure on his adversaries. He told the jefe político that Juan Ignacio had been undercharged for a plot of land measured for him by Reyes Domínguez. The implication was that the pair had struck up a deal. The jefe forcefully replied that neither Domínguez nor Medrano had the authority to set land values, a prerogative of the state government, but we cannot tell whether he voided the bargain.[86] Controversy must have simmered, and after two consecutive years as pueblo presidente Jesús Medrano resigned on May 3, 1890. Jefe González appointed Juan Ignacio Chávez as his replacement, and on June 21 Chávez assumed office.[87] The jefe finally had his man in place.

Judging by the flurry of correspondence between Juan Ignacio Chávez and Silviano González, the community had never experienced a more activist presidente. Juan Ignacio, a resident in town for no more than eighteen months, meant to take charge and enforce his authority. By July he was sending criminal suspects from the area—as well as stray animals—to Guerrero City under special guard. The next month found Gertrudis Holguín charged with cattle rustling and defended by his friend, Manuel Chávez. In a bid for community peace, only a few days earlier Juan Ignacio had named Manuel to serve with Reyes Domínguez on the local electoral board for forthcoming state elections, but now he and Manuel were at odds. Late August found Presidente Chávez defending Reyes Domínguez against land-grab charges levied by the natives Jesús Benito and Santiago Francisfortes; but the presidente was beginning to wilt under the pressure of so many official duties to be fulfilled in such a contentious atmosphere. He asked the jefe to stop ordering the transport of criminal suspects through Tomochic, because the pueblo had no jail in which to lodge them, nor could he spare personnel to escort the prisoners to the district seat at Guerrero. The jefe firmly responded: "Fulfill your responsibilities!"[88] When Juan Ignacio tried to resign in October, the jefe refused to accept, probably more an attempt to bolster his appointee's willpower than a mark of censure. Meanwhile, local resistance to the presidente mounted. The justice of the peace (according to Juan Ignacio) blatantly spurned his duties, so he, the presidente, had to handle local quarrels and enforce order. The municipal treasurer refused to pay the schoolteacher, Santiago Simonet, his salary. People broke the law and defied his authority. For example, Domingo López butchered three cows without securing the required license. The presidente ordered López to purchase the permit and fined him one peso for each animal slaughtered, but López merely ignored the ruling. Now Antonia Holguín had killed a cow without permission. The beleaguered presidente asked the jefe what he should do. Should he just forget the López payment? The jefe thundered back: "Collect it," but we do not know that Chávez ever dared do so.[89]

The new year brought the same sort of turbulence—and much more. The governor's entourage visited in the spring, and Major Cárdenas stole the sacred paintings while Juan Ignacio Chávez looked on—or at least the other way. In an apparent act of conciliation, Juan Ignacio in May named both Jesús Medrano and Cruz Chávez to be local election officials in June's state elections,[90] but shortly thereafter the presidente canceled the religious procession planned by Cruz in search of divine intervention to relieve the drought. A few months later Padre Castelo came to the pueblo to chastise those who worshipped El Santo del Chopeque and Santa Teresa. When the believers stormed out of the church in disgust, Juan Ignacio remained seated. A short time later Cruz and his followers refused to recognize his authority as a public official, so the presidente promptly declared them in rebellion against the state and solicited a peacekeeping force from his patrón, Silviano González. Although the personal ambitions and public performance of

Juan Ignacio Chávez hardly created the fissures that sundered Tomochic society, his demeanor and actions gave added meaning and urgency to the appearances and preachings of Santa Teresa and El Santo
del Chopeque, especially for those who at that moment were in search
of sacred explanation and receptive to divine guidance.

Even as Juan Ignacio alienated the Medrano cluster along with the
devotees of Cruz Chávez (although for different reasons), he attracted
Reyes Domínguez and his cohorts, who appreciated his connections to
the outside, where their business concerns lay. At the same time Juan
Ignacio needed friends. In frustration he had tried to quit his public
post, but the jefe would not have it, and so under his abrasive governance, the pueblo lurched toward tragedy. Moreover, the turbulence in
the village coincided with great commotion and portentous change
evident in all Chihuahua, where the upsurge in mining had awakened
opportunity and aroused its twin, competition. Great old family and
camarilla rivalries regained momentum, and raw new ones sprouted up
to confuse and confront them. Governor Carrillo himself faced political challenges that involved no one less than the country's president.
Let us then trace these diverse and disruptive rivulets of change to their
source, from Tomochic into the Papigochic, on to the state capital, and
finally to Mexico City itself.

5

The Legacy and Temper of the Norteños

WHEN THE SPANISH MILITARY COMMANDER Don Diego Guajardo Fajardo first saw the Valley of the Papigochic in the cold winter of 1649 he was struck by its grandeur. He had approached it from the west, the Sierra side, and so looked down on the rolling hill country carpeted in grass and fringed by mountains, except to the southeast, where it opened onto seemingly endless plains. Below him, the Papigochic River, fed by arroyos, streams, and smaller rivers, meandered south to north along the west side of the valley, then took a sharp turn into the Sierra and transformed itself into a runaway river, cutting spectacular gorges through the mountains. Of course, such a hospitable valley as the Papigochic was quite heavily populated; some five to ten thousand Tarahumaras took advantage of its natural bounty, settling in villages along the high bluffs and sweeping bends of the river. The Papigochic was the center of the Tarahumara nation.[1]

In late 1648 Tarahumaras attacked a convoy traversing the valley, killed its conductor and a number of other journeyers, and made off with salt needed to process silver, as well as a payroll of 4,000 silver pesos in cash. The Spanish government demanded reprisals, and, still making his mark at age 40, Guajardo Fajardo volunteered for the task.[2] Recently married and a Knight of the Order of Santiago, he was reputed to be a "great gentleman" and a "Son of Mars." Moreover, he had in recent years commanded the military garrison in neighboring Durango and briefly been governor of the Spanish colony in the Philippines. Therefore, he had both military and administrative experience in colonial affairs, plus an aggressive will and ambitious bent. The Crown

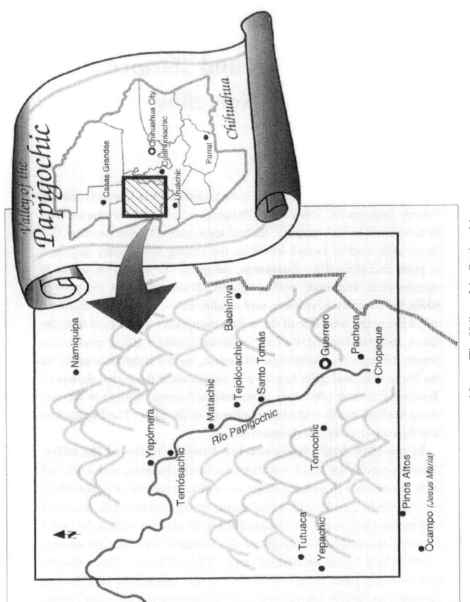

Map 3. The Valley of the Papigochic

undoubtedly appreciated Guajardo Fajardo's achievements, though it could have done without his personal ambition.[3] In temperament and ambition, as well as attitude toward higher authority, this man greatly resembled those who followed and settled into the Papigochic and pueblos like Tomochic.

The "Son of Mars," reinforced by the government with the additional title of provincial governor, opened his campaign of revenge against the Indians in mid-January 1649, but the enemy proved elusive, withdrawing to their redoubts above Tomochic, the center of their resistance. Tomochic's surroundings not only provided a stout natural defense, but the diminutive valley itself was a center of social and religious activity from which the Tarahumara drew inspiration. Guajardo Fajardo responded to the challenge with a scorched-earth offensive, burning cornfields and destroying rancherías throughout the area. Along the way he recovered six or seven hundred of the silver coins stolen from the convoy, which further sharpened his appetite to pursue his quarry. The Indians had never seen anything quite like this sort of wanton revenge; soon many of them sued for peace with the Spaniards, though others continued to resist as guerrillas. Such a cleavage doomed the opposition. Guajardo Fajardo set the surrender of four native leaders as the price for peace, and the severed heads of two of the leaders were promptly delivered to the conqueror. The fate of the other two is unknown.[4]

Guajardo Fajardo halted the campaign to establish a military garrison at a huge loop in the Papigochic River, the future site of Ciudad Guerrero, but then a substantial Tarahumara settlement that warranted surveillance. The Spanish regularly established such garrisons, called *presidios*, in which they would station a small number of professional cavalrymen (nine at this particular presidio, which Guajarado named Papigochic). That force was buttressed with soldier-citizens who agreed to serve as needed in exchange for a tract of tillable land and the farm tools to work it. At the same site Governor Guajardo Fajardo proclaimed into existence a town, which he called Villa de Aguilar (village of eagles) after the birds found there, in the hope its attractions would lure permanent settlers. Spanish law specifically prohibited the founding of new population centers without the explicit permission of the king, but Guajardo Fajardo, like his successors, was much more a man of action than of rules.[5]

The governor's personal motives for establishing the town remain his own, but it would not have been unlike him to have been pondering a new power base for himself, one from which he could dominate the politics of this increasingly important province officially called Nueva Vizcaya. He was already wrangling with the area's other important politician, the Bishop of Durango, and the Villa de Aguilar would help put considerable distance between them.[6] Whatever his ambitions, the governor had a very difficult time populating the new settlement. He lauded the beauty of the site and its potential for mining success; he offered incentives—forgiving the debts of some who agreed to go to the Papigochic, extending the repayment schedules of others—but few took the bait. One who did was Alonso Sánchez, who in search of quick profit registered a claim on April 6, 1649. Sánchez did not know what he might discover, so in the petition for a title to his property he covered himself for silver, copper, gold, tin, "or whatever else" he might find— and to be politic he called his site "Fajardo." A few others also registered property, including Gerónimo de los Reyes, who vowed that if his mine produced wealth, a share would go to the Church. Thus did believers bargain with God, a practice discouraged by the official Church but commonly utilized by Christians in need or hopes of divine assistance. Another claim was held directly by the Church, a mining operation begun by the Jesuits, who were both energetic entrepreneurs and purposeful missionaries, although they had much more luck mining for souls than for silver in the Papigochic.[7]

The Jesuits had begun to proselytize among the Tarahumara in the southern part of what is now Chihuahua early in the seventeenth century. As part of his regional pacification and settlement plan Governor Guajardo Fajardo encouraged them to establish a mission among the natives outside the Villa de Aguilar. The result was La Purísima Concepción de Papigochic, which quickly flourished into the major mission of the region. Padre Cornelio Godínez supervised the building of the church and adjoining rectory at the new site in 1650, and over a brief period baptized hundreds of Indians. But soon "the devil began sowing cockleburs in the hearts of his instruments"; that is to say, some natives became vexed when settlers at the Villa de Aguilar began to abuse their labor. Padre Godínez tried to settle disputes between Indians and their would-be bosses, but the Spaniards accused him of siding with the natives (one irate settler even tried to knife him) while the Indians

resented his inability to halt the exploitation. In June 1650 their simmering animosity boiled over, and they attacked the house of the priest
himself, who, either stupefied by these events or resigned to martyrdom, would not allow the soldier guarding him to fire at the Indians.
The natives assaulted the priest, tied a rope around his neck, and
dragged him toward the church, all the while clubbing him and riddling
his body with arrows. The soldier was next. Then the Indians flung the
corpses at the foot of the Holy Cross erected at the church cemetery.
Finally, they besieged the Villa de Aguilar. Some settlers were killed,
others escaped, and the terrorized remainder holed up in their dwellings in the forlorn hope of military relief.[8]

Governor Guajardo Farjardo soon arrived with substantial reinforcements to save the day, pushing the natives once again back to their
earthen works near Tomochic. There they withstood the siege of the
Spaniards for nearly a week, but once again there were second thoughts
and defections in the ranks. Overtures of peace followed from the Indians, which the Spaniards accepted in hopes that the Tarahumaras
would now recognize colonial authority.[9]

So calm returned to the Papigochic, but not for long. By early 1652
the Tarahumaras had reorganized, this time under the fearsome leader
Teporame, also known as Tepóraca. When he learned of the renewed
hostilities at Aguilar, Guajardo Fajardo hurriedly returned with his
troop to the Papigochic and in a series of hand-to-hand encounters
fought the Indians back to their mountain strongholds. Then, reinforced by contingents from his headquarters at the rich mining center
of Parral some 150 miles to the southeast, he opened another no-holds-
barred campaign against the Tarahumaras. On February 27, 1653, he
took Teporame captive near Tomochic. A few days later Guajardo Fajardo had the native leader garroted to death, and the Spaniards and
their Indian auxiliaries then shot the corpse with arrows. In May the
commander declared the Papigochic once again pacified and returned
to his gubernatorial duties in Parral, a stormy and corrupt stewardship
that within a decade led to his recall by the king himself.[10]

Over the next few decades missionaries and settlers filtered back
into the Papigochic to rebuild their homes, renew their projects, and
pursue their goals: saving souls and digging for gold and silver. Then in
the 1690s hostilities erupted yet again. As in Tomochic two centuries
later, local social realities meshed with spiritual belief to ignite a con-

flagration. Prospectors in 1687 discovered a rich mother lode of silver at Cusihuiriachic, just east of the Papigochic. Miners rushed in and confiscated Indian lands for their wood, water, and cattle-grazing potential, impressing natives into the workforce. Missionaries in the Papigochic could see trouble coming. The Indians in their charge had become sullen and refused to obey orders, so the friars headed for the safety of the garrison at Aguilar, and just in time. Rebellion soon engulfed the entire region. At Bocoyna the natives smashed the altar and baptismal font, tore the priest's vestments to shreds, beat the silver-plated chalice that held the Host against a rock until it broke to pieces. Other Indian groups—Conchos, Tobosos, Jovas, and Apaches among them—joined the uprising.[11]

In 1690 Tomochic was once again the hub of the Tarahumara revolt. There an Indian leader, probably a shaman, had convinced people that through his special powers he had ruined the gunpowder of the Spaniards so that it would not ignite, and Spanish muskets need not be feared. And should a native fall beneath the sword or lance of a Spaniard, he would after three days rise again, alive and well. Here was the Easter story bent back upon its teachers, although the message must also have resonated with more purely Tarahumara spirituality.[12] As we have already seen, leaders of religiously inspired movements frequently promise their subjects immunity from the weapons of their foes and a speedy resurrection should they fall. All, including the Tarahumara shaman, draw upon that primal promise that assures a better world to come and makes the millenarian dream real to believers (who even today far outnumber the skeptics).

To confront this new outburst of hostilities, the Spaniards again centered their defense at the Villa de Aguilar and surrendered the rest of the region to the insurgents. The government ordered one of its most arrogant and rapacious captains, Juan Fernández de Retana, a 42-year-old Basque, to hurry his force from Cusihuiriachic to the Papigochic and await reinforcements. But Retana had never waited for anyone. Once in the valley he quickly took the offensive, marking the route he traveled with the heads of his captives impaled on spikes. With reinforcements from Parral, Retana now had some two hundred soldiers and five hundred native auxiliaries at his command, enough to impose an uneasy occupation on the region.[13]

By 1697 Spanish brute force and peace offerings had once again splintered Tarahumara resistance. The Crown pardoned those natives who laid down their weapons and agreed to fight no more; captives were released to return to their villages in peace. At the same time Retana paid rewards to natives who delivered recalcitrant leaders to him, dead or alive, and continued to hammer pockets of resistance.[14] Spanish-style pacification blanketed the Sierra by the end of the century, and the Tarahumaras never again rose up en masse against the invaders of their homeland. Instead, the majority more or less accommodated to the new ways, many in missions reestablished by the Jesuits. Others retreated into the impenetrable folds of the Sierra to preserve their old customs.

The Papigochic's Blue Bloods

During the eighteenth and on into the nineteenth century mining dictated the fortunes of the Papigochic, indeed all of what is now Chihuahua. As long as the bonanza in Cusihuiriachic lasted, it both required logistical support from the valley and buttressed life there. The great silver strike at Santa Eulalia in 1707 financed the founding of what became the state capital, Chihuahua City, and also attracted shipments of grain and cattle from the Papigochic. The providers were largely of Basque descent, Spanish yes and no, but beneath that genuinely Basque, with all that culture's homogeneity, toughness, self-reliance, and pride in *hidalguía*, a notion of nobility. They saw themselves as pureblooded, uncontaminated by centuries of the Moorish occupation which afflicted so much of Spain. The people of the Papigochic still consider themselves to be of *sangre azul* (blue-blooded or ethnically pure), which translates into their being a step above others, a claim that rankles outsiders and invites ridicule from places like the state capital and elsewhere.[15]

By the mid-eighteenth century surnames that would continue to dominate Papigochic society began to appear in baptismal, marriage, and death records. On February 6, 1742, for example, Francisco Xavier, son of Simón Domínguez and Margarita Morcillo, was baptized. Simón was the son of Juan Mateo Domínguez, first of the Domínguez clan in the valley and an ancestor of Reyes, the man about whom we have already learned so much. Herrera, Chávez, Amaya, Orozco, Hermosillo, Casavantes, and González soon join Domínguez in parochial logs.[16] Very few from these families married Tarahumaras. No doubt the great majority of settler descendants were mestizos, but not by union with the Tarahumaras. Regardless of their bloodline, Papigochics then and now think of themselves as direct descendants of Spaniards and therefore at least a bit better than most other people around them.

Missions along the Papigochic River—places like Santo Tomás, Matachic, Tejolócachic, and Temósachic—gradually attracted Hispanic settlers who coveted the land of the natives and needed their labor. We have already witnessed the process at work in Tomochic; the results across the Papigochic were extremely uneven. Some settlements retained their largely native character with a Christian overlay even into the twentieth century, while others like Tomochic rather quickly acquired a Hispanic character, a function of the amount and persistence of Hispanic pressure on a given site. In any number of scattered native villages only a few Hispanics settled, perhaps just one family, although it most likely became dominant and worked the Indians for its purposes. Such families might even defend "their" natives against the encroachments of other mestizos on the lookout for opportunity, but there was no real appreciation for native culture: quite the opposite. Papigochics felt the Tarahumaras a drag on civilization as crafted by Europeans, a social model the Indians hardly embraced. They mingled some, largely when they felt it to their own advantage, but did not like each other very much. Around places like Tomochic displaced natives established rancherías that accommodated several families, in proximity to the mestizo pueblo but outside its direct influence. And some, as noted, simply faded into the embrace of the Sierra. Those who stayed in the pueblo itself learned to work the new system to some advantage but by and large remained subservient to its demands.[17]

With the Tarahumara question largely settled in their favor, mestizos could divvy up the bounty of the Papigochic among themselves. Land in the valley was by no means partitioned equally, but almost all settler families owned sufficient tracts to live from and work for some profit. They acquired land in a variety of ways—by royal land grant, from politically beleaguered presidentes seeking support and rewarding loyalty, from state and municipal sales, through partnership, squatting, or inheritance, by moving the boundary markers of others to benefit one-self, even by outright theft—or none of the above. Some simply claimed the right to property by occupation.

Many early migrants hoped to strike it rich in mining complexes like that at Cusihuiriachic, but since all such mines slipped in and out of bonanza, during the downturns the settlers shifted to farming and ranching, much of it small-scale but only rarely limited to bare subsistence. Over time the change from mining became permanent, giving the Papigochic its flavor. Just down river from Guerrero City places like Rancho Colorado featured holdings with river frontage, which then stretched back in long, narrow tracts called *porciones*. Owners of porciones grew both irrigated crops, such as wheat, and dry-farmed corn. At Basúchil fifty or sixty families lived in *mancomún*: each held shares in a former hacienda that had been subdivided. Though lots were not owned outright, since the land was held in common, individual plots could be sold or rented with the approval of the group at large. The arrangement prevented any one individual from amassing a large tract within the common property—but still left plenty of room for rancor.[18]

Certainly the Papigochic had its haciendas, but neither in size nor in production did they resemble the holdings of great land monopolists like Luis Terrazas and the Falomirs, masters of immense properties off the fringes of the valley and in other parts of Chihuahua. Rather, the Papigochic contained modest ranches, moderate-sized haciendas, and a kaleidoscopic variety of other types of land holdings, which kindled ongoing disputes over titles and boundaries. Any number of privately owned ranchos existed right inside the property lines of larger haciendas. Even into the early twentieth century many villages still retained smallish common lands for grazing cattle and cutting wood; everyone in the pueblo had a right to the bounty. True, over time local authorities had deeded many morsels (often the best ones) of these public lands to private hands, but even then natural springs within the ejidos remained common property. In sum, a great many families in the valley owned land, a good number in partnerships. When a national survey team came to the area in 1885 to search out available public property to be measured and sold, it found relatively little unclaimed in the valley, although several expanses remained in the northern portions of the Guerrero administrative district. A plat map of the Papigochic drawn in 1885 shows all property (minus the ejidos) in private hands.[19]

Land not only provided subsistence and a living for the people of Papigochic; it was also their greatest commodity. Land was bought and sold, leased and mortgaged through a labyrinth of negotiations. Land secured loans and raised capital. Adjoining parcels might at one juncture be stitched together to form a sizable hacienda like Babícora, which ended up in the hands of the American newspaper magnate William Randolph Hearst. In contrast, families that inherited ample properties frequently split them up among themselves. Individuals then sold off their segments to outsiders, causing a proliferation of relatively small private parcels in some areas. Thus land holdings expanded and contracted over time, not always in a slow and even process, and commercial opportunity accelerated the pace.[20]

The Apachería

Such opportunity did not arise in the Papigochic for a very long time because the valley belonged to that vast region, now encompassing northwestern Mexico and the southwestern United States, that investment capitalists then considered a bad risk. The problem: hostile Indians, specifically in the case of the Papigochic, Apaches. There were other problems that gave entrepreneurs pause—lack of infrastructure, political instability, relative isolation, stronger magnets for investment capital elsewhere, the sheer expense and uncertainty of mining ventures—but more than anything else the Apaches, their image even more fearsome than their reality, smothered capitalistic ambition—and at the same time helped to shape the locale's culture.

For much of the eighteenth and nineteenth centuries, the haciendas and ranchos, the commercial activity and material wealth of the people of Papigochic were menaced by the Apaches. The scourge of these audacious raiders from the north was worse even than disease. As with the Tarahumaras, the Spanish had handled the Apaches with both gifts and guns, but neither had a lasting impact. Following Mexican independence the new state government experienced no better success, largely because the Apaches were composed of a number of tribes, which were in turn segmented into clans. So while one group made its peace with the new occupants and even resettled itself alongside a military garrison, another preferred the warpath. Furthermore, gift giving worked only so long as supplies (meaning also the policy and will to provide them) lasted. When presents of iron pots, blankets, food, and illicit whiskey faltered, as they did in the early 1830s, the Indians promptly returned to plundering.[21]

For their protection the Spaniards erected a line of presidios across the colony's northern frontier. They established other backup garrisons along the more predictable Apache raiding routes further south, one of them at Namiquipa, just outside the Papigochic proper to the northeast, but within the administrative district. What seemed good in concept and on paper, however, did not work very well in the field. The presidios were undermanned and ill supplied, and the Apaches slipped between and around them at will to raid all through what is now Chihuahua and into the fringes of neighboring states. All the damage cannot be estimated, but during 1782–83 alone they killed some thirty people in the Papigochic and stole more than 1,500 head of cattle. On June 18, 1854, Apaches wiped out Yepómera, the northernmost and least protected pueblo in the valley, killing more than forty of its inhabitants. The site was abandoned, but over the next twenty years or so settlers filtered back, furnished firearms by the government. Then in September 1866 some two hundred Apaches struck again, killing one and taking twelve prisoners. The onslaught continued throughout the district into the next decades. Luis Comadurán, a district official, wrote the governor on July 4, 1878, that the Indians were killing at will in his district, Degollado. In the previous week alone they had murdered 49 inhabitants around Temósachic. Even as he wrote, Comadurán learned that Apaches had just killed fourteen residents in Cocomórachic (all probably Tarahumaras) and another five travelers on the route between Cologachic and Namiquipa. Cried Comadurán: "This area is going to be a desert inhabited only by Indians."[22]

Still the toll mounted. Papigochic municipal records attribute deaths to the Apaches into the 1880s. No one was safe: men, women, children, Tarahumaras, Hispanics—all, regardless of ethnicity or social standing, suffered depredations. When the Apaches did not massacre their victims, they took them captive and held them for ransom, or they incorporated some of the youngest into their own Apache clans. Actually, the capturing cut both ways. Settlers needed captives to ransom their own people from the Indians, who drove a hard bargain in prisoner exchange. At one such negotiation in 1881 the natives demanded the return of eight Apaches for the one Hispanic they held. But there were other demands for Indian captives. For example, in 1871 the governor gave Antonio Muñoz of Temósachic permission to raise and educate the Apache girl he had captured. It is unlikely that Muñoz desired an Indian daughter; more probably he wanted a servant.[23]

The state raised militia groups to combat the menace, normally men aged 18 to 48, but not many Papigochics volunteered to serve in such units. Individuals might donate some funding or logistical support, but inhabitants of the region were not particularly anxious to take to the field. Tomochitecos, for example, celebrated the death of the notorious Apache chief Victorio with donations of money to the victors, but few if any were ever engaged in any official campaigns against the Indians—which is not to say that they did not have an occasional brush with Apache raiders out to steal their cattle in the mountains. It normally took the promise of substantial reward to make Apache fighting worth the risk. In 1856 the governor proclaimed that those who voluntarily fought the Apaches could keep the spoils of their campaign, including the cattle, goats, sheep, and whatever else the Indians had stolen. The militiamen were supposed to give the owners of such beasts fifteen days to reclaim their property, and if they did so the proprietors were to pay the militiamen full compensation for cattle repossessed in battle with the Indians. If the Apaches had simply run off at the sight of the patrol, however, the militiamen received only half that amount. But few cattle were returned under these circumstances; the militiamen sold them elsewhere or built their own herds. So not everyone saw the Apaches as a menace; some sought profit in the threat.[24]

By mid-century good pay for Apache scalps was attracting recruits for campaigns against the *bárbaros*, especially because it was hard to tell the scalp of a renegade Apache from that of a peacefully settled one, or for that matter from the hair of other natives. The ever-aggressive José María Bencomo, whose family was among the more prominent in the valley, reported a "small success" against the Apaches in 1863. His troop of 35 from the Papigochic had attacked the Indians in their lair and captured two old women and six young girls. Moreover, they had scalped another elderly woman and a ten-year-old boy. They could have done better, according to Bencomo, but the broken terrain prevented them from charging the encampment with their accustomed gusto, so the Apache braves and their chiefs had escaped. Complaints flowed into the governor's palace concerning these aggressive forays that made no distinctions among their victims. As an example the governor singled out Hermenijido Quintana, a rival of Bencomo for Apache booty and scalps. Quintana followed the footprints of Apaches everywhere, even into their peaceful settlements, and took scalps. The governor tried to tone him down; Quintana should no longer lift the hair of those Indians granted clemency by the government. Nonetheless the pressure on succeeding governors to address the Indian menace was enormous. In 1878 Governor Trías caved in and gave the militia under Captain Jesús de la Rosa carte blanche to track down Apaches. The reward: 150 pesos for each scalp and 100 pesos per prisoner, which was not much incentive to take captives.[25]

Raiding was by no means constant; the most concentrated attacks typically occurred between April and October, reaching a crescendo in August. But whenever they came, attacks were deliberately sudden and unpredictable, leaving Papigochic society quite vulnerable and apprehensive. Such circumstances staggered the local economy, especially commerce; itinerant merchants dared not chance the journey from Chihuahua City to the valley. Mail service was disrupted, and electors chosen from the Papigochic could not get to the state capital to vote for state officials. Small-time rancheros for the most part could protect their interests close to home; not that many possessed holdings worth the risk of attack. But hacendados and rancheros with far-flung herds were at the mercy of the Apaches—and of those who cloaked their illicit undertakings under the Indian menace. Indeed, the *Apachería*, as this long period of Apache incursions lasting into the 1880s is labeled, came to explain many untoward happenings in the valley—deaths, disappearances, and cattle rustling among them. Under such pressures many aspiring entrepreneurs could hardly make a living of it. Take the Hacienda del Rosario, for example, one of the area's largest, propitiously located near the mining area of Cusihuiriachi, and remarkable for its profuse grasses, ample water, and fecund soil, all of which underlined its potential for commercial development. The infamous Captain Juan Fernández de Retana, who so brutalized the Tarahumaras, owned Rosario at the start of the eighteenth century but soon had to surrender it to the Apaches. Efforts to repopulate the estate came and went for a good century and more until the Apache danger diminished and potential profits became worth what risk remained.[26]

Forging a Culture

The Apachería could not help but shape the history of the Papigochic, as well as the character and lore of its people. It reinforced the ways they thought of themselves: first of all, their sense of independence. After more than three centuries, the Papigochics remained geographically and psychologically distant from the formal authority of Church and State, and this made them especially sensitive to official intrusions into their affairs. Although the Indian threat did not entirely isolate the area from the reach of the state capital or its affairs, it did help distance the valley from meddling politicians in Chihuahua City. It forced state governors to earn the support of the Papigochics—and any number did not get it, even in times of national crisis. When the U.S. army marched on the state capital in 1847 during the U.S.-Mexican War, for example, few if any Papigochics responded to the governor's call to defend the nation, although the same might be said of a great many Chihuahuenses and Mexicans in other parts of the country. Some two decades later, with French invaders advancing from the south, the Papigochics did dredge up a company of "volunteers" for the defense, but with more reluctance than fervor, perhaps because the governor himself vacillated on his own political position.

The independence that these people expressed should not be confused with that imagined rugged individualism of the mythical American frontiersmen stretched out in isolated homesteads across an immense landscape. Typically for a Hispanic culture, Papigochics lived in communities reinforced by traditions. Marriages, for example, were often fashioned with community relations in mind (which is not to discount love), and godparentage created strong, virtually obligatory ties to blood relatives and steadfast friends called *compadres*. Papigochic individualism was more in the mold of a brusque, readily expressed "I'm as good as the next person," which they tended to want to prove, and right away. So they were short-fused and much more comfortable with direct action than with go-betweens and negotiation. It was not so much that the Papigochics wanted to be left alone as that they emphasized their own special interests and insisted that their viewpoint carried weight.[27]

The Apachería also nourished that strong sense of pride we have already noticed in Papigochics. As descendants of Basques they understood that their forefathers had successfully defended Christian Spain against the Arab invaders and in recompense had demanded and won special privileges from the Spanish Crown—certain tax exemptions and freedom from compulsory military service outside the Basque provinces themselves. Likewise, the Papigochics considered themselves to be defenders of their country's integrity and heritage; they simply substituted barbarous Indians for Moors and further insisted upon special recognition and compensation. The Apache experience also came to explain dramatic events such as the ability of Cruz Chávez and his followers to defend themselves against a vastly superior federal army. The faithful were said to have sharpshooting skills honed in the Apachería, which allowed them to pick off the enemy's officers with well-aimed shots and toss the leaderless troops into disarray. Never mind that the Tomochitecos seem to have had relatively little contact with the Apaches. Local remembrance has made them expert marksmen, an attribute now preserved in legend.[28]

Despite their particular brand of self-assurance the Papigochics were not hesitant to seek divine intercession through favorite saints and the Virgin herself. As a whole, they were sensitive to divine signs of promise and displeasure. In 1890 Guerrero City had not only two major churches, but five or six chapels where people petitioned their preferred saints for favors and struck their bargains with God. They certainly were not under the tutelage of local priests, who were in short supply and of differing political temperaments. Yet their religion did not render them resigned nor fatalistic. Just the opposite—it gave them hope and could spur them to action in the name of the Lord and under His protection. Remember Tomochic.

The district also knew religious diversity—not a great deal, but more than in many other parts of Mexico. Of course the Tarahumaras practiced a hybrid spirituality that remains with them today, although in ever-changing form. But the Papigochic also had pockets of budding Protestantism and Spiritism that challenged traditional Catholic thought and practice; some, like Reyes Domínguez, who read Jules Michelet, apparently began to do that on their own. Guerrero had 109 admitted Protestants in 1900, among them the highly respected and well-educated Mariano Irigoyen, credited with giving Guerrero some of the state's most progressive primary and secondary private schools. San Isidro had a Congregationalist school in the late 1880s, and Guerrero a Protestant church soon after the turn of the century. Furthermore, Mormons expelled from the United States for their belief in polygamy had begun by then to develop colonies just north of the Papigochic, although the sect did not prove to be attractive to surrounding Mexicans, who were, as much as anything, perplexed by the starchy rigor of Mormon living. What all these religious differences corroborate is the comparative openness of valley society, its exposure to a wide variety of thought and options with the resulting opportunity for freer thinking. Institutional Catholicism never much possessed these people, so there was space for other ideas to flow in.[29]

Competing Camarillas

History and heritage combined to make Papigochics more plain-spoken, self-reliant, and brusquely opportunistic than many of their countrymen, even other Norteños. They were (are) not especially tolerant people, finding themselves easily bruised but rarely cowed. Outsiders thought Papigochics querulous and rebellious. Inhabitants of the valley and its surroundings were even more explosively factionalized than the people of Tomochic, because the stakes (the potential for power and profit) were higher and the actors jockeying for position more adroit and adamant. They pursued the same things as did the contending camarillas in Tomochic: power to tax and fine; power to regulate land, water, and patronage; power to regulate relations with outsiders through an official network. Public office, no matter how menial the job, was an invitation to advantage and advancement. Naturally the fierceness of competition for local posts differed from place to place in the Papigochic Valley and changed over time. In largely Tarahumara villages mestizo strongmen managed to hang on to power for considerable periods, but in most other places the infighting remained fierce and participants had long memories. The documentation features the same contestants challenging each other over and over again. So much rebelliousness had occurred over time in and around the valley that a filmmaker recreating the drama that unfolded at Tomochic located the entire Papigochic on what he called a *Longitud de guerra*, a longitude of war.[30]

Local power groups challenged one another in municipal elections, brawling affairs marked by rancor, coercion, and worse. The declared winner most often faced bitter charges of fraud and a promise of retaliation; contested election results frequently became the pretext for insurrection. These were rifts that never healed, and we can trace some of them right into the great Revolution of 1910. Nests of contention everywhere; the scene is replayed at each political level. With nearly 12,000 inhabitants in 1893, the municipality including Guerrero City had about as much population as the other five Papigochic municipalities put together.[31] It was the administrative seat of the district, which gave it direct entrée into state politics and beyond. As part of this role Guerrero housed the jefe político, that potent political boss responsible for the maintenance of public peace. We have already encountered one of the valley's most prominent jefes, Silviano González, in connection with the troubles at Tomochic. However, González was no stranger to such dissonance in the Papigochic as a whole. For nearly two decades he and his Guerrero camarilla had been hard-pressed by competitors to maintain their dominance, especially by aspiring groups downriver in places like Temósachic, Matachic, and Yepómera, who felt snubbed and given short shrift by those calling themselves the "Patriarchs of Papigochic."

National crises, including civil war and foreign intervention, encouraged contending power blocs in the Papigochic to link themselves to outside causes in hope of forwarding their local ends. Naturally this was a two-way street. Outsiders engaged in struggles of their own solicited support from factions in the valley. Attracted by any new potential for advancement over their rivals, Papigochic groups weighed their best interests against the risks. Not least, they pondered the new political movement's chances for success. None of this interplay had much to do with ideology or even patriotism, and certainly not nationalism. We are speaking here of feuding groups on the lookout for a pretext to rebel openly, of camarilla politics going to war.

The Reform wars, those great Liberal-Conservative struggles of the mid-nineteenth century that culminated in the infamous French Intervention (1862–67), provide a scenario for viewing the process at work. How sides were chosen—or not chosen—had relatively little to do with Mexican nationalism or the ambitions of the French puppet Maximilian and much to do with local concerns and rivalries. In the spring of 1865 the French were closing in on the state capital at Chihuahua City. A call went out to the Papigochic for help to defend the republic with money, weapons, and personnel. Some people responded eagerly with assistance, but many grumbled about forced loans, the need to retain one's rifles to combat the Apaches, the current drought that was creating hardships for everyone. They would rather not contribute to any such cause right now. Then in August certain elements in towns along the northern part of the valley who had long craved autonomy for themselves—groups in Temósachic, Matachic, Yepómera, Santo Tomás, and, farther out, Namiquipa—dramatically declared for the Imperialists. Meanwhile, the advancing French forced the state governor Miguel Ojinaga to flee the capital for refuge among remaining backers in Guerrero City. The newly self-proclaimed Imperialists, mobilized just downriver, routed the governor's troops and began to march on Guerrero itself. A beleaguered Ojinaga carried his governorship into the Sierra toward Tomochic, but French sympathizers from the Papigochic trapped him at Arisiachic and killed him in a brief shoot-out.[32]

The next year found the French army withdrawing from its Mexican adventure and the Imperialist cause in ruin. The lower valley's insurgents scattered into the Sierra, and relative peace returned to the Papigochic. Amnesty was granted to all but the top leaders among the dissidents in the valley. The return of domestic tranquillity was publicly hailed, but rebellion always sleeps with one eye open. Presidential dictator-to-be Porfirio Díaz provided the wake-up call. In 1871 he rebelled against the federal government, gained some support from factions in and around the Papigochic, especially at sorely politically divided mining centers of Uríque and Uruáchic, but not enough strength throughout the rest of Mexico, and was soon forced to surrender this bid for national power. His ignominious surrender occurred in Chihuahua itself, a humiliation he never forgot.[33]

Four years later Díaz was at it again, once more with considerable sympathy in the Papigochic, although much of the enthusiasm seems to have been engendered after Diaz's triumph became assured; pragmatic folks, these Papigochics. The story of how they reacted to the new prospect is a complicated one, but some details are warranted because they say so much about the way in which Papigochics practiced their politics: Díaz rebelled in January. Chihuahua remained calm until June—why show one's hand with the outcome still very much in doubt, especially with the memory of a defeated Díaz still quite fresh? Then movement in the state capital. With the help of some military officers, the camarilla led by the Trías clan staged a coup in favor of Díaz, held the governor under house arrest, and arrogantly assumed control of the state. The bold stroke provoked the resistance of the Trías clan's long-time competitor, Luis Terrazas, who turned for assistance to the most powerful clique in Guerrero City, with which he had long been associated, one dominated by valley elites: Jesús María Casavantes, Celso and Silviano González, and Manuel de Herrera, among others. The political split at the state level and the Terrazas alliance with certain Papigochics encouraged others, at serious odds with this Guerrero group, to side with Trías and thereby hitch their future to the fortunes of Díaz. Restless opportunists like Luis Comadurán and Santana Pérez led the way; we repeatedly see their names in connection with similar undertakings. Pérez, for instance, later wove himself in and out of the disturbances at Tomochic, trying to better his political fortune. A fascinating man, this Santana Pérez—you could never tell which way he would point his rifle. Nevertheless, after a lifetime of rebellion against constituted authority, he still managed to die an elderly man in his own bed in Yepómera.[34]

Understanding the Jefe Político

The public official responsible for maintaining the peace and giving shape to local and regional politics was the jefe político. Not all Mexican states had jefes políticos, but almost all had individuals in some similar role. In essence the jefe was meant to be an agent of the state, linking his administrative district to higher-ups, specifically the governor, and through him to the national regime. In practice, however, jefes frequently represented the interests of their districts more than those of the state. Naturally the blend differed with individuals and changed over time. Like all politicians, jefes weighed their best interests. Up to about the 1890s, they stood more for their district than for the state, at least in the Papigochic, but as the state centralized, becoming more politically powerful and economically self-sufficient, it provided its supporters with significant largesse, and the jefes leaned more toward their increasingly enriched and politically powerful benefactor.[35]

There were of course recognizable benchmarks in this process. In Chihuahua, for instance, we note the change in the state constitution in 1887 that allowed the governor to appoint jefes políticos, formerly elected from their districts. If such elections had hardly been democratic, they had at least allowed competing camarillas to promote different candidates. In the Papigochic it was not unusual to have up to seven camarillas competing for the four-year prize. The new constitution eliminated all that, however, but succeeding governors dared not appoint any jefe from outside the district, even though such practice became common in other parts of the country.[36] It was not the new constitutional provision per se which swayed jefes toward the interests of the state at the expense of their districts, but the reality that interest groups surrounding the governor's palace increasingly established and managed Chihuahua's sources of genuine profit, among them banks, commercial properties, railroads, and industries. Few jefes could resist the lure of participating in the bonanza, and they passed on its benefits to local friends, a practice that both sweetened the pot for the favored few and sharpened the appetites of those left out. Under such conditions camarilla politics could only become more combative.

In many ways the jefe had a wretched job to do. Not only was he (they were all males) responsible for public order—hard to maintain under the best of circumstances—but he was also directly involved in the functioning of community affairs and quite often in the most intimate details of an individual's daily life. His decisions concerned land grants, water rights, public education, religious practices, runaway children, jealous husbands and angry wives hurling charges of adultery, sodomy between two males, disputes that ran from petty personal quarrels to the outbreak of revolution, cattle thieves, and murderers, as well as young people in love but frustrated by the resistance of their parents. The jefe also verified elections (and helped to assure that they culminated to his liking), arranged civic celebrations, approved liquor licenses, and directed surveys of his district's mineral deposits as well as its agricultural pests. When the governor called for militia or the federal army for troops, the jefe had a quota to fill. These, of course, were the official duties; the unofficial ones were endless. So much of the jefe's work involved controversy and attempts to resolve nasty altercations that he could hardly escape criticism or worse, no matter how wise or just he might be. And we should not assume that the jefes were necessarily wise or just. Like all officials they had their favorites, although in the case of Tomochic and the Papigochic we have seen specific cases where they did not hesitate to decide for the underdog. They could be arbitrary and capricious, especially when they sensed their political tenure threatened or when they aimed to impress their superiors with their correctness. But they also conducted campaigns to assist victims of natural disasters and quite often displayed admirable sensitivity toward common people in personal distress. Even if the jefe político does not always earn our applause, the difficulty of his task can still be appreciated.

The jefe whom we have been most closely observing in the Papigochic was Silviano González, the man during whose tenure the tempest at Tomochic erupted. The González clan had come to the valley via Tomochic. Its patriarch, Paulino González, seems to have headed north from his village of Teocaltiche in the state of Jalisco at the behest of a relative, the Franciscan friar Gerónimo González, who headed the Tarahumara mission at Tomochic during the 1840s. Gerónimo probably enticed Paulino with the mining potential in the region or perhaps the area's striking beauty and relative freedom from meddling officialdom. At any rate, 1843 found the González family in Tomochic. Forty-eight-year-old Paulino was married to Guadalupe Mendívil, twenty years his junior and perhaps his second wife. Their oldest child was Celso, age eleven; Silviano was ten, and four younger children follow. Silviano, who developed a special affection for the valley, was the sacristan in the church. We have no idea of how long the González family remained in Tomochic—Silviano stayed for at least twenty years—but by the 1860s it had relocated in the Papigochic valley below. While in Tomochic they undoubtedly knew Jesús José Chávez as presidente of the pueblo and Manuel and Cruz as babies. Silviano had on any number of occasions revisited the pueblo where he had grown up and for which he seems to have held warm sentiments.[37]

The González family became one of the most prominent and richest in the Papigochic Valley. Their entire story is not known, but González interests penetrated mining, rural estates, cattle and sheep-raising, lumbering, merchant houses, retail outlets, blocks of urban property, house rentals, and banks. These were active, modern capitalists continually in and out of business partnerships and financial alliances with kindred entrepreneurs. Tax records of 1903 show Silviano to be among the leading property holders in the Papigochic, his substantial real estate assets neatly balanced between town and countryside.[38] The González clan had its fingers in any number of high-stake financial pies. They were partners in the robust commercial house of González, Herrera, and Salazar and had founded one of the state's first investment banks, the Banco Minero Chihuahuense. They also owned a transport company and a soap factory.[39]

Naturally political prestige accompanied the economic status of the Gonzálezes. Celso was at various times the valley's representative to the state legislature, serving briefly as interim state governor on several occasions in the 1880s. Meanwhile, Silviano González held a variety of public posts in the Papigochic. For instance, in the 1870s he administered the mail in Guerrero but lost that job to a federal employee when Díaz triumphed. He protested the dismissal to no avail.[40] This was one way by which the insecure fledgling president inched his way into local affairs. However, in keeping with Porfirian conciliation González later served as the Papigochic's jefe político on a number of occasions. As such he seems not to have aroused any great antagonism, although other camarillas certainly challenged him. Neither beloved nor despised, he was rather respected (at least by his fellow notables) as a man who well represented the interests of the region to include his own. The dissension at Tomochic, however, undid him. Unable to defuse the discord early on, he gave his political enemies the ammunition they needed to redefine political mastery in the state. The word was out: González could not handle the dispute. To officialdom he seemed indecisive. There were Cruz Chávez and his cohorts wending their way toward Cabora in open defiance of authority, and González still wanted to negotiate with them. Worse yet, he displayed some sympathy toward the dissidents; Silviano González must be replaced. The order likely came from President Díaz himself, always on the lookout to replace one public official with a favorite more dedicated to his regime, which meant himself.

The Power of a Cacique

While the jefe político was officially the ranking political authority in the Papigochic, substantial prestige and political clout also lay in the hands of local strongmen called *caciques* (once again, all males). The power of these caciques tended to be subregional, or local. At times it served their purposes to link their ambitions to higher ups, but caciques could also resist the intrusions of high government. Above all a cacique protected his own turf. Most gained and held their power through family tradition, wealth, influence, and patronage, although the wealthiest and most influential people were not necessarily caciques. A cacique was characterized in the public mind more than anything else by his attitude and demeanor. Caciques tended to be a pretentious lot, blustery and boastful—they liked to throw their weight around, or at least that is how most people viewed them. They were bosses who too often acted like petty despots.

Caciques operated at all levels of society—and of significance. Most in the Papigochic were quite petty, including those mestizos who reigned over largely native settlements. In Tomochic Reyes Domínguez had cacique pretensions, but his detractors never let them take root. There was in the region, however, one cacique who held great sway. His name was Joaquín Chávez, the blustery man so central to events unfolding at Tomochic: he had deeply injured the sensibilities of Cruz Chávez (possibly a blood relative, at least a compadre) by implicating Tomochitecos in the robbery of the silver bullion convoy headed for Pinos Altos in early 1891; he seems to have been family with Juan Ignacio Chávez and was probably involved in his precipitous and controversial ascendancy to presidente of the pueblo; he publicly labeled the dispute at Tomochic a rebellion against the government and personally encouraged the governor to put it down.[41]

Joaquín Chávez was born in 1842 into a fairly well-to-do mining family at Jesús María (later Ocampo), when the complex was in bonanza. His father, Cástulo, was from Parral, the residence of the Juan Ignacio Chávez family. Sent to school in Chihuahua City, Joaquín also worked at the Casa de Moneda, a private mint owned by the wealthy Henry Müller, who held the lucrative contract to make coins for the state government and was allowed to keep a good percentage in recompense. Joaquín Chávez worked at the mint as a teenager and while there undoubtedly made personal contacts that well served his future ambitions. Chávez unfortunately lost his left arm in an industrial accident at the mint, a mishap that may have altered his career plans but hardly dampened his aspirations.[42] While in his twenties, Chávez settled at the small valley pueblo of San Isidro (population 560 in 1882), a few miles east of Guerrero, where he taught primary school and began to invest in his future. Hounded northward by the French Imperialists in 1865, the president of the republic, Benito Juárez, sold national land cheaply in exchange for loyalty, and Joaquín bought 2,511 hectares (6,202 acres) in the neighboring district of Abasolo, not an extraordinary amount of property, but a respectable start. The next year he purchased a small plot in San Isidro for about 25 pesos, probably for a home, but did not pay up within the legal time limit and so lost the plot to another buyer, a good lesson in local politics. At age 31, somewhat later than other bachelors of the period, he married Romana Acosta from Guerrero City, who brought a decent dowry of some 200 pesos (equivalent to nearly the same in dollars) to the marriage, which lasted 35 years until his wife's death. Eight of their children survived her, four others having died young.[43]

Control of communications in and out of the Sierra provided Joaquín Chávez with his real base of power. First he became the region's postmaster, then its police chief. Before the era of telephone and telegraph came to the mountains, mail courier services linked the dispersed mining centers to one another and to the outside. Normal delivery was weekly, in more remote places monthly. Sometimes it took a year for a letter to reach its destination, but people still marveled at the service, perhaps because they had no alternative. Many sites could only be reached through three-tiered delivery: by wagon from Chihuahua to the foothills, thence by mule as far as the trails extended, and finally by Tarahumara runners, paid a dollar a day to lug 30–50 pound packs of mail at a dog trot along footpaths that snow and swollen streams could make treacherous. Still, the natives covered 40, or even 50, miles a day with their cargo. Chávez bid for the service from the federal government, won it because of his contacts, and conducted the operation even after telegraph lines began to crisscross the mountains in the 1880s.[44]

An equally important delivery service involved getting supplies to the mining camps and the precious ore and bullion out. Chávez largely monopolized that service too; he organized the *conductas* that carried the freight. When after the turn of the century railroad lines inched into the Papigochic and beyond, he largely controlled the hub at Miñaca on the spur headed south into the mountains. The rail line stretching north should have passed through Guerrero City, the economic center of the region, and Guerrero's notables badly wanted it. But somehow the builders decided on a shortcut through San Isidro, where Chávez lived—and owned and ran an immense mercantile outlet. So Guerrero was bypassed to the east. No mining company could do without transport, so they all put Chávez on their payrolls to insure a steady flow of goods in both directions. In 1907 the manager at Pinos Altos griped that Chávez was gouging the company. At the time Pinos Altos was then not doing as well as in previous years, but Chávez continued to charge the same high transport costs: 100 pesos per month. The previous month the company had shipped only three silver bars, two of them small. Moreover, only part of that silver belonged to Pinos Altos itself, so it proposed to pay Chávez only 50 pesos for his services. How Joaquín reacted is not recorded, but he normally showed little sympathy for whiners.[45]

Transport of valuable merchandise, bullion, ore, and cash required security. Rumor had it in 1886 that one of the nation's most renowned brigands, Heraclio Bernal, the Thunderbolt of Sinaloa, had begun to work the Chihuahua Sierra, and Carl Lumholtz observed a plethora of wooden crosses on the trails he traversed, crosses marking spots where brigands had killed their prey or where robbers had been shot by some defender or security guard. Much of this sort of criminality in and around the Papigochic concerned contraband. Smugglers beat a sure path from the U.S. border to the valley, and they undoubtedly had accomplices along the way. Julius Froebel, a German who toured the region in the 1850s, found banditry rampant around Guerrero City and on the road to the mines at Jesús María, "perhaps simply to correct the injustice of Dame Fortune at the gaming table."[46] The notorious Chaparro gang, which later joined Cruz Chávez and his religious movement, was in mid-1879 already operating around Tosánachic and Yepachic, and mining capital might well go elsewhere if authorities could not assure its safety. In response the governor named Joaquín Chávez regional security chief, with authority to investigate any sort of behavior he considered disorderly or a threat to public peace. There was enormous arbitrary power here; we should recall that Jorge Ortiz caught a sample of it when a Chávez patrol ransacked his dwelling in search of weapons on the eve of hostilities at Tomochic. Troublemakers could be arrested and consigned to the federal army, and once again in the case of Tomochic we have seen how the accusations of Joaquín Chávez could tar an entire pueblo with infamy.

For all of these responsibilities—mail, transport, and police—Joaquín Chávez needed employees. He had to hire or buy mules and feed, horses and wagons, and purchase supplies and equipment, all of which made him a major employer and customer. He did a lot of people many favors and spurned others. A mail agent at Miñaca had him right: he was a "man of great wealth and therefore prestige, very accustomed to having his will obeyed, believing everyone is obligated to tolerate his imprudences, public employees as well as private citizens."[47] He even pained governors. When Chávez butted into a land dispute around Tomochic in 1907, his opponents communicated their fear of reprisals to the governor, who then ordered the jefe político to tell him more about this man Chávez, who falsely asserted that he held a special commission from the state house in order to conduct all sorts of public business on his own. In fact, that governor, Enrique Creel, already knew all about Chávez; earlier they had been business partners in a mining venture.[48]

Political influence certainly buttressed the economic pursuits of Joaquín Chávez, but he rarely ranked high as a public official. He played his cards right during the Díaz coup of 1876, however, and became jefe político of Guerrero district. The tenure of Chávez as jefe was disastrous, or perhaps his enemies—the Guerrero group allied to Luis Terrazas—only made it seem that way. In August 1879 they rebelled against him and Governor Trías and drove them both from office. After Chávez left, there were complaints he had deposited funds for reregistering branding irons in his pocket instead of in the municipal treasury. He was also accused of livestock theft, specifically that he had declared other people's mules as strays and rounded them up for his own herd. That charge went all the way to the State Supreme Court, which confirmed it, fined Chávez 25 pesos, and ordered him to return or buy the beasts. This was notable symbolic punishment, perhaps, but little more than a slap on the wrist for a cacique with the stature of Chávez.[49]

In succeeding years Chávez held several public posts in the Papigochic. In 1889 he was district judge and tax collector at the same time. He was a tough judge, sentencing the convicted to maximum terms, and as tax collector complained that there were insufficient tax revenues to pay salaries of both the local police and civil employees. But his main business remained personal business. His interests ran from land acquisitions for timber and cattle to mining for silver and coal. In some ventures—coal exploration, for example—he became partners with members of the state's elites, like Governor Lauro Carrillo or the up-and-coming Enrique Creel. In another venture, Chávez joined partnership to invest in mines at Dolores with a ranking army officer who happened to be stationed in Chihuahua. Years later, in 1907, he did business with the U.S. capitalist-adventurer William C. Greene, who sought to establish a gold and silver empire in the mountains above Temósachic. Chávez's sawmills cut lumber for Greene's railroads, and his impressive mercantile warehouse supplied the entire mining community—fine cigars and cognac included. Records of the district's land transactions prove him to have been an active trader in real estate, from modest parcels held in mancomún at Basúchil to ranchos near San Isidro and on to sizable expanses for cattle grazing and timber cutting around Tomochic.[50]

One suspects more than a coincidence between his hostility toward the Tomochitecos and his land interests in the immediate area. There seems to have been no such animosity before the upsurge in mining made land around Tomochic more valuable and Chávez covetous of a share, but that winter of 1891 and on into the following year he pursued the faithful with a vengeance, both with his own security forces and by urging the governor to bring down the repressive machinery of the state on the Tomochitecos. Cruz Chávez considered Joaquín's actions the betrayal of a long-standing trust between the two men, but by the turn of the century Joaquín Chávez reigned as one of the four or five wealthiest property owners in Guerrero District, even if, characteristically, he claimed to be overtaxed.[51]

Silviano González and Joaquín Chávez were not extraordinary individuals. They are best seen as representative of power relationships in the Papigochic. We have sketched out some of their backgrounds and personalities because they became so central to the drama that enveloped Tomochic. Although located outside the Papigochic proper, Tomochic in essence resembled other pueblos in the valley. The people of

all these places had experienced the same sort of historical development and as a result possessed similar personalities: touchy, suspicious,
and possessive. They had grown up together in the same administrative
district and in similar daily lives. Geography provided Tomochitecos
with only a thin insulation from events in the Papigochic, just 26 miles
away, though over difficult terrain. It allowed them to dodge some
edicts of the jefe político, such as voting in those meaningless (to them)
state elections, and to distance themselves from forced contributions of
either manpower or cash for public causes for which they lacked sympathy. But the tactics and strategies, the maneuvers and goals of potent
and forceful politicians like Silviano González and Joaquín Chávez insured that Tomochitecos remained at least aware of, and at times en-
tangled in, regional affairs that could also embody state and national
issues. Reyes Domínguez and his clique in Tomochic would not have
wanted it any other way; Cruz Chávez saw the issues differently.

The steady flow of regional commerce funneled through the pueblo
on the flanks of Joaquín's "mountain schooners" also reminded Tomochitecos of a larger world. Itinerant merchants brought rock salt,
sugar cane, cheap manufactured clothing, chocolate, oranges, and liquor along with news from other places like the state capital, which
supplemented reports and scuttlebutt the locals had picked up in the
mining camps. So Tomochitecos knew about the political turmoil in
the Papigochic—the waves of conspiracies, protests, and rebellions—
and also felt the reverberations, if only because they interrupted commerce and could jump the price of goods sixfold. In fact, in the wake of
the Imperialist cleavage down in the Papigochic, Tomochic's presidente Jesús José Chávez (father of Cruz) held public sessions to discuss
these latest spectacular happenings and to lay out the law as dictated by
the state.[52]

Yet no group in the village seems to have taken sides in these disturbances, and one wonders why. Too much risk? A lack of persuasive
arguments or compelling leadership? Recognition of a need for constituted authority, even while rejecting some of its mandates? Cruz
Chávez said as much when pressed by government negotiators to abandon his movement. Or perhaps we have not fully recognized, or have at
least underestimated, the strength of those bonds that tied pueblo society together before the calamitous events of the late 1880s. Tomochitecos were not unique in their reluctance to join wider causes. Other

pueblos in the Papigochic showed little inclination to embroil themselves in political turbulence outside of their immediate interests, but
the Tomochitecos seem to have been especially wary of such involvement. It took a phenomenal series of blows over a very short period to
break the villagers apart and bring them to naked conflict: drought,
official interference with religious rites, the theft of religious icons, the
imposition of an outsider as presidente, false accusations of complicity
in bandit activities, a cacique who broke faith with them, commercial
competition heightened by new economic opportunity, the appearance
of messengers from God, uneasy politicians protecting their personal
positions regardless of cost to others. All these pummeled social and
moral arrangements in the pueblo and polarized rivals so that one
group rigidly insisted on the letter of civil law while the other vowed to
obey no one but Santa Teresa and Almighty God.

There was much more at stake here than just an argument over who
should rule. Here we witness two entirely different visions of the way
the world *is* and the way it *ought* to be, a reflection of the same dialogue
raging over so much of the world since the nineteenth century. Let us
now witness that debate through the words and actions of people who
did not directly participate in the disturbances at Tomochic but who
sought to shape their trajectory. First we shall meet Governor Carrillo
and then President Díaz, and see how they responded to challenges
such as those hurled by Cruz Chávez. Then we shall examine Santa
Teresa's world so appreciated by Cruz and his devotees.

6

The Governor's Game

THE TROUBLES AT TOMOCHIC could not have come at a worse time
for Governor Lauro Carrillo. The global recession of the early 1890s,
which had dried up money in financial markets and curtailed investment in foreign enterprises such as silver mining, had rocked the state of
Chihuahua. Compounding the downturn, the overall decline in world
silver prices continued as more and more nations turned to the gold
standard and paper currency. Then a fourth year of withering drought
throughout much of the state forced emergency purchases of corn and
beans from the United States. Politically, increased taxation, recklessly
unbalanced budgets, and the raw intention to centralize power as codified in the new state constitution rankled the public. So did the lavish
expenditure on foreign furniture for the new governor's palace. Then
there were the usual charges of corruption and favoritism hurled at his
administration, exemplified by a brewing state lottery scandal. If this
menu of afflictions did not stir ordinary people to open protest, it gave
competing camarillas plenty of grist for their mills. Results of the November 1891 municipal elections at the mining center of Jesús María, at
Santo Tomás and Temósachic in the Papigochic, and further north at
La Ascensión had spawned protest, even some rioting, which threatened to build toward rebellion. In fact, Carrillo was hanging on to the
governorship by his fingernails. His main opposition, the Terrazas camarilla, vigorously challenged his plans for reelection in June 1892, and
it looked as if he might lose the backing of President Porfirio Díaz.
Making things harder, his benefactor and patrón Carlos Pacheco had
just died, not long after leaving the president's cabinet where he had

been in charge of national development. Now Carrillo had no political protector. Then came Tomochic: his opposition was sure to use it as a club, as proof of his inability to maintain public order in the state. No more serious political charge could be leveled against a governor.[1]

Carrillo's path to political prominence and ultimately to the governorship had not been unusual for the times. Born into a fairly well-off mining family that at mid-century had settled at Morís in the Sierra, he naturally turned to mining and also became a licensed land surveyor. He made substantial money from his mining and banking interests, as well as from his connections to federal survey companies, which were often paid off with substantial portions of the huge tracts of the land they measured. Carrillo's mountain mining districts sent him to the state legislature. While in Chihuahua City he worked with the state office of development, and it was there that he met Pacheco, then the president's Minister of Development, Colonization, and Industry. Indeed, Pacheco was personally very close to Díaz. A native of Parral (his only link to Chihuahua), Pacheco had fought in a variety of militia units during the mid-century Reform Wars and then joined the Díaz army to fight the French Imperialists. He and his military comrades helped bring Díaz to the presidency in 1876, and political recompense readily followed. Pacheco was appointed governor and military commander of the State of Puebla and later became the "elected" governor of Morelos. Meanwhile, Díaz also named him to the significant cabinet post. So Carlos Pacheco was both an obedient servant of Porfirio Díaz and a powerful man in his own right, which had put him at odds with Chihuahua's longtime cacique Luis Terrazas.[2]

Terrazas, it will be remembered, had on several occasions fought against the ascendancy of Díaz. Then in 1880 he rode a coup by his supporters back into the governorship. During his four-year term he reached some sort of understanding with the regime: Terrazas would not oppose presidential policies in return for noninterference by Díaz in the personal and business affairs of Terrazas in Chihuahua and elsewhere. Of course, they did not trust one another, and their conciliation was an edgy one. Yet in 1884, when Díaz insisted that Carlos Pacheco become the next governor of Chihuahua, Terrazas quietly departed public office and left his backers to conspire for his return.[3]

As the new governor, but still also the federal Minister of Development, Pacheco allied himself with elites from the Papigochic—individuals such as Celso González (brother of Silviano) and politicians from the Sierra such as Lauro Carrillo. His work at the ministry forced Pacheco to spend long periods in Mexico City, during which the state legislature, which he controlled, appointed Carrillo as substitute governor. The legislature then began work on constitutional changes that would strengthen the hand of governors—legal innovations that mirrored the national ones being promulgated by Porfirio Díaz.[4] The deputies confirmed Carrillo, now an energetic and aggressive 40 years old, as governor-elect in 1888. Toward the end of his four-year term he prepared for reelection, but the Terrazas people had other ideas, as did Porfirio Díaz—and now Pacheco was dead. A political donnybrook ensued with all the attendant dealings, lies, and recriminations. How consummately Díaz played that game—calling the adversaries to Mexico City for private consultations, assuring one and then another of support, spreading rumors, unleashing trial balloons, scolding sycophants for assuming his endorsement. This devious process is all on record in his personal papers; Lauro Carrillo became a victim of it. The governor took a public battering from the Terrazas people, and must have known that behind the scenes Díaz conspired to oust him—not, of course, to be replaced by a Terrazas choice, but by an outsider palatable to the Terrazas people and even to some of his own wavering supporters in Chihuahua, who had become anxious about their own futures.

Political circles even bandied about the name of Miguel Ahumada, who for the past six years had commanded the federal customs zone that included Chihuahua.[5] Customs officials like Ahumada were the eyes and ears of Porfirio Díaz along the border. They monitored dissenters who had sought temporary refuge in the United States to conspire in safety—at times with assertive Americans in search of economic advantage. These fiscal agents constituted a principal pillar of the regime and ranked high among the president's most trusted associates. Under these circumstances it is no wonder that Carrillo became alarmed. The president apparently had not yet made any definite decisions about the next governor of Chihuahua, but he was thinking about possibilities. Then came the tempest at Tomochic.

The governor reacted to the incident in the pueblo like so many public officials who sense their tenure threatened: he ordered the disturbance suppressed by reliable forces, and at the same time downplayed the incident's importance to his superiors and a curious public. He also launched an investigation into the unrest, not so much to uncover its causes or the aims and grievances of the participants as to ascertain the movement's *political* intentions—meaning its stance in the governor's race, as well as its attitude toward the national regime—and to probe the possibility of "outside" complicity. Even before he knew much at all about the upheaval, Carrillo perfunctorily declared it "purely local," of no political consequence, and promised that the culprits would be promptly punished.[6] Such public pronouncements amounted to little more than stock statements authorities regularly issued under such circumstances, hoping to control damage until the trouble could be surveyed.

The governor also began to counter his latest tormentors with labels meant to justify annihilation of the religious movement in the name of the national good. We can see the tactic building in the governor's initial reports on Tomochic to President Díaz. First, the uproar had occurred in a place which was largely "Indian." A day or so later the governor labeled the participants "bandits" preparing to assault a silver bullion convoy, and shortly thereafter fanatics.[7] It mattered little that none of these labels fit the dissidents.

Labeling the Enemy

Let us look a bit closer at the process of labeling at work. Initial contact between the army and the religious movement at Tomochic occurred on December 7, 1891. Two days later Carrillo wired Díaz that the uprising had taken place in an area lightly populated, mainly by Indians. Carrillo knew better. He was no stranger to the village: recall the fracas surrounding the stolen religious paintings during the governor's visit to the pueblo, which caused a tumultuous reaction by the villagers and forced an apology.[8] No, Carrillo knew that Tomochic was predominantly a village of mestizos—of people ethnically like himself. From indirect dealings with Cruz Chávez he understood that Chávez was mestizo. No doubt the governor designated the Chávez group "Indian" with a purpose in mind. Interestingly, Miguel Ahumada played the same hand, wiring Díaz on December 10 about the outburst among the

"Indians" of Tomochic and also dismissing the movement as of no importance.[9]

In his telegram of December 9 the governor stated that the motive for the dissonance was unknown but under investigation. Here we find Carrillo searching for an "explanation," although he knew firsthand of the rift in the village between the followers of Cruz Chávez and the local presidente. That official, Juan Ignacio Chávez, had said as much that late fall of 1890 when, in the matter of the paintings, he admitted to the governor that he was at serious odds with Cruz and that, when it came to spiritual matters and the church proper, Cruz Chávez was in charge and would brook no challenge. The governor might have suspected that reasons for the violent outburst lay in that fissure, but such a supposition would not speak well of his ability to manage politics and maintain order in the state. The governor needed another "explanation," and he soon had it, propitiously provided by another self-interested party, Joaquín Chávez.

Whether Joaquín and the governor conspired to craft a plausible motive for the upheaval at Tomochic cannot be fathomed for certain, but by December 10 Carrillo telegraphed Díaz that he had been informed by Joaquín Chávez ("a person who can be totally trusted and believed") that the Tomochitecos had declared their intention to obey no one but God only as a pretext to arm themselves in preparation for an attack on a mule train laden with silver, which was led by Joaquín and headed for the pueblo.[10] Hence, participants in the commotion were really bandits who intended to camouflage their criminal intentions with a counterfeit spirituality. As we have seen, Joaquín Chávez had previously made a similar allegation related to the attempted robbery of the Pinos Altos convoy in early 1891. Although it had soon become obvious that no Tomochitecos had been involved in that assault, Cruz Chávez and his people did not forget the hurt and resentment caused by the accusation. Nor is there any evidence that any Tomochitecos engaged in banditry either before or after the encounter with the army, though they had ample opportunity to do so had the notion crossed their minds. The faithful were not bandits, although it served the interests of others to label them as such.

The next day, December 11, Carrillo attached yet another label: "fanatic." In reporting to the president he relied on the report of the district judge, Manuel Rubio, who had taken testimony from participants who had either defected from the movement or been captured by the military. "Pure fanaticism," decided Judge Rubio. Those in charge of the group, among them Cruz and Manuel Chávez, had convinced thirty or so "ignorantes," most of them "indios," that they should obey no other authorities but the elderly man and woman they had encountered at El Chopeque, who claimed to be divine and promised miracles. Though Carrillo seized this label, he also argued that such spiritual enthusiasm was little more than pretense. The leaders of the group only encouraged their followers to defend their religion so that they could take up weapons and attack the convoy coming through town.[11] The governor wanted that "bandido" label to stick, and to reinforce it with "fanático."

"Indio," "bandido," and "fanático" conjured up especially powerful messages in the nineteenth-century Mexican mind. "Indio," both then and now, is a term frequently used to denigrate. When today's Mexicans say "Tú eres indio," it means you are stupid. Parents typically tell their children: "No seas indio" (literally, don't be an Indian, meaning don't be gullible around strangers—don't be like those ignorant indios who welcomed the greedy Spaniards into Mexico). Or "Que no te cambien espejitos por oro" (do not trade your gold for worthless mirrors—like the dim-witted Indians who first encountered the Spaniards). The negative connotation of "indio" in a country where the shade of one's skin still carries social significance is well ingrained in Mexican culture and has been for centuries.

"Indio" also suggests aggression, even power struggle, and still does so today as recent events in Chiapas reveal. Conquering Spaniards demanded that the natives swear an oath of allegiance to the king and failure to do so could ignite a "just war." In other words, the Crown could declare the recalcitrant Indians to be in rebellion, therefore unredeemable heathens to be exterminated rather than Christianized.[12] A residue of this practice carried into later centuries, hence the urgency of Lauro Carrillo to label the Tomochitecos "indios." Like numbers of their predecessors, they had forsaken loyalty and obedience to constituted government and were, therefore, the legitimate subjects of "just war"; they could be crushed in good faith.

The label "indio" also raised the specter of caste war, which shadowed nineteenth-century Mexicans. There was a fear—and one not always quietly internalized—that Indian groups would unite to take their revenge on descendants of the colonizers. When the Maya rebelled at mid-century, a national leader warned that the natives were "pursuing with monstrous barbarity the plan for exterminating the white class."[13] Most speakers on the subject at the time advocated assimilation; they envisioned a nation of mestizos. Such absorption would not only eliminate Indians as a race, but also as "bárbaros," enemies of civilization.[14] Listen to this spokesman for Liberal thought: the Indians "in their present state and until they have undergone considerable changes, can never reach the degree of enlightenment, civilization, and culture of Europeans nor maintain themselves in a society formed by both."[15] Therefore, in the name of civilization, "indios" must be changed or subdued. Some, like Pope Leo XIII, discerned substantial advancement toward modernity in Mexico through acculturation of native peoples: "Thousands and thousands of mortals [meaning Indians] were delivered to human society, carried from a barbarous past to the sweet life and to civilization,"[16] but a Mexico City newspaper found much work still to be done. It carried a drawing (copied from a U.S. newspaper) of a "typical Indian" who allegedly had participated in the "rebellion" at Tomochic. Readers were urged to look into that native face, which they were told contained not one trace of intelligence and was a portrait of ignorance and backwardness. Surely such stupid-looking people could never fight for true political ideals. "No, no serious plan can come from the masses of such people [who are] devoid of any high-minded aspirations." Of course, the picture was contrived to drain events at Tomochic of any political significance. The sketch bears no particular resemblance to Cruz Chávez or any of his followers; it could be almost any Mexican mestizo ranchero of the period, and it is definitely not the illustration of an Indian. Still, the newspaper labeled the Tomochitecos "indios," enemies of national progress and therefore appropriate objects of repression.[17] So the nineteenth-century concept of "progress" joined a sixteenth-century view of "fealty" and "just war."

The label "fanático" both underscored and broadened the stereotype in "indio." If "indio" conveyed the idea of lethargic and benumbed thought (even though the natives occasionally rose up in caste war), "fanático" connoted a mind full of peculiar percolating emotions and weird feelings, which from a "modern" viewpoint were outmoded, regressive, irrational, and even dangerous to the constituted social order.

Furthermore, "fanático" was not ethnically specific; it could be applied to anyone—mestizos, creoles, Indians—with no reference to race or social standing. But because "fanático" referred mainly to religious attitudes and practices, those who used the label had to do so with considerable care. They certainly did not mean to discourage the "right kind" of religiosity, meaning that which preached patience and penance, the sort that reinforced patron-client relationships and encouraged the unquestioned support of the national program as designed by national leaders.[18] On the other hand, "fanáticos," driven by "wild superstition" and irrational and unscientific (meaning overly religious) belief, became a drag on "our" progress toward modernity. In sum, "fanáticos" and "indios," were not like "us." They constituted obstacles to "our" betterment which must be removed. "Our," "we," and "us" only included Mexicans who endorsed, or at least did not oppose, the national program for progress as designed by those in charge. Indeed, Tomochic may be seen as a stray spark from a grinding collision that was engaging the nation at large.

"Bandidos" could be even more of an obstacle to progress than either "indios" or "fanáticos." "Bandido" is a word with considerable elasticity, stretching from common criminal to dedicated revolutionary, and it has long been used by the state to discredit all sorts of activities deemed inimical to its interests. However, bandits themselves frequently work both sides of the law; any number have served the state one day and broken its laws the next. Besides, a brigand to one person may be a hero to another. Heraclio Bernal, whom we already have briefly glimpsed in the Sierra, is an example. At about the same period in the 1880s Mexican newspapers labeled the notorious Chucho el Roto a "civilized bandit," and some advocated hiring his expertise for criminal reform.[19] Bandits may be accorded a double identity: "bandit-patriots," "bandit-guerrillas," "social bandits," or "bandit-zealots." When you pin the label "bandit" on someone, you risk creating an icon or an idol for your enemy, but this seemed lost on the likes of Carrillo.

Because of its ambiguity and potential for varied interpretations, "bandido" carries even more force than "indio" and "fanático." In earlier times enemies of a divinely sanctioned social order were deemed to be outside the realm of God Himself: they were bandits. That is what "bandit" literally means: to banish, to force the accused outside the boundaries of acknowledged society—not just to the margins, but out.

Unable to accomplish that goal with any consistency, governments have more recently also relied on cooptation, incorporating bandits into the regime as police. Russia's czars did as much with brigands called cossacks, and at mid-nineteenth century Mexico's leadership turned troublesome bandits into what developed into an internationally acclaimed constabulary, Los Rurales.[20]

But the badge of banditry explicitly aims to drain these activities of their political content, of any challenge to the regime's way of conducting affairs. Genuine political dissent is within bounds, even though it is often not tolerated, but banditry signifies those who have no stake in the national enterprise of which "we are all a part." Political adversaries may find redress in the law; bandits usually do not. For example, those captured in open rebellion against a government may still enjoy constitutional protections, but not so bandits, which is one reason brigands sometimes operate with a political proclamation in their pockets.[21] It is their life insurance policy, even if it rarely pays off. In times of political crisis regimes may invoke so-called laws of exception, carefully embedded in national constitutions. These exceptions remove legal guarantees for highwaymen and their kind. Bandits caught in the act can be summarily executed. Though this may eliminate some unwanted brigands (or political enemies labeled as such), these draconian measures may also reveal that domestic controls are ineffective or have been overwhelmed. They could send a caution signal to foreigners in search of a safe investment or undermine public confidence in the government. Therefore, laws of exception are invoked with extreme caution.[22] Better to try labels first; preferable to attempt to galvanize generalized support for whatever repressive measures may follow.

Unexpected Results

Still, labelers must beware. Their strategy may well budge the mildly dissatisfied into frank dissent and then strengthen their resolve, as occurred at Tomochic. We cannot say how much impetus Joaquín Chávez unwittingly provided the religious movement at Tomochic when he labeled the villagers "bandidos" in 1891. Later, with his movement in full bloom, Cruz Chávez asserted he had felt morally betrayed, a critical concern for a person to whom moral stature meant so much; remember that Cruz Chávez had demanded legal relief when a Tarahumara woman called him a thief. Cruz's followers joined for many reasons, some no doubt with more uncertainty than others. We can only wonder how much the relentless slurs of Governor Carrillo and others helped push them toward martyrdom.

Blind to any unintended consequences, Governor Carrillo continued to apply the labels and report to President Díaz that the movement was of no consequence and would soon be squelched. At the same time he labored to crush it quickly, without arousing the kind of attention that could become a political liability for himself. Specifically, he wished to keep the federal military—the Díaz army, those legions of the president wielding national power—in its barracks. He therefore commissioned his trusted friend, the hacendado Ramón Sáenz, to track down Cruz Chávez and his cohorts. After a brief stopover in Tomochic, Sáenz was off into the Sierra in pursuit of the believers. Meanwhile, Carrillo ordered El Santo del Chopeque and his companion arrested as conspirators in the uprising and brought to the state capital.[23] He must have wondered about these santos (themselves considered fanáticos by the authorities) who wandered around the countryside. Authorities normally paid them little heed, although they could hardly help but notice their appeal to others, and officialdom became wary when santos attracted enthusiastic congregations. Carrillo may have made no connection between religious fervor and political rebellion, but he knew unruly subjects when he saw them.

The detained santo, Carmen María López, naturally denied any complicity in the religious movement at Tomochic. The old man assured authorities that he was no Messiah and in no way instigated sedition. True, the Tomochitecos had visited him at El Chopeque and adored him like the newly arrived Jesus Christ, but he had offered them no counsel, no encouragement to disobey civil authority, and no reason to prepare for battle against the Sons of Lucifer. Certainly he had never been to Tomochic itself, although invited there to rule—"rule" is the word he used—by Cruz Chávez.[24] What was the truth? López was fighting for his life. Although the state normally displayed considerable tolerance toward such religious curiosities, it tolerated no whiff of sedition. So Lopez's insistence is understandable, especially when we recall that followers of Cruz Chávez testified to official investigators that their leader had told them to have no fear, that the Santo del Chopeque had promised to protect them in their forthcoming struggle with the soldiers of Satan and had assured them of glorious triumph.

Unsure of either the content or the meaning of the drama unfolding before him, Carrillo placed López under house arrest. Within a month this santo was taken to Guerrero City (Joaquín Chávez provided the escort), where a judge heard charges that the old man had misrepresented himself as Jesus Christ and dismissed them as too flimsy for further prosecution. Though the court declared Carmen María a free man,[25] the governor did not trust him to steer clear of Cruz Chávez and had him confined to quarters in the state capital, where officials kept him under surveillance well into 1892. A newspaper reporter found him there and declared López a good conversationalist, though a charlatan mystic. To the journalist he resembled a famous hermit, Padre Anselmo de Gil Blas de Santillana, whom the Holy Inquisition had ordered burned at the stake.[26] In a few days López was to be freed—and perhaps he was, for at this point he meanders out of the documentation, with his place in this historical tapestry neither fully revealed nor altogether understood.

7

An Anxious Dictator

IN ONE OF THE OPENING SCENES of the motion picture *Viva Zapata!* we see President Porfirio Díaz, distinguished by his ample white mustache and elegant military tunic laden with medals. Nearing 80 years of age but fit and energetic, he sits comfortably behind a massive table-desk, ready for the day's callers, among them a delegation of campesinos from the State of Morelos who complain that their land has been stolen by a neighboring hacendado. Díaz assures them that the law will resolve their difficulties and even offers the modest farmers his personal lawyer for assistance. Then in a very fatherly manner he ends the session: "Now, my children, I have many other matters to attend to. . . . It's not an easy job being president." The campesinos understand. They murmur and chuckle in acknowledgment and then turn to leave. One member of the group, however, lingers behind and respectfully reminds the president that the farmers cannot await legal remedies. It is the planting season, and they need to get their crops in the ground. Díaz fumes at this challenge to his wisdom, orders the impertinent campesino from the presidential chamber, and when he has left, angrily circles the man's name (Emiliano Zapata) as a troublemaker on a list of the humble visitors prepared for the meeting.[1]

This film vignette reasonably reflects the ambiance surrounding the presidential palace at the turn of the century, an image of the presidency crafted and nurtured for decades by Díaz and his supporters. We see the civilized statesman—Porfirio Díaz exuding an enchanting paternal benevolence edged with law, busily attending to a modern country's many affairs, yet with an understanding moment for those humble campesinos who require his counsel. At the same time it reveals Díaz's firm hand—he is a kind of magnanimous father-king. And finally we see an irascible dictator who brooks no challenge to his word and is on the lookout for dissidence. He resembles a chameleon, changing colors to suit his urgencies. In the film as in life, Mexico's president was an anxious man.

Creating a Nation

Porfirio Díaz and his cohorts had indeed been busy. With an eye to the Western model, they had followed the lead of their immediate predecessors to patch over or simply purge the self-evident diversities in a geographical entity called Mexico and proclaimed the outcome a *nation*. As in the film, the major emphasis in this process was on appearance. The director of Mexico's exhibit at the New Orleans World's Fair in 1885 put it this way: "A country which presents a well-organized display deserves the respect of the entire world."[2] For the administration, then, the key to global respect (and foreign investment) lay in presenting Mexico as a "well-organized display."

Among the country's most renowned displays at world expositions was its Rural Police Force, the internationally famed Rurales, who also paraded on Mexican national holidays in the capital. On one such occasion, this splendid looking constabulary, rode down the elegant Paseo de la Reforma to the cheers of thousands, then across the capital's central plaza, the *Zócalo*, to receive their salute from the world's diplomats mingled with prominent Mexicans flanking the president himself. Dressed in their bolero jackets with swirling designs in silver braid, tight leggings closed at the seams with silver buttons, and magnificent wide-brimmed, lavishly appointed sombreros, these horsemen on their beautifully groomed and well-matched mounts were indeed splendid to behold. That night at a magnificent banquet (French cuisine, of course) staged at the city's most exclusive gaming hall and restaurant, the Elysian Tivoli, the president raised a glass of pulque, Mexico's national drink, and toasted the corps:

Long live, long live the valiant Rural,
Who has spent his life on campaign.

. . .

Our country does itself proud
To have such brave sons
In these Rurales of indomitable spirit
Who are free and are not slaves.
 Brave when on rugged campaign,
Calm and ready to fight,
No enemy is able to conquer
The natural bravery of the Rural.
 This corps of brilliant *charros*
Is the pride of modern Mexico.[3]

In the field, according to their manufactured image, Rurales endured any hardship to "get their man." They were even better than the celebrated Texas Rangers. Foreigners found the rural policemen to be of great strength and courage, taller and tougher than the average Mexican, so that "the evildoer may expect little mercy at their hands." Nor did the corpsmen waste any time with convicted criminals: "The official shooter with his Winchester goes from court and shoots the prisoners as fast as they are condemned." A thunderstruck U.S. cavalry commander, Philip Sheridan, could only exclaim: "With that cavalry I could encircle the globe." And in 1886 a British observer, Solomon B. Griffen, likened them to the "ancient knights of Spain" and then proclaimed: "*THIS* is Mexico."[4]

The Rurales did indeed reflect Porfirian Mexico: a nicely polished skin but rotten at the core. In fact the rural policemen were in the main illiterate common urban types and campesinos. Their practice targets prove that they could not shoot very straight, nor did many possess any real horsemanship. Drunkenness and desertion afflicted the corps, payroll peculations were common, officers mixed in local politics, and the men were frequently abusive and arbitrary toward the populace they policed. Other elite constabularies of the period may have had their own shortcomings, but the rot in the Rurales was especially fetid. Nevertheless, their fabricated image gleamed and especially appealed to those who wanted or needed to believe that after decades of unrelenting turmoil Mexico had become pacified, civilized, and modern. The administration pretended that the constabulary blanketed the country, but instead carefully posted smallish detachments at railroad depots and other high-visibility sites where foreign tourists and entrepreneurs could tout them and common Mexicans would be reminded of their presence as tough-minded hired agents of the state. At any one time during this period called the Porfiriato (1885–1910) there were never more than 3,000 federal Rurales—administrators, disabled, and imprisoned corpsmen included, but strung out along major transportation routes they appeared to be more ubiquitous (and ominous) than they really were.[5] No wonder the dictator promoting this sham was troubled beneath his countenance of stern confidence.

This image-building process—the creation of a Mexico at peace with itself—also required rapprochement with the Catholic Church or at least with the hierarchy of the Church, which had literally gone to war against the mid-century Reform Laws so vigorously attacking its property and authority. But The Reform had echoed far beyond the upper echelons of Church and State; it had jarred the psyche of the entire populace. The Reform had opened minds and focused attention on spirituality, encouraging people to examine not only the ways ordinary people were living their lives but the ways in which they thought life *ought* to be lived, including the proper role of both religious and secular authority. Controversy and debate, frustration and apprehension naturally ensued. Conflict between secularized and more traditional Catholics simmered and periodically bubbled into open struggle. Díaz and his associates sought to paper over the turmoil with images of domestic tranquillity and social cohesion but desperately needed the aura of the Church as peacekeeper. Hence the government's effort to negotiate a reconciliation with the highest authorities of the official Church.

The results of agreements that followed were very uneven. There was simply too much variance of opinion about the role of religion in society and in one's life to make consistent policies possible. As the secular patrón of the country, Díaz himself mediated cases of dissident priests and the complaints of parishioners against their padres. There was mixed enforcement of the laws prohibiting convents, religious processions outside of churches, excessive church-bell ringing, forced donations, and holding of property by the Church. In these ambivalent surroundings Josephine missionaries were permitted to es-

tablish schools in Chihuahua; in Guerrero in 1888 the governor ordered the investigation of a religious procession led by a priest; and in
Durango authorities engaged troops to protect such processions during Holy Week and at the same time obstructed civic celebrations. Even
the bishops openly pursued their differences. Eulogio Gillow, Bishop of
Oaxaca, a personal friend of the president, invested in railroad construction, while Bishop Ignacio Montes de Oca y Obregón, a literary
figure and able politician from San Luis Potosí, railed against the new
civil order both at home and abroad. And as a sample of idiosyncratic
theology (but with little political import) an apostate bishop, Eduardo
Sánchez Camacho, preaching in Tamaulipas, refused to accept the
sixteenth-century apparition of the Virgin Mary that lay at the very
heart of Mexican devotion.[6]

On the question of who should rule the civil state, the president was
understandably firm. For example, in 1887 it was rumored that a group
of clerical conservatives intended to replace Díaz with a member of the
royal House of Bourbon and that the new prince was already on his
way. The president responded with tact but made his position clear:
"The clergy understands well that we are the least objectionable government for them that the nation can have and they are resigned to it,
because they don't see any possibility of the establishment of a clerical
government."[7] The clergy understood nothing of the sort but hesitated
to press its case against the dictator too far. The following year the
regime began to negotiate a concordat with Pope Leo XIII, assuring the
unimpeded preaching of Roman Catholicism and the protection of the
property of Catholics in Mexico. The reconciliation culminated in 1895
with an ostentatious crowning of Christ the King ceremony in the capital, all of which reinforced the appearance—it was nothing more than
that—of national harmony.[8]

Enticing Capital

Capitalists bought the image of a Mexico under resolute guidance—or
at least they found Mexico worth the risk and invested massively, encouraged by incentives such as tax breaks along with cheap leases and
land grants. British and German bondholders agreed to consolidate

old Mexican debts in a new bond issue worth $51,250,000 at 6 percent interest for 35 years, a financial arrangement carrying a psychological bonus in that it induced others to regard Mexico as a good risk.[9] For their own purposes some foreigners further enhanced the image created by Porfirians. Take for instance Dr. James Edmunds, a health officer and public analyst out of London, who with a mining engineer and a professor of agriculture in 1888 surveyed the northern part of the Papigochic region for potential British investors. His "most able guide" was the marvelously double-dealing Santana Pérez—one day in rebellion, the next at the service of government authority. Governor Lauro Carrillo sent along his personal military valet to insure the Englishman's comfort. Dr. Edmunds was euphoric (at least in his official report) with what he saw: "These lands [4,576 square miles of territory] are undoubtedly a splendid country. . . . The country ought to grow everything that could be produced in Great Britain or France. . . . The district should become a great sanatorium for European invalids. . . . [Concerning colonization], it is difficult to imagine anything but success, gratifying alike to the colonists and to the investors who organize the project." Dr. Edmunds expressed only one caveat: pulque, which he called "aloe-beer." Noting that manufacturers earned substantial profit producing the drink, he lamented that it "impoverished and demoralized the community" and concluded, "A population that spends its earnings in rendering itself nerveless with tobacco and stupid with alcohol can never be successful." As a result, Dr. Edmunds recommended the prohibition of pulque in the district.[10] The precise reaction of potential British investors to Edmunds's fabled account is not known, but either they declined to take his bait or the asking price of $2,340,000 proved too steep.[11]

Not to worry; other customers waited. Near the Papigochic, Mexican capitalists (many of them holding high political positions) had invested in numerous speculative properties, among them real estate rich in timber and cattle potential, as well as mining sites. José Ives Limantour—exceedingly wealthy, well educated, and suave, soon to be the country's Minister of Finance, in which office he proceeded to balance the national budget and become the likely successor to Díaz—caught the scent of profit in lumber around Tomochic. In 1846 his father, a prosperous French merchant who worked the sea route between Acapulco and San Francisco, had for "services rendered" (probably gun-running) received from the governor of Baja California (then a federal territory) several strategically important islands off Mazatlán and Baja. In the early 1880s Mexico wanted the islands back in order to shore up its naval defenses on the Pacific coast, and José agreed to give up his inherited islands in exchange for mainland properties. Limantour, educated as a lawyer with economic expertise, still in his thirties, and a friend of Carlos Pacheco, the Minister of Development who sanctioned the exchange, claimed 426,807 acres of richly timbered property around Tomochic and 52,181 acres far to the south in the Tehuantepec region, where the commercial farming of rice, sugar, and pineapples flourished alongside rubber plantations and where the discovery of oil seemed imminent. Railroad construction was either planned or already under way in both districts. In short, the two grants reeked of potential profit, though probably neither Limantour nor his representatives had ever seen them in person. The parcels seem to have been selected in Mexico City from maps prepared during an earlier general survey of public lands. At any rate, Limantour took formal title to the properties in 1888. But not quite all of that acreage was actually his. A good 30 percent of the northern grant belonged to pueblos, haciendas, and ranchos protected by legal titles. Limantour respected those deeds; at least they are carefully blocked out and preserved as such on the maps of the holding. In the process Tomochic, completely surrounded by the grant, retained nearly 10,000 acres and the González brothers, Silviano and Félix, kept their hacienda at Tonachic. Still, those relatively small tracts look awfully vulnerable on the map, especially if the giant decided to swallow.[12]

No doubt Limantour was anxious to exploit his property, or sell it to others who would promptly do so, but the troubles at Tomochic scared off investors so that the minister-to-be did not actually take possession until May 1897, and nearly another decade passed before he sold this northern land for $642,762 to the American owned Cargill Lumber Company, a Goliath in the business.[13] It is doubtful that Cruz Chávez and the faithful ever knew of the early dealings, nor did any of the more business-minded people of the community, like Reyes Domínguez or Juan Ignacio Chávez. At least the district's historical documentation carries no reference to Limantour's transaction, concluded without fanfare far away in the capital. Nonetheless, the plat map of the Limantour grant invites wonderment. There lies Tomochic, a small but recognizable enclave, right in the middle of it. Had they been aware of it, the Tomochitecos undoubtedly would have been suspicious and concerned. After all, they were not accustomed to any fixed boundaries surrounding their community. They cut timber and grazed their cattle where they wished. Survey maps that challenged such customs would have aroused a response, but there is not a hint of such in the documentation. Therefore, we may presume that the Tomochitecos had no idea of the plans ranking members of the regime had made for the eventual use of their countryside, and that Limantour's holdings did not figure in their discontent. Still the survey maps are reminders of the regime's land dealings, which bred dissatisfaction in many locales in the country and further stoked the president's anxieties.

Rumblings of Disorder

While investment opportunities supported by government favor energized the country's economy, they also created competition and disrupted prior ways of doing business. In such an atmosphere the image of a tranquil Mexico became more difficult to maintain, and Díaz became increasingly annoyed by and impatient with rumblings of disorder. One can understand the president's concern in 1890 when rumors circulated that foreign investors were deliberately fomenting internal strife in Mexico in order to depreciate the value of bonds the administration had floated on money markets. The scuttlebutt coalesced around the bellicose activities of one Catarino Erasmus Garza, a firebrand journalist who urged Mexicans to revolution from his base along the U.S. side of the Lower Rio Grande River. Garza was a handsome man with ideals to match his pluck. Born in the northeastern state of Tamaulipas, he had migrated as a youngster to nearby Brownsville, Texas, where he suffered some early defeats in petty business and love, but then honed his social consciousness among radical liberals in St. Louis. The late 1880s found him back in the Rio Grande valley championing the cause of Hispanics and urging them to political action. How Garza could write! With both eloquence and sophistication he leveled bombastic broadsides at arrogant Anglos and at the same time sent endearing love letters to his new fiancée, the daughter of a promi-

nent Hispanic rancher. In the fall of 1891, Garza, still in his early thirties, went to war against Porfirio Díaz. Trying to incite widespread
rebellion, he led brazen raids into northern Mexico, but alas to little
response. Urged by Mexican diplomats to curtail such incursions from
American territory, the U.S. government ordered army contingents to
the Rio Grande. For the next six months Garza and the U.S. military
played cat and mouse, to the delight of a riveted newspaper-reading
public. Meanwhile, Díaz and his associates stewed.[14]

Secret reports reached Mexico City that powerful politicians like
Luis Terrazas were financing Garza's revolution. Several of the president's leading generals—Sóstenes Rocha, Francisco Naranjo, Sebas-
tián Villarreal, and Francisco Estrada—were named as co-conspirators.
Rumor had it that American capitalists like Alexander "Boss" Shepherd, who had launched a huge mining enterprise at Batopilas in the
state of Chihuahua, were anxious to cut a better deal with any new
administration and also backed the movement. In fact, the *Chicago
Times* had it that Shepherd connived to increase the value of his Mexican property up to tenfold by bringing about the annexation of all
northern Mexico to the United States. We know nothing of the details
of his plot, but we can imagine the consternation of Porfirio Díaz when
he learned that Shepherd aspired to take over Baja California, Sonora,
Chihuahua, Coahuila, Nuevo León, and San Luis Potosí.[15]

As Garza's movement persisted in the early 1890s, wealthy Texas
cattle interests who wanted free grazing rights in Mexico also supported him. Moreover, Garza's allies were said to include powerful
financial houses in New York, London, and Berlin that aimed to depreciate the value (meaning the purchase price) of lucrative Mexican
railroad bonds which were at the time the subject of ferocious international competition.[16] Finally, in January 1892, papers found in the sad-
dlebags of a rebel officer named Camilo Muñoz implicated Bishop
Montes de Oca and a so-called clerical party as anxious to redress
through Garza those grievances wrought by The Reform. A concerned
Díaz steadfastly belittled any clerical participation in the Garza revolt
as a "harebrained scheme," and while he did not doubt that the clergy
would hail a successful revolution, he insisted that "they have sense
enough to see that it is out of the question."[17]

One learns to expect such condescending bombast from a dictator,
especially one as troubled as Porfirio Díaz, but his rhetoric hardly stifled

the ceaseless reports and rumors of unrest in the country. All along America's yellow press fanned the flames, ever ready to propagandize the unruliness of Mexicans. Reports in Mexico City newspapers not wed to the regime were not nearly as feverish as those in the U.S. press but still reported the events—incomplete, misshapen, but nonetheless alarming. And Garza's movement seeped into Chihuahua, where a newspaper editor named Francisco Montes de Oca (related to the bishop?) and his accomplices received packets of pamphlets from the revolutionary and printed sketches of Garza's activities in their paper.[18] Díaz ordered the material confiscated and Montes de Oca arrested. Colonel Miguel Ahumada complied and then sent agents eastward along the border to assess the political danger presented by Garza. At the same time, the army stationed several detachments of 50 men each along the border to deter other political dissidents who had taken refuge in the United States from filtering back into the troubled north. Mexican spies kept a wary eye on the likes of Simón Amaya, an especially resolute rebel with a potential following in the Papigochic, who had holed up among relatives in West Texas. In fact the Papigochic was already astir over the arrest of Temósachic's padre, Julio Irigoyen, who had long been an activist in village politics and a thorn in the flank of district authorities.[19] So there was plenty of unrest in the north even though the president's lackeys, such as Ahumada, with their own ambitions and reputations to protect, reported nothing to worry about. Nonetheless, Díaz had to balance their assessment of conditions against that of the *San Francisco Chronicle*: "The people of the northern part of the state of Chihuahua are in sympathy with Garza, and a leader is all that is needed to induce them to join his forces." A leader? Garza himself? Cruz Chávez, perhaps? Or even just the challenging words of a folk saint?[20]

So while Ahumada's account may have temporarily reassured Díaz of the security of his regime, it hardly calmed the president's worries about the nation's image. First reports of dissension at Tomochic only confirmed the dictator's apprehensions. General Rangel, federal military commander in charge of the Chihuahuan district, wired Díaz on December 9, 1891, about the hostilities in Tomochic. Typically, the general accorded them no importance but pledged to remain on guard. The president's priorities are evident in his immediate response: Be sure you have sufficient forces on ready-alert, because it is important not only to contain the disorder but to do so in such a way that when news of the disturbances reaches foreigners, they will understand that the outburst has been squelched and that the nation's credit has not been damaged.[21] The next day, when Ahumada insisted that the so-called Indian uprising carried little importance, Díaz emphatically countered that even though the outburst seemed inconsequential he had ordered the army to treat it as an emergency because of the damage such incidents could do to the national credit.[22]

The tenor of the president's messages is clear: Díaz wanted the movement crushed as quickly and quietly as possible and its promoters punished. Although certainly not the first Mexican authority to do so, he used the word *escarmentar*, which means to punish, but in a way that would make an example of the offenders, that others in society might learn a lesson about challenges to authority. Díaz rarely spelled out the specific punishment to be accorded his antagonists; he left the details up to his underlings so that he could criticize them if they went too far or not far enough. But in this instance, he commanded that the punishment be "exemplary," thus giving his military commanders carte blanche to do as they saw fit. Furthermore, the term *escarmentar* reinforces our broader image of Díaz as president. The word frequently refers to punishment meted out to unruly children, the kind of castigation that hurts but is mainly meant to teach immature youngsters a lesson. Here we see Díaz acting in his role of president-as-stern-father who brooked no discord in his patrimony.[23]

Tracking the Tomochitecos

On December 11 Governor Carrillo declared the Tomochic incident concluded and assured the president that he would continue surveillance along the international boundary, on the lookout for any reverberations from the Garza movement. Díaz was pleased that the nasty affair had ended, but the very next day a new, ominous alarm sounded. In the mountains near Tomochic a scribbled message had been found nailed to a post; in the note Cruz Chávez had invited Jesús Medrano to join the faithful on their trek to visit La Santa de Cabora at her rancho in Sonora. Jesús Medrano had long been counted among Tomochic's more influential people, as we have seen. He owned considerable land, had a muleteer business that supplied the mining districts, and had frequently held official local posts. Certainly Medrano had experienced his differences with the Reyes Domínguez clique as well as with the newcomers to the village, the presidente, Juan Ignacio Chávez, and his associate, Pablo Porras. But still, on that fateful day when Cruz Chávez and his group stalked out of the village church in protest against the admonitions of Padre Castelo, Jesús Medrano had stayed put. Nor was Medrano present at the skirmish on December 7. Instead he was off provisioning his mule train, probably in Guerrero City, and he does not seem to have been part of the buildup toward the crisis. But the authorities certainly did not want Jesús Medrano aligned against them, which is why they found Chavez's note so disconcerting and suspected the worst. Medrano was then conducting a mule train of supplies— food to be sure, probably clothing and blankets, but perhaps also guns and ammunition—to mining camps in the Sierra. Cruz knew this, made sure their paths would cross, nailed his message to the post, and then moved on. When Medrano encountered the invitation—and it was nothing more than an invitation—he made his decision. He jettisoned some of his cargo on the spot, took the mules, some provisions (including flour and miscellaneous cargo), most of his hired hands, and cast his lot with his brother Carlos and the religious dissidents, leaving the incriminating note behind.[24]

Governor Carrillo had all these pieces of the puzzle at his fingertips. His latest information was reliable enough, reported to authorities by a sorely frightened peon employed by Medrano, who deserted the mule train when his boss resolved to join the faithful. Carrillo must have recognized the dangers posed by the dissidents, their movement now reinforced with proven leadership and fueled by substantial supplies. Yet he conveyed no such concern to Porfirio Díaz. Instead he reported the religious movement too fragmented to warrant military pursuit. Carrillo insisted that the devoted were traveling either alone or in pairs along remote trails. In fact, the faithful seem to have traveled pretty much as a group along well-known routes through pueblos such as Yepachic and Tutuaca where they were counted and observed (and helped?) by villagers whom they had known over the years. At a rancho near Tutuaca, two young boys were spotted escorting two mules laden with provisions, including ammunition, to the Tomochitecos. The faithful made no secret of where they were headed. At Maicoba, already over the state line into Sonora, they told villagers that they were Tomochitecos en route to Cabora, even as Carrillo assured the president that the movement had been fractured and for all intents and purposes ended.[25] No doubt the governor weighed his comments to the president in light of his own precarious political future. Why alarm Díaz by asking for military support? Such a request would only have underlined his own inability to handle the eruption of disorder in his state.

Which is not to say that the governor did nothing; the potential for the discord to filter into and swell other channels of discontent was very great. Circular Number 114, issued from his office on December 19 and widely disseminated throughout the region, listed the names of the rebellious Tomochitecos. Carrillo also suspended the sale of arms and ammunition in the Sierra. At the same time he unleashed groups of security troops in pursuit of the faithful—40 men each from the mining centers of Pinos Altos and Ocampo. Residents of Temósachic donated 128 pesos to outfit another 21 men to reinforce the group led by the ever-available Santana Pérez, who was said to be tracking the 30 Tomochitecos in the Sierra. Volunteers received no less than one and one-half pesos daily (about $1.20) for their services, and in this case they planned for a 20-day campaign. Judging by their performance in the field, these volunteers had much less interest in law enforcement than in getting a daily wage, or some food, a rifle, and perhaps an overcoat. Another party of eighteen set off from Morís. The aforementioned Ramon Sáenz had also taken after the devotees with his own troop, although he gave up by Christmas Day. The bitterly vengeful presidente of Tomochic, Juan Ignacio Chávez, had a suggestion for catching and punishing his tormentors. He recommended that the Tarahumaras from Arisiachic, with their long-standing acrimony toward Tomochitecos—natives who not so long ago had been well paid to track down and scalp Apaches—now be turned loose on Cruz Chávez and his followers. He asserted that if offered a liberal price for the scalps of the faithful, the Tarahumaras would lift hair.[26]

Nor did Governor Carrillo only count on his own resources. He also contacted his fellow governor in Sonora, Rafael Izábal, who promptly alerted authorities in settlements along all possible routes open to the Tomochitecos toward Cabora, ordering that he be informed of their progress. Izábal also gave official permission to those forces pursuing the quarry from Chihuahua to enter his state and ordered the federal army commander in the region of Cabora to dispatch to the rancho a detachment of soldiers "in which you have confidence." The admonition "in which you have confidence" is an indication of the wariness with which authorities considered the mesmerizing powers of folk saints like La Santa de Cabora. Indeed, they feared the defection of "illiterate, superstitious" soldiers to her blandishments. Quite a substantial military presence already existed in the area, where the army had only recently concluded its latest war against the Yaquis, who still offered sporadic resistance. Nor were the previously subjugated Mayos any less resentful and restless. Amidst all these preparations and activities Carrillo sent to Cabora a delegation of agents from the Papigochic who were well acquainted with the faithful and who could identify them on their arrival to the waiting military. Cruz and his cohorts, it was planned, would then be arrested and escorted under military guard to Chihuahua City. So the trap was set, Santa Teresa herself the lure: the devotion of the faithful would lead them into the grasp of their persecutors. Meanwhile, Carrillo emphasized to President Díaz that Tomochic itself had returned to order. The movement had attracted little notice and no support from the mining camps and pueblos of the Sierra. "Todo sigue su curso": all is normal.[27]

Díaz was not so sure. A military man with considerable field experience, he understood how quickly seemingly innocuous brush fires can suddenly flame out of control. He may have been uncertain about the folk saint Teresa—authorities frequently waffle over the appearance of such religious figures—but he understood well enough that insurrection had to be quickly snuffed out, and Carrillo's accounts did not reassure him. As the major military action seemed to be centering in Sonora, Díaz promptly contacted both Izábal and the state's military commander, Luis E. Torres, and ordered them to corral the Tomochitecos. Furthermore, he wanted to know more about the setting of the coming confrontation. Exactly where and what was this place called "Cabora"? In response he learned only that Cabora was a rancho where the single authority was the father of the "supposed" santa.[28] So the country's senior military tactician, President Porfirio Díaz, who insisted on personally managing his army's maneuvers from the national palace in Mexico City, had relatively little intelligence on which to base this operation. Still, an effective strategy in this case must have seemed simple enough. In cooperation with Carrillo, Sonoran officials had set the trap.

Part II

La Santa de Cabora

8

Romería at Cabora

GOVERNOR LAURO CARRILLO CALLED the massive gathering at Cabora a *romería*, one of those buoyant, impressive assemblages of people
that were part religious revival, part country fair.[1] He knew romerías
could get unruly, even threatening to public order, but this one was
merely vibrant and uninhibited, hardly licentious, and not at all aggressive. It was not the kind of raucous carnival that frequently commemo-
rated a village's patron saint's day, but neither was Cabora steeped in
sadness and doleful prayer. People prayed, to be sure, both out loud
over their rosaries and in more quiet, personal ways. Tears flowed
abundantly. Certainly the pilgrims reassured that child with misshapen
limbs (Mexicans lovingly call such youngsters *los preciosos*, the precious
ones) and consoled that coughing, grizzled, tubercular man. But they
also chatted openly with one another, told stories, made jokes, and had
fun. A healthy liveliness permeated the place; periodically someone
plucked a guitar and sang out a familiar song, religious or otherwise.
These were mostly common country folks free of the restraints and
burdens of everyday life, and they acted like it. In a word, they appeared
to be uplifted.

Among the devotees these early months of 1891, hawkers peddled
simple, inexpensive religious articles like *milagros*, shaped from cheap
metal to resemble an arm, a leg, or a heart, whatever the purchaser
sought to heal. Crucifixes shaped from straw, printed pictures of La
Santa de Cabora, and prayer sheets, plus a few banners stitched with a
"Viva!" to La Santa were also up for sale or barter. Among favored
articles purchased were scapularies, small cloth rectangles attached to

ribbons to be worn around the neck as protection and to invite luck. These carried embroidered mottoes: "Hail, Blessed Teresita," "The Great Power of God Rules the World," or "La Santa de Cabora." Other vendors offered pottery, huaraches, straw hats, leather belts, and chewing gum. At the same time folks readied country food—corn tortillas, chicharrón, menudo, cabrito, carne asada, potent coffee—cooked on the spot. Watered-down mescal was also available.

Participants in this colorful pageant milled around the locale, seeking forage for their animals, twigs and branches for fires, and materials of any sort to fashion a temporary shelter, usually a simple lean-to with mesquite poles and bushy covering or, even more simply, an enclosure of cane mats, propped up and pulled together. A few ne'er-do-wells, pickpockets, prostitutes, con men, gamblers, and the like also made the rounds. Teresa had called for the renovation of society, especially in the ways people thought about and treated one another, and her listeners seemed to embrace the ideal.[2]

The physical setting of this romería could hardly be called comfortable. Cabora lay in ruggedly inhospitable, near-desert terrain in southern Sonora, where two great rivers, the Yaqui and the Mayo, descend from the high Sierra to begin their relatively short journey across the plains to the sea. There were no real population centers near Cabora. Tiny Boroyeca, a miners' outpost, lay huddled in the foothills 21 miles northwest, while 25 miles in the other direction was Navojoa, only a secondary town in the 1890s but still the region's agricultural marketing center. The district's political seat and most familiar geographical reference point was 66 miles southwest in the silver mining complex at Alamos, which had oscillated in and out of bonanza since colonial times, while Sonora's major Pacific Ocean port, Guaymas, was a very long 150 miles northwest.

Worse yet, Cabora was often hot and buggy. In Mexico's hottest zone record summer temperatures can reach more than 130°. In the early 1890s, the region was suffering through prolonged drought and blistering heat. Most trees had long lost their leaves to the dryness. Only the distinctive *palos jitos*, which can grow up to 30 feet in height and at a distance resemble a lollipop, guarded their dark green foliage and granted some shade for man and beast. The heat brought maddening plagues of flies. A welcome rain squall might bestow temporary relief from the flies but only encouraged hordes of mosquitoes and chiggers. Plenty of snakes and thorny scrub made it even less inviting. No, Cabora was hardly a garden spot to human beings.

Yet beginning in late 1889 Yaqui and Mayo Indians, mestizos and Creoles—Mexicans mostly but also other Latin and North Americans, with a sprinkling of Europeans—eagerly trekked by the thousands to this uninviting venue. They probably followed railroad lines or old carriage tracks between cities, and then from places like Navojoa shadowed a horse trail over partially flat, partially hilly dry scrub forest to Cabora. Each step by mule, burro, horse, or human roused a puff of dust from the fine dirt. If they traveled in April, they might have been lucky enough to find a fruit-bearing *guamuchil*, similar to a tamarind, but otherwise nature yielded little for human nourishment. No matter; most of these pilgrims were driven by the expectation of spiritual and physical healing along with that of communion and ecstasy. At the sight of Cabora's hazy outline of ranch structures, many of the journeyers would shout and sob in exhilaration and sing euphoric hosannas to the Lord.[3]

Once at Cabora the pilgrims centered their attention on the comely mestiza teenager they called "La Santa." Her name was Teresa Urrea, addressed by some as Teresita, or more simply, "la niña" or "niñita," little child. Descriptions vary, but only in minor detail. At 5 feet 7 inches she was a bit taller than the average Mexican teen-aged girl, slim, and still seemingly without breasts in her long black dress with a homemade *reboso* draped loosely across her shoulders. Her thick dark hair hung to her waist when it was not in braids. She was light-brown-skinned (some called her color *rosada*, a kind of reddish bronze), and her pleasant childlike face was distinguished by her dark eyes, which were quite large and projected a brilliance that, while not harsh or piercing, was compelling.[4]

Word at the romería, confirmed by Teresa herself, had it that while she was in a profound trance, during which those tending the adolescent thought her near death, the Virgin Mary had appeared and counseled—even admonished—the young girl about the need for all people to love one another, to treat each other as equals, to live more holy lives, and to respect the Word of God. Some years later Teresa revealed that the Angel Gabriel had delivered to her a letter emanating directly from God, which empowered her to teach and to show her followers the righteous path. The letter was a notably threatening communication with an ominous, one might even say apocalyptic, tone:

If my sacred heart had not burned with woe for men, I should long ago have cast them into the depths of hell for their terrible offenses. . . . I have shed my precious blood upon the cross in order that they may have time to repent of sins. Now, if they do not so, I will make them feel the rigor of my justice; I will visit them with sickness, and I will hasten the judgment day when the good will be separated from the wicked: "Go, sinners, to the fires of hell for all eternity; you would not hear me when I spoke nor have you paid attention to my advice. Go, go to live in the eternal flames of hell." And to the good I shall say: "Come, blessed of my father, who listened to my words, come and share in my glory as your reward for submission and obedience, come and enjoy everlasting life."[5]

The Virgin Mary also gave Teresa special powers to heal the sick, especially the poor and hopelessly infirm. Miracle cures occurred, many of them documented by eyewitnesses, who soon spoke to journalists and other interested investigators. A vaquero, Simón Salcedo, had been partially paralyzed when a horse kicked him in the head. The man's right leg was stiff, his right arm useless, and the right side of his face distorted. Teresa placed his crippled hand between her own, then picked up some dirt from the ground at Cabora and spat in it, making a paste which she applied to the man's leg, arm, and face. Witnesses later said her spittle was blood red. She stared at Salcedo and spoke to him in a low voice. Then Teresa took Simón's crutch and ordered the man to walk, and he did so; then to raise his right hand, and he raised his once useless arm. Smile, she said, and the once flaccid muscles on the right side of Simón's face responded. Salcedo was among her earliest cures; many others followed. A woman suffering from hemorrhaging lungs arrived in agony. Teresa told her, "I will cure you with the blood of my heart," and she repeated the dirt and saliva treatment. The bleeding ceased; the woman was cured.[6]

One day an oxcart lurched into Cabora, guided by a man in his forties. On the cart, cushioned by straw, lay a stricken woman, the man's wife, still in her twenties. Two years earlier she had contracted a fever that left her paralyzed from the waist down. Teresa serenely awaited them: "I knew you were coming," she said. The Santa gazed into the sick woman's eyes, most likely hypnotizing her. Then she softly stroked the woman's legs and hips. "Stand up," Teresa gently commanded, and the woman did so. She needed some support at first, but then, released from her trance, took several hesitant steps on her own.[7] Santa Teresa healed lepers and others with supposedly incurable oozing sores; she cured nervous disorders, including those of people said to be insane. The deaf heard and spoke, and many doubting observers who had traveled to Cabora only to test and debunk the Santa confirmed these cures. Not all came away believers, but most agreed that she was a remarkable young woman with highly unusual and difficult-to-explain powers—mystical forces whose source and precise nature may perplex us. The details of her early life, however, are less controversial and more commonplace.

The Making of a Folk Saint

Teresa was born on October 15, 1873, on a rancho near the Tehueco Indian village of Ocoroni in Sinaloa, the state just south of Sonora. The Tehuecos were one tribe in the Cahita group (of which the Yaquis and Mayos are the best remembered), and some 13,000 of them farmed the middle stretch of the Fuerte River Valley when the Spaniards arrived in the sixteenth century. The natives resisted the invaders, but disease and forced labor took their toll, and by the start of the next century the Tehuecos had been pretty much reduced to Jesuit mission sites. Reports of silver deposits attracted several great Spanish clans to the region, among them the powerful Urrea family, whose forebears were Christian Moors (*Moriscos*). In colonial Mexico, Urreas counted as governors, generals, hacendados, wealthy mine owners, and potent politicians. Lieutenant Manuel Urrea helped to found the town of Culiacán, oldest Spanish settlement in northwestern Mexico and later capital of the state of Sinaloa. Mariano Urrea fought Apaches in Sonora and Arizona, and his son José led a column to put down rebellious Texans in 1836. José Urrea later governed successively in Sinaloa, Sonora, and Durango. Miguel Urrea, the brother of Mariano, was commissioned by the government to mediate the boundary between the states of Sonora and Sinaloa, and having accomplished that delicate task, he allied himself to the dominant family of southern Sonora, the

Almadas, and like them settled into highly profitable mining and agriculture. Thus, Teresa's father Tomás, a nephew of Miguel and Mariano, came from a family of considerable political and social note.[8]

Of course not all the scions of these clans live up to the reputation and potential of their lineage. Tomás Urrea seems to have been one who fell a bit short. His father died soon after his birth, but his well-to-do Uncle Miguel filled in the gap, insuring that Tomás married well (to Loreto, the only child of Miguel's sister), and appointed him administrator of his large ranch called Santa Ana, which spread north of the largely Tehueco settlement at Ocoroni. The union with Loreto soon bore children, but Tomás also enjoyed his amorous diversions with Tehueco women on the rancho. One such encounter with the fourteen-year-old daughter of a ranch hand produced Teresa. Well-off ranchers, often with pretensions of ethnic superiority, frequently fathered children among their workers. Whether or not they acknowledged and cared for their offspring is another issue. Some did; others did not. Tomás Urrea did both.[9]

In this case, Tomás at first paid scant attention to his illegitimate daughter, who lived with her mother and aunt in a humble hut. The aunt seems to have been a scold and a bully, and Teresa caught much of her ire. When the child was three, they moved from the rather isolated hut to a settlement of ranch workers where Teresita had plenty of playmates and became a sort of tomboy, given to pranks and roughneck activities despite a periodic pensiveness and propensity to withdraw into herself. Still, she rather cheerfully did her daily chores—feeding the animals, grinding corn on a *metate*, breaking up clods of clay in the family garden—and in the evenings seemed to enjoy listening to her elders reminisce about the past and their traditions so infused with the religiosity of the rural people in the region. In other words, she heard from them and believed—and later said it many times—that God both healed and punished, that His will would be done, that direct communication with the Divine was possible, that the Holy Spirit was active, and that miracles occurred. Yet she did not seem to be overly devout and paid little attention to the rituals and doctrine of the official Church. If she was like other children of this locale and epoch, however, strong folk beliefs—including spirits and maybe even witches—crept into her life along with knowledge of plants, buds, and bark said to bring good health and luck. Teresita had no formal education, but taught herself to read and write, if only in the most rudimentary way; she could write her name but not much more, and her reading was limited to the simplest texts. As she moved toward puberty there seemed to be little that was extraordinary about this young girl.[10]

Then her life dramatically changed. Sinaloa experienced a tumultuous gubernatorial election in 1880, and Tomás Urrea had forthrightly endorsed the loser, an Urrea defeated by the candidate supported by Porfirio Díaz. Revenge and persecutions were bound to follow, so with the backing of his uncle Miguel he fled with his family to the safety of Sonora, to the rancho called Cabora, which Miguel had given him as a wedding present. He planned to develop that forlorn site and at the same time manage three of Miguel's cattle ranchos in the vicinity. Tomás, his wife, their four children, and an adopted son arrived at Cabora to discover it had recently been sacked by Yaqui raiders. They would have to rebuild. So Tomás, still a self-assured and aggressive young man, settled his family into the comforts of one of his uncle's homes in Alamos and turned to reconstructing his rancho.[11]

Cabora lies in rigorous but potentially productive ranching country. It only gets about eighteen inches of rain a year, the bulk of it during the rainy season from July through September. The spring might bring a few short-lived downpours, not enough for commercial cultivation but vital for cattle forage. Frost is uncommon but arrives every few years. Vegetation ranges from thorny scrub to low forests. Rangy criollo cattle—all hide, stringy muscles, and bone—do fine there, but the life of a cowboy is unenviable, thanks to the vicious thorns and irksome, sometimes painful vermin, such as scorpions, which thrive in the area. Don Tomás searched the region for better bulls than those he had brought north to breed some fat onto his cattle, and he dammed arroyos to store precious water for irrigation, but much of his attention went into the construction of his large adobe home on the edge of the 25-foot-deep arroyo called Cocoraqui, which coursed the northern boundary of his property.[12]

Original building plans called for a dwelling of rock masonry, but stone proved so hard to come by that the patrón turned to adobe, and the result was a truly impressive dwelling of two wings, one with a chapel and kitchen besides bedrooms, the other with Urrea's bedroom and library, plus a veranda with its traditional arches, all faced by an extensive patio enclosed by a high picket fence. Inside walls were painted

Sonoran style, halfway up with white lime, partly for its artistic look, but also because lime protected the adobe and tended to control bugs and vermin. The hacendado's field hands and vaqueros, up to a hundred recently hired Yaqui Indians, lived with their families in a mixture of housing styles around the main house. The total population of the place hovered around four hundred, a mid-sized undertaking.[13]

With capital borrowed from his well-to-do uncle, Tomás Urrea put the ranches to work. There was not much of a local or regional market for cattle on the hoof, so he subsidized his enterprise by working the by-products of slaughtered cows into soap, tallow, tanned hides, and beef jerky. He and his wife met only periodically, either at Cabora or in Alamos, but it was enough to keep their family growing. Tomás was returning from just one such visit to Alamos in 1885 when he stopped for a respite at the small rancho of an acquaintance, Ramón Cantúa. There his roving eyes fell upon Cantúa's fifteen-year-old daughter, Gabriela, and within a few weeks the uninhibited Urrea took the young girl to Cabora as his mistress. When Loreto protested, Tomás ordered his wife from Cabora. Loreto never returned, although from time to time Tomás consorted with her in Alamos.[14]

Meanwhile, Teresa was growing up on one of Urrea's other ranches near Cabora. To her playmates she seemed healthy, cheerful, and outgoing, but she also knew personal affliction. Her demanding aunt and the sharp, petty bickering and tumultuous disputes unsettled the household. Then in 1885 her mother died or disappeared, and Teresa came to know a heavy heart. Three years later she moved to the Urrea mansion at Cabora, perhaps at her own request or at the suggestion of an employee who wanted help or at the insistence of Don Tomás, who had apparently grown quite fond of this daughter he had once ignored. Once at Cabora she fell into a profound relationship with the elderly housekeeper of the place, a mestiza woman named only Huila, who was also a *curandera*—that is, a healer who used natural herbs and native beliefs to effect cures, some of them quite magical. A cripple who walked with a homemade wooden crutch, Huila had been a member of the Urrea household since the Sinaloan days at Santa Ana, where she evidently knew Teresa as a child but had paid her little attention. At Cabora Huila, who could read and write, supervised the kitchen, housekeeping, washing, and ironing in the Urrea household, and also administered to the sick and troubled on the ranchos. Tomás accorded her enormous respect.[15]

Huila began to take an inquisitive Teresa on her sick calls, where the young novice learned to use bark and branches, leaves, reeds and seeds, berries and cacti, hens' eggs, a rattlesnake skin, and the dried stomach of a cow along with magic and ritual in healing the infirm. At times Teresa assisted her teacher. She would reassure sick people by touching them lightly on the forehead or brushing a cheek while confiding soothing words. Huila noted the extraordinary tranquillity that Teresa brought to the afflicted. When a vaquero suffered a particularly nasty broken thigh, the curandera probed the hurt and applied her remedies. As Teresa fastened her eyes upon those of the agonized patient, however, he promptly became transfixed and much relieved of his convulsions and pain. Huila concluded that her pupil possessed special healing powers far beyond her own. After all, it is not the herb that cures—it is what the healer says with the herb that counts: the healer prays to God to give power to the herb to cure. Huila sensed that Teresa seemed to heal with divine inspiration.[16]

Then apparent tragedy struck the Urreas. At about midnight on the night of October 20, 1889, Teresa lurched into fearsome convulsions. Her shrieks of terror brought her father and several household servants to her bedroom, where six strong men struggled futilely to still her shakes and hold her in place. For four hours the torment continued. Finally Teresa became fatigued and quieted down. The youngster noted a fierce pain in her heart and in her soul. She wept uncontrollably, yet at the same time she had a smile on her lips as if she were experiencing pleasure. She called out to Lola—someone she seemed to know well— but there was no Lola at Cabora and, as far as anyone remembered, never had been. An hour later the attacks returned but not quite so violently, and they continued intermittently for the next thirteen days, diminishing in length and intensity. On the second day she asked for a cup half-filled with soil. She took a spoon and started to remove the dirt, but the cup instantaneously filled up and overflowed with earth. Teresa then ate a bit of that soil, or at least placed some on her tongue. It was the only thing she ate during those bedridden thirteen days. From time to time she went into a trance, once so deeply that her father thought her dead and ordered a coffin constructed. The thirteenth day she suffered extreme pains in her back and chest, which her attendants relieved with hot plasters. Then the pain moved to her head, so Teresa mixed some soil with her saliva and applied the concoction to plasters which she placed on her own temples. The pain disappeared and she got up from her bed.[17]

For the next three months Teresa lingered in a daze that periodically deepened into a trance. Visitors said she spoke the words and in the tone of voice of a four-year-old child but attributed it to her malady, which they assumed had affected her vocal cords. Periodically she also acted childishly, one time showing off the toe of a new shoe saying, "Look, I also have shoes like those of my nanny Virgin." However, on other occasions Teresa spoke more maturely, particularly when she placed some soil on the tip of her tongue, but even then she seemed distracted, as if something physical were disturbing her. From time to time she placed her hand on her heart. Loved ones and other onlookers sought to chat and reason with her, but Teresa could not hold a conversation. In answer to questions she only blurted out a word or two and then might babble off in an entirely different direction, as if on a journey of her own. She also spoke vaguely of conversations with the Almighty and of commissions received from the Virgin Mary—including the mission to cure the sickly and to give them moral advice. It is even said that she healed Huila's crippled leg but at the same time sadly predicted the curandera's impending death. Three days later Huila died. Teresa foresaw other events: a rogue tornado would strike one of the ranches (it did); a cowboy had fallen from his horse and fractured his leg (which proved true). These were pure coincidences, assured the girl's fretting father, who thought his daughter demented.[18]

La Santa's Spreading Fame

In January 1890 Teresa slid into another heavy trance for a few days, but when she emerged, she had changed. There was no more childishness, and one could have a reasonable conversation with her. During the previous three months people had flocked to her from the surrounding country; she had put her hands on the sick and crippled, and they got well. "Of this [the specific cures]," she said, "I remember nothing, but when I came to myself, I saw they were well."[19] By the spring she had plunged deeply into her ministry. Word of her healings and other mystical proclivities, often exaggerated by hope and distance, seeped into pueblos like Tomochic, where her reputation caught the attention of Cruz Chávez and others. Murmurs and then reports of La Santa and her miracle cures spilled into population centers like the Papigochic, then spread to surrounding states and on to the United States, Puerto Rico, Europe, and South America. The sick and curious, believers and doubters, flocked to Cabora by the thousands to see the Santa for themselves and to experience, if not revel in, her mystical powers. There they camped in considerable physical discomfort, some for weeks, manifesting their faith coupled to hope.

Teresa worked from sunrise to late evening among the pious, some rich and many poor, of various ethnicities, cultures, and nationalities: cancer victims, the crippled and paralyzed, the blind and deaf, people with nervous disorders and the raging insane, those suffering from family conflicts, and those with missing limbs. Testimonies to her kindly composure and healing efficacy are remarkable. In 1890 she told a man who had not heard in fourteen years, "You have eyes that do not see. You have ears that cannot hear," and he heard those words, though not very distinctly. She then placed cotton wads mixed with soil into his ears and his hearing gradually returned.[20] Teresa normally fixed her engaging eyes on those of the ill and took their hands into her own. She did not clasp them tightly, but simply pressed her thumbs against those of the infirm. Then, if, for example, an ill person was having unbearable headaches, she would place one of her thumbs on the forehead or gently rub the afflicted area. "When sick people come to me, I can see where they are sick, just as if I were looking though a window."[21]

Teresa also used herbs, as she had learned from Huila. La Santa was said to emit a perfumed scent—an odor of sanctity—from her person, and a similar flowery aroma flowed from the mixtures of saliva and soil she prepared for the healings. Pilgrims soaked their handkerchiefs and bandannas in water she used for her work, saying that it smelled sweet; water has always been considered a purifying and holy element. "I don't know how I have the power [to heal]," Teresa said, "but I am positive that I can cure any disease with which I come in contact. I do not claim to have supernatural power, but I have the wonderful will power and magnetism strong enough to cure any and all diseases."[22] In

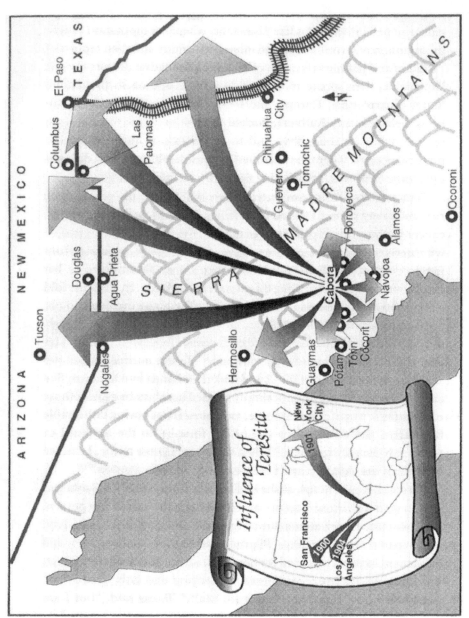

Map 4. The Influence of Teresita

the same breath, however, she admitted that she could not cure every-one; some must continue to pay for their sins. Or perhaps those who failed to respond did not believe in her ardently enough. Yet she in-sisted, "I seldom fail. If I fail to effect a cure on some, I have never failed to greatly benefit them."[23] Teresa had an intuition about whom she could and could not heal, and in particularly puzzling cases she retired to her modest adobe dwelling, alongside the main Urrea house, to meditate on possible remedies and to seek sacred guidance. She was on one occasion perplexed by the ulcerated sore on a man's leg and so went to her room to contemplate. A kind of phantom appeared before her—a man leaning on a staff with an oozing sore on his leg. Two pieces of bone gradually eased their way out of the sore, and when they were gone the specter tossed away his crutch and was well. Now Teresa knew what to do for her patient. She thoroughly washed his festering sore and then drew from it two little pieces of bone like those she had seen in her vision. The man threw away his crutch and walked; within several days his leg had healed.[24] Those who witnessed these happenings, mar-veled, glorified, and celebrated the compassion of the Lord and his servants on earth.

Proclaiming a Saint

Teresa's followers soon declared her a saint. She disavowed such titles and insisted that she was no saint but had only received special powers from the Divine. "I do not ask any ceremony of you; God is the one you should worship. My body is the same as yours, but my soul is very different."[25] Yet the congregation insisted. After all, its members com-prehended that God conferred special grace on some individuals and gave them powers in His name. They could appreciate a saint when they found one. Teresa finally capitulated. If they considered her to be a saint, so be it. They called her "La Niña de Cabora," which shows how personal she had become to them and how they meant to shield her assumed innocence and purity from the vulgarities and corruptness of adulthood. The pious brought humble offerings, not only to reward and venerate her, but to praise God, and while she might accept a tortilla laden with refried beans or an orange, she took no money, admonishing those who offered coins to give them instead to help the poor. When patients could not afford to feed themselves, she offered them one of her own meals and politely asked the Urrea servants to bring her more. Certainly her actions were saintly.

We have ample evidence that all this happened at Cabora, but how might it be explained? A few have speculated that the original convulsive attacks stemmed from some form of epilepsy, but no history of such a malady has been found among her relatives. Others relied on psychological trauma for a rationale. It was said that Teresa had suffered a similar convulsive attack three years earlier in 1886 when she was thirteen, as a result of the persistent and virulent arguments between her mother and aunt. Or perhaps the first attacks had occurred a bit later, when her mother died or disappeared.[26] Some people (mainly her detractors) believed a failed love affair triggered the first major seizure in 1889. They explained that a young miner named Millón from Boroyeca had fallen deeply in love with Teresa, and when she spurned him, he tried to rape her, which shocked her into convulsions and trance. A slight variation asserted that Teresa had discovered her beloved having sex with another woman and that the resultant frustration and despair caused her malady: According to one of Mexico City's leading newspapers, *El Monitor republicano*, when Teresa caught him in the act, she screeched and otherwise scandalized her family, "and after a brief fainting, declared herself a saint, inspired by God."[27]

But these sorts of supposition do not gratify. They may not be all that ridiculous or far-fetched, but they ring hollow—or maybe they are just less interesting than other possibilities. For example, many people deliberately drive themselves into convulsion and trance because they believe that in such a state of mind they are closer to their divinities. Only in this altered state of consciousness can they begin to communicate with one another—we humans can at last speak with our gods. Certainly working with Huila among the Yaqui, Teresa came to know peyote as a hallucinogen.[28] Perhaps her convulsions and trance can best be seen as self-induced or at least as the result of the mystical ways in which she thought about herself. After all, she would not have been the first or the last to welcome such developments. Today these experiences are the stock-in-trade of a good deal of religious expression—I am thinking of the many offshoots of African spiritualism as well as the wave of fervent Protestant Pentecostalism now sweeping over Latin America and elsewhere. Believers flocking to the evangelical movement joyously welcome trances and convulsions in their hope to be filled with the Holy Ghost. Teresa was possibly on the same sort of search.

The Spirits in Teresa's Life

Teresa insisted that she regularly communicated with Christian divinities such as the Virgin Mary, but also revealed that she was similarly moved by spirits—not only the Holy Spirit of Catholic teaching, but those spirits that were an integral part of local belief, spirits that influenced people to do both good and evil things. It was said that Teresa could see the soul leave a person who had just died. She claimed that the soul left all parts of the body at the same time, like a swirl of vapor, and then took form, although she went no further to describe that form. She said her own soul traveled where she desired, even to celestial regions, and her friend Josefa Félix, a 23-year-old from Boroyeca, recounted just such scintillating journeys with Teresa: "She woke me up when we were sleeping together and sent me to some place, and I was there immediately. We walked together and chatted."[29] However, not all encounters with Teresa proved to be so friendly. A few residents of Boroyeca revealed that a vision of Teresa had sorely frightened them: "She appeared at night with her eyes closed. Then she opened them, and to the background noise of voices and steps, she vigorously shook their beds, spilling them out and onto the floor, where she stripped them of their sleeping clothes. Then she sent them on a long journey," but we do not know their destination. When queried about these ventures, Teresa admitted being in the visions and frightening these people but did not elaborate on why she had done so.[30]

La Santa de Cabora heard everything, everywhere, regardless of distance, even—or especially—those who criticized her. She said that God had led her to understand all languages. She foresaw death, people lying inert in their coffins before they actually died. Spirits supplied her with cures and news of far-off families of the afflicted. They revealed to her a person's most private secrets and told her when her half-sister would be married and to whom. To free her spirit Teresa went to her room and lay down on her bed. Observers thought her asleep, yet noted she was in subdued conversation with some force: "People think me crazy, not that I am violent, but I pay no attention to their questions, and I say strange things."[31] No doubt her stare was hypnotic; many spoke of the magnetic power of the young girl's dark eyes.

Hypnosis, visions, dreams, spirits, shamanic ecstasy—these all shaded into the imagined (but certainly not false) world of the faithful. Mystical experiences, like all other experiences, mirror and nourish the social environment from which they arise. Teresa was no anomaly to her listeners; she was of their culture and lived and practiced well within its boundaries. People came to her with their dreadful sicknesses and high hopes, not because she offered new healing techniques or wonder drugs, but because they thought she could have been touched by the Divine in some special way. They believed that only God cured, that no healing occurred beyond His will, that the power to heal is a gift of God, and that divine miracles do occur. Teresa herself insisted that she was quite an ordinary person to whom the Lord had given a special gift. The Santa de Cabora healed—but only through the grace of God. So even as we wonder about the myriad symbols and beliefs swirling about such conclaves as the one at Cabora, we can appreciate their dynamic and vital relationship to local culture.[32]

La Santa's Critics

Naturally a good many debunked and dismissed the goings-on at Cabora, especially those who had without reflection come to equate science with progress and many aspects of religiosity with backwardness. *El Monitor republicano* editorialized about the events at Cabora this way: "This is certain, she [Teresa] is no saint, but the result of the highest ignorance. There is no catalepsy, no hypnosis, only a young girl imprisoned by nervous attacks and a multitude of imbeciles who pay her tribute because of a lack of intelligence. Saints do not belong to these times; their age has passed, and fortunately for the honor of civilization and progress, they will never return."[33] Skeptics and cynics included government officials, their supporters, and others who had hitched their future to that vision labeled "modern." We have already noted that Porfirio Díaz and Lauro Carrillo uncompromisingly held such convictions.

Nor was the *San Francisco Chronicle* much more generous after it observed her healing practices and interviewed her in 1900: "Like all people of her class, she attracts the superstitious and ignorant and her followers number a legion. Certainly possessed of animal magnetism above the average, combined with firmness of character and undoubted belief in herself, she has those peculiar attributes necessary to make a good hypnotist or pseudo 'Divine healer.' " The reporter had watched her gently rub the legs of a partially paralyzed man who said he felt tingling sensations all over his body during the treatment and professed to stand better than he ever had since his affliction. Nevertheless the journalist denied seeing any such improvement. Another San Francisco paper, *The Call*, breezily mocked the curer: "Santa Teresa also tried her magnetic touch on reporters. One of them had a roaring headache all day, and she banished it by a few Svengali-like passes. It is not believed he will suffer from headaches until he makes a night of it again. Another of the reporters took treatment for a verse-writing habit, but it is feared the cure will not be permanent." Earlier *El Sábado*, of Hermosillo, Sonora, accused her of selling a simple mixture of soil and cooking oil as some supposed holy remedy, as well as common foods like milk at elevated prices.[34] In sum, these journalists claimed, Teresa and her father were running a scam on her admirers for profit. Such charges were unwarranted. In fact Tomás Urrea furnished a good many pilgrims basic foods free of charge, along with pasturage and space in his corrals for their animals, all of which added up to substantial financial hardship for him. Friends feared he courted bankruptcy because of his generosity.[35]

As was to be expected, the official Catholic Church railed against Teresa. The Church has never been patient with those who assume sacred functions it considers to be its own and has always insisted upon monopolistic control over miracles. So-called santas who lured parishioners from clerical control were a bane to Catholic officialdom, always quick to label local religion as "primitive" and "pagan." And there is in popular spirituality a spirit of defiance toward all authority. Yet the

Church also had its more down-to-earth concerns. It tended to tolerate native healers, therefore, especially when they associated their practices with the official religion, and it even endorsed miracles such as those at La Salette and Lourdes in France when it needed impressive crowds to support its political struggle against the secularizing state.[36] But no such scenario emerged in Mexico, at least not with Teresa, who had some searingly deleterious things to say about Mother Church. No, Mexico's official Church went after Teresa early on. In October 1890, when parishioners in Guaymas presented a diversity of images, icons, and relics to be blessed by Sonora's Bishop Herculano, His Excellency was shocked to discover among the hallowed objects any number of lithographs depicting Teresa. Why not? By then an entrepreneur named Fermín Tapico had sold for 50 centavos each thousands of such images in Sonora, and more rolled off the printing presses every day. In a surge of disgust the bishop ripped off his cassock and angrily swept it like a majestic broom through the pile of icons to be blessed. When Teresa learned that the bishop intended to excommunicate her, she told her anxious followers: "Don't worry about it; it is nothing. God has commanded me."[37]

Besides the institutions of Church and State that so forthrightly disdained Teresa, and those individuals who debunked her out of hand, there were the inevitable doubters—those stuck between what they witnessed at Cabora and what they thought they believed or should believe. Foremost among them was the girl's father, Tomás. A well-read man who projected himself as modern, he could not comprehend the early hullabaloo surrounding his daughter, whom he first thought to be mentally unbalanced. The excitement at the rancho only caused her undue stress and himself considerable expense, so in the spring of 1890 he ordered her to desist from her spiritual activities. Instead, he would send her to school in France or the United States; he could arrange a splendid marriage for her. Teresa was amused by her father's offerings. "Yes, Papá. I do intend to marry some day, but when I do, it will be a simple, quiet affair. That will not be until I have completed my commitment to the Blessed Virgin. When I do marry, people will no longer consider me a saint, and that will make you happy." One night Tomás stood frantically at her bedroom door, pistol in hand. "Do what you wish, Papá," she calmly advised, "but in the end you will be convinced." That did it. Tomás calmed himself. He remained mystified by his daughter's powers and skeptical of their origin, but he was converted to her cause and remained devoted all of his life.[38]

Other skeptics designed various schemes to test Teresa. They had noted her strength; she effortlessly carried hefty patients in her arms, and at times, as she lay on her bed, onlookers tried but could not lift her limbs. On one occasion a burly man from the nearby settlement at Nuri challenged her to a game of *vencida*, a kind of arm wrestling. "I don't want to beat you," said Teresa, and turned the game over to one of her friends. The girl protested that she could not hope to win the contest with the husky man, but Teresa responded firmly, "I order you to do it." She did and won.[39]

As her fame spread internationally as well as throughout Mexico—Teresa received more than 100 written inquiries a day, and her father would have needed a secretarial staff to answer them all—the government became uneasy about all the commotion. Her spiritual claims and practices challenged state power and rallied crowds, which could be infused with political goals. Officials remembered that in the mid-1870s in Sinaloa Tomás Urrea had zealously opposed Porfirian designs and further recognized that a good many of those drawn to the site were Yaqui and Mayo Indians with whom the regime had recently (in 1886) forged a clouded peace, still only loosely guaranteed by a substantial army presence. So the central government ordered the military to sniff around the edges of Cabora for any symptoms of social turbulence. Tomás Urrea was justifiably apprehensive that the army might try to repress the activities at Cabora as politically subversive. Teresa advised him not to worry. If the soldiers arrived with any such thoughts in mind, she would erase them.[40] Teresa seemed prepared to test her powers against the military, if necessary, but nothing surfaced to implicate the Urreas in suspect practices. Commanding officers periodically conversed with Tomás Urrea, and soldiers witnessed the spectacle of his daughter's healings all during 1890 and 1891 but apparently did not consider anything politically inflammatory or socially destabilizing.[41] One wonders why. Had the government wanted to quash the romería, it could easily have invented a pretext. Perhaps it had reckoned that tampering with people's religiosity could backfire and ignite a conflagration. Besides, if the Mexican army marched every time a Santa Teresa or a Santo del Chopeque turned up, or when the Virgin Mary appeared on a cactus or in a tree, it would constantly be on the move. It seemed better to disparage these events as inconsequential and hope that after a time they would burn out and dissipate, which in other cases they frequently did.

Spiritists in Search of a Medium

Besides the government and its military arm other groups across the spectrum of social interests cast a wondering eye on Cabora, none more so than the Spiritists. Throughout the second half of the nineteenth century the international Spiritist movement had gained momentum in Mexico. For some, spiritism was a revelation; for others, simply entertainment. While a good many people amused themselves at parties by practicing magnetism and hypnotism and watching chairs and tables wiggle and tip over, there were significant numbers who extolled spiritism as a progressive philosophy and science. Composed mainly of educated middle- and upper-class followers, including a surprising number of former army generals, important Spiritist centers flourished in Guadalajara and Mexico City, as did groups in smaller cities like Mazatlán and Guaymas, and even in unlikely hamlets such as Boroyeca, located not very far from Cabora. In fact, it was a Spiritist, Francisco Madero, whose political movement in 1910 finally toppled the Porfirian regime.

Spiritists did not believe that life ended with death or that after death one's soul departed to reside permanently and more or less quiescently at the side of some divinity or devil. Rather, they anticipated the reincarnation of the spirit and posited the existence of an active spirit world. When people died, their spirits were freed for the next embodiment, in this world if errors in the previous life warranted punishment or in that other, more splendid world through which spirits progressed from the lowest plane into a purer, more noble type until they eventually reached union with God. All could progress and no one could backslide—a comforting premise. As an adjunct to their philosophy many Spiritists also saw the evolution of worldly society as neverending progress toward the perfection of a human utopia overseen by a Supreme Being. And because all Spiritists claimed to investigate, analyze, and base their conclusions on observed data, they considered themselves to be scientific. They expected communication between freed spirits (liberated after death) and those present in living human beings, and proffered "scientific proof" of such contacts.

This communication was mostly accomplished through mediums, those certain few whose extraordinary faculties allowed them to communicate with spirits. Such power was not theirs by choice: spirits had selected and then tutored them as mediums who then became conduits for exchange between spirits in both worlds. Spiritists considered Jesus to be the greatest of all mediums; He fit in with their doctrine of progression because he had reached the side of God in only one lifetime. Ever on the lookout for a truly convincing medium, they now wondered about this remarkable teenager, Teresa Urrea. Just how assiduously had the spirits prepared this young woman for mediumship? At first glance she seemed to fit the Spiritist concept of a perfect candidate: female (and therefore unburdened by traditional leadership responsibilities), humble, uneducated, powerless, and by all appearances without a well-formed identity. There was nothing about Teresa's "self" to impede the endeavors of spirits to teach her. Spiritists in France and Spain, Colombia and Puerto Rico had learned of La Santa de Cabora, especially her miraculous cures and conversations with beings not of this world, and they were eager to learn more of her. But even as they asked, Mexican Spiritists had already begun to make inquiries at Cabora.[42]

Members of the fledgling Spiritist circle at Boroyeca first visited Cabora in November 1889 at the time when Teresa was lapsing in and out of convulsions and trances. Their group of only five or six associates was barely three months old and not at all sure of the doctrinal questions to be addressed, but at that point it hardly mattered. Teresa was too childlike to hold any coherent conversation, and the Spiritists declared her insane. Nevertheless, under the proddings of the movement's main office the group returned to Cabora in the spring of 1890 and discovered an entirely different, much more mature, purposeful, and serene Teresa Urrea, whose behavior and accomplishments they now thought certified her communication with spirits. Enlightened spirits advised her how to heal the afflicted. They guided her to foresee the future, to hear far-off conversations and travel through space, to perform a repertoire of "miracles" that the uninitiated attributed to the Divine.[43]

Elated by their findings, the Spiritists invited Teresa and her father to their meetings in Boroyeca, made both of them honorary members, and then declared the Santa honorary president. According to Boroyeca's Spiritists (we have little directly from Teresa herself on this subject), she affirmed that she regularly consulted with "protectors" (the Spiritists termed them spirits), whom Teresa identified as Agustín, Felipe, and "Hermano" ("Brother"). The first two were constantly at her side and "Hermano" at her back. Teresa called Spiritism the true religion, but insisted that she could not wholly adhere to its tenets because it denied (which it did) the existence of the "celestial court," an impassable stumbling block for her. Teresa resolutely refused to deny the divinity of Jesus Christ and the concept of the Trinity, an anathema to Spiritists. She believed in the mystery of the saints and the cult of images and other elements of Roman Catholicism even if she sharply criticized major practices of the official Church. So she could not be a true Spiritist, even less a medium, but the Boroyecans did not give up on her. They appreciated her difficulty in discarding her religious upbringing along with the "superstitions" of those among whom she ministered, and vowed to work on such intellectual shortcomings. They would teach and she would learn. In one session they asked, "Is religion necessary?" and Teresa replied, "No." Morality existed without it. "I believe one serves God with one's deeds and one's examples and not by useless demonstrations."[44] To the Spiritists such comments represented "progress," and they claimed that by November 1891 Teresa no longer believed in the divinity of Jesus Christ. Still, she continued to insist that the spirit proceeds from God rather than man. The Spiritists cringed at such reasoning but concluded: "We hope to change that thinking too."[45] They never did.

Teresa flirted with spiritism and may even have adopted some of its precepts. No doubt she wavered on many of the doctrinal teachings of the Catholic Church, but it is doubtful that she ever abandoned those beloved divinities that shaped and infused so much of her life. Like most people Teresa begged and borrowed bits of belief from a variety of sources in order to help smooth, explain, and organize her course through life. Catholicism loaned her its divinities, magic its phantoms, and curanderas their expertise with herbs and other medicinal powers. Astrology could well have made its contribution, and en route La Niña de Cabora seems to have discovered some Spiritist ideas that fit her purposes and eased the passage. After all, a good many of today's Spiritists are baptized Roman Catholics and still call themselves Catholics.

Nor did Teresa necessarily encounter contradictions between the spiritism being urged upon her and the brand of Catholicism she had long favored. The Holy Bible is full of miraculous phenomena not all that different from those practiced by modern mediums: inspired trance messages, paranormal healing, apparitions, prophetic statements, and physical healings. There is a good deal of possible interaction between Catholic and Spiritist beliefs, and in its repudiation of official Church trappings and intermediaries spiritism can appeal to those in search of a more primitive Catholicism. Spiritism may disavow the divine nature of Jesus and miracles, the existence of angels and devils, the sacraments of the Church, and the physical reality of heaven and hell, but it embraces—it insists upon—Christian morality and values. So it is no great wonder that it attracted Teresa. Spiritist views joggled her imagination, responded to some of her questions, touched her realities, and offered alternatives. The composite that emerges from such human creativity is the essence of local religion—people using what they know of the world to mold a belief system that makes sense and is useful to them.[46]

La Santa's Would-Be Mentor

Of all local Spiritists convinced that Teresa had been tapped for mediumship, Lauro Aguirre was the most persistent, and we find him woven into her life from Cabora onward, though we have few details of his background. Aguirre was born June 21, 1857, in the mining district of Batopilas, deep in the Sierra Madre of southwestern Chihuahua.[47] He grew up in the vicinity of Batosegochi, a mining center near Chihuahua's border with Durango. Nothing is known of his parents or his childhood, but his youth must have included an element of money and influence, for as a young man he enrolled in the elite Colegio Militar in Mexico City, where he specialized in topographical survey engineering. Like so many fellow army officers who were graduated from the academy, he soon shucked his military uniform for more promising civilian employment, and by 1879, at age 22, he was working out of Tapachula,

Chiapas, with the federal Boundary Commission along the Guatemalan border. Then he transferred to the Geographic Commission with headquarters in Jalapa, Veracruz. In the mid-1880s he surveyed around Guaymas and Hermosillo for one of the companies mapping public lands in Sonora, a wickedly competitive, high-stakes game, controlled in the main by state politicians and their wealthy friends. Aguirre's employer, the German immigrant Luis Hüller, a giant among giants in the survey business, at one point owned a third of the Baja California peninsula as well as enormous properties in Sonora and elsewhere. Aguirre too seems to have acquired considerable Sonoran real estate.

About 1890 or so Aguirre ran into a savage land dispute with state notables right at the time when courts in the Arizona Territory of the United States were airing others of his business difficulties. One of his adversaries could have been Hüller himself; if so, it was a battle Aguirre could not win. He later complained about the monopolistic practices of Hüller and his ilk and their tendency to silence surveyors who protested their greed. In 1892 Hüller's company surveyed nearly 7,500 acres around Alamos and ran into local protests which carried through the courts for the next eight years. Although we do not know whether Tomás Urrea was one of the litigants, at about this time Aguirre claimed that Urrea was victimized by powerful interests looking to usurp his property. At any rate, the business heat became too intense for Aguirre, and in the summer of 1892, now aged 35, he took refuge in the border town of Nogales, Arizona, where he commenced to vent his anger as an inflammatory journalist committed to the downfall of the Porfirian reign, his personal and business reversals transformed into rabid political dissent.[48]

Aguirre was well known as an articulate and committed Spiritist in Guaymas, where at his modest home he regularly engaged members of the port's higher society in séances (though himself no medium), occasions on which he also aired his distaste for the Porfirian regime. Before his flight to Nogales he had taken an abiding interest in the commotion at Cabora, and by some accounts had even traveled there to observe the Santa and to converse with her father. Urged by fellow Spiritists to report his impressions, on July 28, 1892, he wrote from Nogales, concluding that Teresa was indeed a medium with diverse Spiritist faculties, some of them quite rare. Aguirre emphasized that it had not always been that way—that before spirits had shaped her character, Teresa was a most vulgar and ignorant young girl, imbued with all those lamentable superstitions which only served the self-interests of the Catholic clergy. Then powerful spirits cloaked in convulsions and trance states transformed her into a medium and began to converse with her, to advise and move her, all of which was plainly evident to Aguirre in Teresa's words and behavior.[49]

Spirits gave Teresa answers to difficult questions and authorized her to reveal the intimate secrets of her listeners, Aguirre wrote. At times in person and on other occasions through sketches and drawings, spirits furnished her with foresight. Mediums like Teresa radiated inspiration. First she might speak like an untutored country bumpkin and then, especially during a trance, as a person familiar with reasonably sophisticated contemporary thought about philosophy and religion. Concerning her cures, he continued, "She says that she is not the master of her own hands, but that they are directed by the spirits who protect her and . . . use her as an instrument to heal."[50]

Teresa herself was not so sure of the origin of her powers. While at Cabora she asserted that she had received the power as a gift from God, but a decade later in 1900 she equivocated, saying, "I have no knowledge from whence comes this power. It has been given me to heal the sick and the poor. Yes, I have had visions, but no particular person has appeared to me. Indeed, in all these visions there have come before my eyes numberless people. This gift has been given me for the benefit of mankind, and it would be wicked for me not to exercise it."[51] She told the press in early 1901 that she intended to seek the source of her power abroad—in Paris, Oberammergau (site of the famous passion play), Jerusalem, India, and finally Egypt—where she hoped, "Maybe I can find someone to tell me the secret."[52] Still, she insisted, "I believe in God and in his ability and willingness to endow human beings with a portion of his Divine power to banish pain and suffering."[53] As Teresa became more worldly, her religiosity became more complex, which only affirms that a person's spirituality is rarely static.

Lauro Aguirre found Teresa's moral character beyond reproach and granted her impeccable Spiritist credentials. He also promptly utilized her fame and following to serve his own anti-Porfirian political bent. In their widely circulated publications, such as *La Ilustracion espírita*, a monthly newspaper out of Guadalajara and the capital, Spiritists shied away from overt political pronouncements and assessments, although they could hardly argue that spirits never talked politics. Teresa also publicly denied any political intent in her mission, even after the faithful of Tomochic and other dissidents took up weapons against the government in her name. Did she not recognize the political nature of her crusade or just not care to admit it?

9

Priests, Money, Doctors

AUTHORITIES AND THEIR ALLIES are wary of folk saints like Teresa, not only because the miracle cures they perform enhance their political potential, but also because they are prone to preach wellness for the society at large and in doing so rarely hesitate to identify existing maladies. Teresa was no exception. "I should like to heal all humanity," she declared. "I wish I might gather it in my arms and heal it so."[1] What was it about society that she yearned to heal? What had gone so wrong in the world, as evidenced in northwestern Mexico? On this subject Teresa minced no words; she unhesitatingly identified priests, money, and doctors as the greatest evils on earth. She also assured that the Roman Catholic Church would be reformed—that such overhaul was already at hand in Italy—but that she could not predict its future shape, only that in the changes under way the true story of Jesus Christ would be revealed. Here she harked back to a simple Christianity devoid of hierarchy and intermediaries—and who could miss the connection of such an admonition to civil government? Or did she mean to go one step further, to remind all that the meek (among them her followers) shall inherit the earth? Teresa hinted at the destiny of mankind, but in such opaque images that her listeners could make little sense of them. She prophesied that clarification would come from two other divinely touched youths, soon to appear, who had suffered more than she and who also possessed more God-given qualities.[2]

Meanwhile, Teresa warned of God's growing impatience with an errant humanity. In 1896 she revealed to the public the aforementioned doomsday letter, addressed to "My Daughter," which she said the

Archangel Gabriel had delivered to her (she did not say when) from an angry Almighty: "If my sacred heart had not burned with Divine love for men, I should long ago have cast them into the depths of hell. . . . I have shed my precious blood . . . that they may repent of their sins." Although somewhat cloudy about the precise nature of the sins that caused the Lord's anger, the letters laid out a general prescription for reform: "Therefore I desire that they [all people] should repent in their hearts, have care of their souls, adore and venerate the Holy Mother Mary who is the one that pleads with me most for the salvation of sinners and happiness of men, recite the rosary, revere the Holy Cross, respect your superiors, give to the needy and do evil to no one." In other words, God enjoined mankind to return to a true Christianity. If not: "Go, sinners, to the fires of hell for all eternity"; but for those who did return, "I will be merciful." More than that: "[I] will fill them with prosperity and will cause them to succeed in all their enterprises or business."[3] How interesting that the Almighty promised prosperity in "enterprises" and "business," a decidedly "modern" notion. Furthermore, one can only wonder at the intent of His words: "Respect your superiors." Teresa herself said nothing in this regard, nor did she attempt to interpret the profoundly conservative declarations in the letter. In fact, she railed against money and pointedly discouraged her followers from obeying some "superiors," such as the prelates, priests, and other representatives of the official Church, many of whom had embraced the Porfiriato. Therefore, although her relationship to the contents of the letter remains ambiguous and even contradictory, its appearance purportedly placed her in contact with the Almighty.

This communication from God conformed to a tradition of occasional letters from Heaven, an aspect of popular religion long evident in Mexico and elsewhere. Such letters tend to arrive in periods of crisis, identify the catastrophe as the result of sin, and insist that the calamity can only be ended by conversion. They underscore belief in a living God, in His concern with the world and active participation in it, and in the ability of mankind to mollify the Lord's anger through good acts. In this environment Teresa preached that "God is the spirit of love, that we who are in the world must love one another and live in peace, otherwise we offend God."[4] In broad ways she implied the need to renovate and regenerate Mexican society.

For Catholics, much of God's nineteenth-century anger, as revealed in such letters, visions, and prophesies, had to do with ways in which the modern world impinged upon traditional belief or, one might say, the manner in which secularization everywhere nipped at the flanks and sapped the strength of the Catholic Church. Mankind had surrendered to pride in human reason and material greed, thereby separating itself from dependence on God, who responded with vengeance: sickness, drought, floods, personal misfortune, social calamity. Teresa remarked on these generalized human failings as revealed to her and, as noted, identified priests, money, and doctors as those specific shortcomings that impeded God's goodwill and harmony among all peoples.[5]

The First Great Evil

To Teresa priests were not needed at all and neither was the Mass they celebrated. The faithful needed no intermediaries but should communicate directly with God through prayer. Here is Lauro Aguirre describing La Santa's relationship with prayer (although with Aguirre we can never be sure if we are hearing more of him than of her): to Teresa, "praying was like talking to a revered friend, one in whom she felt the utmost trust. Prayers should be offered with profound feeling, should be soul-stirring and heartfelt. She objected to the prayers of priests— empty, external, impersonal, without feeling; simply memorized passages, alike for all persons and all occasions. A parrot could perform as well."[6] Away with the external trappings of the Church, the soaring cathedrals with their gilded altars. Off with the gorgeously adorned vestments of priests. Teresa certified that the faithful need not confess to priests (not that many rural people did so anyway): only God can forgive. Furthermore, she preached, people should baptize, confirm, and marry themselves. In fact, Teresa herself performed a couple of baptisms. On Christmas Eve 1889 she baptized the newest son of her father (and presumably his wife, Loreto, but one cannot be sure) along with a Yaqui baby. La Santa insisted that God actually performed the baptisms, and when others asked her to baptize their children, she declined, pleading that the Lord had authorized her to baptize only those two children, no more.[7] Widely practiced by many religious groups, baptism is of course a master symbol of the Roman Catholic Church. It is the initial sacred milestone in the passage through life; baptism admits one into the institutional Church. Most religious sects do their own baptizing because it ushers recipients out of old religious habits and into an entirely new world.[8] On this occasion we have Teresa urging all to baptize themselves—to initiate themselves into God's realm, to escape that of Holy Mother Church, and to join her crusade.

It is difficult to decipher the full nature of La Santa's rancor against the Church, but the antipathy ran exceedingly deep and extended even to the Pope himself. She came as close as she could to declaring His Holiness the Antichrist. "The greatest of the priests is the most evil," and "God had declared all their [priests and Pope] acts void." Those are remarkable accusations to hurl at the Church she insisted would soon be reformed: "In Italy, discussion is already underway with the Pope, and Truth will triumph." Indeed, she revealed that an Italian initiator of the reform wished to visit her at Cabora; he and his children wanted to come but the man's wife was opposed and apparently her wishes prevailed. At any rate, no such visitors are known to have reached the rancho.[9]

Teresa evinced the virulent anticlericalism long evident in Mexico and elsewhere that had reached high tide in the wake of The Reform. There were the old standard complaints about priests—that they said Mass and gave the sacraments only to receive excessive fees, got drunk and violated their chastity vows, engaged in commercial ventures, did not pay their debts, and meddled in politics (as for example Padres Irigoyen and Portillo in the Papigochic, although from opposite sides of the fence). Many felt that priests got something for nothing, that they were parasites on society who confiscated donations meant for others. In cartoons urban newspapers lampooned priests as pompous busybodies who stuck their big, sniffing noses into the private lives of parishioners, especially their sexual pleasures.[10] All of these accusations were observed realities; even if exaggerated, they still could be verified. Padre Portillo had children and sizable private parcels of real estate, while Irigoyen reveled in local politics said to be none of his business. As might be expected, Cruz Chávez had it in for Manuel Castelo, the itinerant priest who in Tomochic had condemned La Santa de Cabora along with El Santo del Chopeque. Castelo had bought a horse from Chávez the spring of 1891 but never paid for it. During the following year's upheaval Chávez demanded his due, punctuated with a death threat. Moreover, he tripled his price for the horse, way out of line with going prices in the region.[11]

Chávez may have had good reason to scorn Castelo, and many common country people undoubtedly had their quarrels with individual clergymen, but the aversion that these people (and countless others elsewhere, then and today) felt toward priests was much more generalized and had largely to do with the way in which ordinary folk thought about and practiced their religion. Their spirituality was rooted in their own history and daily experience. What did the priests who came to them, first as missionaries and then as representatives of the official church, know of or even care about the past of these folks? Could anyone point out a priest in the Papigochic who labored day after day in dry farming, who knew drought or deprivation, or who had died of malnutrition? Who had ever seen a priest lugging a leather sack overloaded with rocky silver ore up one of those treacherous, hand-hewn ladders at the mines? *Our* religion stems from *our* reality. What clergyman experiences *our* sort of daily life? Many people harbored reservations, therefore, about priests, not so much because of an explicit grievance against a representative of Holy Mother Church, but because they felt nothing in common with them. They simply lived different realities.[12]

Teresa's sessions with the Spiritists confirmed for her the worst about the Church and its clergy, and a good deal of what she said about the failures of the institutional Church echoed the intemperate stance of Spiritists. For its part, the Church had aggressively condemned Spiritism as high on the Devil's menu for the downfall of mankind. Lauro Aguirre thought Teresa, before her conversion by the spirits, imbued with those ubiquitous Roman Catholic superstitions that "so well served the exploitations of the clergy," lamenting that self-interest had delivered most of her well-to-do and cultured relatives (the Urreas in Alamos, for example) to the designs of a manipulative clergy.[13] Teresa picked up some of that language: the faithful needed no intermediary in their interaction with God and even less allegiance to a corrupt Church with its fraudulent and immoral deputies—or perhaps all along La Santa's thoughts on the matter had coincided with Aguirre's.

The Devil's Dinero

Money was the second great evil identified by La Santa de Cabora, and her attack on money resonated with the Church's own moral arguments against the commercialization of the mind wrought by science and secularization. But while the Church sought to regain the power and populace it had lost to modernization, Teresa emphasized the unwelcome ways in which the new reasoning had altered human relationships and goals. In the modern order, people paid more attention to material gain than to spiritual need. Suspicion existed that money (but not necessarily all by itself) dissolved traditional community and other familiar human relationships, that it created competition where there had been harmony, that it was anonymous and impersonal, and measured human quality by crass wealth instead of moral worth. Teresa sensed all this when she implored her devotees to love one another, treat each other charitably, or face eternal damnation: "God is the spirit of love; we who are in the world must love one another and live in peace; otherwise we offend God."[14] She seems to have said nothing precisely about income inequities, although in a general way she preached the necessity of equality among all peoples, excoriated greed—that "confused love of riches"—and in later years decried the poverty of the Yaqui Indians among whom she labored.[15] Once again, the Spiritists may well have influenced her thinking. They declared: "Selfishness is the source of all evils, as charity is the source of all virtues," words that certainly approximated those of Teresa. Moreover, Spiritists collected no money at their services; it was against their doctrine to do so, and they passionately condemned the Catholic Church for its money grubbing.[16] One simply did not accept monetary payment to forward God's work, regardless of how one conceived of that Supreme Being.

None of this implies that Teresa and her followers were strangers to money. Some undoubtedly bartered in kind, even at Cabora, but most made their commercial exchanges in hard cash and had done so for generations. In this epoch Sierra mining, fueled by the founding of private banks by the area's elites, pumped money into the regional economy as well as into the pockets of humble workers. Significantly, all of the mining labor disputes in the area involved money: in 1883 at Pinos Altos where laborers protested the receipt of half their pay in tokens instead of cash and demanded weekly instead of bi-weekly wages; in 1885 at Cusihuiriachi, where miners complained of being paid in less valued copper coins instead of silver pesos; and in 1889 at Los Bronces in the Sahuripa district bordering Cabora, where Mexican employees demanded salaries equal to those of foreigners for the same work. The superintendent of this latter large mining complex pleaded that his laborers (mainly Yaquis) already received the highest pay in the country for their toil: 75 centavos to 3 pesos a day (60 cents to $2.40). But the workers insisted—equal pay for equal jobs.[17]

While this outcry pertained to money per se—that is, coins in one's purse—it also echoed a moral dilemma for the great majority of Teresa's followers. In their working world, money—inherently a measure of worth—was increasingly equated with human quality, with status and prestige. That is why the miners at Los Bronces demanded equal pay for equal work. "Equal pay for equal work" meant to them, "We're as good as you are, by God! Pay us our worth." But even as these miners and other workers rioted and struck for justice in money matters, tradition tugged at their consciousness. Why all this fiery concern about money? After all, most of these people still had one foot planted in traditional prestige systems where elders, community, and moral obligation were what counted. So they oscillated between the lure of what seemed to be a better way to fulfill their lives and hallowed customs which had long served their culture. Just how *does* one shift from one prestige system to another? While Teresa did not directly address their quandary, her ministry offered to restore what money seemed to be siphoning from their lives: precious feelings of community, security, and self-respect. Simply said, the goings-on at Cabora made her enthusiasts feel good and right about themselves.[18]

Usurpers of God's Work

Doctors—the third of Teresa's chief evils—also bore the stain of being unprincipled money grubbers. Actually, Teresa knew few if any doctors. There were perhaps only three or four in the entire region, virtually all of them well-paid foreigners employed in mining complexes. The government certified others with some claim to medical knowledge to practice and charge fees, but these "physicians" tended to be people with political connections who could buy their certification. They may have had some medical competence, but they were not really doctors. One such medical person from Boroyeca is said to have attended Teresa at the height of her convulsions and to have pronounced the young girl near death, living only on "reserve vitality." He could do nothing for her, so he offered his condolences and left.[19] We have no idea if or what he charged for the visit, but his diagnosis probably confirmed what country folks already suspected of doctors: they promised more than they delivered but still collected their fee.

When an American doctor, E. P. Schellhous, visited Teresa in the company of several friends in the spring of 1891, La Santa revealed that physicians had told her she was suffering from an ailment that had numbed her brain, a diagnosis that must have made her bristle and lose any confidence in "scientific" evaluations. For his part, Dr. Schellhous reported her in good mental and physical health. He noted that Teresa was certainly not the first person who healed by the laying on of hands, that Jesus and his Apostles had done as much. Dr. Schellhous then proclaimed Teresa a Spiritist medium: "She is simple, innocent, and without pretensions and has a lucid understanding of her elevated mission and complete knowledge that she is only the instrument of superior and benevolent spirits who consider her invaluable in spreading good and kindness to suffering humanity."[20] So we learn that Dr. Schellhous himself was no impartial observer, but although sympathetic to his kind, Teresa could hardly agree with his finding. The Almighty had given her the power and mission to heal, period. Other than these sorts of medical practitioners—Schellhous and the rest—Teresa knew no professional doctors, only local healers like Huila.

For the most part country folk around places like Cabora turned to curanderas and their likes for both practical and supernatural reasons. Aside from the dearth of doctors, theories about the causes of most illnesses ran from sorcery and witches to chastisement by God, and all of these people acknowledged the connection between the natural and supernatural. No cure was possible without God's will, and the Lord only granted the gift of healing to certain individuals, such as Teresa Urrea, or perhaps an unexpected visitor like Carl Lumholz, and true curanderas. Who were these other so-called doctors who claim to do the work of the Lord? What was this science that pretends to skirt God's volition? In response, we can appreciate that Teresa's admonitions about doctors not only pertained to their scarcity, ignorance, and greediness, but to their interference with the workings of the Divine. She labeled doctors "evil," which put them in league with Satan.

Furthermore, Spiritists had their irreconcilable differences with professional physicians and no doubt discussed that dissonance with Teresa. Doctors called Spiritists "quacks." They saw nothing scientific in their practices, which they found either inconsequential or harmful for patients. Here you can taste the flavor of the Spiritist response to such accusations: "If the majority of the men of medicine would not be so pretentious about their knowledge and not squander the opportunity to investigate those deeds [healing practices] which have repeated themselves for centuries, medical practice would not be an art but a science, doctors would not be robots but learned people, humanity would not suffer as much but find more relief and security. Unfortunately, most doctors deprecate those ideas which do not originate with themselves and physicians do not understand that behind practices which may seem ridiculous [to them], . . . lies a true science, a new truth, a surprising revelation, and a marvelous world whose virtue is still unknown." Spiritists proclaimed that Teresa Urrea worked "with noble disinterest" toward this exalted end.[21] This debate about religion and science continues, at times repugnantly shrill, but on other occasions remarkably thoughtful. Based on what they know about the world, most people seem to have definite personal feelings about where to seek relief for what ails them.

Weighing Teresa's Advice

These, then, were Teresa Urrea's most robustly argued points of view—at least the ones most visible in the documentation—but this tells us nothing of how her listeners received her counsel. We cannot climb inside their heads, nor is there much written evidence to draw on, but we may explore cultural connections and infer a good deal from the actions of the faithful in this case. We may also presume that each cultural cluster, not to speak of factions and individuals within such groups, brought its own interpretations to Teresa's messages. Mayos,

Yaquis, and Tarahumaras, as well as mestizos and Creoles, all tucked her pronouncements—or more likely just those chunks and tidbits which most appealed to them—into their respective cultural baggage.[22]

What we know of the Mayo comes mainly from military reports of the period. During the 1880s agricultural entrepreneurs, largely Mexican but also foreign, had with the assistance of the military steadily occupied more and more Mayo farmland and appropriated native labor along the Mayo and Fuerte Rivers. After initial resistance many Mayos went to work for the newcomers, but the army, battling relentless Yaquis just to the north, still kept a wary eye on the Mayo. Therefore, when in August 1890 Colonel Antonio Rincón, in charge of keeping peace among the Mayos, received word of a huge, ebullient gathering at a native settlement called Jambiobampo, just south of Cabora and within his jurisdiction, he became truly apprehensive. Smart and experienced enough not to barge into such an assembly, Colonel Rincón unobtrusively worked his way, unarmed, into the midst of the mass— some 1,200 strong—to investigate the object of their commotion. There he encountered a sixteen-year-old Mayo youth named Damián Quijano, surrounded by a coterie of protective sacristans, elders, and ritual dancers. What was going on here? Damián spoke no Spanish, but Colonel Rincón was able to converse with him and his father in Mayo, and after some courtesies to ease the tension, the boy revealed that in communications with God and La Santa de Cabora he had learned of the forthcoming great flood that would inundate all humanity. Only those who took to the slightly elevated Rancho Jambiobampo would be saved. God was sending the flood to purify mankind.[23]

The pronouncement about the impending inundation must have resonated strongly with Mayo mythology, which possessed its own accounts of the great-flood-to-come. From time immemorial Mayo settlements along the Fuerte River had periodically been devastated by flash floods spawned by downpours in the Sierra, and their flood myth, which accounted for the destruction of the wicked along with the survival of the worthy few, may well have been reinforced by the Old Testament tale of the flood brought to the region by Christian missionaries. Both emphasized a Father's punishment of His errant children. Therefore, Damián felt obligated to summon his kinsmen to the site in order to save them from God's wrath, and within a day or so they had congregated, peons and sirvientes from surrounding haciendas and from much longer distances, lugging their personal belongings mixed with some possessions pilfered from their patrons.[24]

Colonel Rincón was flabbergasted. Not only had these people left their workplaces without the permission of their employers and their pueblos without the consent of local authorities, but the colonel feared that this gathering might be one more of those that in the past decade had escalated (he used the word "matured") into overt rebellion against authority. He thought these people in league with Mayo compatriots who in smaller groups had been attracted to similar santos in the nearby Forest of Cuirimpo, noting that Damián's uncle, Cirilo Quijano, had campaigned as a general in the forces of the most dreaded of all Yaqui war chiefs, Cajeme, only recently brought to bay. In these circumstances, and unable to convince Damián's listeners to disperse and return to their respective locales, Rincón arrested Damián along with some sixty of his most fervent followers. He delivered fifteen of his prisoners to the civil authorities at Maciaca and escorted the remainder to a military post. Then he began to collate the influx of intelligence reports concerning all those other santos who had popped up among the Mayo.[25]

While Colonel Rincón himself went to investigate the crowd at Jambiobampo, he ordered his trusted and trained subordinate, Captain Emilio Enríquez, with a squad of thirteen men, to look into similar assemblages in surrounding hamlets. Santos had sprouted up everywhere in the socially disturbed region: Santa Camilia in the forests of Ilibaqui; Santa Isabel at Macochi; Santa Agustina at Baburo, venerated by sixty men and women. Enríquez arrested a few of the santos and their followers, but others fled at the approach of the soldiers. The junior officer marched on to discover more of the same: San Juan and La Luz at Cohirimpo, San Luis at Tenanchopo, and San Irenio at rancho Sapochopo. He arrested them all and took them to the military jail of the Eleventh Cavalry Regiment, where most were interrogated, admonished, and transported with their families across the Sea of Cortez to labor at 1.25 pesos daily ($1) in the mines of Santa Rosalía in Baja California.[26]

Throughout the repression, the Mayo apparently revealed nothing about Teresa Urrea that alarmed the military. Though they may have prompted the army's inquiries at Cabora, there were no immediate actions against La Santa and her followers. Meanwhile, Captain Enrí-

quez did gain some further expertise about these santos and their devotees, knowledge he intended to put to work in late December 1891
when he was ordered to Cabora with his detachment to arrest the elusive Tomochitecos headed there from Chihuahua.

How we would have enjoyed eavesdropping on that conversation in
which Damián consulted Teresa—two youngsters, both in their mid-
teens and claiming divine knowledge, discussing the end of the world.
We may wonder what language they used. Teresa apparently spoke no
Mayo, although her mother was a Tehueco in the same general language group. Their native clans were neighbors and no doubt inter-
mingled, or perhaps Damián's father, who also attended the meeting,
spoke Spanish. Regardless of the linguistics involved, Damián had experienced a conversation with the Divine about the great flood to come
and had gone to converse with Teresa, perhaps to ask her advice. Certainly she attracted many Mayos—and in mid-May 1892 a force of
Mayos crying "¡Viva la Santa de Cabora!" attacked Navojoa, a significant regional town not far from Cabora.

Indeed, in a meshing of Mayo and mestizo belief systems, Mayos still
celebrate the third of May as a saint's day dedicated to Teresa and also
exalt her in their own cultural myths. Here is but one of them:

> During the time of Santa Teresa, Napoleon was leading his cav-
> alry and riding his horse through the Mayo area. His horse and his
> men were very tired. Napoleon said, "We must go on," and he
> continued to drive his horse. When he came through here, Santa
> Teresa said, "Now look, it is time you should rest." Napoleon
> replied, "I am not going to rest." And on he went. Because he dis-
> regarded what Santa Teresa said, because he did not respect Santa
> Teresa, suddenly his horse's sweat turned to blood. The horse was
> sweating blood out of his body. This was the miracle that was
> performed because Napoleon did not respect Santa Teresa.[27]

In this lore the identity of Napoleon is unclear. Are we remembering
Napoleon Bonaparte or Napoleon III, who in the 1860s had fostered
the French Intervention into Mexico? Perhaps we can envision the
Mexican military marching through Cabora, as it eventually did, or
sense a great French general's imperialistic adventure as representative
of the enduring conflict between mestizo and Mayo in the indigenous

mind, or more directly, Napoleon might have been a mythic metaphor for a usurping state with its priests, money, and doctors. Whatever the case, Mayo devotion to Santa Teresa and her God-given power to perform miracles remains embedded in their culture.

With the Yaquis it was much the same, albeit from their own distinct cultural perspective. To them Cabora was—and is—a holy place enshrined in traditional myth:

Rabdi Kowame [a preeminent Yaqui prophet] preached to those who accompanied him that day, the sixth of the first month of the innocent children of 1414. "Travel over all of the forests, hills, and villages to come out at a place called Takalaim. Preach the holy division line and announce the gospel of the reign of God." And he said, "Go ahead, do honor, and preach the Holy Hymn." Passing from there a little further, they arrived at Cocoraqui [the arroyo on which Tomás Urrea erected his home], where they taught the holy doctrine and commandments of Dios [God]. Leaving Cocoraqui, en route to Cabora, Rabdi Kowame said, "*Eli Eli lama sabactanti* [sic]," which means, "My Lord, come forth and do honor." Proceeding from there, and further on, arriving at Cabora, he speaks again to those who accompanied him, "Watch that no one deceives you, for many men will come, and he will deceive you, [the charlatan will assert that] 'I am he, sent by Dios,' and he will deceive many of you and our children. Do not hear those who come after this. War will be seen, and we will be upset, and there will be no end."[28]

This is ardent prophesy that places Cabora at the center of the myth. The Yaquis believed that the universal flood had already occurred.[29] A few virtuous Yaquis survived, and God warned them to beware of false prophets. Then sacred apparitions and holy visions preceded the birth of Christ, redeemer of the world. From 1414 to 1417 several prophets appeared, among them Rabdi Kowame, who warned, "War will be seen, . . . and there will be no end." The Yaquis had indeed been suffering through war without end. Had they yielded to false prophets—Christian missionaries, civil officials, some of their own holy people, or even Santa Teresa? Judging by the zeal with which so many flocked to Cabora, by the uninhibited veneration with which they adored Teresa (insisting over her passionate protests that she *was* a santa), and by the fervor with which some soon died in her name, we may safely conclude that this young girl who ministered to Yaquis from sacred sites once trod by their own holy men was to them godly.

Teresa reciprocated the admiration and healed in ways familiar to the natives. Yaquis called their own curers "one who has good hands," and these indigenous healers also blended their saliva with dirt or white mesquite ashes and rubbed the mixture on their patients, all the while reciting prayers and making the sign of the cross over the diseased or injured place.[30] In later years, Teresa told the *New York Journal*: "I never led the Yaquis to battle, but I did sympathize with them. My father employed them on his hacienda and I knew and loved them. I have seen the many wrongs. Before my eyes children not three years old have been lynched, hanged from trees . . . by order of the military commander of the Sonora District to keep the Yaquis down. Do you wonder why the tribe fights the forces of such a government? My poor Indians! They are the bravest and most persecuted people on earth. They will fight for their rights until they win or are exterminated. God help them! There are few of them left."[31] This was a ringing indictment, to be sure, but one made from a foreign country fully a decade after she had ministered to the Yaquis in Sonora. Time and retrospect may have honed La Santa's political consciousness and sharpened her tongue, and it was certainly safer to hurl accusations from the U.S. side of the border than in Mexico itself. The Mexican government would not have tolerated such belligerency from Cabora. While on the rancho around 1890 Teresa seemed to realize this, or perhaps her father told her so; at any rate, while in Sonora she shied from the sort of pointed political pronouncements that would have brought the troops down upon her ministry. Still, we have no idea what she counseled her followers off main stage, out of public view. We only know that people took up arms in her name.

It is true that the Yaquis suffered terribly. For several centuries they had resisted the encroachments of outsiders onto their lands and into their culture along Sonora's Yaqui River. There were long periods of uneasy peace, but sooner or later a broken promise, a disregarded treaty, greed, or arrogance triggered a new revolt. In April 1886 the renowned Yaqui war chief Cajeme had been captured and executed by the military, but his death only shifted the hostilities into guerrilla war-

A typical Indian pueblo in the Sierra Madre. (American Museum of Natural History, neg. no. 2583, photo by Hovey, courtesy Department of Library Services)

"Mountain schooners" transporting heavy machinery to mines. (American Museum of Natural History, neg. no. 25832, unknown photographer, courtesy Department of Library Services)

Mexican workers' camp at Ocampo mine. (American Museum of Natural History, neg. no. 109811, photo by Hovey, courtesy Department of Library Services)

Pinos Altos silver mine near Tomochic. (American Museum of Natural History, neg. no. 109879, photo by Hovey, courtesy Department of Library Services)

Ocampo mining center where Tomochitecos worked. The large central building is the church. Much of the old town still stands. (American Museum of Natural History, neg. no. 109863, photo by Hovey, courtesy Department of Library Services)

One-handled wooden plow of type used at Tomochic. Such plows are still occasionally used in the Sierra. (American Museum of Natural History, neg. no. 109891, photo by Hovey, courtesy Department of Library Services)

The rugged terrain of the Sierra through which the army tracked the fleeing Tomochitecos. (American Museum of Natural History, neg. no. 109856, photo by Hovey, courtesy Department of Library Services)

Three Tarahumaras from Yépachic in 1890. (American Museum of Natural History, neg. no. 109917, photo by Hovey, courtesy Department of Library Services)

Cerro de Miñaca in the Papigochic Valley near Ciudad Guerrero, said to point gold seekers toward fabulous lost mines. (American Museum of Natural History, neg. no. 109904, photo by Hovey, courtesy Department of Library Services)

Administrators at the Ocampo mine. (Author's collection)

A political rally at the Ocampo mine. (Courtesy Sra. María Rosario)

Joaquín Chávez, the cacique and security chief of the Papigochic, with a favorite child perched on bars of silver that he transported. (Courtesy Sra. María Rosario)

Reyes Domínguez (right) with a youth band he organized for Tomochic around 1905. (Author's collection)

A surgeon performs an operation at a mining complex in the Sierra Madre. (Author's collection)

Weddings attracted huge gatherings of extended family and friends in the Papigochic. (Author's collection)

Schoolboys undergoing militia training in Ciudad Guerrero.
(Author's collection)

A village musical group, possibly from San Tomás; such groups were much
cherished among Papigochics. (Author's collection)

Spirits and demons pervade the lives of Mexicans. (Author's collection)

A priest warns his flock of the Almighty's wrath. (Author's collection)

Religious pilgrims headed for Cabora to see La Santa. (Author's collection)

The martyred Santa de Cabora. (Author's collection)

Jefe Político Silviano González. (From Juan Carlos Chávez, *Peleando en Tomochi*)

General Jose M. Rangel,

JEFE DL LA
Campaña de Temóchic.

General José María Rangel,
federal commander.
(Author's collection)

Santana Pérez, militia chief
and political maverick.
(Author's collection)

LOS SUCESOS DE TEMOCHIC.

The battle of Tomochic, October 1892. (Author's collection)

Gutted adobe home of Doña Antonia de Medrano in Tomochic. (From Juan Carlos Chávez, *Peleando en Tomochi*)

TERESITA URREA,
(LA SANTA DE CABORA)
á quien se atribuye por los periódicos gobiernistas una participacion directa en los
sucesos de Temóchic.

Teresita, "said by government newspapers to have directly participated in the events at Tomochic." (Author's collection)

Santa Teresa healing her followers. (Southwest Collection, Texas Tech University)

Teresa with her father, Tomás Urrea. (Southwest Collection, Texas Tech University)

La Santa's techniques of healing.
(*New York Journal*, March 3, 1901)

Lauro Aguirre, the Spiritist and fiery
journalist allied to Teresa. (*El Paso
Daily Times*, January 10, 1925)

Raiders killed attacking Nogales, Mexico, in the name of Santa Teresa in August 1896. (Special Collections, University of Arizona Library, Tucson)

At the time of Teresa, the Virgin Mary made other appearances in Mexico, this one on a cactus in the state of Jalisco. (Author's collection)

The mystery woman, photographed around 1900, whom some have recently identified as Teresa. (Courtesy Silver City Museum, Silver City, New Mexico)

Teresa Urrea. (Southwest Collection, Texas Tech University)

fare. Santa Teresa began her ministry in this tense atmosphere and attracted numerous Yaquis to Cabora. No one has yet uncovered exactly who they were. They may have been *broncos*, who raided from the Sierra de Bacatete not far to the northeast, or *pacíficos*, who labored in commercial agriculture and ranching on the haciendas and ranchos of patrons who had bought up or otherwise preempted the best properties in the region. Most likely there were some of both, for the line between broncos and pacíficos was blurred; the latter by day might become the former at night.[32]

Teresa became known as the "Queen of the Yaquis"; they sought solace from her at Cabora, and some later fought and died with messages from La Santa tucked into their pockets and protective scapularies with her image around their necks. Teresa could only have attracted such devotion by doing and saying things that resonated with her audiences. She does not seem to have been overly calculating in this regard. Rather she drew naturally upon those local and wider traditions that in fundamental ways were already her own, nurturing that partnership of faith and hope that encourages daring among many diverse peoples.

Unlike the Mayos and the Yaquis, the Tarahumaras were not attracted to Santa Teresa in any numbers, perhaps because of differences in spiritual belief, social organization, or historical experience. As we have seen, the Tarahumaras had their own santos, or similar supernatural leaders, who led the opposition to early Spanish incursions, and such holy personages do not seem entirely to have disappeared from their midst in later times. Unlike the other indigenous groups, the Tarahumaras tended to live in smallish family clusters on separated rancherías rather than in larger settlements and villages, and though subdued and scattered by the aggressive colonizers, they were less brutalized and decimated than the others. Still, such generalizations are subject to qualification. In the Papigochic Valley, where Tarahumaras were concentrated in reasonably large pueblos such as Pachera and Tejolócachic, an occasional "Viva" to the Santa de Cabora could be heard, which proved she had penetrated their mentality if not moved their feet.[33]

We have already noted the great diversity of mestizos and other light-skinned people who proudly proclaimed their Spanish ancestry and who were drawn to Teresa out of faith, hope, curiosity, or malice—to be healed and uplifted, or to feed their disdain for things institutionally religious. They came to contemplate the miraculous, play politics and seek support for their ambitions, or just witness the spectacle and participate in the drama. Tomochitecos certainly must have empathized with her condemnation of priests, money, and doctors as the greatest evils in the world. We already know of the villagers' dispute with Padre Castelo, and we soon shall encounter other examples of their contentiousness toward the priest, along with their concerns about money per se and doctors who did God's work. People and institutions approached Teresa out of all sorts of self-interest, not only out of desperation or crisis. And we should recall that many among the poor and miserable, the downtrodden and humiliated who had heard tell of her spiritual powers were not openly attracted to them. They, as well as those who flocked to Cabora, are good examples of humble human beings exercising their choice.

Her Own Woman

No doubt a good many among those thousands who turned to Teresa Urrea did so to advance their own interests, but she was by no means putty in anyone's palms. We have observed how she laughed off her father's doubts about her mission, and she later forthrightly rejected his objections to the man she wished to marry. When that marriage quickly failed, she hardly paused before taking a lover and having two children by him. As resolutely as the Spiritists, for whom she felt considerable empathy, sought to force-feed her their doctrine, she steadfastly refused to deny her belief in Christian divinities. The military harassed her; she stood firm. Yet she did not hesitate to admit her limitations and failings, and she did all this in a society said to be male-dominated. In this way she resembled those Papigochic women who could hold their ground and then some. After Cabora, when her career shifted to the United States, we shall see that Teresa dressed in high fashion crowned by a fancy coiffure, sedulously defied authorities on both sides of the border who sought to curtail her activities, and contracted with a cunning entrepreneur to make money as a traveling faith healer, although she continued to cure the poor for free.[34]

In historical perspective it is not surprising that such a teen-aged girl held forth so impressively at Cabora. Among Catholics there had been increasing devotion to the Virgin Mary and female saints since medieval times, and women have led and continue to guide any number of militant spiritual movements, such as the religious riots during the French Revolution and the still simmering Holy Spirit millenarian uprising in Uganda.[35] While at Cabora Teresa does not seem to have openly advocated armed rebellion against the state, but she did call for a revolution in the ways that people thought of themselves and behaved toward one another, and in doing so she shook three mighty pillars of the reigning regime: priests, as local agents of an intrusive and stubborn Church that sought to stifle local forms of religiosity; money, which measured human worth by material possessions instead of virtue; and doctors, who had usurped the work of God in the name of science.

Nor was all this just so much talk, for Teresa also influenced movements such as the one at Tomochic, with its vow to obey no one but God and Santa Teresa. Let us now rejoin those villagers in their trek toward Cabora. Dogged by soldiers nearly all the way, by Christmas Day these crusaders descended from the western flank of the Sierra and cautiously moved toward their nirvana—a place but also a state of mind. Meanwhile, the federales had dispatched the unit commanded by Captain Enríquez to intercept the fugitives as they put down their weapons and settled in to pay reverence to La Santa. The president himself, two state governors—Izábal in Sonora and Carrillo in Chihuahua—and two military zone commanders checked and rechecked their strategy and anticipated no problems. They were resolved to pluck out this painful splinter before it festered any further.

Part III

———————

Armageddon

10

Forsaking Forgiveness

EMILIO ENRÍQUEZ, the smart and experienced cavalry captain who little more than a year before had so effectively quashed the religious revival among the Mayo, felt quite confident that he could do the same at Cabora. His orders in this case were specific: arrest the band of fanatics who had come from Tomochic to visit Santa Teresa. On the day after Christmas, 1891, Captain Enríquez self-assuredly rode into the rancho with his troop of 2 fellow officers and 40 horsemen, all of them with at least four years military duty on record. Their quarry had not yet arrived, but Cruz Chávez and the faithful were not far off—only some ten miles northeast—and military intelligence had sketched out the anticipated route of their approach.

What to do? The strategy at headquarters seems to have been to await the arrival of the Tomochitecos in Cabora and then, after the believers had laid down their weapons to venerate their Santa, to pounce on them and quickly send them off shackled and under heavily armed escort back to Chihuahua where they would be tried, sentenced, and judicially silenced. But Enríquez decided not to wait. Did he fear making the arrests among thousands of Teresa's followers, who might protest and riot? Did he underestimate the resourcefulness and tenacity of his foe? Was he after glory and promotion? Although the Porfirian military system did not encourage its officers to take real initiative or to make bold decisions on their own, there were many able and ambitious men like Enríquez among the junior officers. At any rate, he decided to intercept and overpower the Tomochitecos before they reached Cabora. The issue was joined six miles to the northeast at an isolated rancho called El Alamo de Palomares.[1]

Cruz Chávez and his band knew the federales were on the way. Perhaps they saw them coming, or someone from Cabora tipped them off, or one of their own scouts had spotted the army patrol. Enríquez had no detailed knowledge about the location of his adversary, and so there among the thick mesquite and other hardy foliage that could camouflage predators, the Tomochitecos deliberately laid their ambush, and the unsuspecting Porfirian military marched right into it that early morning of December 26. The eruption of rifle fire lasted but a few moments. In the first volley alone, Captain Emilio Enríquez fell dead along with one of his fellow officers; six federal cavalrymen along with thirteen horses, dead; nine soldiers wounded alongside any number of injured horses. The remaining terrified corpsmen scattered into the bush, many of them wounded, to die, desert, or scramble their way back to their posts as best they could. A surprising number returned to their units despite the supposed propensity of Porfirian soldiers to defect. At least 28 of these battered and bewildered troopers wandered about the wild countryside until they came upon a dwelling or settlement, received aid and directions, and then gradually filtered back to their duty stations—where superiors hardly greeted them as returning comrades. Instead, officers sharply interrogated the shaken men to judge whether they had too quickly given ground and fled as cowards.[2]

As for the Tomochitecos, they picked up the rifles and ammunition of the fallen soldiers along with other potentially useful particulars and resumed their trek toward Cabora, which soon was in sight. Like so many pilgrims, they were overcome with emotion. Spilling uninhibited tears and wailing hosannas mixed with declarations of eternal victory to their adored Santa, they cast down their weapons and crept on their knees toward the modest chapel from which Teresa frequently ministered to her enthralled flock. Cruz and his cohorts cheered their arrival at the entrance to the holy place and gave thanks for the moment at hand. Then a shock: Teresa was not there nor anywhere about the place. Where was La Santa de Cabora? No one knows, and herein lies one of the great mysteries of our story. If only some more immediate recorder of these events—one of the multitude of journalists who later interviewed her, for example—had thought to ask; but none did. The official government record insists that she fled Cabora at the approach of the Tomochitecos because she did not wish to become involved in the political conflict of the faithful from Chihuahua. Her father Tomás was also gone. As a result, officialdom presumed they had left together and were hiding out until Cruz and his band left in frustration. Perhaps so; without doubt she had known for some time that her followers from the small pueblo of Tomochic had taken up arms in her name and had vowed to visit her at Cabora. Or she could have fled at the sight of Enríquez and his troop. The captain died before having the opportunity to render a report on his findings at Cabora. It is also possible that she simply could have been "elsewhere"—say, at Boroyeca with the Spiritists.

Without the solace and advice of Teresa, the Tomochitecos had to decide for themselves how to proceed. They could have pushed on, perhaps northward toward the border and refuge from the army in pursuit; others at odds with Porfirian rule had done as much. Or they might have surrendered to the army, although they had not yet received any offers of amnesty—and it seems highly unlikely that they would have accepted them had they been made. They could have tarried in the region hoping for a prompt return of the Santa. Instead they made the fateful decision to return to Tomochic and their families. They did not attempt to recruit any followers from among the masses at Cabora, nor did any outsiders at the site join their movement. Yet they must have attracted some attention, for they camped for four hours on a slight hill facing Cabora, sobbing in their anguish and disappointment, and singing songs of praise to Santa Teresa. But they knew they dare not tarry at the site, and so under the cover of night resumed their journey.[3] Sadly they left behind one of their own, one of the four Chávez brothers, Jesús José, at age 32 a year or so younger than Cruz. Jesús José may have been wounded in the initial confrontation with the military and brought by his comrades to Cabora for healing by Teresa. When a heavy fever settled upon him and he could travel no farther, the faithful had no choice but to make him comfortable and leave him behind to the healing powers of Santa Teresa or the mercy of the army.[4]

The Regime Responds

The disaster at El Alamo Rancho stunned Mexico's military. Armed insurrection (as it is always labeled by the powers that be) is a threat to any government, no matter how minor it may seem. For personal dictatorships, especially those more image than substance, such setbacks are intolerable, making them appear weak and unable to defend their interests and those of their backers. Political jackals sniff out such flaws and exploit them to incite more formidable opposition to the regime. In fact, word of the defeat was already out and even abroad. Just a few weeks after the incident at El Alamo, the *New York Times* reported: "News of the victory over the troops in Sonora spread rapidly and caused people to take up arms and join the revolt [of the Tomochitecos]. . . . People are gathering at many little towns [to rebel]."[5] No doubt the rout was the talk of the day throughout the region and beyond, but whether or not the setback had encouraged rebel clusters to form is another question. The American press had a tendency to associate any disorder in Mexico with impending revolution. Yet the government feared that a fuse had been lit in the public mind, one that had to be stamped out before an explosion occurred. Debacles, such as El Alamo, need to be explained away, the perpetrators quickly corralled and punished in exemplary fashion.

In this case, military superiors found blame easy to place: Captain Emilio Enríquez had recklessly exceeded his orders to stay put at Cabora, ignored proper military tactics as outlined in the official training manual, and blundered into ambush. "Only an unpardonable carelessness can explain the defeat of Enríquez. He went beyond his orders. He was to wait for the fanatics to arrive, but he went out in search of them. He could have caught and killed them all after they had surrendered [laid down] their weapons and turned to pray to the Santa."[6] How interesting! Was that really the plan? Was Enríquez ruthlessly to slaughter the faithful as they knelt in worship before their Santa? The captain probably had some discretion in the matter based on developments at Cabora, but as he was dead there could be no rebuttal. President Díaz concluded: "There is nothing we can do about such carelessness but learn a lesson so that it will not happen again."[7]

Meanwhile, a new chase began with the zone's most aggressively determined military officer in charge: cavalry Colonel Lorenzo Torres, ex-Apache hunter, still vigorous at age 55, the scion of one of the state's most prominent families and once Sonora's governor. Torres promptly ordered dragoons from the army posts at Pótam, Tórin, and Bacojori into the chase, along with infantrymen from the large army base at Cócorit. One cavalry unit circled through Cabora itself, discovered the stricken Jesús José Chávez lying helplessly on a makeshift bed, and executed him on the spot, the government's demonstration of "exemplary punishment." Hastily recruited militiamen from communities like Batacosa, Quiriego, and Boroyeca, all of which lay along the suspected travel route of the Tomochitecos, further reinforced the overall mobilization, and Governor Izábal issued circulars identifying the quarry to all public authorities in the region and urging them to be on the lookout.[8]

The first response to this flurry of military activity was not encouraging for the government. The municipal president of Nuri, a substantial agricultural community in the northeast corner of the district, reported that their prey had passed through the village on December 29, but as the travelers had nonchalantly identified themselves as pilgrims heading for Cabora, a common sight in the pueblo, he had suspected nothing and allowed them to pass on unchallenged.[9] By now Chávez and his followers were further east, ascending the spectacularly formidable Sierra de Juliana, occasionally splitting up into groups of three to five, only to reassemble further up trail. This was no country for cavalry, and pursuit by infantry was exceedingly tedious and tiresome. Díaz warned his field commanders not to allow the enemy to escape to Chihuahua. Jesús G. Coronado, presidente municipal of Sahuaripa, assured the president that the flight of the rebels "must be desperate. They must know that they will have to surrender before entering Chihuahua or be exterminated."[10] But the Tomochitecos knew nothing of the sort.

Chihuahua sent security forces from its side of the state line to participate in the hunt, and Colonel Torres ran into them late the morning of December 30 at the hamlet of Peñitas high in the Sierra. Pursuing military units had spotted the refugees from time to time; they even exchanged some rifle fire. On each occasion the Tomochitecos had found shelter in the deep folds of the mountains. Governor Carrillo urged his forces to pursue the faithful pitilessly and transferred the remaining few soldiers in Tomochic itself to garrison the important and restless mining complex at Pinos Altos, which Chávez and his followers would pass en route home. Above all, he reasoned, unrest must not be allowed to spread to the already surly and restive miners.

To everyone's surprise, the governor forwarded a new strategy to the Guerrero district's jefe político, Silviano González: let the Tomochitecos return unmolested to their pueblo, and once there swoop in and capture them. "The [remaining] people [in Tomochic] are in no danger, because we may presume that the fugitives are already looking for a way to return to order."[11] Had the military tactics meant for the faithful at Cabora been communicated to Carrillo? Ever on the lookout for a negotiated resolution to this nasty affair, González must have concurred, for on the afternoon of January 25 Cruz and his followers, all well-armed, reentered the pueblo to the emotional embrace of their families.[12]

It had taken the group a good month to reach Tomochic, most of that time spent in the Chihuahua portion of the Sierra with which they were already quite familiar. Admittedly, they had needed precaution and time to dodge the military; still they passed a considerable spell in the mountains, one suspects, debating their future. As they approached Tomochic, several members of the band filtered down into the pueblo, presumably to make contact with friends and family. A few who had not joined the movement and had stayed in the village went into the mountains to meet the returning group, which is when they learned that the faithful had decided to come back and die with their families. But of the 30 men who had left Tomochic, 8 now seemed to be missing. Was Chávez suffering some defections? We do not know the names of the absent. Nevertheless, when we compare rosters of the group circulated after the first encounter with the army in December 1891 with one assembled about a year later, all the names on the first list—except Jesús José Chávez—appear on the second, which means that if defections occurred on the return from Cabora, they were not permanent.[13]

Typically, these kinds of religious movements breathe. Members, all of whom tote personal motivations and possess different levels of commitment, join, leave, rejoin, desert. One cannot expect complete concurrence when such fateful decisions as "to die with our families" are made. Was only Cruz Chávez speaking, or did such dire determination reflect the resolve of his group? And just what was the intention here? No doubt the faithful believed that they would soon be pounded by the army, and like other historical characters faced by such prospects they flaunted a willingness to die for their cause. But was something more at play? Did the faithful anticipate (or were they told) that they *must* die in order to usher in a new world of justice and plenty? In short, must they induce the apocalypse in order to bring on the millennium? Did they believe that if martyred they would be guaranteed salvation and a place at the side of God, or even be bodily resurrected to return to a new epoch on earth—a Mexico devoid of the anguish and suffering of the moment—a place of abundance and harmony? Such belief resides in many religious movements, some of them politically radical, and many hold that the succession of ordained events is promised in sacred scripture, it is just a matter of when. Humanity certainly has produced its enthusiasts anxious to hurry the moment.[14]

Grievances and Redress

The return of the faithful naturally stirred Tomochic. The jefe político, alerted that Chávez and his band were headed back to the village, ordered the place cleared of guns and ammunition. Then, to open the trap (as well as to stabilize an important mining site), the security force stationed there after the original outbreak of hostilities in December was transferred to Pinos Altos. The presidente municipal, Juan Ignacio Chávez, argued with the jefe político that any troublemakers in the area, knowing that most of the adult males had joined the religious faction, just might attack the defenseless homesteads in the valley. He did not identify the potential "troublemakers," nor were there reports of brigandage in the immediate environs. More likely the presidente feared the potential revenge of the faithful and therefore sought official permission to rearm the populace (meaning himself and his friends, but certainly not the kin of the pious). Juan Ignacio apparently did not like the answer he received from his superior, however, for he resigned office, and on January 19 the jefe named Bartolo Ledesma to the presidencia. But then Ledesma did his own quickstep out of town, advising the jefe político that he could neither read nor write and was, therefore, not qualified to be presidente (although he had previously held other public posts in the pueblo). Anyway, he could not possibly remain in the village because he had made promises to be elsewhere. This was deliberately vague, to be sure, but it worked. So the position fell once more to Reyes Domínguez, who reported in late January that he was trying to talk some sense into the returnees—to get them to recognize and submit to civil law. He told the jefe político, "If I get something out of them, I'll let you know."[15] Obviously he did not, because by mid-

February he too was begging out of the municipal presidency: Domínguez regretted having to leave but explained that his mother was sick in
Basúchil, near Guerrero City, and pleaded that he must remain at her
side until she recovered, which turned out to be until the dispute at
Tomochic had finally been settled. The jefe político then named the
schoolteacher Jesús Armenta as presidente, nothing more than an administrative formality. For all intents and purposes Cruz and his cohorts had control of community affairs. Could they be negotiated out
of their resistance, or did the faithful have other plans for themselves?[16]

Lauro Carrillo kept close track of all these maneuvers from the governor's palace in Chihuahua City, but now his personal political standing was truly precarious. With the gubernatorial election less than six
months away, President Díaz, anxious to calm political strife in the
state as well as to assure his own position, had abandoned Carrillo in
favor of outsider Miguel Ahumada, who could be counted on to mediate the president's differences with the powerful Terrazas clan. Moreover, in early January electoral differences in Ascensión, just south of
the frontier with New Mexico, had erupted in savage bloodletting. In
the wake of a disputed election there the secretary to the presidente
municipal had been killed, along with three other citizens, and it took
army units hastily summoned by the governor to quell the ensuing
riot.[17] Some suspected Catarino Garza, still on the loose along the
Lower Rio Grande, to be implicated in the upheaval, all of which further rattled Carrillo's rickety political structure. With the business of
Tomochic unfinished, Governor Carrillo feared further confrontation
and opted for negotiation. On February 7 he ordered Silviano González to cease all pursuit of the religious fanatics until the government
decided what to do.[18] That left the matter wide open but made a settlement possible, or so the governor thought.

Four days later—on February 11 in Chihuahua City—the government's appointed negotiator, Tomás Dozal y Hermosillo, rendered
Carrillo the report of a remarkable meeting with the Chávez brothers,
Cruz and Manuel, at which the dissidents aired their grievances. Carrillo's mediator, a longtime, respected resident of the Papigochic, was a
good choice to test the temper at Tomochic. He had held high public
office, and though not a trained lawyer, he possessed a certificate to
practice law. On different occasions others had employed him as a go-
between in disputes involving all levels of authority; indeed, he had

competently represented the interests of Papigochics to President Díaz himself. Furthermore, he had relatives among the Tomochitecos, a personal touch that enhanced chances of conciliation. On arrival at the pueblo, Dozal y Hermosillo was greeted by 30 members of the religious group—all toting rifles—who then designated Cruz Chávez to represent them in the talks. After a rest the negotiator settled into conversation with Cruz in the company of his brother, Manuel. To open, Dozal y Hermosillo assured his listeners of the sincerity of his mission and the benevolence of the governor, and then rather gently inquired why they had chosen to forsake civil authority. In response he received an earful.[19]

According to Cruz and Manuel, the only reason the faithful had armed themselves in late November 1891 was that a regional security force, acting on the orders of Joaquín Chávez, had a week or so before the initial encounter tried to arrest one of their followers, Jorge Ortiz, with the intention of forcing him into military service. Reyes Domínguez had told them as much. Furthermore, they had not meant to confront the troops when the military first arrived at the pueblo. They only left the church to consult over their concerns with the jefe político, Silviano González, but the soldiers had opened fire on them so they had to defend themselves. While en route to and returning from Cabora they had maintained this defensive attitude (apparently meant to include the ambush at El Alamo, although this was not specifically discussed). Moreover, they were neither bandits nor common thieves; while traversing the mountains, they had stolen nothing. However, at the start of their journey they did take two boxes of crackers, a couple of bundles of cloth, some sugar, and other items from the pack train entrusted to Jesús Medrano, but they would pay the owners for any losses. From the federal soldiers who fell at the El Alamo Rancho they took only five rifles and a saber, and then to avoid any accusations that they had looted the cadavers they sent a courier to the presidente municipal of nearby Batacosa telling him of the incident and suggesting he survey the blood-drenched site for himself. This sort of moral concern—a steady vision of the way things ought to be done—permeated the comments of Cruz and Manuel at the conference.

The pair saved the expression of their most profound indignation for Joaquín Chávez, whom they called their "tío"—more than uncle, or even a relative, but a trusted personal friend. How Joaquín had betrayed them. Beyond the Ortiz matter, he had reproached them for their religious beliefs and falsely contrived and circulated to authorities the wicked rumor that the believers at Tomochic intended to assault the silver bullion mule trains Joaquín periodically conducted through the mountains toward the mint at the state capital. Nothing, they averred, could have been further from the truth. In fact, Cruz and his followers offered to serve as security guards for any such precious shipments; they would guarantee its trouble-free transit, so strongly did they desire to prove their trustworthiness to their "tío" Joaquín, along with any others who doubted their intentions, integrity, and veracity.

But all this circled the real issue. That is, Cruz and his followers demanded the right to practice their religion as they saw fit—a *right*, they insisted, guaranteed by law and the national constitution. (At this point you hear Cruz, the stickler for law, speaking.) The leader of the religious movement denied telling the pueblo's former presidente that his group would recognize no authority but God, because the faithful duly recognized the need for government—they agreed that no society could exist without government. Thus the quarrel here was not with the state or national government per se, or even with the obnoxious presidente of the pueblo himself. In fact, Cruz emphasized that he and the others were disposed to obey officially designated local authorities like Juan Ignacio. They did not see themselves in rebellion against the state; rather "rebels" was a label fastened on them by the government, one the faithful did not care to wear. However, they did mean to worship, to pursue their spiritual lives, as they wished, as enabled by law, period. When Chávez and his followers berated curate Manuel Castelo and stormed out of the village church that momentous day, they in effect declared: "We are going to determine what our religion means to us and how we will practice it." As far as the faithful were concerned that was the heart of the matter plain and simple and a principle to be defended.

Dozal y Hermosillo countered immediately and very forcefully: even if the law offered freedom of religion, it also mandated restrictions on religious practice. It was "imprudent conduct," contrary to these prohibitions, that had led to the grave consequences Tomochic now suffered. Precisely what Dozal y Hermosillo meant by "imprudent conduct" is not clear. Certainly civil laws instituted by the Reform movement had restricted various religious practices such as processions without the permission of local authorities. One recalls the conflict between Cruz Chávez and Juan Ignacio Chávez over just this matter, and perhaps this was the mediator's point. More likely, however, he was referring to the declaration of the faithful to follow only the will of God (and Santa Teresa) over that of civil government. The only way out of their dilemma, he continued, was to plead for amnesty and to rely on the goodwill of the governor, who the mediator assured them was disposed to pardon the Tomochitecos and welcome them back into the body politic. This was no alternative for Cruz Chávez and the devotees. Call it amnesty or something else, they would neither confess nor make acts of contrition to ecclesiastical or civil authorities for exercising their rights. They had moved far beyond that sort of ritual cleansing. On this issue there was for them no justice but God's.

How to counter Cruz's intransigence? What to recommend to the governor? In his report to Carrillo, Dozal y Hermosillo first called attention to the clashing camarillas in Tomochic—the seemingly unbridgeable rifts between the Medranos and Reyes Domínguez, between Juan Ignacio Chávez and Cruz, between Padre Castelo and the faithful—and suggested that the governor name an outsider as the new municipal president, a person who held the confidence of all factions. Such an appointment would, he thought, calm the village and keep the restlessness from spreading to other inhabitants of the region. He also advised that the state finance a primary school in the pueblo. At the same time, he still saw the possibility that Cruz and his band would not disarm and could become lawbreakers in the surrounding Sierra. Therefore, he proposed in his report that the faithful be treated with "prudence and moderation until they themselves disband, for their religious fervor will soon become lukewarm, and they will comprehend that the promises of La Santa de Cabora and El Santo del Chopeque were nothing more than vulgar superstitions." Once they had disbanded, Dozal y Hermosillo thought it best that a military picket be permanently stationed in the village in order to assure the safe passage of convoys to and from the mines as well as to suppress any recurrence of unrest in the district. So the mediator remained unconvinced about the intentions of the faithful. Did he not take Cruz at his word that the faithful guaranteed the safe passage of mule trains through the village? Possibly his concern with the potential spread of turmoil in the Sierra simply swamped any trust he had for the faithful. After all, this mediator considered himself a "modern man," and while plainly well intentioned, he was blindly ignorant of the steadfast principles and irrepressible certitudes that compel the likes of a Cruz Chávez.

Fixing an Election

Governor Lauro Carrillo received the counselor's report in good faith, but was too distracted by his own personal political problems to act immediately on its conclusions. He fended off the concerns of President Díaz by shutting down two newspapers in the state capital that had reported to enthralled readers the holy marvels at Cabora and suggested that the governor of Sonora "finish with this fountain of miracles [Teresa] who has captivated the ignorant people of the region."[20] But he neither appointed an outsider as village presidente nor reestablished the primary school in Tomochic with state funding. He seems to have bought the negotiator's conclusion that if treated with "prudence and moderation" the religious movement would soon dissipate—that the devotees would lose faith in the visions and promises of their santos and recognize the error of their ways—though remembrance of the explosive controversy over the paintings must have given the governor pause.

Even if the governor had some misgivings about this approach to the troubles at Tomochic, it was about the best he could manage at the moment. By March it seemed that his most detested political rivals, the Terrazas group, had made unexpected headway. Despite rumors of a compromise candidate dictated by the president, Terrazas threatened to claim the governorship for himself. Early the next month Carrillo took a train to Mexico City to address Díaz face-to-face. At first the president demurred; he would not even grant the governor an appointment. It was not so much that he wished to rebuff Carrillo, but rather that he was doing everything he could to make it appear that he had no direct hand in Chihuahua's forthcoming elections, even though everyone knew the opposite. Finally, about April 10, he granted Carrillo his audience. We know not what words passed between them, or even if Díaz forthrightly confessed his intention to remove Carrillo in favor of Miguel Ahumada, but a deal does seem to have been struck: Carrillo agreed to step down in favor of Ahumada as long as Díaz blocked

Terrazas from the state house.[21] So Carrillo became the federal senator from Chihuahua, and on July 22 the legislature confirmed Miguel Ahumada as governor.[22] The president now had his man in the governor's chair and could get on with settling the troubles at Tomochic once and for all.

Building Their Utopia

Cruz Chávez and his people hardly leaped at the amnesty lure tossed by the mediator, Dozal y Hermosillo. It would be instructive to know how seriously they even considered amnesty, although they undoubtedly discussed it. Not a person that we know of ever defected from the cause and accepted amnesty, and one suspects that the offer—as such propositions often do—only further firmed the resolve of the pious to follow their own path and to accept (or welcome) their fate.

No public officials now remained in the village, and without their record keeping we have no idea what if any sort of governance took place. The faithful were in charge, but they certainly did not participate in June's state or national elections. Yet there must have been at least some discussion about the kind of world that they stood for. Cruz himself left some hints about such a vision in some very brief communications he had with authorities: first the reviled priest, Manuel Castelo, and then the district's civil officialdom. Recall that Cruz had sold a horse to the priest the summer of 1891; Castelo had promised a yoke of oxen in payment, but then the troubles intervened. Now, in June or July, Chávez sent an emissary to the priest's quarters in Uruáchic to collect the debt. Cruz no longer wanted the oxen in recompense; the faithful needed pesos right now to buy food, and he demanded 50 pesos ($40.00), a pretty hefty price for a horse at that time in the region. When Castelo could not be found at home, the courier left the note and departed, but Cruz did not receive the prompt response he expected, so in late August he sent a second note by carrier, and this time he meant business.[23]

The letter, written on official stamped paper but full of simple spelling errors, carried a well-drawn cross in one corner. It began in friendly enough fashion, "Estimado amigo," but then became threatening: "If you do not pay up, I will be forced to come and get it [the money] with my companions." Moreover, Cruz had upped the asking price to 60 pesos, plus travel expenses for the messenger, and reinforced his demand with a note to the municipal president saying that if the padre did not pay up, he would personally come to Uruáchic to collect. Chávez could have left the matter at that, but in his letter to the priest chose instead to emphasize the nature of the enterprise under way at Tomochic: "Each person who accompanies me earns four pesos daily, for in this [social] group there is no distinction between classes; we are all equal and we all enjoy the same *haber* [meaning assets or pay]."[24]

This statement both critiques Papigochic society as Chávez and the others knew it, and at the same time becomes a resounding proclamation about the way the world should be: Here we are equal; there are no classes. And as if to punctuate his resolve, one more thing: we pay our followers four pesos daily. Now, we may presume that no such payment was possible. Not only were the group—and the village—suffering extreme deprivation even as Chávez wrote the communication, but four pesos would have doubled or even more than tripled the accustomed daily wage in the area, even that earned in mining. No, Chávez intended that four pesos as a metaphor to declare that he and his followers were every bit as good as those who had money—that money was not the true measure of man—and in this he echoed the admonitions of Santa Teresa.

The sort of equality the faithful of Tomochic craved did not exclude the right to private property, and owners who sold or in other ways gave up their property deserved recompense, as we have just witnessed in the case of the horse. But the group's ethics and moral insistence in such matters became even more evident when they ran out of food and faced starvation in late July. Seeds were in the ground but harvest was still a good three to four months away. The state government had earlier alleviated the shortage of primary necessities with a few donations, but now the faithful and their families knew genuine hunger. Under such pressures the believers first begged relief from townsmen like Domingo López and Lisandro Domínguez (son of Reyes), who had left the pueblo when the faithful returned. Domingo and Lisandro periodically checked on their holdings, unimpeded by the hungry faithful, but while they had corn stored at their homesteads, they refused to surrender a grain of it to the increasingly desperate Cruz and his comrades. Instead they complained to authorities in Guerrero that in July the faithful had seized their corn and other (unspecified) property, and demanded that the government protect their interests.[25] Toward mid-August Chávez made ever more urgent appeals for assistance to the jefe político, Silviano González, and then to Reyes Domínguez himself, but again to no avail. The famished campesinos broke into the storehouse of Reyes Domínguez on August 17, but as they did so they sent a note of apology to the jefe político explaining that they were near starvation and had approached Reyes Domínguez for relief. They did not expect charity or goodwill, but at present they had no money to pay for the corn and would give Domínguez a promissory note to be paid off with appropriate interest out of their next harvest. An implacable Reyes Domínguez, however, would have none of it and carried a bitter grievance to the top, first in two letters to the military zone commander, General José María Rangel, and then directly to Porfirio Díaz. He demanded to know when the federal government was going to do something about these fanatical rebels who had turned to robbery.[26]

The president was not ignoring Tomochic, but had a good many other pressing matters on his mind. First of all, even those who had supported his reelection at their national convention in the capital had openly wondered about his advancing age (Díaz was a very fit 62), his possible successor, and the need to build some substantial administrative and legal structure in government—that is, to ease it from the unpredictable hands of a personal dictatorship.[27] Furthermore, Catarino Garza was still on the loose in the northeast, and Santa Teresa remained nettlesome; indeed some around her had taken a more aggressive stance against the Porfirian regime. There had been other outbursts of discord, headlined in newspapers, that had stained the country's image and made it less attractive to capital investors. Quoting a miner from Chihuahua's Sierra, the *New York Times* reported Mexico "in an unsettled and troubled condition [with a] revolutionary movement backed by the lower classes to a man," an exaggeration to be sure but nonetheless disturbing to moneyed groups.[28] Then there had been Chihuahua's tumultuous elections, the smoke of which had hardly cleared. Despite his other presidential priorities and pestering notes from the Reyes Domínguez types in his camp, Porfirio Díaz had hardly forgotten Tomochic and soon planned to pluck the burr from beneath his saddle.

Since January the faithful had more or less settled into their routines of worship, farming, and family life, knowing that the government was by no means done with them. Drought continued to hound the inhabitants, although July's rains, however scant, raised expectations for forthcoming relief and allowed the farmers to plant corn, especially down toward the river, now rushing with mountain runoff. Most of the farming had to be done by hand, because so many of the community's draft animals had been slaughtered by the military for food. It was said the pious farmed with one hand and held a rifle in the other. Yet the Tomochitecos chose to seek no remedy for their plight. They could have gone to work in mines that had started to recover from their downslide. Shipments to and from the mines passed through the village, but the faithful paid them no heed. They might have left the pueblo altogether and sought refuge higher in the Sierra or even the United States, but they preferred to stay and pray. Here were people awaiting the inevitable. Meanwhile, their reputation as ferocious, resolute fighters (perhaps with divine guidance) spread. It was murmured that they might take the offensive, and Ciudad Guerrero was named as a possible target. Other rumors had the political maverick Santana Pérez stirring up the miners at Pinos Altos, encouraging them to join the Tomochitecos in their struggles.[29]

Still, despite all the commotion surrounding the spectacular happenings at Tomochic, no outsiders came either to join or even support the faithful or to hinder them. Did no one care? A curious few wandered in and out of the pueblo, and the pious were amiable with all who did so, but nothing much else stirred. Both inside and outside the village people just waited. A flurry of excitement occurred in April when Mauricio Mendoza, one of those taken prisoner after the original battle, broke out of Guerrero City's jail and headed for home. Nine days later Julián and Antonio Rodríguez and Felipe Acosta did the same; shortly thereafter, three others followed. The same judge, Manuel Rubio, who initially had investigated the causes of the outbreak of hostilities, ordered the prisoners rearrested but had no heart for the chase. Authorities knew the escapees had returned to Tomochic but did not (or dared not) pursue them.[30] The ranks of faithful therefore swelled a bit, but only thanks to those already closely related to the pueblo; they were simply Tomochitecos coming back home. No doubt Cruz and his congregation had sympathizers as well as detractors among the general populace outside Tomochic, but all steered clear of involvement. Or so it seemed.

In the waning days of July a Tarahumara named Juan de la Cruz was rambling around a rancho called Arañas near Tomochic when he came upon a tattered leather pouch containing correspondence, broadsides, religious articles, and four small balls of a white powder that he recognized as a kind of saltpeter commonly used in native healings. There is no telling how far de la Cruz investigated the items in the bag, but he quickly realized their import and the possibility of official recrimination if they were found in his possession, and he almost certainly knew of the troubles at Tomochic. He hurried the pouch to Judge Rubio in Guerrero City, but when he could not find him, he turned to Temósachic's politically active priest, Julio Irigoyen (who we may recall had himself been in touch with Teresa). The curate then sorted through the contents of the bag: various lithographs of the Virgin of Cabora and other saints, seven scapularies (which remain undescribed), two pieces of (holy?) cloth (also undescribed), and the four little balls of ground saltpeter. Then he dug into the written and printed materials: circulars printed in Sonora and signed by Lauro Aguirre, the Spiritist, who seemed to be, at least to some degree, Teresa's mentor; three pages of maltreated and now all-but-illegible letters that appeared to be signed by Teresa Urrea in answer to queries by Carlos Medrano, one of the most socially prominent and more literate individuals among the faithful. Finally, there were four other letters addressed to Cruz and Manuel Chávez and dated from both 1891 and 1892.[31]

But this list is all we have; the exact dates and substance of this correspondence were not recorded. Nor do we have any idea of who owned the pouch and its contents, although we can assume it must have been one of these Tomochitecos we are studying. But now at least we have some evidence that Lauro Aguirre was campaigning actively (presumably against the Porfirian government) with broadsides that in the summer of 1892 were circulating far beyond Cabora. It was said that those broadsides were printed in Sonora, which could date them to the spring of that year before Aguirre fled to the United States. Most important, the contents of the pouch place the political radical in continuing close contact with Teresa Urrea. And we know that Carlos Medrano held a considerable correspondence with Teresa, as did Cruz and Manuel Chávez, some of it dating into the past year, although we do not know how far back. Quite possibly Teresa, or whoever wrote for her, addressed the Chávez brothers, while Medrano answered for them and the others. At any rate, we have Medrano among the leaders of the faithful along with Cruz and his brother Manuel, which is in keeping with the reality that the leadership of such religious movements normally involves more than the one highly visible figure purportedly touched by the Divine. Then we have the lithographs proclaiming Teresa to be La Virgen de Cabora and in the company of other Catholic saints at the side of God, all of which confers enormous power on La Santa. The scapularies found in the pouch probably were meant to protect the faithful against the bullets of their enemies and the little balls of white powder to heal the battle wounds of the pious. The contents of the leather bag seem to have been urging the Tomochitecos to battle with guarantees of divine assistance and salvation: this was a war pouch.

Authorities tussled over the spectacular find. Padre Irigoyen, who had always had his differences with officialdom, held the contents and the state demanded them from him. But the priest insisted that the material should be forwarded to Church, not civil, authorities—and at that point the paper trail ends. A search of both ecclesiastical and civil archives failed to uncover them.

Military sources heard early in the summer of 1892 that the faithful intended to return to Cabora for consultation with La Santa and that they were ready to fight it out with anyone who tried to impede them. In fact, the trip was not made, perhaps because about this time another santo had appeared closer to home. This new holy figure, named San José, was no itinerant like El Santo del Chopeque, but had settled down with his family at Piedra de Lumbre, a cluster of dwellings near the mining camps around Maguarichi in the neighboring district of Rayón. Tomochitecos had in other times worked those mines, but now they visited to converse with this tall, robust 60-year-old mestizo with a thick beard whose name was José Antonio Rodríguez. Reports had it that he originally hailed from the Papigochic and had visited Santa Teresa, where some Yaqui ranch hands noted his resemblance to Saint Joseph. They called him "San José," and the name stuck. Upon arrival at Piedra de Lumbre, San José commenced to baptize, marry, and perform other rites normally reserved to the official Church. In return the stream of pilgrims honored him with small gifts of money, crops, and animals. Some labeled him a *sucursal*—a kind of branch office—of Santa Teresa. A few Tomochitecos visited San José, who, while he did not openly endorse their stand against authority, was said to sympathize with it and to have reiterated that their faith would protect them from the bullets of their enemies. Teresa's influence seemed to be spreading and deepening, and now the faithful had further confirmation of the rightness of their course wherever it led them.[32]

Meanwhile, Santa Teresa, her followers, and the district around Cabora had been in turmoil. On May 15 Mayo Indians, shrieking "¡Viva la Santa de Cabora!," had in considerable number fearlessly assaulted the important regional center at Navojoa. Public officials and their supporters had been shot down defending the town's main plaza. The army had been summoned for emergency assistance, and blame for the bloody assault pointed directly to Teresa Urrea.

11

Exile and Exultation

THE MORNING OF May 15, 1892, broke clear over Navojoa, a fast-growing community of some 2,000 mostly mestizo inhabitants busily engaged in the commercial farming boom that had begun to energize the district. The town was a business hub on the north-south route along Mexico's Pacific coast, dealing in cotton, beans, chilies, tobacco, and grains grown along the nearby Mayo River and on the Yaqui River further north.[1] Because the Indians of the region continued to raid and otherwise aggressively resist the encroachment of others, people still referred to Navojoa in terms of its potential. But Navojoa was nonetheless a symbol of the sort of progress that Porfirian Mexico endorsed. In this largely desert area the two rivers had long been lifelines (both spiritual and material) for the Mayo and Yaqui Indians, but to the new regime they represented capitalistic potential. Something had to give. The government had spent much of the previous decade clearing the land and taming the natives and converting them into a responsible workforce for the new enterprise while driving off recalcitrants. Since this process took some doing, much of the area remained under martial law well into the 1890s. While the army struggled to keep a kind of peace, surveyors connected to the country's official Scientific Commission mapped out tracts for investors, who dredged the rivers to increase their flow and cut gaps in the banks to irrigate their fields.[2] Flourishing crops made the Navojoa district a showcase for what could be achieved with money and military muscle—at least until the Mayo challenged this symbol of Porfirian progress.

That morning more than 200 rebellious natives, some with firearms but most armed with their traditional bows and arrows, stormed Navojoa shrieking vivas to God and La Santa de Cabora. The town's presidente, Cipriano Rábago, rallied the few militiamen and soldiers available along with local volunteers and made a futile stand at the main plaza. The Mayo wave swept over the twenty-odd defenders, leaving Rábago and some others dead, along with eleven Indian attackers, and numerous wounded on both sides. The town's survivors retreated to the relative protection of the local flour mill, imposingly modern and the strongest structure in Navojoa, and from there continued the fight, awaiting the military assistance they had frantically solicited by telegraph. While the majority of Indians kept them busy, other Mayos looted the town for weapons, clothing, provisions, and cash—at one place, probably Navojoa's biggest general store, 4,000 pesos (well over $3,000). The fighting and sacking continued for three hours. When the natives learned that army reinforcements were approaching, they fled into the dense woods outside town, toward Cabora.[3]

The previous night the army in fact had learned through Mayo informants that armed groups of natives had gathered with the intention of attacking a pueblo in the region. Not knowing the precise target—Huatabampo, San Pedro, or Navojoa were named as possibilities—they had guessed wrong. Still, even as Navojoa suffered the assault, the army was on general alert and responded with dispatch.[4]

Army General José Tiburcio Otero, a tough officer who believed in reprisals as object lessons, headed the pursuit and within sight of Navojoa shot down ten or more Mayos said to be part of the assault party. Then his troop fanned out over the countryside, searching villages, coercing information from whomever they encountered, executing those Otero suspected of complicity. His daily reports recorded the mounting toll: "Four more killed; thirty-two captured, seven with rifles; others with bows and arrows."[5] Otero also reported that native families were coming to him to ask his protection against the renegades in order to return to work. No doubt a good many Mayo did just this to avoid persecution. At the same time some of the assailants sought refuge with their families and acquaintances, and when refused protection, they did not negotiate. For instance, when the comisario of Cuinampo, a village to which a group of the rebels belonged, refused them sanctuary, they killed him. But most of the original raiders sought safety away from their kin and friends, and the hoof prints of their horses pointed to their intended refuge: the rancho of Cabora.[6]

Meanwhile, at military headquarters in Cócorit, zone commander General Abraham Bandala interrogated prisoners and awaited orders from Governor Izábal and President Díaz. Two leaders of the attack on Navojoa, Juan Tebas and Manuel Torigoqui, convinced the general that their assault had no overtly political ends; they never aimed to unseat recognized political authority. Asked about the recklessly daring aggression against Navojoa, the natives responded that they had been driven to such action by their belief in La Santa de Cabora. Teresa had inspired (ordered?) them to attack Navojoa. Bandala recalled in a telegram to Díaz that in the past the army had not acted decisively to expel the Urreas "who exploit these ignorant people." This backhanded slap at the zone's former commander, the late General Marcos Carrillo, with whom he had frequently been at odds, was a cheap one, for Bandala understood as well as anyone else that decisions to remove political antagonists came from above.[7] That is why he himself rather knavishly reminded the president that Teresa's name had been invoked in the uprisings at Tomochic, as well as Navojoa, and inquired of Díaz what should be done to prevent further bloodshed in the district. The president responded as if he had already made up his mind on that issue; he had now had enough of the Urreas. At orders from Díaz, Governor Izábal consulted with General Bandala about a place to which the Urreas could be exiled and silenced. That issue settled, the general marched on Cabora.[8]

La Santa's Travail

On May 19, four days after the Navojoa affair, General Bandala resolutely set out toward Cabora with 100 infantrymen from the Twenty-fourth Batallion and 28 cavalrymen from the Twenty-eighth Regiment. En route he linked up with General Otero's troop. This was a sizable military force, a show of strength, for the government was plainly apprehensive of what might happen to its armed forces in the presence of La Santa de Cabora. The troop arrived at dawn that day, and Bandala called the scene he found ugly: all those crippled and blind people, so

much filth. But calm prevailed. Sighting horse tracks on the rancho that
indicated those involved in the attack on Navojoa had indeed come to
Cabora, Bandala ordered the mayordomo of the place to use his vaqueros to round up suspects. He corralled fifteen, but most of their
quarry had fled further on toward the Sierra at the sight of the soldiers.
With the situation under control, Bandala brusquely arrested Teresa
and her father, Tomás, and formally charged them with the attack on
Navojoa. He told them that their days at Cabora had ended; the government had decided to exile them far from the rancho. He gave them
only enough time to assemble a few personal items for the journey, for it
would not have been wise to tarry too long among the followers of
Teresa. No good-byes, no public promises to return, but this hardly
dampened the expectations of the faithful.[9]

The Santa and her father offered no resistance, and neither did the
hundreds—perhaps thousands—of her devotees camped at Cabora.
They did nothing. Only God could prepare the path and decide the fate
of saints: let God's will be done. Bandala escorted the pair from Cabora
to his headquarters at Cócorit to await further orders. Meanwhile, a
very troubled President Díaz pondered his next move. He so feared the
power of Teresa to incite religious enthusiasm that he ordered Bandala
to separate her from the ordinary soldiers at the army post: "Those
men are also ignorant and could become troublesome. Perhaps it is
best that you transfer her to Guaymas."[10] The move occurred the next
day under an armed escort of some two dozen soldiers. The Urreas
traveled in a closed carriage, shielded from most onlookers, but as
the entourage approached the outskirts of Guaymas, people who had
learned of her coming, most of them Indians, flocked to catch a glimpse
of her. Some watched from the surrounding hillsides while others knelt
at the roadside in order to adore her—and undoubtedly a fair number
showed up out of plain inquisitiveness, disdain, or disbelief.[11]

Teresa later asserted that once in town she was lodged in the governor's mansion, an uncomfortable, smelly place overlooking cattle pens,
where the mosquitoes and stifling heat bothered her all night.[12] In fact
none of this happened; Teresa was only embellishing her story for journalists eager for spicy details of her quarrel with Mexican authorities.
Instead, the officials entrusted her to the guardianship of a noted lawyer, J. M. Gaxiola, who seems to have done her no disservice. There
was a good deal of commotion around the attorney's house itself, how-

ever. Crowds of curious people and others anxious for Teresa's blessing thronged the site, among them notables from the port's upper class as well as humble Indians from the native barrios. Only a police cordon around the house kept the mass of people at any distance. Still, religious enthusiasm can build spontaneously and quickly breach police lines, so the government decided to remove the Urreas from Guaymas and to hasten them to some far off destination.[13]

Urgency with good reason. Inflammatory (and wildly inaccurate) statements about the government's intentions toward Teresa had leaked out. F. M. Hartner, an American businessman with a mercantile outlet in Guaymas, had told the curious in San Antonio, Texas, that a judge in the port city had already convicted Teresa of witchcraft—that is, that she preached harmful magic and worshipped the Devil (still a vital strain in Mexican popular culture and punishable by authorities who have a mind to do so)—and sentenced her, along with her father (identified as a very poor goat rancher), to be shot, although the sentences had been commuted to imprisonment. The *New York Times* picked up the story and added that her fame among the Mayo and Yaquis and in Chihuahua was so great that the government had decided to "put her away." According to the report, Teresa had offered no defense at her trial and now quietly awaited her fate. Angry Mayos, meanwhile, had gone on the warpath (a reference to Navojoa), "and have devastated vast amounts of property and created much terror among ranch owners."[14]

Díaz must have boiled at such adverse publicity, and now he offered the Urreas a choice: prison or exile. Prison quite likely meant the dank cells of San Juan de Ulúa, the massive former colonial fortress in Veracruz. This amounted to a death sentence from malaria or yellow fever, so Teresa and her father chose exile and were told to go either far to the south to an obscure village on the Pacific coast near the boundary with Guatemala or north to the United States, not too close to the border, but fairly well into the country, say in a city like Tucson in the Territory of Arizona. The Urreas chose Tucson.[15] We know no further details of the agreement. Was the exile to be permanent, or was there a time limit that would allow the family to return after a cooling-off period? Had the U.S. government been consulted? What of the Urrea properties at Cabora? Were the ranchos protected or to be confiscated?

Did Lauro Aguirre, in Guaymas at the time, help the Urreas make up their minds about "the best course to follow"? It was a decision Díaz lived to regret, but perhaps it could have been no different. Even for dictators choices can be limited, and the president dared not chance martyring Santa Teresa. Thus when Governor Izábal reported that the Urreas were on their way to exile in Tucson, Díaz responded simply, "Thanks for the news."[16]

On June 2, Teresa and Tomás journeyed by train from Guaymas to Nogales, a bustling young (only ten years old) town of 4,000 literally split in two by the international line. Once on the U.S. side, they received a tumultuous welcome from town officials and the business community as well as those in need of miraculous healing. The merchants knew a tourist attraction when they saw one and began to take up a collection among locals to finance the purchase of a house in Nogales for the Urreas. Meanwhile, authorities lodged Teresa and her father in a comfortable downtown hotel where the surrounding scene soon resembled a street fair. Hawkers by no means outnumbered the devoted, but they surely made more noise and bustle. At the same time the *New York Times* printed a retraction of sorts concerning its earlier report on the impending execution of Teresa. Now the paper blamed the Mexican government for deliberately circulating accounts of Teresa's death in order to "quell the excitement among restless Indians flooding to Nogales to see her for cures."[17] The Mexican government understood the repercussions of martyrdom, however, far better than did the editors of the *Times*.

The Glory of the Coming

Mexican authorities were indeed troubled, but not so much by those who truly sought to be healed by Teresa. They learned that Yaquis who went to Teresa for cures were returning with rifles and other weapons, and perhaps—we can only speculate—advice from La Santa about how to use them against their enemies. Or maybe she guaranteed them divine protection against the projectiles of their foe. At the same time Tomás Urrea, plainly angered at the expulsion, had become overtly anti-Porfirian in his public statements, and a patently aggressive poem dedicated to Santa Teresa emerged from the underground to appear in print. Here was a strident plea from the pained:

> You are named by heaven
> Because the Lord chose you,
> Teresita was your name
> As soon as dawn broke through.
>
> Wake up, loving girl,
> For God has chosen you
> To be our defender
> As soon as dawn broke through.
>
> . . .
>
> Protectress and advocate,
> Blessed the sun that shone on you
> Upon your divine beauty,
> As soon as dawn broke through.
>
> Thank goodness we've come
> To this rancho to rest a bit.
> Come, come, all you sinners,
> To pay this girl a visit.
>
> . . .
>
> Sinners we have been
> Who will always say to you, lead on.
> Here you have a slave for you
> In your heavenly home.
>
> . . .
>
> Here you have your peoples,
> Fill them with your blessing
> And beg the Virgin in heaven
> To pray for our forgiving.
>
> In you I hope, beautiful girl,
> And in the Archangel Saint Michael
> That in life and in death
> We shall win against the Devil.[18]

This poem recognizes the people surrounding Santa Teresa in Nogales and is the clearest statement we have about their condition. First
of all, they have refigured the border town of Nogales into a "rancho," a
place perhaps like Cabora, but certainly one where common country
people frequently gather and feel right at home. But there are (unspecified) troubles, a terrible oppression, weighing them down. They blame
themselves in moral terms for their afflictions; they freely proclaim
themselves sinners and seek the intercession of the Virgin Mary for ab-
solution. But then Teresa appears among them, and a new day dawns.
She has been "chosen by the Lord" to be their "defender," their "protectress and advocate." "What a lucky morning" continue passages of
the poem, "the day that gave birth to you. . . . At that moment / your
invocation around us flew / through cities, towns, and villages." Teresa
has become a wake-up call to these people, who transformed her into a
kind of Holy Deliverer. American newspapers even called Teresa the
new Joan of Arc. One might wonder what the Yaquis knew of that
fourteenth-century visionary who identified with prophesies about a
virgin who would rescue her homeland from invaders and inspired
French armies to turn back the English, but her image to this day
inspires believers of Mexican origin.[19]

Nor was La Santa de Cabora to act alone as defender and advocate
of these people. The poem also summoned forth Saint Michael, the
archangel, the guardian of Christian armies in their battles with heathens. There stands this archangel, sword in one hand, scales of justice
in the other, in combat with (or victorious over) the dragon—the per-
sonification of evil, of Satan and his accomplices. The words of the
poem are worth repeating: "In you I hope, beautiful girl, / And in the
Archangel Saint Michael / That in life and death / We shall win against
the devil." They remind us of humanity's continuing struggle against
the forces of the Devil. But we are going to fight them, even to the
death, and we shall win. The political connotations are also clear, in
all their desperation and ardor. This was a commitment, whether La
Santa de Cabora endorsed it or not.

"As dawn broke through"—over and over again, we hear this refrain.
What is happening in the minds of these enthusiasts "as dawn breaks
through"? Here the poem seems to refer to the Second Coming—the
Promise fulfilled. Christ is returning at this Golden Daybreak to set

things right. This theme—"Some glorious morning, sorrow will cease. / Some glorious morning, all will be peace"—reverberates through the militant millenarian strain in religious fervor today.

Healing and Politics

Whatever Teresa's influence in this mood both joyful and ominous, it frightened Mexican officialdom to the point that authorities sought to move her farther from the border, as they originally had planned, at least to Tucson. General Bandala asked the U.S. mayor of Nogales, Manuel Mascareñas, to remind the Urreas of their promise to settle in Tucson, which the mayor did, but he did not insist that they do so. In support of the mayor, American newspapers rattled the sword. For instance, the *Phoenix Weekly Herald* noted that Mexican authorities were harassing Teresa and that the residents of Nogales were "hot at the annoyance. Teresa and her father refuse to obey further mandates [from Mexico]. Should any attempt be made to spirit them back across the line, there will be a lively time of it."[20]

For their part, the Urreas moved into an ample, well-furnished house provided by the "grateful citizens of Nogales" and declared that they intended to remain in Nogales and build a large hospital there for the infirm who journeyed to see Teresa. An estimated crowd of 5,000—Americans and Mexicans of all social classes—surrounded the home each day and all night. Teresa ministered to her followers daily, while petty business swirled around them: pushcarts and stalls vending their milagros, candles and more candles, statues of Jesus, charms to ward off the evil eye, and scapularies in cruciform, reading on one side, "Salvé, O Teresa Amada" (Hail, Oh beloved Teresa), and on the other "The great power of God reigns upon earth." The scene was one of both joy and longing. Noise and color bombarded the senses, along with the smells of *chicharrón* frying in deep, bubbling fat, smoke from the charcoal fires that heated strong coffee and seared *carne asada*. Foods fed the body; these scents fed memory and the soul. People wanted others far away to know they had been part of this grand theater, and the city's local newspaper, the *Southwestern Advertiser*, announced that it had "arranged for a large number of photos of the lady

[Teresa], a 14″ × 22″ copy of which will be forwarded to any address for fifty-cents American or seventy-five centavos Mexican."[21]

Despite all this hullabaloo, Tomás was deeply worried that the Mexican government would attempt to kidnap his daughter and himself and whisk them back across the border to an uncertain fate. For his protection he had a document notarized naming the Mexicans responsible for "anything serious" that might happen to him or his daughter. Then the pair traveled to Tucson to inaugurate legal proceedings for U.S. citizenship. Quite probably the Urreas had no particular interest in becoming U.S. citizens, but sought the sanctuary of American law that sheltered political dissidents as long as they did not try to raise revolution in places deemed friendly to the United States. It was a law that could be stretched over a variety of diplomatic dilemmas or not invoked at all. All depended on the politics of the moment, and Mexico had yet to make a successful case for extradition.[22]

An unhappy Mexican government dared not create an international incident over it. Its consul in Nogales, Felipe A. Zabadie, kept a close eye on the Urreas while investigating Tomás's political activities at Cabora; Zabadie concluded that Tomás had decided not to re-engage himself with Sinaloan politics, "because he has had some run-ins with justice there." Nor had he gone into the Sierra to encourage the Tomochitecos who had "risen up shouting 'Viva la Santa de Cabora!'" At that time, Tomás had steered clear of outright political involvement. However, the consul did note that the American press had cast Teresa as a "martyr, unjustly expelled from her country, despoiled of her wealth, sentenced to death, pardoned, and exiled."[23] And Lauro Aguirre, already considered a political firebrand and angered by failed business dealings in Guaymas, had moved to Nogales to be near the Urreas.

For the time being, at least, the Urreas settled into a kind of routine. Gabriela, the much-loved mistress of Tomás, arrived from Cabora to console him. We wish that she had brought us some news of the rancho since the departure of Teresa and her father, but the record is silent on that point. The great gatherings there seem simply to have melted away in the absence of their beloved Santa. Perhaps they received a bit of a push from the military, and we have no idea of how many of the believers may have journeyed to the border to renew their adoration of the young girl. A good many undoubtedly anticipated her return. Still, silence from Cabora. Rumors sprang up that Teresa had recrossed the

border and headed for the rancho, where she rallied masses of Indians
to her cause, now said to have a sharp, antigovernment political edge.
Nothing of this sort ever happened. Teresa was "sighted" here and
there in Mexico's north, but she never really materialized. The chances
are she never left the U.S. Southwest, even though in their minds people placed her where they wished. But as for Cabora itself, the spectacle
there had played its last.

Teresa was by no means through, however, and she continued her
spectacular cures in the Nogales area. By one report she restored to
sanity a mentally ill woman who had impulsively stripped naked on a
Nogales street. Teresa persuaded her to sit on a swing over an open irrigation ditch filled with water. La Santa firmly pushed the swing and
set it in motion back and forth, back and forth over the ditch. Then
she suddenly cut the rope that held the swing and the confounded
woman splashed into the water below. The result: she never again dis-
robed in public.[24]

Now for Tomochic

With Teresa exiled, although still bothersome, the Mexican government resolved to cure its problem at Tomochic. Let us remember the
complaints of Reyes Domínguez directly to Porfirio Díaz that Cruz and
his people had looted in the pueblo. Díaz had asked his regional military commander, General Rangel, what could be done about it. Rangel
had replied that the only way to protect the interests of Domínguez and
the others who had not "rebelled" was to launch the long-delayed military campaign against the village. The general's telegraphic dialogue
with the president went as follows:

RANGEL: Should we start up the campaign [against Tomochic]?
DÍAZ: Do you believe that with the elements [of war] that you have
    at your disposition you can end the campaign in short time?
        Do we still need a permanent force at Palomas [a small Mexi-
    can village just south of Columbus, New Mexico, thought to be
    threatened by Catarino Garza]? Or can we remove the unit?

RANGEL: Yes, the campaign can be ended in short order. Yes, the forces on hand are sufficient, including those provided by the state government who know the terrain. We do not need detachments in either Palomas or Ojinaga [across the Rio Grande River from the Texas hamlet of Presidio], because the bandit Garza has disappeared.

DÍAZ: Reconcentrate [into the garrison at Chihuahua City] the troops at Palomas and Ojinaga. How many men do you have, including assistance from the state [Chihuahua]? What are your operational plans?

Then the president wired General Bandala in Sonora: "Rangel is opening the campaign against Tomochic. Send Colonel Lorenzo Torres with *gente de país* [state militiamen and volunteers] to form a rear guard."[25]

Now the president was serious. Even if Rangel felt he could solve the problem on his own, Díaz wanted Torres there to ensure that no one escaped—no more futile chases in the Sierra, no further sparks that could ignite other dissidence, no additional speculation and publicity that belied the government's propaganda about a contented, peaceful country. State politics had been decided in favor of Ahumada, and the ousted Carrillo tucked out of the way. So now—finally—the campaign against Tomochic could commence with the expectation of a speedy resolution.

12

A Terrible Swift Sword

A SINGLE-MINDED GENERAL RANGEL arrived with his troop of some 200 soldiers on the heights to the northeast of Tomochic on September 1, 1892. The next morning he confidently planted the colors and readied for the attack. Prudence, not to speak of the president's orders, dictated that General Rangel await the arrival of supporting units from the west, those of Captain Francisco Castro from Pinos Altos and of General Torres from Sonora. Even if not needed for the direct assault on the pueblo, they would help prevent the defenders from fleeing into the Sierra. But Rangel thought he could handle all that himself. Victory at Tomochic offered a splendid opportunity to curry favor with the president. No doubt Rangel foresaw only limited resistance, such as that which had occurred in the initial encounter at the pueblo.[1]

With no probing and little rest, with limited intelligence about the enemy, and with no intention of waiting for those supporting troops headed from the west, Rangel readied for the clash. The general calculated that he would confront 38 rebels; in actuality nearly twice that number were ready for him. In keeping with the strategy outlined in the official army training manual, the general divided his forces into three small columns, one of 70 soldiers at the center commanded by Lieutenant Colonel José María Ramírez, the other two on the flanks, 44 local militiamen under Captain José María Vergara, and 40 federal infantrymen led by Captain Melitón Ordóñez. The attack plan resembled a huge V—a wedge with Ramírez at the point and Vergara and Ordóñez at the sides. Santana Pérez with his contingent of 30 provided the rear guard from the heights of the Cordón de Lino overlooking the valley from the east. Rangel, his small staff, a military doctor, and Joaquín Chávez, plus an escort of six cavalrymen, commanded the engagement from the opening of the V. All appeared picture-perfect for the assault.[2]

Ramírez advanced his contingent down the mountainside along the main road into the settlement at 9 o'clock the morning of September 2. A contingent of maybe fifteen or twenty Tomochitecos hunkered down behind the stone walls of the cemetery where the road leveled out into the pueblo. When the troops passed close by, they opened fire, virtually at pointblank range: "¡Viva la Santísima de Cabora!" Devastation followed. A bullet from the first volley shattered an arm of Lieutenant Colonel Ramírez and put him out of action. With little natural protection from the terrain, soldiers became easy targets. The two flanking units, pinched in by the topography, came to the rescue but were themselves quickly engulfed by contingents of defenders who struck their flanks. Ramírez's troops bent and then broke. Captain Vergara was shot dead straightaway, and with him down his unit split and ran. Officers who tried to rally the terrified soldiers themselves fell, wounded or dead. Rangel moved forward with his staff and escort to stem the impending catastrophe, but to no use: Major Abraham L. Prieto, chief of staff, was killed and the escort overrun. A headlong retreat followed. Soldiers screamed and fell dead; others lay wounded in agony; dozens surrendered. The furious episode lasted little more than an hour.[3]

The defeat of the federal army was total. Vergara lay dead, along with twelve of his security force. Seven others had been wounded and nine taken prisoner, five of those nine also wounded. The militia unit also saw its commander, Ordóñez, and four men killed, one wounded, and nine taken prisoner. The federales had 11 killed, including Major Prieto and Lieutenant Domingo Manzano, an unreported number wounded, and 33 taken prisoner. Most devastating of all, General Rangel and his party were missing and presumed captured.[4]

The remaining members of the decimated military contingent limped back into Guerrero, and we can imagine the consternation—indeed horror—with which residents of that city witnessed their return. Nothing like this had been remotely foreseen. Rumors rapidly circulated that the victorious Tomochitecos might soon try to take Guerrero itself, and the *New York Times*, though it again had its facts badly garbled, darkly predicted "the beginning of [widespread] hostilities" in

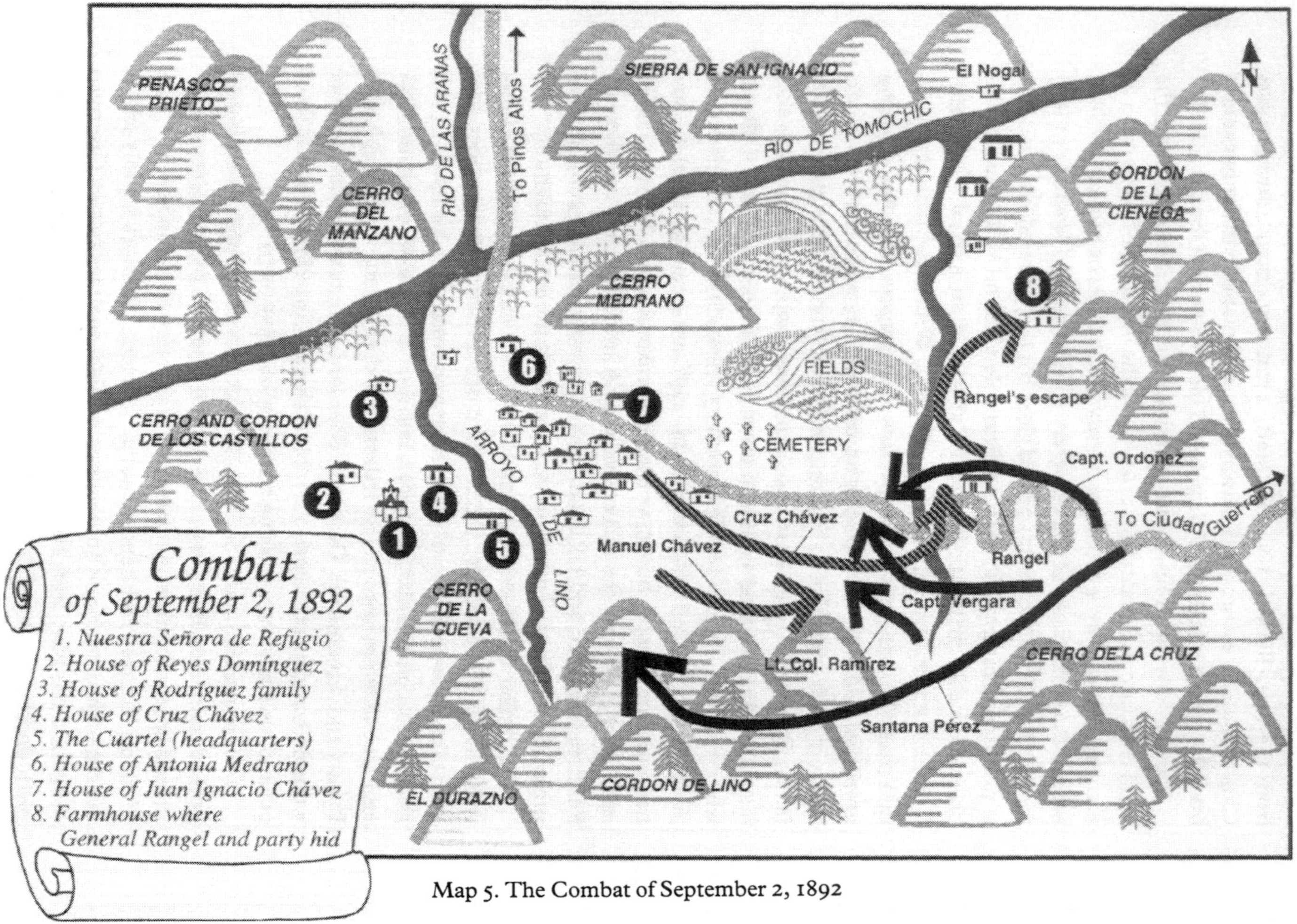
N
PENASCO PRIETO
CERRO DEL MANZANO
RIO DE LAS ARANAS
To Pinos Altos
SIERRA DE SAN IGNACIO
El Nogal
RIO DE TOMOCHIC
CORDON DE LA CIENEGA
CERRO MEDRANO
FIELDS
CEMETERY
CERRO AND CORDON DE LOS CASTILLOS
ARROYO DE LINO
Rangel's escape
Capt. Ordoñez
To Ciudad Guerrero
Cruz Chávez
Manuel Chávez
Rangel
Capt. Vergara
Lt. Col. Ramírez
Santana Pérez
CERRO DE LA CUEVA
CERRO DE LA CRUZ
CORDON DE LINO
EL DURAZNO
Combat
of September 2, 1892
1. Nuestra Señora de Refugio
2. House of Reyes Domínguez
3. House of Rodríguez family
4. House of Cruz Chávez
5. The Cuartel (headquarters)
6. House of Antonia Medrano
7. House of Juan Ignacio Chávez
8. Farmhouse where General Rangel and party hid

Map 5. The Combat of September 2, 1892

which "the success of the Indians will encourage the dissatisfied element of Mexico to a general uprising."[5] Porfirio Díaz and the backers of his regime feared the same.

Causes of Disaster

Preparations for the army's attack on Tomochic had not gone smoothly. As in all such Mexican military offensives of that time, the government combined federal units with state and local security contingents. The strategy augmented troop size and provided local intelligence, but more important, it gave the impression of broadened community support for the venture (a campesino or a merchant would be much more likely to support an operation in which his son was a militiaman) and aimed to create the aura that one's own neighbors would not tolerate public dissidence.

When it came to enlisting local men for his campaign, General Rangel recognized that militia are only as dependable as their leaders, and that more often than not it is loyalty to their leader, usually a well-known local personage, that holds these forces together in combat. Battle experience had taught that once their leaders fell or faltered, the militia units dispersed—which is why the enemy targeted ranking militia officers from the start. With this in mind, Rangel naturally turned first to leadership of known sympathies. Captain Joaquín Chávez could be counted upon to serve with his security unit, and Major Santana Pérez, decidedly less predictable, probably would raise a troop for pay. Both had participated in the earlier pursuit of the Tomochitecos, although in the case of Pérez, how vigorously is another question.

Governments tolerate such security groups when they have few reliable units of their own, as was the case in late-nineteenth-century Chihuahua, but Captain Chávez ranked among the notables of the Papigochic, was therefore no threat and could be kept on retainer. Santana Pérez was another matter—cross him and you could have a dangerous adversary on your hands. Then again, you might have the same even if you didn't cross him, for Pérez would bargain his support with almost anyone. The arrangement was chancy, but Rangel had few other options and he planned to move quickly. The general's strategy was to catch the enemy off guard, to surprise the faithful with one swift, crushing blow. As a tactic (probably recommended by the president himself) he encouraged the negotiator Tomás Dozal y Hermosillo to return to Tomochic in order to parley with Cruz and his cohorts; to tell them that amnesty remained a possibility if they would only agree to respect civil authority, lay down their weapons, and surrender. All along Rangel suspected what the answer would be "None but the justice of God!" but he banked on the talks misleading the faithful about the government's real intentions, to bind the defenders in place at least long enough for his final preparations to jell.[6] The general did not want any forewarned and frightened Tomochitecos escaping to the mountains.

In his effort to deceive the enemy, Rangel also decided against a general mobilization, which would have sent reverberations throughout the region as individuals scurried to evade military service. Instead, he picked small contingents from several locales: fifteen soldiers from the detachment at Pinos Altos, only a couple of hundred from his own large garrison in Chihuahua City, most of the unit of thirty-odd men at Ciudad Guerrero, and the militia units. In late August he sent out word to rally all these forces in Guerrero, but when he arrived on August 29, nothing had been accomplished; no one had been assembled. Why the breakdown? Authorities claimed they had received no orders to mobilize the units. With marching orders to Tomochic delayed, Rangel feared that he had lost the element of surprise. Now his prey might scatter to the winds.[7]

When Rangel finally drew into sight of Tomochic on September 2, he found that no one had fled for the asylum of the Sierra; instead the Tomochitecos were spoiling for a fight against the Sons of Satan. The raw numerical odds against the defenders were great, but when terrain and other customary defensive strengths were added in, not overwhelming. No doubt the general underestimated his enemy.[8]

Porfirio's Army

The Porfirian military, of course, had its own agenda and mind-set. Among top-ranking officers, the generals (and there was a huge surplus of generals) were for the most part as committed to the president, himself a renowned general, as he was to them. A large number of these officers had originally enlisted in a variety of local, state, and federal military organizations as relative youngsters and been promoted through the ranks, a path eased by civil war and foreign intervention, during which they had the good fortune to ally themselves with the eventual winner, Porfirio Díaz. As president, Díaz repaid that loyalty with military advancement, padded payrolls, and political appointments. In the case at hand there are several examples. Rangel had previously been both political prefect and military chief of the port of Guaymas and later jefe político and military commander of the federal Territory of Baja California. Carlos Pacheco, badly wounded retaking the city of Puebla from French interlopers in 1867, two decades later was a Díaz cabinet minister and at the same time the governor of Chihuahua. Abraham Bandala joined the national guard in his home state of Veracruz at age twenty, fought with Díaz at Puebla, and was promoted to lieutenant colonel some ten years later when he supported Díaz's successful challenge for the presidency. About the time of the troubles at Cabora, Díaz made him brigadier general, and Bandala later served as governor of the state of Tabasco on no fewer than nineteen occasions. Lorenzo Torres, now well into his fifties, also fought the French and endorsed Porfirian aims; he became governor of Sonora. The pattern held for two other generals we are about to meet: Felipe Cruz and Rosendo Márquez. Cruz hailed from the president's home state of Oaxaca and at age eighteen joined the army as an infantry soldier. Díaz named him colonel in 1880 and within six years promoted him to general. During his career Cruz was jefe político and military commandant in the region of Tlaxiaco in Oaxaca. Márquez was only twenty in 1857 when he joined the national guard in the federal territory of Tepic, and Díaz secured his potential support with appointments to cavalry colonel in 1871 and brigadier general five years later. In the 1870s he was jefe político at various times in the state of Jalisco and the territory of Tepic as well as a deputy to the national congress, later becoming the governor of the state of Puebla. It is clear, then, how Díaz treated his army comrades and how civil and military authority melded during his regime.[9]

At times, of course, the mesh between generals and the state unraveled, and of course there were important generals who all along had not much favored Díaz, but by and large the president made the rank profitable enough to insure the allegiance of his generals. Often the relationship involved a personal loyalty, seemingly a kind of affection, that cut both ways. Rosendo Márquez reflects the pattern: Governor Már-

quez was the first ranking politician to propose that the country's constitution be altered to permit presidents to seek consecutive terms of
office, a change of which Díaz took advantage in 1888. A bit later, when
Díaz suggested that the governor name one of the president's friends a
jefe político in Puebla, Márquez responded, "You know, señor, your
slightest indication is a command for me."[10] The president regularly
called in his generals for personal chats, or they stopped by to see him
with face-to-face reports. In fact, Rangel could not wait to tell his commander-in-chief about the curious religious fanatics at Tomochic.[11]
For his part, Porfirio Díaz was extraordinarily sympathetic to his former comrades in arms, even when they courted military disaster.

Although this "old boy" practice filtered down into the ranks of
lower officers, there was a publicly proclaimed endeavor to profession-
alize the military corps as part of the government's overall intention to
make Mexico modern. French and German advisors helped to reorganize the old Military College and to introduce the latest in weaponry,
tactics, and administration.[12] Such professionalization hardly removed
the army from civil matters; just the opposite. It honed skills in mathematics, surveying, foreign languages, telegraphy, and detailed record
keeping, all of which could be (and often were) used to strengthen the
military's hand in normally civilian affairs. We have as examples an
army survey crew mapping out and dividing up Yaqui lands to be delivered to private enterprise, and army personnel as fiscal agents along the
borders. The military used the blanket of martial law and extraordinary
powers granted by congress to assume judicial and administrative control of troublesome regions. Under such authority it could exile the
likes of Santa Teresa. While the Porfirian army is best remembered for
how the president used it to forge his dictatorship, to capture, centralize, and maintain his power, and to show off his nation-building project
to the world, its real importance lay in the myriad ways it worked to
regiment the lives of ordinary people to coincide with the objectives of
the dictatorship.

Filling the Ranks

With reason, common folks feared the army for its demonstrated brutality, its arbitrary confiscations of private property, its swaggering ar-

rogance, but most of all for the forced conscription that fed its ranks. Of course, merchants with food and brew to sell, as well as local officials with buildings to rent, welcomed a detachment of soldiers in their midst. And certainly there was a steady trickle of volunteers for military service, some to escape personal unpleasantness at home, others in search of social mobility, a good many to get some equipment, perhaps a rifle and a horse, and then to desert, but the great majority of rank-and-file soldiers were either drafted under the guise of local lottery or brazenly dragooned directly into the army. If they expected to keep their jobs, local civilian officials had military quotas to fill, so within their jurisdictions those judged to be ne'er-do-wells, unruly, or otherwise troublesome, political antagonists and commercial rivals alike, ended up in army uniform along with those suspected or convicted of crimes, both petty and more grave.[13] The political opponent of a municipal president might lose his workers or even a son or two to the draft. Exemplifying this practice, Rafael Pimentel, the president's watchdog in Chihuahua, wrote to Díaz in July 1892: "Among replacements [levied for the army] are some ten electoral pen-pushers [officials], who have caused me great trouble. Therefore, I want to send them under escort to Yucatán [fearsome military dumping ground for political malcontents, who, once there, faced the rebellious Maya as well as rampaging yellow fever]. These people must understand the respect due the government, and even more so when for more than a year, they have been compromised." The president immediately wired back his concurrence with Pimentel's position.[14]

Naturally, there was resistance. Faced by the draft, men ran off and hid in the tangle of an urban barrio or in the craggy mountains near their pueblo. Bribes bought freedom in any number of cases, or the better-off might pay someone less fortunate to do their military service for them. With the assistance of a parent or patron, others turned to the legal system, where a surprising number of judges, much to the irritation of Porfirio Díaz, granted them relief.[15] However, only a relative few could count on the influence of others or raise the money to pay for an advocate. Even then they faced the reality that too many judges favored the regime over the law. Once again we see Pimentel writing to the president that summer of 1892: "[I have] sent replacements today. Have recommended to judge that he not grant them *amparo* [a constitutional guarantee against forced-labor]. Do not want them back, especially Amado Porras, employee of [Luis] Terrazas."[16] Without a doubt, most caught in the conscription nets, some literally swept off the streets or out of cantinas, ended up as soldiers of the regime.

In the 1880s Guerrero district's municipal government examined its military draft procedures and reasoned that the system would be less arbitrary if expanded to include all bachelors ages 18 to 35 in good health and of decent physical stature (that is, at least 5 feet 4 inches tall), not the sole support of their families, and free of burglary convictions. It recommended that those levied into service under these guidelines be assigned "normal" military duties. At the same time, the council ordered that a separate list of convicted criminals and inveterate troublemakers be kept and advised that these miscreants be sentenced to hard labor (spade and shovel work) in the army. These sorts of distinctions outlined on paper, however, were disregarded in practice. Married men, boys in their early teens, and older men, some well into their fifties, along with habitual drunks, robbers, political protesters, and other painful thorns in the sides of local authorities all found themselves levied into service.[17]

In response to a call-up in the Papigochic in 1888, for example, José A. Blanco, presidente at Santo Tomás, sent in six names, five convicted of crimes or otherwise quarrelsome and difficult to handle. He judged them brave and capable of learning weaponry. Blanco added the sixth, Estanislao Morales, because he came from a broken home; he had no more family than his mother and therefore apparently was judged to be prone to vagrancy or worse. At Temósachic Presidente Benedicto Acosta came up with no names at all by the July 20 deadline. Why? Because those men of bad reputation he intended to enlist seemed to have stolen some horses and ridden off to the mountains. Five days later Acosta forwarded the names of two young men said to be "disaffected with authority." He thought it best that they calm their animosities in the army. Juan N. Bencomo, the presidente at Mátachic, made no bones about his choices for the military: "I believe that people recruited for the army ought to be the most pernicious in the pueblo where they reside." He then named a Sr. Rodríguez, "who has only dedicated himself to vagrancy," and Estanislao Rodríguez, who claimed he was ill but was not believed by the presidente. Finally, the police chief of Pinos Altos, Luis J. Hernández, offered for service a man from the local jail, really a cave that served as the prison. Hernández noted that he was transferring the prisoner to the more secure jail at Jesús María because the cave dripped water on the inmates, and he did not want this recruit to develop a sickness that could incapacitate him for military duty.[18] This, then, is a small sample of how recruitment proceeded for the Porfirian army, as revealed in the official record. Off the record it was much more indifferent and cruel, and the military itself, as well as the society it policed, paid a very stiff price for such practices.

Los Pelados

Desertion rates soared in the Mexican army, while alcoholism, malingering, misbehavior, and unrelenting ignorance elevated the turnover rate to some 40–50 percent.[19] One wonders what kept any of them in uniform and so many steadfast when under heavy fire in combat. We know relatively little of their training and barracks life, only that it was rigid and harsh. Recruits, nicknamed *los pelados*, or "the peeled ones," were threatened with beatings and imprisonment, even execution, for infractions of regulations. Furthermore, presuming that the Porfirian military employed training techniques common in many other countries then and today, instructors sought through the most malicious sort of coercion to replace memory of family and pride in local place with those of allegiance to officialdom and dedication to national purpose. Forget your backward pueblo and join the national enterprise to make Mexico modern and great—a respected member of the world community of nations. Forsake your Indianness with all of its dimwitted superstitions and idiotic practices and become modern. In keeping with this sort of indoctrination, the official *Boletín Militar* viewed the Yaqui uprising in the 1880s this way: "[In Sonora] the shriek of the primitive races contrasts in a terrible way with the whistle of the locomotives that, proclaiming culture and progress, plow our country in all directions. The leap from civilization to barbarism has set back the fabulously and legendarily rich state of Sonora three centuries."[20] Now we can see why the government so deliberately termed the Tomochitecos "indios" and why the public mind (especially in the country's capital) frequently linked the troubles at Tomochic to the Yaqui Indian wars.

During their initial processing recruits might be held incommunicado from family and friends; the parents of youngsters plucked off the

streets for military service did not even know where their children were.
They might not see one another for a month or longer, if then. It is
impossible to gauge how deeply these sermons of indoctrination delivered by training officers take root, but we know that soldiers learned to
challenge the Tomochitecos for their religious beliefs, and that soldiers
everywhere reject their families and their culture, and while mouthing
the dogmas of the training cadre, invent rationales for turning their
guns on their own people.[21]

The *Boletín* noted in 1886 that Porfirian troops came from the ignorant and indolent lower class of society, "weighted down by the most
crass ignorance and most absurd superstitions." It speculated that
"bad sons of Mexico," those "constant and hidden enemies of your
institutions [especially the clergy], who work tirelessly to deprecate our
institutions and government and the wise laws that govern [us]," had
exploited this ignorance to keep the country in rebellious turmoil.[22]
After last roll call in the barracks, these soldiers gambled, drank, quar-
reled, fought, and deserted. Such free time must be replaced with
classes—at least an hour a day—in the (officially prescribed) history of
Mexico, geography, cosmology, and hygiene. Noncommissioned officers could study the national constitution "in order to awaken their
patriotic spirit" and learn the civil penal code so that soldiers would
come to understand the consequences of their actions.[23]

All this was meant to lift the veil of base ignorance from the soldiers,
but more crucial to the aims of the military, it encouraged dirt-poor
campesinos and the urban damned to compare their old lives with the
new and in doing so to feel better about themselves. "See how well the
government treats you? Now you have a real bed and regular meals. We
deserve your loyalty. Help the nation grow powerful by eradicating
those among us who because of their [religious] superstitions retard
progress. Make Mexico up-to-date and esteemed!" Somehow, the lit-
any worked its magic.[24]

Recommendations to improve one's physical strength as well as
one's stature in society were poured into these Mexican recruits: take a
hot bath at least once a month, or even better every two weeks ("thousands have taken no baths since being Baptized"); trade in your huaraches, which only wreck your posture, for modern leather boots; lay off
the alcoholic drinks which "are a species of liquid fire that apart from
disturbing one's reason, consume one's life and open the door to a

thousand vices and sicknesses"; and brush your teeth twice a day.[25] While we have no statistics on how often Porfirian soldiers took hot baths and brushed their teeth, we do know they drank a lot of mescal, tequila, and pulque, were not all strangers to marijuana, gambled routinely, consorted freely with female camp followers, and regularly scaled the walls of their quarters to get out on the town. Maybe they were only reacting to those abusive officers who arrogantly discounted their pay, demanded personal services, and failed to issue them promised clothing and equipment. Just observe those soldiers who first arrived at Tomochic in December 1891, dressed in thin cotton shirts and pants meant for summer campaigns, who soon suffered the numbing cold of a week-long snow and freeze high up in the Sierra.[26] Yet these same soldiers did not hesitate to train their gun sights on the Tomochitecos, to suffocate and incinerate the faithful, some of them women clutching their children to their breasts, all the while howling vivas to the government and their country.

A Tense and Wary President

Porifiro Díaz, experienced in ways that the military can overturn regimes, took his precautions with the army. He kept it small, about 15,000 in actual strength. (His budgets financed nearly twice that number and ranking officers skimmed the overage. In other words, he bought their loyalty.) The president also regularly rotated units so that they would not become complicit in the ambitions of local politicians.[27] At the same time his limited army enjoyed good, up-to-date weaponry. Infantry soldiers carried 9-pound Remington Rolling Block rifles— rugged guns, not subject to jamming or other breakdowns, easy to operate and their use easy to teach. Because of its simplicity and modest cost (only $18.00 apiece), armies around the world favored the Remington Rolling Block. These rifles were notably accurate at 1,000 yards or more and could effectively harass an enemy at twice that distance. Moreover, they carried a 12–14 inch bayonet for close-in encounters. Porfirian cavalrymen carried a sister weapon, the Remington carbine, a couple of pounds lighter, and among single-shot military carbines about the easiest to load. While the Díaz army had shortcomings, its weaponry was not among them, and the president wanted those Remington Rolling Blocks trained on the resistance at Tomochic.[28]

The president's personal controls on his army extended to the battlefield, where the commander-in-chief insisted on dictating strategy and tactics from Mexico City. Such practices cost the military in initiative and mired its field commanders in petty controversy, typified by the Tomochic campaign. On August 22 Díaz telegraphed Bandala in Sonora that Rangel had opened preparations for the campaign against Tomochic, but because the federal troops in Chihuahua had no experience in mountain fighting, the president found it indispensable that Torres provide a back-up force of national guardsmen from Sonora. The country's commander-in-chief promised to arm such units with whatever they needed. But a chink appeared in his plan; Rangel rejected the support of the Sonorans. Instead, the general proposed to make the assault with federal soldiers from Guerrero and Pinos Altos, plus units of local guardsmen from the Papigochic. Rangel suggested that the Sonorans be posted in the distant mining centers of Trinidad and Mulatos "to await further orders." It seemed to Díaz that Rangel meant to exclude Torres from the engagement altogether, and the president would take no further chances with a campaign that already had dragged on much too long. He wanted the enemy throttled—all of them, now, and he took special pains, therefore, to explain to Rangel that the soldiers from Sonora were accustomed to military activities in the mountains where they had campaigned against the Yaquis. He assured his compadre, "Torres will be under your command," and more insistently, "Make your arrangements with him [Torres], so that the rebels cannot escape to the mountains or plains."[29] Following the old Spanish colonial tradition, Rangel listened but for his own reasons did not obey and blundered into catastrophe.

Rangel Resurrected

Preparations to rescue Rangel, presumably a prisoner of the faithful, were hurriedly set in motion on September 3. Díaz himself ordered that 200 soldiers under the state's now elderly but still renowned Apache fighter, Joaquín Terrazas, be reinforced by militamen recruited from the region and rushed to Tomochic. But before the new units could be mobilized a bedraggled Rangel reappeared in Guerrero. He explained that when the enemy scattered his forces, he and several of his aides, along with the doctor and Joaquín Chávez, had taken refuge in a farmhouse on the edge of the village and then under cover of night slipped into the Sierra where Chávez knew the route to refuge. They had taken some food at Arisiachic and eventually worked their way back to town. Not everyone believed that explanation, however. Another account circulated that Cruz Chávez and some of his followers had come upon the general and his staff cowering in the outlying farmhouse but that as they started to take them captive, a young girl dressed in blue, apparently La Santa de Cabora, had intervened, urging the Tomochitecos to savor the victory that she had assured and to let their enemy go free, which they did. This supposition about Rangel's escape carried important implications for public thinking about Tomochic, because it cast Santa Teresa as a divine apparition at the scene of the battle. God's hand was at work here. Others later swore that they had seen Rangel being captured by the Tomochitecos and therefore surmised that the general had struck some sort of deal with the defenders to effect his release.[30]

To this day Rangel's escape remains a mystery. Certainly there were those anxious to invent stories that would discredit and otherwise belittle the general, especially in the eyes of Díaz. On the other hand, the nightmare of battle always produces its close calls and miraculous escapes. If Cruz Chávez did make some agreement with the general, he soon had ample opportunity to make that known and to collect his due, but no such thing occurred. Following their stunning victory the Tomochitecos did not vigorously pursue the battered remnants of the army. Had they done so they could have inflicted additional mayhem, but to what end? Attacking the army and capturing Guerrero—these were not aims of their crusade. They only wanted to live as they saw fit, or to die for much the same reason.

Placing Blame

Rangel and others now tried to explain away the calamitous defeat, and attention focused on Santana Pérez and his hand-picked troop of locals recruited from around the maverick's home base at Yepómera. It will be

remembered that Pérez had already displayed a strong streak of oppor-
tunism and over the years had become known for his political side-
jumps; one could never be sure where he might land. The accusation
followed that as the debacle unfolded, Pérez and his men, assigned as
the reserve unit, had not come to the aid of the beleaguered military.
Worse yet, some alleged that during the melee his troops had fired on
the army instead of its enemy; soldiers claimed to have been hit in the
back by bullets coming from the direction of the Pérez contingent.
Santana naturally denied any such treason, saying he had not joined the
attack because Rangel had ordered him elsewhere. He was on his way
to the other side of the pueblo when the fighting broke out, he claimed.
By the time his men were in a position to support the attack, Rangel and
his staff had been captured, and Pérez contended that he feared hitting
them with rifle fire from such a distance. This sounds reasonable,
though that does not make it true, and the simmering animosity between the federales and Pérez's outfit finally boiled over in Guerrero.[31]

When they returned to Guerrero following the debacle at Tomochic,
Pérez and his men had been lodged with federal soldiers in the military
cuartel. Pérez was preparing his battle report when an army officer
named Fernando Antillón, purportedly drunk, burst in along with
some raucously aggressive comrades, sassed Pérez, and insisted that his
militiamen surrender their weapons, placing Pérez and his troop under
arrest. Sharp words and then shots followed. Terrified citizens of Guerrero thought the Tomochitecos had attacked their town, but the bullets
zinging around came from the confrontation between Pérez's troop
and the federales. One soldier fell dead. A bullet winged Pérez in one
leg, but along with a number of his comrades he managed to scale the
parapet around the barracks and escape through adjoining corrals into
the night. A few days later Pérez was recovering from his wound at the
governor's palace in Chihuahua City (he must have known where to
seek refuge), where he told his side of the conflict, assured Ahumada of
his allegiance, and returned to the somewhat suspicious graces of the
government.[32]

Santana Pérez was but one scapegoat. Recriminations flew in all directions. Pimentel blamed the disaster on the impulsiveness with which
Rangel had approached the entire campaign, the general's brazen over-
confidence, and his ignorance of the mountainous terrain and lay of the
pueblo, as well as his inexperience in fighting Indians. The likes of

Pimentel never tired of designating the Tomochitecos "Indians," and Díaz himself played the same tune for public consumption. Even if they knew or suspected differently, Porfirian mestizos (especially those in power) would hardly admit that their own kind had delivered them a resounding blow. As word of the startling defeat spread, people so inclined increasingly pondered the claims of the faithful that God led and protected them. Others questioned the ability of the regime to defend itself. If a handful of campesinos could lick the federal army, how about a force of revolutionaries? Pimentel wired Díaz on September 5, "We must attack immediately, or the Tomochitecos will attract help."[33] Díaz agreed. The president ordered the mobilization of new troops, and as was his predilection named an old comrade-in-arms, General Felipe Cruz, to supervise the fresh operation. When Rangel limped back into Guerrero and telegraphed "Things did not go well for lack of supplies," Díaz comprehended the reality and rather curtly replied: "I thought you were captured. I have named Felipe Cruz commander and sent reinforcements."[34] With Rangel thus nudged to the sidelines, Cruz assumed the task of reconstructing the campaign.

Reviving the Campaign

Now 53, Felipe Cruz may have been a good soldier in his day, but by 1892 was an unrepentant alcoholic. During the ensuing mobilization his aides carried the besotted general to bed more than once. Still, as federal army reinforcements spilled into Guerrero, Cruz and his staff began to remount the operation against Tomochic. First they needed to reorganize the militia; recruits would receive one peso a day for their service. Díaz made money available, but warned about "putting weapons in the hands of Indians whose loyalty is not well established."[35] In fact, the president's growing concern encompassed masses of country people over a widening area who he feared would scavenge military equipment left on the battlefield and turn those guns on the government. But Cruz could ill afford to be choosy about his replacements. The presidente municipal of Matachic struggled to raise ten militiamen but reported that all candidates had fled town: "I can see their horse tracks headed for the mountains." At Santo Tomás Presidente Rafael

Márquez Quesada tried to rally support but "people just mocked me." The presidente municipal of Temeychic reported, "Can't find people to recruit. Some are in Sierra; others in Chihuahua [City]." As for the pueblo's presidente himself, he could not report for duty because he had broken an arm and a leg when a carriage overturned on him.[36]

The famous leader-to-be of the Revolution of 1910, Pascual Orozco, and his brother Tomás were ordered to sign up or send replacements for themselves, but answered that they needed to care for their businesses and families and therefore claimed exemptions; the Orozcos never did involve themselves in the Tomochic campaign.[37] But here and there, with pay, promises, and coercion, authorities managed to dredge up a bevy of recruits, including ordinary workers forced to fulfill the military obligations of their bosses. As the remobilization moved deeper into September, new army infantry and cavalry units filtered into Guerrero, and the militia forces started to take shape. At the same time General Bandala reported Torres nearing Pinos Altos with 200 Sonoran soldiers, and more militiamen were being recruited from that state for the next attack.[38] Now, if only all this mobilization somehow could have been coordinated into one cohesive movement—but that could hardly happen, because the command structure of the operation was itself embroiled in backbiting disagreement about who was in charge of what.

President Díaz had placed the alcoholic Felipe Cruz in command of the expedition, to be assisted by Colonel Terrazas, now 63, as if the colonel's reputation for Apache-chasing was relevant to Tomochic. The real problem, however, was Rangel. Despite his humiliation, Porfirio felt for his longtime military chum and sympathized with his dejection over the calamity at Tomochic. Thus, the president quietly advised Cruz, "See if he [Rangel] wants to reverse the defeat he suffered, and [if so], give him some operation under your direction. If you lead the campaign, let him stay [behind] in command of the garrison at Guerrero."[39] Cruz complied with his president's wishes, but Rangel pleaded with his compadre: "Allow me to vindicate myself, to complete the Tomochic campaign, and then I will resign from the army." Díaz waffled. He had the secretary of war name Rangel chief of operations for the campaign—not a battlefield assignment, but one with enough authority to muddle the lines of command. "I hope that you will take advantage of this opportunity to repair the damage you have suffered," the president wrote, and the resurrected Rangel responded by quickly cashiering Joaquín Terrazas as too old for a tough campaign in the Sierra. Díaz concurred but counseled sensitivity: "You can tell Terrazas that he is too old, but do not offend him so that he refuses to serve."[40] The old warrior understandably did take offense and refused to collaborate with the campaign. Rangel had won another point but was not satisfied. He requested full command of the assault—a second chance at the Tomochitecos. At that point, Díaz drew the line. When Rangel said he wanted to come to Mexico City for a private audience with the president, Díaz wired right back, "Stay right there. You can come to see me when the campaign is over."[41]

Similar kinds of internal discord permeated the civilian side of preparations. Bandala, for example, carped that Chihuahuan officials had ignored his advice to quash the disgruntled Tomochitecos early on and now were paying the penalty. Pimentel continually undercut the decision-making authority of the new governor, Miguel Ahumada. When Pimentel spent state money on the purchase of arms and ammunition for the campaign, Ahumada flared up and complained to the president: just who was giving orders in Chihuahua? Díaz, donning his mask of conciliation—after all, the president deliberately encouraged and thrived on these sorts of skirmishes among his subordinates—maneuvered to soothe the governor: "You are to participate in all decisions. Pimentel should not do anything without your approval. He should know that."[42] One could believe that Porfirio initialed that telegram with a chuckle.

On September 19 General Cruz, a few drinks under his belt and a dozen bottles of brandy in his baggage, ordered the new attack on Tomochic to commence. He telegraphed the president: "I leave tonight to attack the rebels at Tomochic. I have no money [a persistent complaint], but I always march."[43] An extremely disconsolate Colonel Terrazas remembered the scene this way: "At midnight with bands blaring and uproar in the streets, General Cruz had himself carried in his bed, where he gave the order to march to Tomochic—tomorrow."[44] Amidst this incredible spectacle the army plodded off for its next encounter with the Tomochitecos.

13

Revival

AFTER ROUTING THE FEDERALES on September 2, the Tomochitecos reveled in nothing less than ardent religious revival. For a good six hours a day the faithful dedicated themselves to prayer and ritual in the village church, where they repeated the "Our Father" and "La Salvé": "Almighty and everlasting God . . . grant [that] we may be delivered from present evils and from everlasting death." They endlessly recited the rosary and many other Catholic prayers, which they spontaneously punctuated with shouts of rapture and cheers of joy, vigorously clapping their hands and hollering raucous "Vivas" to their spiritual guide, La Santa de Cabora. After the ceremony Cruz Chávez blessed his followers, giving them a sign with his hands: "My brothers, I give my blessing," and in response, members of his flock raised their right hands as if taking an oath: "We receive it."[1] No doubt about it—Cruz himself had come to communicate a divine presence.

But there was immediate work to be done. Three contingents of the faithful mounted up their horses. One group rode the main route up the Cerro de la Cruz and chopped down the telegraph poles that carried the line between Pinos Altos, Guerrero City, and the state capital. Then the villagers cut down a line of pine trees in the area, leaving stumps about 5 feet high as a parapet for their next defense against the army. Another band scouted the area to the west of the village, around El Rancho de las Arañas and along the Cerro del Manzano, for remnants of the enemy, especially troops from the west, which had been expected but had not arrived in time for the battle. The third unit went to the village cemetery to dig graves for those Tomochitecos killed and mortally wounded in combat. About midday on September 3 the villagers, apparently all of them, gathered at the house of Cruz Chávez to begin their mournful journey to the cemetery. Four wagons pulled by mules carried the cadavers; men, women, and children trailed behind.[2] We have no precise count on how many of the faithful died in the previous day's battle: perhaps only four, one carried in each wagon. But if we compare the army's estimates of enemy strength before and after the encounter, those defenders killed could have reached eighteen, which would represent a staggering 25 percent of their fighting strength, losses not inconsistent with the sort of close-quarter combat in which they were engaged. Whatever their losses in manpower, their victory sustained their purpose.

Tending the Prisoners

During and after the battle the Tomochitecos had taken 51 federal soldiers and local militiamen prisoner. These captives were made to attend the religious festivities—the unrestrained singing and soulful incantations to the Lord and Santa Teresa—where they prayed (probably for their safety), but in general did not join in the general enthusiasm of the moment. Cruz tried to proselytize them—and in this regard Chávez could be very forceful and persuasive—but as far as is known only one of the captured soldiers ever joined the movement, and we know nothing of his personal motivation.[3]

By all accounts the prisoners were well treated. Much of the time they were locked up and guarded in the dwelling of José Dolores Rodríguez, next to the home that served as headquarters for the defenders. The prisoners must have been cramped, but periodically they were allowed to stretch out and wander around outside under surveillance, and they ate reasonably well—a portion of roasted corn mixed with water and two tortillas a couple of times a day, which was about all the hard pressed Tomochitecos could afford them. On occasion one of the movement's leaders, Cruz or his brother David or one of the Medrano brothers, brought extras to the captives: some milk, boiled potatoes browned in lard for flavor, a bit of hardtack, or some scrap of carne asada.[4] Few of the prisoners tried to escape, although one finally did so; most simply awaited rescue.

Some captives were wounded, as was Cruz Chávez, who had taken a bullet in the leg. Most seriously hurt was the assault's leader, Lieutenant Colonel Ramírez, who had almost immediately suffered a severe arm wound and was in danger of slowly bleeding to death. The Tomochitecos tended to him as best they could with plant medicines and local cures. Ramírez suffered great pain until he could stand it no longer and pleaded with Cruz to permit his return to Guerrero for treatment. Short of that, he implored Cruz to amputate his battered arm or simply shoot him dead. Chávez pondered his options. Then he received a request by courier from his (former?) friend, Jefe Político Silviano González: Could he send the military physician Dr. Arellano to attend to the wounded? After a conversation among themselves, the faithful acquiesced.[5]

Arrellano treated the wounded soldiers with medicine and bandaged up their injuries. He offered the same to Cruz, but Chávez declined, saying he preferred to rely on local herbs and traditional curing practices, along with soap and beef suet mixed with earth the Tomochitecos had brought back with them from Cabora. Above all else, Cruz relied on faith and prayer. Ramírez, however, was another matter. In anguish, with neither confidence in local medicine nor credence in miracle cures, he lay near death. Arellano asked that the lieutenant colonel be released to return to the hospital in Guerrero. Always in consultation with others in his group, Cruz took the matter under advisement. Discussion and seemingly some controversy followed, but the faithful finally agreed to release the sorely wounded officer and even provided him an escort back to Guerrero City. When Ramírez arrived, rumors spread about his release: he had paid off the enemy (the same conjecture had greeted Rangel) or had been converted to their faith, so his captors let him go. But no evidence indicates that the Tomochitecos turned the lieutenant colonel free out of anything but compassion.[6]

The defenders also demonstrated benevolence toward other prisoners, like the two captured militiamen, Francisco Caraveo, teen-aged son of one of the Papigochic's best-known well-to-do families, and Gabriel Calzadillas, likely a young worker in the same household. Simón Caraveo, patriarch of the clan, traveled to Tomochic in the company of a Guerrero schoolteacher, Marcelino Arias, and successfully pleaded for the release of the pair in exchange for the promise that the boys would fight no more for the enemy.[7] The pious treated another local guardsman, Lieutenant Esparciano Guerrero, much the same way. Cruz Chávez gave the young officer a tongue-lashing for traveling in the company of troublemakers, stripped him of his uniform down to his underwear, and told him to go home to his mama, an act that may be seen as humorous or cruel humiliation.[8]

The Tomochitecos could also be tough. When a repairman went to the village to fix the severed telegraph line there, the faithful took him captive and held him eight days. Then he escaped from custody (for unexplained reasons) and returned to Guerrero with important intelligence. The repairman established the number of defenders at 50, a total later confirmed by Dr. Arrellano, who also collected vital knowledge about the Tomochitecos while performing his medical tasks. Yes, the faithful intended to continue the fight, and the repairman had overheard talk of confronting the federales—better said, ambushing them as they had done six months earlier at the rancho El Alamo—at a juncture in the mountains called "Guajolote." Equally crucial, the repairman had learned that Santana Pérez had sent word to Tomochic that he could *not* support their cause, that as far as he was concerned they were on their own.[9] The government was glad to learn that for the moment, at least, Pérez stood on its side—for pay, of course. Then quite unexpectedly some strange, potential allies rode into the pueblo offering their services: some dozen bandits headed by their fearsome chief, Pedro Chaparro.

New Recruits

Posses were on the hunt for Chaparro when the brigands arrived at Tomochic with their offer of assistance. All the Papigochic knew of Chaparro's escapades. He once masqueraded as a padre, wearing his black mackintosh as his priestly garb and baptized Tarahumaras, charging a fee of one goat per baptism. By the time he was about to leave, he had collected quite a herd. The natives finally caught on to the ruse and grabbed him, but the bandit's accomplices learned of his plight and freed him to pursue his plundering ways.[10] Early 1892 found the bandit, his main confederate, Eufemio Escudero, and their band of ten to twelve outlaws terrorizing communities on the southern edge of the Papigochic, their escape routes open into the nearby Sierra. Reports in the spring had them higher up in the mountains, around Sisoguichic and Bocoyna. Chaparro visited his girlfriend weekly in Siso, and when Pedro came to town, all hell broke loose in the pueblo. He and his band got drunk and shot up and plundered the place. Accounts had it that the gang raped some women and actually hanged a few folks who objected to their rampage.[11]

Cruz Chávez and the faithful needed help, but how could they reconcile notorious banditry with their fervently moralistic religious beliefs? Cruz told the brigand chief about the occurrences that had fueled and then perpetuated the troubles at Tomochic. He and his party had been wronged; they had been defamed by authorities—all those slanders and lies. Cruz emphasized the rightness of his position and then his mission: "We are condemned to die. . . . Only God will assist us and will defend us to the last. We do not expect to win; we will lose and die." Once again, Cruz spoke of an anticipated death; God would defend them but only to the last moment. The Lord would not save them; they would die. The pious understand that this denouement by no means indicates God's indifference to their plight; just the opposite. They view their lives as a God-given mission—Cruz Chávez said explicitly that he was on such a mission—and know that the Lord intends to take them to His side when the mission is completed. They recognize that the Almighty in His wisdom will choose the moment of their resurrection and the inauguration of the Golden Age. This kind of resolve edges very close to the belief that one *must* die to bring on the Millennium— the predestined route to justice and plenty. Quite possibly Chávez envisioned himself and the others as martyrs who at God's command would be resurrected bodily into a new earthly world—even a new era of Mexican history—devoid of the sorrow and torment of his present one. He insisted that Chaparro be of this same frame of mind. The bandit could join the faithful in their encounter with the battalions of the Devil, but he and his men must swear not to steal anything from then on, to defend the faith as a community, and to fight to the death— to martyr themselves for the cause.[12]

Chaparro and his band rode out in late September to find weapons and ammunition for the defense. They came upon a ranchero, Tomás

Ramos, working his fields outside the pueblo of San Isidro down in the Papigochic and demanded money and guns from him. Ramos protested his lack of both, so they trussed him up and took him to a site near Bocoyna. They must have left word of their whereabouts and indications that a ransom was being sought for the release of Ramos, for shortly after, a brother of the captive arrived and learned the price of freedom for Tomás: 500 pesos (about $400), or else the brigands would take their prisoner back to their lair in Tomochic. The brother quickly met the ransom, Chaparro then took the brother's rifle, and the bunch headed off toward Tomochic. Ramos immediately sought help from the municipal president of Bocoyna, but to no avail. The president was either in sympathy with, or afraid of, the Chaparro gang. Whether the money actually furthered the defense of the pueblo is not known, but Chaparro was not done. The presidente municipal of Pachera anxiously advised the jefe político on September 15 that Chaparro, Escudero, and their cohorts were out to kidnap him—that they had promised Cruz to raise eighteen men for the protection of the village and that he was to be one of the forced recruits. Perhaps Chaparro was only out to settle an old score with the presidente, or the official may have been overreacting to the bandit's threats, but one wonders how far Cruz Chávez might have gone in seeking reinforcements. At any rate, the defense was growing in number. Juan José Madrid, who had just come from Tomochic (where he went to see his father Encarnación, being held there as a military prisoner), reported the strength of the faithful now at 81, including the bandits.[13]

Chaparro's brash kidnapping, ominous threats, and other intrusions certainly added a new dimension to the way people viewed the happenings at Tomochic. First, a smallish band of ordinary country people who claim divine protection defeat—no, utterly vanquish—the legions of the dictatorship. Then the region's most feared bandit begins to pillage in their name. Alarm along with wonderment gripped the region. One person who felt especially vulnerable in this ominous atmosphere was the padre, Manuel Castelo, who had recoiled from the admonitions of Cruz Chávez to pay for that horse he had bought in the more tranquil spring of 1891—or suffer the consequences. The stunning victories of the curate's bedevilers over the army followed, and now Chaparro was on the loose.

Enough was enough; in August Castelo wanted out. He had written the vicar in Chihuahua City that he feared for his life and intended to leave his post at Uruáchic and seek refuge in Chihuahua City. Castelo explained that the Tomochitecos had communicated to Uruáchic's officials that they intended to assault the town in order to take their revenge on the priest. Moreover, influential people in the important mining center had become devotees of Teresa. The Tomochitecos had sympathizers in all of the surrounding villages who would, if given the opportunity, gladly surrender him to his tormentors. For that reason the padre would have to approach the state capital by a circuitous route, but in any case, he was on his way. On September 16 the vicar passed on the message to his bishop in Durango City, adding that a number of pueblos had rebelled and that the army had been unable to suppress them. "It appears that these poor people are returning to their old ways of idolatry." Still, when Castelo arrived in the state capital he received the bishop's blunt response: Go back at once to your congregation in Uruáchic. The priest pleaded that this was impossible; the Indians had already sacked one convent and were plundering elsewhere. The bishop seemed to sense Castelo's exaggerations and felt the padre's personal fears unwarranted.[14] Nevertheless, Castelo did not return to Uruáchic, even months later when the Sierra settled down some, and it was probably wise that he did not.

Even as they prepared for the next assault, the Tomochitecos learned that another of their beloved santos had been arrested amidst tragedy. This time it was José Antonio Rodríguez, the former resident of Guerrero now revered as San José at Piedra de Lumbre. General Lorenzo Torres thought San José a threat, lured him into custody at Yoquivo, and had him brought for safekeeping to military headquarters at Pinos Altos. Then the general ordered the gathering of devotees at Piedra de Lumbre broken up. At four o'clock on the afternoon of September 26, 40 militiamen from Sonora under the command of Captain José María Ayala surprised the prayerful at the religious site. Rifle fire erupted, several of the faithful fell dead, and 25 were taken prisoner. When he heard of the incident, President Díaz demanded details. Torres reported three killed: Sacramento Pérez, his son Gabriel, and "an old woman." Then came the justification and once again the scapegoat was Santana Pérez, who happened to share a surname with Sacramento. Torres averred that Santana had cast his lot with the Tomochitecos who were organizing reinforcements at the locale. Perhaps so. Who knows what, if anything, the double-dealing Santana Pérez was up to at this point?

Torres turned over the other prisoners to the army for shipment to Yucatán, but he released the twelve-year-old daughter of the slain Sacramento Pérez, one of the dead man's surviving seven children. Her name was Barbarita, and when she returned to Piedra de Lumbre, crowds quietly began to gather at her side. Quite spontaneously the young girl became Santa Barbarita to her admirers. She effected cures and promised to protect them from the bullets of their enemies. Concerned authorities noted that these sorts of folk saints seemed to be emerging everywhere in the Sierra.[15]

But by now the army was closing its pincers on Tomochic. General Felipe Cruz approached his prey with purpose and bravado, if not altogether soberly. The Tomochitecos prayed "La Gloria" and loaded up their weapons behind their parapets in the pueblo. The climactic battle between God and Satan was imminent.

14

Glory

GUERRERO'S POPULACE WATCHED the army's campaign to crush Tomochic get off to a chaotic start. While dead drunk the night of September 27, General Cruz ordered 50 infantrymen and 25 dragoons under
Captain Herrán to march to the Rancho La Generala, some six miles
outside Guerrero, in the general direction of Tomochic, but still more
than fourteen miles from the target. He also commanded Captain
Chávez at Pinos Altos to close in from the west, but in his stupor authorized the officer to take only two mules to carry ammunition and other
provisions for the troops. None of this made any sense, but subordinates obeyed the general's orders. Off they went from Guerrero about
midnight. Citizens who watched the spectacle were thunderstruck and
terrified. Was the Porfirian military really this hapless? Why did the
president countenance the likes of General Cruz? Could this corps
hope to defeat the Tomochitecos? Would another victory over the army
embolden Cruz Chávez to attack Ciudad Guerrero?[1]

Rangel too was dumbfounded, and because of irregularities in the
orders he received from his superior he requested leave from the site,
intending to go to Chihuahua City and to contact the president about
the impending disaster. Colonel Terrazas wired Pimentel in the state
capital about the bizarre affair, warning that the military force assembled by Cruz was about to be destroyed by the enemy and the morale
of the entire mobilization effort devastated. The colonel minced no
words: "Cruz was drunk."[2] But how to stop him in his folly?

There was no halting the hallucinating Felipe Cruz. When he arrived at La Generala he noticed all the tall, mature corn stalks outlined

in the moonlight, and thinking them the enemy, ordered a charge. Off he galloped through the fields, slashing at the corn stalks with his saber and undoubtedly slicing a few tassels to the ground. Following their commander's lead, the cavalrymen did much the same, although undoubtedly less wholeheartedly.[3] Whether Cruz eventually came to his senses or simply became fatigued is not clear, but the charade finally wound down to a close.

Imagine the delight in Tomochic when news of the farce at La Generala reached the faithful. Cruz Chávez led a prayer session to thank La Santa de Cabora for deceiving the army; but how joyous, even jovial, that moment must have been for the devoted.[4] Here they had further proof of the divine hand at work on their behalf. God's will was being done.

A Tenacious and Hard-Hearted General

At the opposite pole, Porfirio Díaz fumed, outraged. What would happen when his countrymen, not to speak of foreigners, received word of the latest debacle? After all, the president himself had selected Felipe Cruz to finish the business at Tomochic. The regime would be a laughingstock or worse. Díaz determined to rid himself of this nasty irritant once and for all, and to do the job, he called upon one of his closest companions (to be sure, another former comrade in arms) well known for his tough, at times brutal, no-nonsense approach to nettlesome challenges. Enter General Rosendo Márquez, age 56, for the past seven years governor (albeit a controversial one) of the important central state of Puebla and proven loyal follower of the dictator.[5]

Pending the arrival of Márquez in Chihuahua, the president ordered Felipe Cruz to suspend all military operations. When the secretary of war ordered the scandalized general to Mexico City, Cruz balked. The president then lost patience and had Cruz escorted by a military squad to Chihuahua City to await transfer to Mexico City. When Márquez arrived at the state capital on October 9, Cruz had still not appeared there but was said to be on his way. All Márquez could tell the president was that Cruz "is in bad shape." At the same time he assured Díaz that preparations for the next campaign against Tomochic had already begun.[6]

Immediately, Márquez inspected the headquarters of the two main army forces in town, the Eleventh Infantry Battalion and the Third Cavalry Regiment. He pronounced the dragoons in decent shape but found the men of the Eleventh poorly disciplined and badly trained. Moreover, the infantry had been stationed in Chihuahua for two years and may have begun to take sides in the dispute at Tomochic. Márquez decided to take no chances. He had 250 men of the Ninth Battalion stationed in Mexico City hurried north by train to the theater of operations.[7]

Then the general took stock of his overall position. He placed (deliberately overestimated?) the enemy at 100 to 120 fighters. "I have faithful informants," he insisted (who else could better recommend such spies than our old friend, Reyes Domínguez?). Márquez knew that the Tomochitecos were well armed with Remington rifles and carbines, swords, and bayonets they had taken from fallen and captured federal soldiers, as well as an assortment of other weapons: 1873 Winchesters, including the famous .44-40 repeaters, perhaps a Sharp's Buffalo gun or two, some Colt single action pistols or maybe a Smith and Wesson. As for the disposition of the dissidents themselves, "They are arrogant, and I am sure that they are waiting for us." Márquez had thought of having the twelve-year-old Santa Barbarita delivered from Piedra de Lumbre to Tomochic in order to transfix the devoted in place. "With her there, they won't leave, and it will be easy to destroy them"—but that strategy never came to pass.[8]

However, other tactical details were ironed out. He replaced the alcoholic Lieutenant Colonel Pablo López with Colonel Juan B. Morales and insured that Lorenzo Torres was in place at Pinos Altos in order to cut off any possible retreat of his foe into the Sierra. Finally, he sent the president an enigmatic telegram: "I believe that I am not mistaken to say that this public disorder has been motivated by some high-placed people in the state."[9] Unfortunately for us the general did not name names, and the public record mentions the pregnant observation no further. No doubt political adversaries of the state government, most likely members of the Luis Terrazas camarilla, took advantage of the dogged resistance and army defeats at Tomochic to further their aims, but no proof has surfaced that they actively aided the faithful or in any calculated way attempted to bend the religious crusade to their own ends.

With General Rangel once again in tactical command (Díaz must have agreed to give his compadre another chance), the federal march toward confrontation began on October 17. Márquez stayed behind in Guerrero, in part to give Rangel free rein as promised by the president but also because reports placed an unidentified armed band of 180 men around the Rancho Serupa some twenty miles northwest of Guerrero, and the general needed to insure that support for the Tomochitecos was not building elsewhere. He ordered Santana Pérez (the maverick somehow had managed to regain the trust of the government) to investigate the makeup and whereabouts of this latest threat and secured Guerrero with reinforcements from the state capital.[10] Meanwhile, the army marched in three columns toward its objective. The first was under Lieutenant Florencio Villedas with 8 commissioned officers, 136 soldiers, and a martial band of 5. This was followed by a slightly larger contingent under Lieutenant Colonel Emilio Gallardo. Last came the reserve, which featured an artillery unit toting a disassembled Hotchkiss (light artillery) mountain cannon—the latest innovation in Porfirian armament, which the military eagerly desired to test on the battlefield.[11]

In all, Rangel's army totaled some 450 officers and men. General Torres approached from the west with about the same number, including a group of Pima Indian scouts. This meant that the federales outnumbered the defenders about 15-to-1, a substantial numerical advantage even against a well-prepared enemy dug in for the defense.[12] On October 19 Rangel was encamped on Cerro de la Cruz overlooking the village from the north, and later that day the traditional bugle calls— "Atención," "Parte," "Diana"—announced the arrival of Torres on the Cerro del Manzano, with contingents on the Sierra de San Ignacio rising to the west. A seasonal frost chilled the air that last night before battle. Soldiers nervously counted and recounted the 100 cartridges allotted to each of them, stuck them in pouches and cartridge bandoleers, and then settled down for the night's uneasy pause, their private concerns blunted (or boosted) by hard drink and nervous boasting. Their officers, conscious of the tactics employed by the Tomochitecos in earlier encounters, covered up or removed altogether the epaulets and other insignia from their uniforms that might attract fire.[13] All could hear the prayerful intonations of the faithful wafting up from below, beseeching the Almighty to favor their holy cause in His name.

The Climactic Struggle

Dawn broke clear over the valley of Tomochic. At 7 A.M. Torres ordered his columns to attack: two columns up, one back. Forward units would form a gigantic pincer, squeezing the enemy on its flanks, while the third column would be held in reserve to reinforce the advance groups as needed and to round up any of the foe fleeing the trap. The Twelfth Infantry under Captain José María Corona spread out and descended the hill that bordered the main road through the pueblo. A detachment of twenty men slid slightly north to secure the strategically critical Cerro Medrano, that dramatic rocky outcropping which rose from the valley floor and dominated the village. Troops under Captain Nicolás D. Luna covered the Cerro del Manzano to the south, where Torres had located his command post. Companies of militiamen from Guaymas and pickets from Navojoa and Sahuaripa were held in reserve. Captain Corona's force edged cautiously across the river and into the valley proper. And all hell broke loose.[14]

The defenders had posted sentries at strategic sites, including the bell tower of the church, and divided their main body into three guerrilla groups of ten to twenty or so each, ready to strike the enemy where most challenged. Because Rangel was slow to mount any offensive from the east, the defenders could concentrate on the advance ordered by Torres. Shouting vivas to the Santa de Cabora and hailing the power of God, the devoted burst from the cuartel. Pedro Chaparro and his band, plus a half dozen others, headed for the cover of the cave in the mountainside above the east side of the village. Others took up positions in the belfry of the church. In skirmish lines, firing as they went (their Repeater Winchesters giving them somewhat superior firepower at short range), the Tomochitecos crashed into the forward elements of the federal forces under Captain Corona and sent them fleeing in terror back up the slopes on the western outskirts of the pueblo. Torres watched anxiously as his left flank disintegrated and hurled his right into the fray, down the Cerro del Manzano, across the river into the valley. The defenders quickly turned their wrath on the new challenge, and the antagonists clashed in frightful hand-to-hand combat on the low land along the river, amidst the fields of corn, which now stood high. Bullets and bayonets took their ferocious toll on both sides; death howls rent the smoke-clouded air along with cries of pain and protest from the wounded, but the soldiers could not long stand ground against their zealous and unforgiving foe. Within an hour they gave up the fight, turned tail, and ran, confused and mutilated, to the heights of Cerro del Manzano where their distressed commander, Lorenzo Torres, struggled to regroup his forces and ponder his options. He had never before suffered or even seen anything like this.

Across the valley Rangel could see, hear, and smell the battle developing, although he could not gauge its outcome. Too much smoke from exploding black powder soon veiled the scene. Whatever his personal thoughts and emotions at this horrendous moment, he did not exactly rush to the aid of Torres, but instead ordered Lieutenant Colonel Emilio Gallardo down the Cerro de la Cruz to menace the village proper and sent a unit under Lieutenant Colonel Florencio Villedas along the Cordón de Lino to overrun the enemy holed up in the strategically located cave. A furious firefight ensued there; Villedas fell wounded among numerous federal casualties, and so the attack was abandoned, leaving the army saddled with yet another abject defeat. Meanwhile David Chávez held the force of Gallardo at bay long enough to allow help to arrive from companions who had routed Torres on the other side of the pueblo. These mobile units of the faithful, already flushed with victory, then smashed into the flanks of the federal column with predictable results. Confused and terrified soldiers sensed themselves surrounded, put up a cursory resistance, then broke and scattered back up the Cerro de la Cruz to the shelter of the army reserves.[15]

These latest reversals did it; Rangel had suffered enough frontal attacks on the faithful. He dared not chance another calamity, judged that his antagonists could not be overwhelmed by brute force alone, and so determined to place the pueblo under siege; that is, to ring the valley with troops and slowly bleed the faithful to death.

The purpose of laying siege, of course, is to weaken one's opponent. First of all, it deprives the enemy of potential outside support, and Mexico's military remained apprehensive that political rebels known to exist in the Sierra and along the lower fringe of the United States might ally themselves with the Tomochitecos. Siege also aims to exhaust a foe's food and water. The faithful had undoubtedly stockpiled what they could, but they were short of grain, and the year's crop still stood unharvested in the fields. Furthermore, siege dribbles away ammuni-

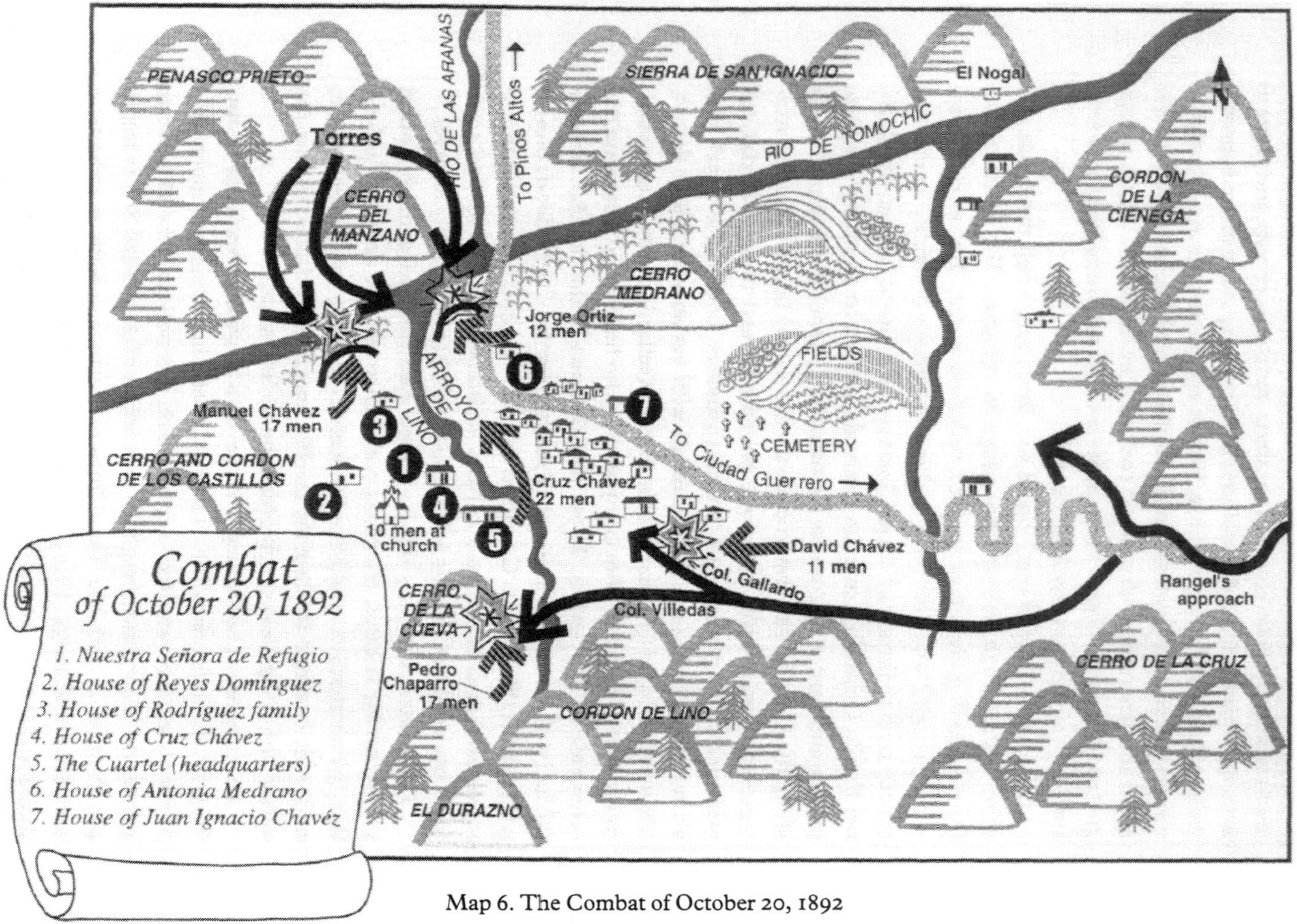

Map 6. The Combat of October 20, 1892

Combat
of October 20, 1892

1. Nuestra Señora de Refugio
2. House of Reyes Domínguez
3. House of Rodríguez family
4. House of Cruz Chávez
5. The Cuartel (headquarters)
6. House of Antonia Medrano
7. House of Juan Ignacio Chávez

tion as the contenders fire off periodic bursts just to let one another know they are still present and able to do damage. The army had at least 10,000 cartridges in reserve and more to come, while the Tomochitecos must have expended a good portion of their ammunition in that first day's encounters and could not count on replenishment, a problem sorely exacerbated by the variations in make and caliber of their rifles and pistols. Also, among those under siege disease spreads, the wounded suffer and the dead putrefy, morale deteriorates, women and children need to be cared for. The ability to break out diminishes as siege continues; the strength to fight off assault declines. The defenders are uncomfortable and under stress, and can never rest. On the other hand, their adversaries can be rotated, shifted to back areas, reinforced, and replaced. Bombardment, even by a single Hotchkiss mountain cannon, may do little consequential damage but further increases tension; a bursting Hotchkiss shell hurls shrapnel at a frightening speed of 800 feet per second. Rangel knew what he was doing and what he wanted when he placed Tomochic under siege.[16]

Normally commanders offer their beleaguered opponents a negotiated surrender during siege, perhaps amnesty or some other terms. But not Rangel, not now. Without doubt the faithful would have rejected such offers anyway, but the general never contemplated talking this enemy into submission. Instead he intended to fulfill the president's demand for "exemplary punishment" and to revitalize his own reputation doing it.

When Rosendo Márquez learned of yet another disaster for the federales beleaguering Tomochic, he took 30 dragoons from the garrison at Guerrero and headed for the front. En route he met the stream of wounded, suffering soldiers hobbling from the valley toward respite and medical attention in the city. A rough count of dead and wounded placed the army's first-day casualties at more than 100; some later said 300, but that seems exaggerated.[17] We have no idea how many of the faithful fell during that initial combat, but judging from the hand-to-hand struggle in which they were locked, their losses must have been heavy. Despite the disarray in its ranks the army still mustered a lot of firepower (a soldier could load and fire off eight to ten aimed shots a minute), and not all soldiers cut and ran. With a lull in the fighting, the faithful returned to their fortified positions to check their losses, regroup, and to thank God for the day's successes, costly as they may have been. But sorely outnumbered defenders cannot long pay the price of open combat, while siege (assuming its success) can only prolong their agony.

Before he reached the battle site, Márquez received word that Guerrero itself was threatened by Santana Pérez turned traitor. As such a turnabout seemed entirely credible, the general hurried back to the regional center and ordered reinforcements from Chihuahua City. Whatever the intentions of the unpredictable Pérez, he did not assault Guerrero at this time, but instead went off to the state capital to profess once again his loyalty to the governor and secure additional pay for his troop.[18] It was blackmail, to be sure, but a cost the government willingly paid for peace with this risky security chief who enjoyed a following among certain country people in the Sierra and also knew the territory.

With Pérez bought off, at least for the moment, Márquez felt more secure. Remarking that he felt deeply saddened, he sent the president a chagrined account of his labors: "Would that I could say to you, as did a certain emperor, 'I came, I saw, I conquered,' but I can only say to you that I have worked to fulfill the trust that you have placed in me."[19] At the same time, however, Márquez assured Governor Ahumada that the rebels at Tomochic had been throttled, another of the formulaic obfuscations that regularly flitted among Porfirian officials and administrators. The governor sent back his congratulations and promised the resources necessary to pursue any rebels who had escaped, but this was only wishful thinking. How perplexed Ahumada must have been a day or so later to learn the truth: another resounding defeat at Tomochic and the outcome there still in grim doubt.

The Siege at Work

Meanwhile, Rangel moved to secure the siege in place. With the faithful mainly pulled back to their bastions—the church, the battle-readied home of Julián Rodríguez that now served as their headquarters, and the dwelling that housed the federal prisoners—the general was free to occupy the Cerro Medrano in the center of the valley and to make direct contact with Torres. The bandit Chaparro and his men remained up on the hill at the fortified cave, dangerous still but quite isolated.

Now Rangel could proceed to pick away at the edges of the valley, then the outskirts of the pueblo proper, so he sent squads of militiamen, preceded by wary Pima Indians from Sonora, to probe the position. Plundering as they moved deliberately from house-to-house (they only got a few pigs and chickens, a shirt or horse harness here, a couple of musical instruments there, religious icons, some jars and plates), the probing squads piled up dry straw, branches, and corn stalks against anything wooden inside the dwellings—frames and beams, chairs, chests, and tables—soaked them with kerosene, and lit them up. So Tomochic began to burn, including the house of Cruz Chávez, as the military drew its net more tightly.[20]

As the siege deepened on that second day of the confrontation, October 21, a stir suddenly flared up around the headquarters of General Torres. Unrestrained vivas to the Tomochitecos and Santa Teresa incongruously echoed over the military site. The prisoner called San José had broken from custody and was rampaging among the decimated Ninth Battalion, haranguing the men to desert the army for the holy cause of those who defended the besieged pueblo and assuring them that if they did, the Lord would protect them from the bullets of their foes and reward them with Eternal Glory. "God is with them. . . . Teresita, La Santa de Cabora, blesses them." Those who believe in a divine presence in their world do not take such words lightly, even if some think the herald deranged, and Torres feared the worst from his soldiers, the great majority of them untutored country people. When General Rangel learned of the incident, he acted. Although he declared San José insane, Rangel had him executed military style, in full view of his troops and overlooking the Valley of Tomochic. That's the way that "modern" generals like Rangel and Torres dealt with such dark characters; that's how they quelled the threat—but only for the moment. Even as he faced the firing squad, the holy man professed no fear, saying that within three days he would be resurrected.[21] Whether he achieved salvation and sat at the side of God is not known, but the matter of bodily resurrection also remains open, for soon enough another "San José" appeared among these believers.

With the stench of carnage filling the air, along with the pungent smell of black gunpowder, the siege stretched into its third and then fourth days. The main body of troops bivouacked above the pueblo, soldiers eating what Porfirian troops normally stuffed into their pockets: tough but flavorful and nutritious jerky and pinole, eaten with brown sugar or made into gruel. Loose cattle, confiscated, slaughtered, and butchered into strips and tossed on hot coals, provided a feast, and stray chickens quickly found their way into the cooking pot. Army rations—maybe some refried beans and tortillas or fresh boiled potatoes—supplemented this country fare made just that much more palatable by plenty of hard drink: pulque, mescal, tequila. Soldiers also spent their few centavos for an apple, orange, or something much stronger brought to the site by an opportunistic petty merchant or the women who quickly become part of such military stalemates. But the overall atmosphere above Tomochic was hardly a relaxed one. It was, instead, permeated by apprehension, an anxiety that the fearless Tomochitecos might at any time come forth to challenge the siege, and when a squad of soldiers went to the river to fetch water, the men dressed as common country people, they blessed themselves and feigned reverence as if to reassure any defender who might be watching them that they too believed and should not be sniped at.[22]

Overall, the federales maintained their military regimen. Rifle squads sporadically fired rounds at the enemy below, just to remind their foe of the army's presence, and the artillery crew periodically sent five or six fifteen-pound shells from the Hotchkiss whizzing into the pueblo. Exploding missiles dug pockets into adobe walls and scattered some dogs and chickens grubbing for food but were too small to do any real physical damage to the defense. Still, they kept the Tomochitecos on their guard and apprehensive. What did they know of an artillery shell arching in on them from considerable distance? Yes, they knew dynamite explosions from the mines, but this was different, a new weapon in the arsenal of the Devil.

The faithful could do little more than praise God, tend to immediate necessities, and prepare for the next assault. They had poked loopholes through the walls of their dwellings, making the houses compact little fortresses from which they fired occasional rifle bursts at their enemy just to let them know that the defense stood firm. To show their colors and boost morale, they shouted hosannas to La Santa de Cabora and sang vigorous hymns to the Lord. There were also common daily chores and heartbreaking labors to be done. The wounded needed to be comforted and the dead buried, now inside the dwellings themselves or most frequently in the church. Under the gaze of federal marksmen they fetched water from the Arroyo de Lino, which still ran with water from the seasonal rains. Women did most of this work; remember that perhaps as many as 200 women—sisters and wives, widows, and long-time friends—and children ranging in age from infancy into their early teens still counted among the faithful. Many of them were living in the church, still the most spacious and strongest structure in the pueblo, but at the same time the main target of army snipers and the Hotchkiss. The few accounts that we have render some details of the military operation but little of the day-to-day lives of the defenders, only that the faithful had prepared as best they could for siege and trusted the outcome to God.

At 2 A.M. on October 25, the fourth full day of the siege, an army contingent of some seventy men attacked the cave at which Pedro Chaparro and eight or nine of his bandit gang were positioned behind a barricade of stout timbers and small boulders. As the soldiers approached, their comrades far across the valley on the Cerro del Manzano peppered the mouth of the cave with rounds from their Remington Rolling Blocks. A wicked firefight followed; in only fifteen minutes of combat the military, forced to climb a steep, open approach to the cave, suffered 23 dead, including the commander of the operation, Captain Eduardo Molina. Seven of Chaparro's men also died in the fierce assault, but not the brigand chief himself. Astoundingly, somehow, he and at least one of his comrades escaped during the melee to the safety of the surrounding pine forests, later to return to banditry until authorities finally caught up with them a year or so later. So Chaparro did not fulfill his vow to Cruz Chávez to stand firm and, if necessary, to die for Santa Teresa and Christ, but before he fled he put up a ferocious fight against the Sons of Satan.[23]

With the strategic cave now in army control, federal units advanced after dawn into the village proper, burning and looting as they went. As they moved forward, pickets of soldiers occupied the scorched ruins of the dwellings to insure that if any of the faithful tried to escape the tightening ring they could be dispatched. Then, an unexpected breakthrough for the military. All along one of its major objectives had been to rescue the fifty-odd soldiers still held captive. No one knew the intentions of the faithful toward these captives. One had escaped on the second day of the siege and reported that the enemy had treated them as best they could and had tried mightily to convert them to their hallowed mission with no apparent success. Still, the possibility existed that Cruz Chávez and his people might try to ransom their own escape with the lives of the prisoners, and what might the president say in that eventuality? But the question did not have to be answered, because on this same day, October 25, the defenders turned the captives loose to rejoin their military ranks. They simply could neither feed nor tend to them any longer. Rangel, still smarting from the earlier debacle and now mired in another campaign that was dragging on far beyond his liking, had the returning soldiers thoroughly interrogated. Why were you captured? Did you surrender? What did you tell the enemy? Eustaquio Santiago, it seems, a member of a local security force, had waffled during his captivity; he had temporarily allied himself with the faithful and then rejoined the prisoners. So Rangel had him shot; there was to be no mercy for those tempted or tainted by the creed of the enemy.[24] This campaign must end only one way.

The next day military headquarters were transferred, along with the Hotchkiss, to the sizable dwelling formerly occupied by the Medranos, although a wary Rangel and a cautious Torres did not arrive until the following morning, when their safety was more assured. First the village church, the symbol and center of enemy resistance, had to be captured and that bell tower from which sharpshooters persistently harassed the besiegers silenced. Now militiamen crouched behind the stone wall bordering the large patio at the main entrance to the edifice. Four or five soldiers, protected by the heavy covering fire of others, crawled on their bellies, dragging behind them sizable bundles of dried corn stalks and other light tinder, edging toward their objective, the large, main wooden doors of the church. Then they were there, the kerosene-soaked bundles pushed up against the doors and lit. Flames rapidly consumed the dry wooden doors and leaped to the frames and beams around them. Once inside they devoured the stairs to the choir loft, then the loft and supports of the structure itself, including the bell tower, which collapsed with a roar into a rubble of heat and dust. Then the roof of the church fell in on the terrorized occupants below. Stored ammunition exploded; thus the Apocalypse came to be.

Screaming women, some with children in their arms, scrambled to flee the suffocating smoke and flames, only to be shot down by the soldiers waiting outside. For the military it was a turkey shoot. In their panic, the Tomochitecos did not try to shoot their way free of the trap; instead, they tossed down their rifles and fled in hysteria toward the last few homes that shielded their cause. Doña Felicitas Villatel, clutching her year-old child at her breast, became disoriented in the smoke and fury and ran straight at the soldiers who aimed to slay her. The child took the bullet which would have killed his mother, and so she survived to tell of her loss. In fact, a number, including women and children, found safe refuge with the remaining defenders, sufficient to suggest that more than a few soldiers showed compassion, but more than sixty men, women, and children died in the bloodbath at the church. Beyond that, soldiers took five men and various women prisoner; they shot the men that afternoon. As night fell, the army doubled its sentry watch in and around the pueblo to insure that no defender escaped. Pairs of guards walked the Cerro Medrano. The military plugged up the arroyo that carried their enemy's last water supply and then poised itself for the kill. Meanwhile, the church continued to burn and smolder. Periodically, one heard another chunk of church wall fall. It took days for the ashes of the fallen structure to cool down enough so that the remains could be probed.[25]

The eighth day of the campaign—seventh of the siege—found the surviving Tomochitecos surrounded in their last redoubt, their cuartel, and the federales itching to storm the place. Still, the adversaries exchanged few shots that day; the faithful must have been preserving any ammunition they had left for their final glory. No doubt they prayed, but their boisterous singing and haughty hosannas had been stilled as they waited inside the dwelling where the bodies of loved ones lay rotting in corners next to the horribly wounded and dying. All able survivors, men and women, found themselves tending the stricken, caring for the children, eyeing their adversaries through loopholes, awaiting attack. Food about exhausted; water running out. What should be done? How should one die? Cruz's ministry had never been free of consultation and debate, and at this desperate moment some pressed their leader to petition Rangel to spare the women and children the final assault, but Cruz would have nothing of it.[26] He meant that they should—or must—die for their beliefs. Others were not so sure. Such rifts characterize even the most fervent and steadfast religious movements, indeed social movements of all persuasions. We have no idea who specifically counseled with Cruz at this extraordinary moment, but his brothers Manuel and David still lived, and the pitiful pleadings of some women, and the plight of the children, must have been overwhelming.

It is said that about this time General Rangel sent an old friend of Cruz Chávez, a Yaqui Indian named Enríque, nicknamed "Chavolé," with whom Cruz had earlier worked as a muleteer, to negotiate the release of the women and children—and even to suggest the surrender of the remaining defenders whose lives Rangel guaranteed. But Cruz had replied: "I do not have anything to save. . . . The temple has been destroyed. Tomochic is erased from the world. It is not worth living; besides, God calls me. Teresa has announced that my mission on earth is complete."[27] This meeting may be the invention of writers who were not privy to the events but who later cared to recall them in their own special ways, yet by all that we now know of Cruz, these words would have reflected his sentiments as well as those of many of his followers. Cruz rendered his judgment, apparently without regret. He was ready to go to his reward, perhaps to be resurrected, brought back, into a better world, and now he could release the others to follow their own paths. A surprisingly large total—some forty women and more than sixty children—streamed from the cuartel through the soldiers filled with awe and pity, and on to the rear lines of the army to await the end of the onslaught.[28] They carried only a few pathetically small bundles of personal belongings with them. At the same time a few women, who would not leave their menfolk or feared to face the soldiers, stayed behind to accept their destiny.

A hard rain fell throughout that night. All the next day the army awaited a surrender flag that never flew; Rangel displayed restraint. Did he mean to take anyone alive? Certainly not the men, who were firmly slated for "exemplary punishment." But for the remaining women and children, saving them, he thought, would demonstrate the humane side of the dictatorship, and early the next morning, October 29, a few more women and children left the cuartel for the custody of the military. At seven o'clock bugles blew and elements of the Eleventh Infantry and Twenty-fourth Militia advanced against the stronghold. As their army comrades laid down a fusillade of cover fire, a few men crept to the walls of the building and then onto the rooftop, composed of soil and timber. With their bayonets they broke holes through the roof; some then shot at anything that moved below, while others dumped burning fagots on the enemy. At the same time soldiers hacked away with axes at the wooden doors to the entrance of the bastion. For almost an hour those inside—only thirteen remained—managed to shoot back at their adversaries through the loopholes in the walls of the structure, and occasionally a careless soldier fell wounded or dead. Then, no more shots from within; only thick, black smoke belching from the loopholes. The door splintered apart, and wary soldiers cautiously dared to enter, their bayonets at the ready. No confrontation, however, took place: the enemy, including a few women and youngsters, lay about dead and dying. Then some slight movement among the fallen occurred, perhaps a groan or an agonized cough of blood. Six men still lived, though all fearfully wounded, too weak to resist any longer or perhaps now prepared for their final glory, among them all the Chávez brothers—Cruz, Manuel, and David. Their survival was probably reported to Rangel, but even if not, we know his instructions. The six were taken outside to the adobe wall of a nearby building and shot. Soon afterward the field commanders communicated to their superiors that the Tomochic affair had successfully ended. Fulsome congratulations about bravery and duty raced in all directions.[29] Rangel reported the "enemy eliminated to the last man." Tomochic had been leveled. "Only the house of Reyes Domínguez remains. He has rendered us good service." General Márquez assured the president that peace and public order had been restored in the zone and because of the "energetic punishment administered to the fanatics of Tomochic," others would now think twice about opposing government intentions.[30] But these events always have their more-or-less predictable repercussions as well as their more surprising aftermaths; they are never really forgotten.

Today, those who know what happened there approach the valley of Tomochic with wonder and respect. The Cerro Medrano is no less impressive than it was a century ago, and the cave where the brigand Pedro Chaparro stood still yawns above the village. When it rains, the Arroyo de Lino, etched somewhat deeper by a century's torrents, still continues to carry away thin layers of the soil once soaked in blood. Poking carefully in the dirt on the valley floor, one may still turn up a century-old bullet, a cartridge shell, or an army buckle. A new church, less imposing than its predecessor, has been built just off the foundation of the old one. Recently some random excavator dug a pit at the edge of that foundation and struck charred beams—the remains, no doubt, of the earlier structure. I have preserved a piece of that charcoal in a plastic bag, and when exposed to air it crackles as if alive.

Part IV

Echoes

15

The Ceaseless Quest

THE STENCH OF DEATH hung over the Valley of Tomochic for days. Dogs and other animals gnawed at abandoned corpses, while soldiers, who so frequently join armies just for the right to loot, scavenged the burned-out buildings. There was nothing much left to be had—a few farm tools, some metal pans, and damaged leather horse gear, maybe a dozen rifles of different make and caliber, religious icons, a runaway horse, and personal items, all saturated with the foul aftermath of battle. The ruined church, of course, excited the troops' greatest hope for booty—raging fire might blacken and blemish silver chalices and ornamented candelabra but did not destroy them, and rumor, imagination, and greed had enriched this temple beyond the fabulous. Even as timbers of the structure smoldered and hot ashes challenged human touch, expectant soldiers poked the remains for treasure. In order to maintain a semblance of orderliness, General Rangel had to declare the place off-limits. He posted sentries to reinforce his order, but such precautions do not deter clever booty-hunters.[1]

Over the next few days the military conducted an inventory at the church and reported (God only knows what they did not record and kept for themselves) a very substantial find: priestly garments, altar clothing, and most coveted, considerable silver, including three chalices, a lamp, a small cup trimmed with gold; the *hisopo* from which holy water was sprinkled; the silver chains used to suspend the incensory, metal ornamentation that had decorated a wooden cross, and several candelabra damaged by bullets—more than the usual appointments of a small country church. Those articles that survived the fire were probably kept in the curato, and the most lucrative finds undoubtedly wound up in the hands of the soldiers. The army was supposed to turn over the inventoried goods to Church authorities, but at this juncture the record of what really occurred falls silent. As for the valuable holy materials themselves—*se fueron*; they simply went away.[2]

The army did not linger at the scene. For three or four days details of soldiers stacked the decaying corpses, doused them in kerosene, set them afire, and later returned to heave a few shovels of dirt on the remains. But the bodies were hardly covered, and pigs could easily root them out. Rangel also had his men round up any loose horses and mules, along with the few remaining stashes of grain the defenders had left behind as they fled their homes. The general's intention was to return these few paltry possessions to the families of the faithful. He arrived in Guerrero City on November 4 with 40 women and 71 children, who had survived the cataclysm by surrendering themselves to the enemy; he also had 18 horses, 5 mules, and 28 burros, plus some weapons and other materiel that had belonged to the pious.[3]

General Márquez telegraphed the president that "the true story of Tomochic is horrible beyond belief; one could write a novel about each of its episodes." Then he added a rather observant, reflective note: "I have submitted my official report, but it only gives you an idea of what the nation and the army have gained or lost."[4] Márquez sensed some sort of trade-off here—victory, but at a price. The general was not known as a remorseful man, but he may have been touched by the senseless slaughter. Or perhaps he overheard the whispered conversations among the populace of Guerrero about a government that so relentlessly and callously pursued its goals. He may have sensed troubles ahead. Márquez promised to discuss all this with Díaz on his impending trip to Mexico City. How do dictators (as well as presidents) respond to such contemplative remarks by their trusted generals and personal friends? Díaz lauded his "old brother in arms" and his soldiers, saying "my spirit was there, along with my desire to fulfill your needs." The president lamented "so much bloodshed" and admitted the government should have acted more decisively sooner, but he blamed the outcome on "their [own] savage stupidity." In a summary phrase, "They got what they asked for. No other result was possible without sacrificing your dignity and the authority which is the basis of social order."[5] This was hardly surprising from Porfirio Díaz, but still a revealing restatement of his priorities.

Maybe the Tomochitecos got what they were looking for, but not everyone saw it that way. "A Second Alamo: The Brave Defense Made by a Few Tomochicans" proclaimed a headline in the *El Paso Daily Times*, and the body of the story read, "A second Alamo was fought in southwestern Chihuahua last Monday morning, the only material difference being that the men who went down before overwhelming numbers then were a swarthier hue than the brave defenders of the Texas Alamo. They fought for the same causes, life and liberty, and the cry of *'Viva la libertad'* with which they met their death sprung from fearless hearts." In a Spanish-language newspaper published in Paris, Mexico's Minister of Foreign Affairs assured the international community that events at Tomochic were purely local and devoid of political import, yet much of the foreign press spoke of Tomochic as a dedicated rebellion against the regime. At the same time, two of Mexico City's most influential newspapers, *El Monitor republicano* and *El Diario del hogar*, questioned the government's reasoning and intentions even as they elaborated upon circumstances surrounding the tragedy. These accounts led another of the capital's leading newspapers, *La Voz de México*, to demand "a full investigation of this affair, because it has been said that against these valiant Indians the government violated all rules of war, which at this moment, toward the end of the nineteenth century, amounts to High Treason by the nation." Reiterating this moral stance, *El Tiempo* exclaimed: "Extermination is not permitted by a civilized country." These were very strong words indeed, and the newspaper wanted those responsible for the massacre punished.[6]

Even as these challenges were hurled, Márquez and Rangel traveled to Mexico City to present their accounts face-to-face with the president. We can only surmise the response of Díaz by what happened next: Rangel thanked the president for affording him the opportunity to restore his reputation as a capable army leader, returned briefly to Chihuahua (but not in active command), soon resigned from the army as promised, and died within three years. The president also interviewed and severely reprimanded Colonel Florencio Villedas for his battlefield failures, and the chastened officer soon after died of a heart attack.[7] Márquez quickly returned to Guerrero City to excise—forcefully so—

any hint of rebellion that lingered in the region, but his command was brief and soon passed to another general, Juan A. Hernández, deemed to have more expertise and experience in stamping out rural dissidence. *La Voz de México* counseled Díaz to go easy, to give any remaining insurgents time to reflect, arguing they would then surrender of their own will and return to work. *El Tiempo* urged the government to reestablish church missions, like those that had previously imposed a kind of peace on the district. Porfirio Díaz was in no mood to compromise, however; he would extinguish any sparks kindled by Tomochic lest they feed the smoldering rebelliousness along the northern frontier. From over in Sonora General Bandala assured the president that the carnage at Tomochic had had "a calming effect on the entire area. Victory helps to assure peace in the country."[8] But the general was overly optimistic.

Tomochic as Symbol

As news of the outcome at Tomochic spread, the pueblo's name came to symbolize the variety of ways in which people reflected upon the tragedy. For some it connoted brutal government and a ruthless dictator, for others the pity of human ignorance and superstition, as well as the pain of becoming modern. Political dissidents used "Tomochic" as a battle cry, civil authorities to promote mandatory education and the need for domestic peace, generals and commanders of militia to advance their careers, and Díaz to cement his presence in the troublesome North. Opportunistic entrepreneurs throughout the region sought to gain an advantage over competitors by accusing them of complicity in the affair and denouncing them to authorities. Any number of personal disputes were settled in the same way, and parents scolded unruly children saying that the Tomochitecos (that is, savage Indians) would get them, if they did not behave.

As a result, two more years of unrest and military oppression gripped the district, and by the time it finally simmered down, Tomochic and its aftermath had planted their historical benchmarks. Never before had the Papigochic and its surroundings been brought under the hegemony of the federal government; never before had the area's notables of all political circles become so tied to federal favor. Some say the seeds of future revolution were sown at this moment; it is one reason the Papigochic is called the cradle of the Mexican Revolution of 1910. Naturally the place did not shed its history, its tradition, but the dominance of the power and purse of central government not only created opposition but presented opportunity and conflict that split people and communities, sometimes widening long-standing rifts. We saw an early version of this process at Tomochic—and witnessed the group that felt itself being suffocated by the new order quickly strangled. But the cries of such people do not cease and can incite others to action. Authorities dedicated to maintaining both the peace and their own tenure tend to clump these sorts of disparate elements into "the enemy," and in this case Porfirians took advantage of the discord at Tomochic to justify a mop up of its adversaries throughout the region.

The same day, October 27, that the final defenders of Tomochic were executed, Governor Ahumada issued a circular warning the citizenry that anyone in the district "who directly or indirectly assists the rebels of Tomochic or their accomplices or sympathizers, or offers them any sort of protection—tries to hide them or fails to report them to authorities—will be punished."[9] So would those who treated with army deserters, for example, by buying their military weapons, ammunition, and equipment. Such edicts amount to a hunting license for those out to settle personal grudges or to eliminate a competitor, and a flurry of denunciations followed. None of the accused had much if anything to do with the occurrences at Tomochic, but their adversaries labeled them "accomplices" and the military finished the dirty work. The wellto-do hacendado Ramón A. Sáenz, presidente municipal of Rosario, in November 1892 denounced Alvino Rico, one of those captured by the Tomochitecos, saying that Rico had provided the faithful with weapons. Even Jesús María Ortiz and Felipe Nevares, residents of Tomochic who had opposed Cruz Chávez and his group and left the pueblo, suffered arrest. They insisted that in no way had they participated in the work of the faithful, but Sóstenes Beltrán, the presidente municipal of Pachera, put them under house arrest anyway. Pointed questions, near accusations, insinuations, doubts where none had existed—all these infiltrated the district, frightening and stifling its inhabitants. The *New York Times* reported that "sixteen Indians taken prisoner in the massacre at Tomochic two months ago have been brought to Mexico

City by the Eleventh Mexican [Infantry] Battalion. The prisoners will be shot after they are questioned in regard to the uprising, which has not yet been quelled."[10] But just who were these "Indians"? There were no captives taken at Tomochic.

As abuses multiplied and complaints mounted, Governor Ahumada turned conciliatory. First, he placed blame: obstinate religious fanaticism had caused the Tomochitecos to reject constituted government authority and to take up arms. Early on, the government had attempted to negotiate a solution with the disaffected. When that did not succeed, alas, the army had to be summoned. But now, inspired, he said, by his intention to restore public peace and foster social and individual progress, Ahumada urged all inhabitants to resume their daily work "in the knowledge that the government offers you all guarantees of the law and will contribute what it can to your welfare and betterment, with the assurance that no one will be bothered or persecuted without cause and that local authorities are at your service." At the same time, the governor urged municipalities to contribute money, food, clothing, and other goods for the relief of the survivors of Tomochic. Díaz approved the governor's approach, "Very good," he commented. "This interests me. Let me know the results."[11]

Resurrection and Rebellion

Within days the president had his results, though not as desired. Rebellion had erupted here and there in Guerrero district and threatened to ignite the entire Sierra. Flash-points occurred at Tosánachic, a major crossroads in the mountains northeast of Tomochic, and then Yepómera, at the northern end of the Papigochic proper. Trouble had been brewing at Tosánachic since the army's frustrated campaign against Tomochic in September 1892. Some residents of the community seemed to sympathize with the faithful, and Silviano González, the jefe político, had on October 14 removed the elderly Estanislao Lozano as the pueblo's presidente municipal for lack of confidence in the local authority. Estanislao promised General Márquez the following month that he would disband his local security force and swore obedience to the government. Márquez posted 50 federal cavalrymen at the pueblo to make sure that Lozano kept his word. Rumbles from Yepómera were much more threatening to the government; there Celso Anaya, who had been engaged in controversial village politics and threatened rebellion since the 1880s, gathered a band of twenty, confiscated weapons from the local citizenry, and announced that he was recruiting people to go to the aid of the Tomochitecos. Even if he meant it, he was already far too late, and by late December soldiers sent by General Torres had broken up the budding movement in Yepómera.[12]

The spring of 1893, however, brought outright rebellion to the Papigochic. On April 1 some fifteen conspirators gathered at Rancho Corral de Piedras near the pueblo of Cruces in the vicinity of Namiquipa to launch a revolt headed by two old hands in such matters: Celso Anaya had resurfaced, along with the more formidable Simón Amaya, a former jefe político in the district who had fallen from favor and been exiled to the United States but now returned claiming support for his revolution in 23 of Mexico's 30 states. The rebels took Cruces, forced loans of money, weapons, horses, and supplies from the well-to-do residents and recruited another 40 men to their ranks.[13] Then they marched toward Temósachic, and quite spontaneously the campaign became a religious crusade infused with the enthusiasm of an old Tomochic revival. Aghast, Temósachic's presidente hurried to the state capital: "The rebels follow the same customs of the fanatics of Tomochic. They pray; they carry a banner of La Virgen de Guadalupe, and only differ in that they demand loans and say they will take the war to the government. This last point is impressed upon them by Simón Amaya, who hopes it will give more substance to his movement. Amaya is no fanatic, nor is he religious; he only seeks to exploit the ignorant people in the pueblos for his purposes. He has made them believe that all the dead of Tomochic have been resurrected."[14]

Indeed, it was commonly believed among Mexico's faithful that God's work is never done and that martyrs to Christ's cause would be resurrected—that those who perished defending the Holy Faith were guaranteed salvation and a place at the side of God in heaven. San José, Santa Teresa, and perhaps Cruz Chávez himself had promised as much, and the pledge of invulnerability to the bullets of Lucifer's forces plus the reward of salvation for those who died for their faith are recurring themes in popular religiosity. Furthermore, not all of the pious limit resurrection to the afterlife. They anticipate bodily rebirth by divine hand in the here and now, not back into their old world of pain, but into an ideal environment of peace and plenty.[15] Martyrs can be brought back to life, which is why heroic Tomochitecos continued their struggle in the minds of so many. In fact, some claimed to have seen these fearsome warriors for years after the climactic clash at the pueblo. In this instance nothing is known of Amaya's religious bent. Perhaps he was a believer or only used the theme of resurrection to recruit and inspire followers. But Tomochic was churning the public mind and testing its temper.

In further show of extreme concern, if not desperation, President Díaz in early April hurried General Juan Hernández into the expanding theater of operations. Still vigorous at age 50, Hernández was another of those Porfirian generals who had worked his way up through the ranks, fought against the French, supported Díaz's presidential ambitions, and later directed operations against the Yaquis. His charge was to bring some coordination to the chaos of command in Chihuahua. Temósachic fell to the rebels on April 3, 1893. The victors forced more loans, recruited another thirty-odd supporters, and burned the municipal archives, an act of defiance against all things official, but also, more opportunistically, to rid themselves of records that might at some later date be used to challenge plans they had for rearranging matters like power and land in their own favor. They rested up two or three days and then resumed their march up the Papigochic. Santo Tomás lay next in line. Rumor had it that Cruz Chávez led one contingent of rebels and the brigand Pedro Chaparro another.[16] How emphatically and how quickly Tomochic had stamped people's imagination.

The president ordered the enemy stopped at Temósachic, a fiat that came too late for implementation. In fact, Simón Amaya and his band of 72 had already occupied without resistance two square blocks in the heart of Santo Tomás, farther upriver and the remaining major pueblo between the rebels and Ciudad Guerrero. Federal strategy calculated to dislodge them was the same as that employed at Tomochic—starve out the enemy by siege. After five days of siege and with reinforcements on line the federales began to tighten the noose on the last rebel stronghold at the main plaza. Then, in one of those utterly desperate yet courageous human lunges for freedom, the rebels, led by Simón Amaya, burst from their redoubt and firing their rifles as they ran, hurled themselves against a link in that chain of soldiers that shackled them. Though few of us will ever know, or want to know, such fervor, we may still marvel at it. Amaya and his followers, some forty in all, actually fought their way through the front ranks of the infantry, but at terrible cost to both sides—and they were still a terrifying distance from the safety of the Sierra beyond the village. Three miles of carnage unfolded as the federal army unleashed its cavalry upon the fleeing rebels. Sabres mercilessly cut them down; infantry bayonets mopped up behind. This was battle turned to ghastly slaughter. Simón Amaya stumbled down dead. Celso Anaya was mortally wounded and died the next day. Somehow— these affairs almost always have their astounding surprises and miraculous escapes—ten or twelve defenders made it to the countryside, although half were captured and shot within a day. Still, six or seven seem to have escaped, and a vengeful Porfirio Díaz ordered them tracked down. We do not know their destiny; some may have taken advantage of a general amnesty offered the next year. Meanwhile, as an object lesson authorities placed the corpse of Simón Amaya on public display in Guerrero City. The regime should have realized (and perhaps it did) that people grasp different meanings from such lessons.[17]

Although only a handful escaped the grip of the military at Santo Tomás, the government deliberately made it appear that the Sierra still seethed with revolutionaries. To its way of thinking that situation justified wanton repression. First it offered a sizable reward—100 pesos (about $80)—for information on anyone who had associated, or even sympathized, with the aims of Simón Amaya or the ideals of the Tomochitecos, and named Pedro Chaparro, the bandit who had joined and then deserted the faithful at Tomochic, as most wanted among the fugitives. Two months later Sinaloan police caught up with Chaparro and escorted him back to Ciudad Guerrero to stand trial for his alleged crimes. Instead, General Hernández ordered him shot in the town cemetery and his cadaver hanged for public viewing in the nearby mountain pass at Puerto de las Manzanillas, scene of the mule train robbery of which the Tomochitecos had been falsely accused. Through the corpse of the man who had allied himself with the Tomochitecos, Hernández meant to tie Cruz Chávez and his followers closer to the earlier assault and thereby further legitimize the government's harsh repression of the pious and anyone who sympathized with them—but hangings and tough talk could hardly erase the specter of Tomochic.[18] For example, about this time four or five gunmen, wildly shouting "Long live the power of God and the banner of Teresita," rode into Temósachic with their rifles and pistols blazing, broke up the early morning dance party at the home of Eufracio Sotelo, and then disappeared like mystical wisps into the dark.[19] Then came the worst possible news for the government: a new santo—or the resurrection of an earlier one—had appeared in the Papigochic.

Yet Another Santo

San José, El Santo, appeared in the valley in the late spring of 1893, encouraging listeners to defend their religion against the Sons of Lucifer, who looked an awful lot like Porfirian soldiers. Among those who worshipped him and looked to the santo for guidance were 30 widows and a number of children who had survived Tomochic. This new rabble-rousing prophet from Rancho Colorado, just downriver from Guerrero, was warned to desist but did not. As devotion to San José burgeoned in June, authorities decided to finish with him. Soldiers arrested El Santo and with neither explanation nor ceremony shot him dead. His execution only heightened the incantations of the women and children from Tomochic, however, causing General Hernández to urge the removal of these "troublemakers" from the district. He wanted them far away to avoid further sympathy and support. Porfirio Díaz concurred and put the women at Governor Ahumada's disposition. "I have thought of bringing them here [Mexico City] to work in a cigarette factory and of sending the children to primary school in Texpám [a small pueblo fifteen miles north of Mexico City]," the president told the governor, "but you use your judgment."[20]

We do not know the fate of these or many other survivors of Tomochic. Some later returned to the destroyed pueblo to build a new life as best they could, while others settled with relatives in the Papigochic. Some orphaned children were adopted (probably as servants) by families in the state capital. Still, the memory of Tomochic haunted the valley, and vivas to the martyrdom of the faithful and to La Santa de Cabora erupted from time to time.

Tomochic Remembered

Government repression had only led to further glorification of the To-mochitecos. One band of rebels forayed into Mexico from the El Paso area, shouting their vivas to an imagined "Society of Cruz Chávez," believed to be a dedicated, militant society in the image of Jesuits as soldiers of the Pope. Although invented by the raiders, the prospect of such a "Society" lost none of its power to inspire. At the same time that chameleonlike renegade Santana Pérez, who for years had walked the tightrope between service to the government and rebellion against it, finally decided on the latter. He had briefly fought with Simón Amaya at Santo Tomás but fled before the army closed its circle around the pueblo. Afterwards, with a band of perhaps a dozen, Pérez had zig-zagged about the nearby Sierra trying to raise recruits here and eluding army patrols there. Authorities stripped his ranch at Yepómera of its cattle and tracked their prey northward into the United States, where Pérez, invoking the martyrdom of Tomochic, issued proclamations calling for the overthrow of the Mexican government and urging sol-diers to desert to his cause.[21]

Other dissidents such as Victor L. Ochoa, a U.S. citizen committed to the ideals of radical liberalism with its emphasis on democratic in-stitutions and human equality, hovered around El Paso weighing the prospects of a raid into Mexico. Ochoa too raised Tomochic as his battle standard, elaborating as necessary to serve his cause. The 27-year-old newspaper editor claimed that "In 1892, the prefect [presi-dente] of the district of Tomochic committed a crime. His soldiers killed a young woman's parents and her brother. When neighbors heard of the brutality, they rebelled and organized to form a new state." Government repression followed: "Soldiers killed 600 people in To-mochic, [all] except 114 women and children. My own family was slain."[22] In this manner Ochoa deliberately declared himself to be a resident of Tomochic, which, of course, was not true, nor were the details of his reportage even remotely accurate. Still, through his words we can see one of the ways in which rumors are planted and nurtured, how a real tragedy may be sifted for embers to spark other ambitions and embellished for political purposes.

In January 1894 Victor Ochoa launched his own attempt at revolution in Mexico. He vowed "to concentrate 5,000 men near Chihuahua and march against the prefect of Tomochic." In "prefect" one wonders who Ochoa had in mind, Juan Ignacio Chávez or Reyes Domínguez? Juan Ignacio, so intricately involved in the breakout of hostilities in the pueblo, left the village for good in early 1892 when Cruz Chávez and the faithful returned from their visit to Santa Teresa. Then when the soldiers withdrew after the final battles, Domínguez became presidente and effectively ruled the pueblo well into the next century, even when someone else held official title. Whoever his prey, Ochoa intended to hang him, but later lamented that "the government learned of our intentions and our six divisions were unable to rendezvous. I had only 500 troops and was forced by government troops to retreat. We had to disband to save ourselves. I escaped [back to the U.S.] in the uniform of a Mexican soldier."[23]

Rebellion and Risk

No doubt Victor Ochoa was a dreamer, but he certainly was not the first rebel, nor will be the last, to envision armies that never materialized. And why did these invitations to rebellion fail? First of all, the valley and environs were under stringent military rule; soldiers were everywhere. Díaz wanted to replace the federales with local militia, but his field commanders talked him out of it. The regular army officers did not (or claimed not to) trust the militia to douse any new flare-ups of dissidence and so made a case for a continued federal presence. After all, their reputations, already bruised, were on the line. Such military occupation not only cows the public but creates a frightful mood of uncertainty in which neighbors begin to distrust neighbors and friends suspect friends. One had better not discuss rebels unless one was prepared to join them. And what were the alternatives offered? A breakaway religious group that did not so much detest government as wish to be left alone; political discontents from downriver whose disputes were mainly local and chronic; and finally, outsiders, even foreigners, with radical ideas that hardly resonated with regional tradition. Not much choice in these possibilities for disgruntled people of the Papigochic, especially in the absence of some overarching issue or concern to stitch together, or at least blanket, their diversity. Under the circumstances the government could gradually diminish its overt military presence and offer amnesty to those who had grown weary of the fight, to those who feared that military arbitrariness would extend to their families or who felt that revolution no longer served their interests—or at least for the moment seemed futile. They would await a more propitious moment to further their objectives. The amnesty decrees of the spring of 1894 brought more than 100 home to the Papigochic. The unpredictable Santana Pérez soon followed.[24] Governor Ahumada visited the valley in April, offering land and water reform in exchange for public order. And one could only grin (or grimace) when the governor in September of that same year ordered residents of Tosánachic to stop bothering Santana Pérez and to return to the "reformed" rebel any of his cattle they had confiscated but not already sold.[25]

Amnesty, of course, does not guarantee domestic tranquillity. It only affords the regime a respite in which to reinforce its power. In this case amnesty cut both ways: it brought an uneasy peace to the Papigochic but amplified the voice of protest just to the north along the international line where agitators and insurgents continued to test the will and mettle of both Porfirian and American authorities to silence them. Officials for both governments prepared lists of candidates for prosecution, extradition, exile, or worse. The name of Teresa Urrea—La Santa de Cabora—appeared prominently and repeatedly on those registers in recognition that even from exile Teresa's influence still excited passions, moved feet, and could cause a disciple to pick up a gun.

16

A Santa's Many Masks

THE CITY THAT STRADDLED THE BORDER, or "both Nogales" as the locals called it, a desert border town of only some 6,000 inhabitants in 1892, was a busy international crossing, with traffic moving steadily in both directions on paved streets and through railroad connections. Up-to-date telephone and telegraph communications plus a couple of newspapers kept the populace aware of events in the town and elsewhere, and news of Teresa's presence and feats attracted thousands of curious and hopeful visitors from around the globe. Actually, the place could claim elements of sophistication; opera companies visited, along with magic lantern and steriopticon shows. The circus came to town, and the local drama club offered seasonal productions. Residents knew Mozart as well as high-fashion clothing, and the imposing Moctezuma Hotel had by this time been "completely rebuilt." Moreover, the town claimed a Methodist Seminary and a Masonic Hall, along with a Young Men's Athletic Club whose monthly "social" attracted a crowd. But that summer of 1892 La Santa de Cabora was the talk of the town.[1]

Accounts of Teresa's healings astounded audiences. In one example, Teresa treated a young man paralyzed from an early age along one side from his hip to the ground, one leg muscular and healthy, the other nothing but skin and bones. Under her magical touch the useless leg gained strength and the man walked. Vidal García, about 60 years old, had been entombed in a daze for four years; he could not hold a conversation and could hardly see. Teresa worked with him for four days, and the man recovered his speech sufficiently enough to be understood, and his eyesight to the point that he could guide himself about town.

Word of other miraculous cures circulated: habitual liars now told the truth, and she rid several people of the envy and greed that had caused them to covet their neighbor's goods. Of course, there were doubters. In the summer of 1892 a reporter for Arizona's *Willcox News* questioned four blind people "who firmly believe their eyes will be opened, and they will be made to see," and concluded, "They will probably be made to see clearly that the saint is a fraud."[2] Still, as many as 5,000 pilgrims a day continued to come to bask in the spirituality reflected by La Santa de Cabora.

But Teresa did not have only healing on her mind, and the ensuing years of her life became a mix of show business, revolution, and religiosity, colored by a sensationalist press and the bombast of politicians. Between 1892 and 1895 Teresa and her father took up residence for months at a time in locales such as the large Yaqui colony at Palo Parado, on the Santa Cruz River, some thirty miles north of the border along the main road to Tucson or El Bosque, another largely Yaqui community nearby, where Teresa was said to have lived in a humble reed hut. Escorted and promoted by her friend Lauro Aguirre, she periodically visited the Yaqui barrio in Tucson where she was received with ecstatic adoration. Many of these Indians had been displaced during Sonora's long Yaqui wars in the 1880s, and although a good number had taken up permanent residence and found work on the area's railroad construction, the scars of tribulations suffered in Mexico remained. No doubt many yearned to return to their traditional land. Certainly Teresa sympathized with the Yaquis. "I have gone among them healing their sick and trying to relieve their wretchedness. . . . They have no rights [in Mexico], and I fear that they will be exterminated. I would do anything for them, but I do not pretend to have any power to lead them to better conditions."[3] Regardless of these self-admitted limitations, La Santa regularly ministered to the natives and heard their pleas for justice. Country people like these Yaquis did not attribute all their misery to punishment by God for their own shortcomings. They possessed a sturdy sense of justice and knew injustice when they suffered it, and urged healers to use God-given powers to cure these wrongs. In doing so, they must have given Teresa quite a lesson about human misery and injustice. But to what use did she put the knowledge?

And Now at Ojinaga

As we have seen at Tomochic and Navojoa, religious movements exploded upon the countryside and swallowed up towns and villages in Teresa's name but without her physical presence. In the spring of 1895 a woman carrying a small stone idol emerged from the mountains near the pueblo of Mulato, six miles south of Ojinaga, the port of entry on the Rio Grande below El Paso. She claimed to have gotten the idol from Heaven. Local residents called her La Santa de Cabora, and she quickly raised a lively following of 300, then 500 devotees. More arrived every day from both sides of the border. La Santa—as her followers called her—informed the faithful that she was a messenger from God, with Whom she was in daily contact. She regularly issued bulletins about her conversations with the Almighty and collected money from her flock around Ojinaga. Said an eyewitness: "I know dozens of men who gave her all their money and left their families with nothing to eat." Another (unfriendly) report had her selling 19-cent horseshoes for a dollar each to her admirers and retailing pictures of herself along with medicines said to resist bullets. A journalist put the take of this Santa at a very substantial $2,000 to $3,000.[4] Could this actually be Teresa Urrea at work?

Fearing an outbreak of rioting, the Mexican government ordered the enthusiastic crowds to disperse. When they did not, authorities attempted to arrest the Santa and to confiscate the idol. Before they could catch her, she fled to the safety of U.S. territory, where hundreds of devotees, mainly Hispanics from both sides of the border congregated to protect and adore her. Meanwhile, in April the police arrested several of her followers in Mulato and lodged them in the Ojinaga jail. Now the faithful resolved to rescue their fellow-believers, and, led by a hunchback named Encarnación Zares, assaulted the town jail. In the initial firefight, six men died, but the defenders—150 police and volunteers—held their ground, and the confrontation settled into a standoff periodically punctuated by exchanges of bullets that killed another half dozen. Meanwhile, the government dispatched help for the beleaguered town, and when troops arrived from Chihuahua City, the faithful panicked and sought sanctuary in the United States. There a band of itchy-trigger-fingered Texas Rangers waited to turn them back into

Mexico. Some seventy then surrendered to the pardon proffered them by the governor. Still, seven of the faithful, including Zares, refused to give up. They holed up in a modest adobe dwelling in Mulato, hanging what a journalist described as "magnets" (they must have been scapularies or metal icons) around their necks, and swearing that they would never yield and that their santa would protect them and deliver victory. But the Santa, whoever she was, had already departed the scene.[5]

For four days the soldiers endeavored to starve out their foes or otherwise coax them into surrender, all to no avail. On the fifth they marched on the dwelling. As the military approached, the hunchback could be seen making mysterious passes with his hands and arms as if to ward off the bullets. The firefight lasted a bloody 25 minutes, before the faithful, outnumbered and outclassed in weapons, were overcome. Zares and two more lay dead; the other four desperately wounded, one shot four times. "So ends the religious war on the Rio Grande, although with another leader," warned the *Brownsville Daily Herald*, "trouble may break out again, as many Mexicans still believe in the supposed woman and her magnets, and that if they had been more careful in following her, they would have overcome the authorities."[6] The power of a santa to mobilize a fierce following was well understood here.

Indeed, many continued to believe in Santa Teresa, who denied any responsibility for the spectacle at Ojinaga, claiming she was at the time more than 100 miles west of the place. Even as Teresa said what she must to avoid complications with U.S. authorities that could lead to her extradition to Mexico, other reports put her at the site of the revival. Perhaps it was time to move on. At the last of October 1895 Teresa and her father packed up their considerable belongings in no less than twelve horse-drawn wagons and moved to a rancho owned by Ramón Montoya, just outside San José, an agricultural community of 1,000 on the Gila River in eastern Arizona, nine miles above Solomonville and within easy reach of the great mining centers at Clifton and Lordsburg with their thousands of Mexican employees, among them a considerable number of Yaquis. While residing at the rancho, she was said to be connected with a Spanish-language newspaper published in Solomonville, edited by Pedro García de Lama, a sidekick of our old acquaintances Victor Ochoa and Lauro Aguirre, as well as their radical leftist friend, Manuel Flora Chapa. One account had it that Teresa Urrea had founded the paper, which regularly "handled the Mexican government

without gloves."[7] If so, where did she get the money? Most likely any
funding was not her own but that of accomplices in the newspaper project. Nevertheless, those who insisted that Teresa had incited the bed-
lam around Ojinaga remembered the alleged contributions of $2,000,
even $3,000, which some santa supposedly had received there.

In early March of 1896, U.S. authorities learned that Aguirre and
Chapa planned to launch their long-expected revolution against Mexico to coincide with upcoming federal and state elections in that country—always periods of great challenge and unrest. The U.S. military
sent Seventh Cavalry Colonel E. V. Sumner, commander of Fort Grant
in eastern Arizona, to investigate. At Solomonville Colonel Sumner
found no evidence of any stockpiled weapons, although he noted that
plenty of people in town supported dissident political factions in Chihuahua and Sonora. The colonel also discovered that the local newspaper editor, García de Lama, a prime suspect in the conspiracy
against Mexico, had fallen out with Teresa, Aguirre, and Chapa when
the editor refused to print a bombastic proclamation calling for revolution in Mexico. In fact García de Lama had turned traitor to the cause
and carried the proposed proclamation to Governor Ahumada in Chihuahua City, thereby ingratiating himself with the Mexican government. García de Lama became Ahumada's paid spy, and Colonel Sumner took advantage of the situation: "I do not consider any of these men
reliable, but they are willing to cut each others throats."[8]

In his search for clues and evidence, Colonel Sumner wheedled
intelligence from Solomonville's leading citizens, among them the lawyer Wiley E. Jones, county district attorney, who also happened to be
on Ahumada's payroll, and the postmaster, Pedro Michelano. The latter rendered some very provocative impressions of La Santa de Cabora:
"One: Teresa is opposed to the Mexican Government and wields a
powerful influence over the lower class; Two: she would not hesitate to
use that influence to violate [U.S.] neutrality laws in order to overthrow
the Mexican government; Three: leaders of the revolution [Aguirre
and Chapa] associated themselves with this woman to make use of her
influence."[9] The *Denver Republican* added: "Her adhesion to a revolution would be an alarming circumstance to the Mexican government,
as thousands would blindly follow her lead for direction."[10] These are
resounding indictments of Teresa as Revolutionary.

Authorities took Aguirre and Chapa—but, for unknown reasons, not Teresa—into custody, bringing them before government officials for questioning on March 21, 1896. The pair undoubtedly admitted their distaste for things Porfirian but denied intentions to foment revolution in Mexico. Whether the United States found insufficient evidence to move on the case or perhaps did not care to do so, no charges were filed. Meanwhile, Mexico's Foreign Minister in Washington, Matías Romero, downplayed the entire incident with a stock statement: "The people engaged are cattle stealers and marauders. . . . The leaders are of no [political] standing and represent no one but themselves."[11] Still the pot continued to boil.

June found the Urreas in El Paso, where Teresa said she intended to write for Aguirre's aggressive journal *El Independiente,* which liberally stirred the gospel of Teresa's sacred mission into the brew of revolution in Mexico. If herself not divine, Aguirre declared, she was at least an inspired leader, chosen by God to free ordinary Mexicans from their bondage. Throughout, Teresa steadfastly denied any connivance in revolutionary intrigues aimed at Mexico. From a house on Overland Street in El Paso she assiduously tended to the hundreds of afflicted who came each day in search of a remedy, or more simply to bask in a divine presence. Who knows what else Teresa was up to? Tensions continued to simmer along the border, occasionally boiling over into bold, brief forays by rebels against lightly defended border customs stations on the Mexican side.[12] Then came an electrifying assault against the critical communications hub of Nogales: "¡Viva La Santa de Cabora! . . . ¡Viva el poder de Dios! . . . ¡Vivan los Tomochis!" To inhabitants of the region and Mexicans everywhere it must have seemed that the ghost of Tomochic would never be laid to rest, and now Americans had been drawn into the fray.

Nogales Under Attack

At 4 A.M. on August 12, 1896, rifle shots suddenly rent the early-morning stillness, and some seventy rebels, mostly Yaqui Indians wielding a few rifles but also bows and arrows and machetes, assaulted the customs house on the Mexican side of the line. One night watchman, Manuel Delahanty, sensing his family endangered, bolted from the customs post toward home and was shot dead in the street. His father-in-law, Crescencio Urbina, heard the commotion, rushed to the scene, saw his daughter's husband crumpled on the road, and waded into his assailants, who greeted him with death. The remaining guard at the customs house grabbed a rifle from the bank of weapons kept there and started to defend the place, but the attackers quickly took him prisoner. Others arrived only to be captured, then released after they had identified the homes of the presidente municipal and the administrator in charge of customs, along with those of a well-off merchant and a local doctor. These rebels needed money: plunder and ransom were ways to get it.[13]

Residents of Nogales rallied to the defense. In a stroke of quick thinking, Manuel Mascareñas, the Mexican consul in the U.S. part of the city, rang the city's fire bell for help. Fires were the true curse of these towns largely built of timber, and a clanging fire bell always aroused a hurried response. Some sixty men answered the clanging, both Mexicans and Americans, including a contingent of U.S. national guardsmen spoiling for a fight with these revolutionaries.[14]

The battle raged for a couple of hours, during which the insurgents in their frenzied search for guns, ammunition, supplies, and money sacked several private businesses and public buildings, including the municipal palace. From the customs house they took eighteen rifles, two pistols, and plenty of ammunition, but they missed the big prize— the safe with $80,000 in cash. It had recently been moved to a nearby structure pending repairs at the customs house. In the confusion, a few Americans stumbled right into the ranks of the rebels, who admitted to no quarrel with the gringos and allowed them to return to the U.S. side unharmed; captured Mexicans would not have fared as well. As more and more people joined in defense, including a good many American civilians armed with weapons from the national guard armory, the rebels cut and ran.[15]

Nogales reeled from the assault. Business and transport, even saloons, closed down as the citizenry braced for another anticipated attack. Rumor had it that rebels into the thousands were on their way from places like Tubac and the Sonoran mining center at Altar, 80 miles south, to support their brethren, who were themselves regrouping in the surrounding hills. Eight revolutionaries and six townsmen had been killed in the initial attack, while many more lay wounded. A captured raider, Francisco Vásquez, claimed (as might be expected) that he was forced under the threat of death to join the insurgents. He filled in for authorities important details about the attack, but the most revealing evidence was found on the corpses of the assailants, now arranged side-by-side against a customs house wall for viewing and picture-taking. One of the dead leaders, Loreto Rivas, carried a letter dated June 28: "We will be near Nogales on the night of August 11, and in conjunction with your men, we hope to secure all the weapons at the place. Tell your men not to be afraid: that we are all brothers and sisters, and that the rich should share with the poor, and tell them to remember that the 'Santa' is always with them in spirit." The letter was unsigned but carried the sense of Lauro Aguirre. Another letter dated July 25 stated: "Remember the eleventh of August is the day when you are to go to Nogales, capture the town, and right your wrongs. Remember, Santa Teresa is always with you, and through her miraculous influence, no harm can befall you." The Nogales newspaper that printed that letter labeled the entire affair: "Lauro Aguirre's long-promised revolution."[16]

The paper had good reason to suspect Aguirre. Copies of his news-paper, El Independiente, were discovered in the pockets or under the shirts of the dead rebels along with pictures of Santa Teresa, scapu-laries, and other icons meant to protect them against the bullets of their enemy. One carried a photo of Teresa wrapped in a piece of mosquito netting and carefully tied with a pink ribbon; another, a lock of her hair in a little pouch looped around his neck. Investigators also found a list of nineteen men who had agreed to join the movement, all said to be "Santa Teresa fanatics," some of them misidentified as "Tomochic In-dians." There is little doubt about the authorship of this daring raid, although Aguirre categorically denied involvement and did the same for La Santa de Cabora: Teresa, he asserted publicly, did not even know the leader of the group: "Her only desire is to relieve the poor and suffering. She represents what is good and true against the oppressive powers that be."[17]

Teresa spoke for herself in September, assuring the public that her overall intentions were hardly political and regretting that some groups had rebelled in her name: "I am not one who encourages such upris-ings, not one who in any way mixes up with them. . . . If more rebellions follow . . . I will say once more that I am taking no part in them."[18] More uprisings certainly followed, and Teresa denied a connection to all, even if there was a significant amount of circumstantial evidence to involve her. She openly associated with Lauro Aguirre and sharply criticized conditions in Mexico. If she did not help to plan and finance the revolts, she surely inspired many who joined them.

Next day the round-ups and interrogations in Nogales started in earnest, accompanied by the sort of official heavy-handedness we noted earlier around the Papigochic. It was as if the authorities concurred wholeheartedly with the editorial in Denver's *Rocky Mountain News*: "Evidently the mountains in that vicinity are infested by a class of men better dead than alive, and if in effecting their capture some of them should be shot, the corpses will be even more joyfully received by the civil authorities than the live criminals."[19] The weight of official repression fell most heavily upon those Yaquis who had settled around places like Tubac, and once again the corrupted atmosphere permitted a good many personal scores to be settled in the name of pacification. Furthermore, the attack had focused attention on diplomatic arrangements between the United States and Mexico, specifically on neutrality and extradition covenants. Under the new pressures the U.S. Attorney General's office seriously began to investigate Teresa, Lauro Aguirre, and their companions for possibly exporting revolution to a friendly neighbor, while the Mexican government demanded their extradition for crimes against the state.[20]

Teresa, meanwhile, was making newspaper headlines throughout the United States. The *New York Herald* promulgated her as the "Indian Joan of Arc" who "leads another horde of fanatics in a religious war," attributing to her the assertion that the "Virgin Mary has appointed her to lead her people from bondage. Fiery enthusiasm rules her. She proclaims that the downfall of the Mexican government is at hand."[21] Ever on the lookout for revolution among "volatile and violent" Mexicans, the press liberally placed words in Teresa's mouth, many of them eagerly furnished by her close friend and counselor Lauro Aguirre, while La Santa herself publicly lamented that rebels used her name for their purposes. In other words Teresa seemed to be trying to avoid legal snares while advancing her ambitions.

Fulfilling Holy Promise

While authorities on both sides of the border investigated and hounded Teresa, her spiritual followers elevated her to new heights and enveloped her in millennial belief. To them she became that long-awaited culture hero who had promised to return one day to create a world devoid of sadness and injustice, one in which *they* would reign in peace and good health. The myth of the returned Toltec God Quetzalcoatl, the Feathered Serpent, looms large in Mexican culture. Many of the faithful insisted that Teresa had been at Tomochic all during the struggle against the forces of Lucifer and that she had disappeared during the climactic conflagration, had been carried to Heaven alive, and that she would return. Now she had done so. Some even identified her as a Tomochic Indian, bodily resurrected or escaped. Others endorsed the label of modern Joan of Arc, bearing a charmed life and returning to defend her people, even if, as a few insisted, she wore a modified cowboy costume with a short skirt, a brilliant neckerchief, and wide sombrero. Some saw Teresa as the mother of Moctezuma, the majestic Aztec king deposed by Spanish treachery. They called Teresa *el soñado Mesías Mexicano*, the long-dreamt-of Mexican Messiah "who had returned to liberate the servile peon and to re-establish the throne destroyed by Cortez."[22]

How wondrously the spirit builds and lifts. Teresa had first been elevated by her followers from a healer with certain (but limited) divinely granted powers to a full-fledged Santa, who could intercede with the Lord about various petitions from the sick and downtrodden; and now she had become a divinity herself, a woman-god, returned as promised in a blazing millennial vision of the glorious world to come. A cultural hero to some, however, may symbolize someone much more earthly for others eager to exploit the enthusiasm of the faithful for their own ends. For his readers Lauro Aguirre molded Teresa into much more of a down-to-earth revolutionary, and money-grubbing entrepreneurs (some of the pious considered them to be the agents of Satan) tempted La Santa with the prospect of personal pecuniary profit. Despite her earlier denunciation of money, Teresa caught the scent and took the bait.

Becoming Bourgeoise and Doubting Divinity

In June 1897, the Urrea clan, headed by Tomás and at least fifteen strong, moved from El Paso to the extensive mining complex at Clifton and nearby Morensi, Arizona, where thousands of Hispanics, American and Mexican, mined copper for long hours at low pay and under harsh conditions for Phelps Dodge, among the most overbearing of capitalist barons. There Teresa fell in love with a 21-year-old laborer named Guadalupe "Lupe" Rodríguez, whom she married over the objections of her father on June 22, 1900. Lupe went berserk the day after their wedding night, tried to shoot Teresa, was arrested by the police and shortly thereafter remanded to an asylum in Phoenix. The distressing affair left Teresa despondent. She and her family thought it best for her to seek a respite in San Jose, California, where she ministered to the three-year-old son of a family acquaintance who was afflicted with spinal meningitis. Five doctors had pronounced the boy incurable but in Teresa's hands the lad greatly improved, an astonishing feat reported with photos and flair in the *San Francisco Examiner* on July 27, 1900.[23]

News of this "miracle cure" caught the eye of a bamboozling petty businessman from San Francisco named J. H. Suits, who purportedly offered Teresa $10,000 to tour the country as a faith healer. While details of the agreement cannot be verified, La Santa soon began a carnivalesque adventure in the company of a 21-year-old family friend from Clifton who became her translator and lover. With much ballyhoo she reached New York City in March 1901, where newspapers reveled in her personal life and dealings with the Yaquis but did not say much about the latest healings. They pictured her groomed and dressed in a high style far from her origins at Cabora.[24] Had La Santa gone bourgeoise? If so, at what cost to her God-given mission?

While on tour Teresa announced that she intended to travel abroad to seek the source of her healing power. Formerly she had spoken of God's intervention in her life, but now she proposed to seek explanation for her magnetism in places like Paris, Egypt, and India: "Perhaps somewhere I may find some one wise in such matters who can tell me the secret."[25] What might her followers have thought of all these changes in La Santa? Before, she had accepted no payment for her cures and reviled money as one of the world's greatest evils. She had preached the gospel of the poor, and now she paraded with the rich. Teresa previously had pronounced herself subject to the will of God, and now she was looking elsewhere for insight. The faithful who adored Teresa knew that the Almighty grants powers to certain individuals to forward His work; Teresa had been so chosen. But they also recognized that the Lord, when somehow displeased with his designee on earth, may reclaim those remarkable powers. Indeed, Teresa's popularity had waned. There would be no journey to foreign places, and her traveling faith-healing spectacle shut down.

In the aftermath of her brief business career, Teresa (apparently in the company of her lover) moved to Los Angeles, where in December 1902 she settled in with a married sister in an attractive cottage at the corner of State and Brooklyn. Since the trolley ran by the house, the site soon became a rendezvous for the sick and curious.[26] These were not, however, the tumultuous crowds of Cabora and Nogales, nor was Teresa as steadfast in her ministry. Saying that she must prepare herself for ever more wonderful demonstrations of her powers, in mid-1903 she took a long retreat at the seaside resort of Santa Barbara, where she apparently lived off the income garnered during her cross-country medicine excursion.[27]

Now in her late twenties, Teresa seemed tired; it was time for her to go home to Clifton, Arizona. Her father Tomás had died in 1902 of typhoid fever, a loss that Teresa felt deeply, despite their differences. On August 25, 1903, her Los Angeles home burned to the ground, consuming possessions and remembrances of her colorful and rewarding life. By her lover she had a daughter, Laura, named for her friend, Lauro Aguirre—and was now pregnant again. In 1904 she obtained a legal divorce from her demented husband, Guadalupe, but did not remarry. That same year Teresa paid $300 for property on the south (and most desirable) side of Clifton and had a handsome two-story adobe and stone house of eight rooms erected there at a cost of $3,000. Although she cherished her new baby Magdalena along with her first daughter, Teresa grew increasingly listless, moody, and melancholy. Soon it became clear that she had contracted tuberculosis, that scourge and incurable malady of the times, and La Santa de Cabora died on January 11, 1906, at age 33. Her hometown newspaper, *The Copper Era*, lamented, "While yet in love with life and enraptured with the world, she passed to silence and to dreamless sleep."[28]

More than four hundred people attended the funeral, to that date one of the largest ever held in Clifton. No fewer than 21 wagons decked with whatever greenery could be gathered in wintry Arizona—evergreens, pyracantha with its red berries, branches of juniper—carried relatives in a somber procession to the gravesite, and a friend of the deceased Santa wrote a commemorative verse:

> Lay her in the earth;
> And from her pure unpolluted flesh
> May violets spring;
> I tell then, priest and minister,
> A ministering angel hath this woman been.[29]

Teresa was buried in a Roman Catholic cemetery on Shannon Hill next to her father, but in the Clifton area the relentless search for copper periodically displaced cemeteries in the name of enterprise, and Teresa's remains soon were moved to an unmarked grave in Ward Canyon Cemetery, on the other side of the San Francisco River outside of town. Why an unmarked grave for such a renowned person? Did the official Church seek to obliterate her ministry, to erase it from the minds of the devoted? We cannot say, but Clifton's priests do not seem to have been overtly hostile toward Teresa. Besides, if the faithful care to persevere, such deletions are not possible. The pious worship whom they wish and when they want. One would think that given her reputation, her followers would have converted Teresa's burial site into an enduring, vital shrine where they could have continued to pray and present their petitions to La Santa. But this did not happen in Clifton. The *Arizona Daily Citizen* later noted, "Her magical power had disappeared. The 'sainted girl of Sonora' had been forgotten."[30] Teresa's enthusiasts may well have sensed that once she detoured from the Lord's true work for money, travel, and luxury (although Teresa hardly died wealthy), God indeed had stripped her of her healing and prophetic powers.[31] It became apparent to the faithful that the Almighty no longer favored her to do His bidding in this world at that time. But such santas never wholly disappear from human memory and can always be recalled for succor and inspiration.

17

The Village Son of a Bitch

EVEN AS THE ARMY BURNED and buried the fast-decaying bodies left
on the battlefield at Tomochic in late 1892, inhabitants of the pueblo
who had avoided the strife filtered back to pick at the remains of the
devastated place. First on the scene was Bartolo Ledesma, the frequently abrasive police comisario and local judge, who owned a fair-
sized ranch at nearby Pahuiriachic; shortly afterward, Reyes Domínguez arrived. Even if the dwellings of Tomochic lay in charred ruins
(except the home of Domínguez, which the military had spared as
payment for its owner's active cooperation), there remained numbers
of stray animals, unharvested crops in the field, tools, guns and bayonets, and—most important—the question of control over how the
pueblo was to be realigned and rebuilt.[1]

Anxious to restore some semblance of normality in the valley and at
the same time to eradicate all tracks of the deed done there, General Rosendo Márquez appointed Domínguez along with the ex-presidente,
Juan Ignacio Chávez, who had done so much to ignite the initial troubles there, to oversee the cleanup and resettlement of the pueblo. Several widows of the fallen faithful, however, including those of Cruz
Chávez and Julián Rodríguez, protested, urging that someone more
trustworthy be sent to the village to inventory the remnants. In order
to avoid controversy and cool passions, the government more or less
agreed with the widows and consented to allow a ranchero from the
district's pueblo of Santa Inés, José de la Luz Córdova, respected for his
intelligence and impartiality, to do the survey and insure that whatever
property remained ended up with its rightful owners.[2]

Córdova arrived at the devastated site on November 13 to find dozens of corpses decomposing in the sun, tugged from their thin dirt covering by rapacious animals. The corpses had become an acute health hazard, so he hired ten Tarahumaras from the pueblo of Arisiachic to pile up, burn, and then bury the remains where they lay. They could hardly do otherwise, for the bodies were too putrefied to be moved to a mass grave or a cemetery. In ten days the Tarahumaras, each paid 50 centavos a day, disposed of 73 corpses.[3]

While proceeding with the gruesome details of burial, Córdova also started to round up stray horses, cattle, goats, and pigs, to study their brands and other markings and relate them to rightful owners; in the first week alone he corralled nearly five dozen animals. Reyes Domínguez, Jesus María Ortiz, and Bartolo Ledesma—the core of the old camarilla that had opposed the faithful and eventually fled the pueblo—battled him every step of the way. Tarahumaras saw Ortiz, for example, carry off burros that had belonged to Juan Rodríguez, a martyred defender, and there was no telling what Ortiz had confiscated from the ruined home of Dolores Rodríguez. For his take, Ledesma boldly invaded the property of Jorge Ortiz, harvested the deceased man's corn, and lugged off three cartfuls of grain for himself. Reyes Domínguez also scurried about: he took 30 bushels of corn from the fields of the dead Macario Ruiz, plus a couple of saws that had been the property of Dolores Rodríguez and branding irons that carried the mark of Jesús Medrano. Questioned about his horse, which carried the brand of Carlos Medrano, a Tarahumara named Hilario González claimed that General Rangel had given him the animal. Córdova tried hard, but there was no way he could straighten out the lies and obfuscations. "All has disappeared from the houses of the people, and no one knows who took what: benches, boxes, leather sacks, and wrinkled hides."[4] At one point he expressed regret at having to report the details of these matters to his superiors in pencil, explaining that Reyes Domínguez possessed the only ink in town and would not give him any. Córdova ordered Domínguez in writing to return those items he had lifted from the homes of the fallen, without success. Then he demanded receipts from Domínguez for the confiscated goods, again with no response. On November 16 Domínguez left the pueblo for Guerrero carrying a rifle and two large sacks packed with articles he had taken from the village, some belonging to Tomochitecos and some military materiel he had gathered up. Córdova hurried a note to the jefe político: "I presume that he will surrender these to you, and I presume that he will discuss the other items that I mentioned [he had taken]."[5] Nothing indicates, however, that Domínguez was ever questioned about these matters.

Indeed, Domínguez and Juan Ignacio Chávez demanded indemnification for alleged losses incurred during the attack on the pueblo. Domínguez wanted to be paid for the ten days in December 1891 when the army rented his house for its cuartel, as well as for the intelligence and other help he had given the army during its campaigns against the village. Moreover, Domínguez wanted to punish the dead even further, demanding his indemnification from what remained of their property. Whether the government gave Domínguez any remuneration for his part in the calamity is not known, but the jefe político officially rendered him no property that had belonged to the faithful. These scant goods were instead secured for the survivors. For his part, Juan Ignacio billed the government for 1,800 pesos (about $1,400) to cover the loss of his two houses and commercial establishment, including the furniture and billiard table, burned by federales in the attack.[6] Earlier we noted that each of these little country villages seemed to have its own "son of a bitch," and that Reyes Domínguez played the role well for Tomochic. His buddy Juan Ignacio made an apt understudy.

A few of the women who survived the holocaust returned to pick up the meager articles restored to them by Córdova, mainly unharvested corn and beans, plus some of their identifiable animals. Most, however, like the widows Mendías and Medrano, did not even bother to pick up their property. The women and children were being cared for by families in Guerrero, which did not spare them a sharp interrogation by General Márquez and his staff but gave them temporary shelter, even if under surveillance and a sort of house arrest. No one knew quite what to do with them. Governor Ahumada publicly expressed regret for their afflictions, urging a public subscription for their welfare. Small amounts of money, as well as offerings of corn, beans, potatoes, and clothing, trickled in from the pueblos in the Papigochic. Rancho Colorado, for example, immediately raised $10\frac{1}{2}$ pesos and $6\frac{1}{2}$ bushels of corn. In mid-1893 the relief fund was still delivering benefits to 21 widows and their children: more than 310 pesos in cash, 152 bars of soap, 222 packages of cigarettes, 148 boxes of matches, and 12 pounds of tallow for candles. In the early summer that year the involvement of these refugees with the new local santo, San José, sorely concerned authorities, who feared a resurgence of religious fervor that might attract multitudes. However, when this did not occur, and with El Santo eliminated, the governor forgave the survivors their involvement in the Tomochic affair and released them to their future.[7]

A number of families—Chávez, Calderón, Medrano, and Rodríguez—returned to Tomochic to restart their lives. By the time they did so late in the spring of 1893, José de la Luz Córdova had completed his inventory, and Reyes Domínguez ruled as the pueblo's officially appointed presidente. Authorities apparently forgot, or just did not care, that one of their respected own, Tomás Dozal y Hermosillo, sent early in February 1892 to defuse the troubles, had found the village hopelessly factionalized, had noted that Reyes Domínguez and Juan Ignacio Chávez had become lightning rods for discontent, and had recommended that an outsider trusted by the populace at large be placed in charge of the pueblo's affairs. Instead, governance in Tomochic now became a Domínguez family affair.[8]

True to form, Domínguez fired a parting shot at the state-appointed intervenor. He complained to higher authorities that Córdova had not done his job well and that unburied bodies from the armed encounter were still being discovered in the countryside (undoubtedly those of mortally wounded soldiers who had crawled off to die). This was typical Domínguez, who hung on to grudges like a bulldog and was now more truculent than ever. While attending to out-of-town business, he left his relative Cirilio in charge, while his nineteen-year-old son, Lisandro, also got paid from the public trough for various municipal duties. Everything in town was more or less up for grabs, and Domínguez worked hard to assemble and oversee all in his favor. As might be expected, however, villagers frequently ignored his commission and otherwise challenged him. They literally turned their animals loose on him—or better said, his authority. For a very long time (one might say customarily) these country people had used pigs, goats, cattle, dogs, and the rest of the farm menagerie to help settle up scores. Just easing open a gate did the trick, or perhaps pulling apart a few of the branches that made up a fence. The animals wandered out to freedom and trouble, carrying vengeance into some quarry's vegetable patch or cornfield. Loose animals drove Reyes Domínguez to tantrums. He complained to the jefe político (and it is only fair to say that some of the beasts must have broken loose on their own): "People won't help to control them. If they do, they want to be paid. Can I fine those who refuse to help?"[9] He received no such approval; the jefe político hoped to calm disputes in the village, not to rekindle them.

As might be expected, land was also at issue. Relatively few property titles had been perfected by law, and many claimed their right to possession by occupation; that is, on the basis that they had worked the land for considerable time. Now, with so many landowners dead, property rights could be challenged. Widows with broods of children to support might sell off parcels, and with the Domínguez camarilla in charge village authorities orchestrated the process. Isabel Rodríguez, widow of José Dolores Rodríguez, had an especially knotty claim concerning title to her property, and we do not know its outcome, only that Cirilio Domínguez reported in December 1893, "We're working on it." On December 12, the jefe político confirmed land titles to the surviving families of ten defenders (still officially labeled "fanáticos") who had died in the confrontation. These titles were anything but gifts. Those who received them had to prove they owned the land and had occupied it previously, and did so with old records somehow still in their possession or by tracking through registry books in the municipal palace at Guerrero. Nonetheless, in succeeding years Domínguez and his group—but especially Reyes himself—managed to monopolize valley property. By 1908 Domínguez was secure enough in his holdings to ask the state to formalize them through a resurvey of the entire village. Whether the survey was ever done cannot be confirmed, but it did not matter. In the 1920s, when Tomochitecos looked back at their pueblo around the turn of the century, they remembered that "Reyes Domínguez controlled or owned the majority of the land."[10]

All this maneuvering and manipulation temporarily ousted the local justice of the peace, Bartolo Ledesma, who had clung to the title all during the troubles. "I have been judge for four years even though I do not possess the qualifications. I cannot write. The administration of justice has suffered because of my personal difficulties, and I am a judge against the letter of the law. Now resources for living are so scarce I have to catch as catch can in order to support my family." And Ledesma went on to suggest as a replacement for himself, Jesús José Montoya, Nicolás López, or Luriano Herrera.[11] This is the first mention we have of a Montoya, proof that outsiders quickly appeared to stake a claim in the stricken pueblo. The Montoyas arrived as a family of ten with Vicente in his early forties as patriarch, and it seems unlikely that they would have come without an invitation from the ruling clique. Certainly the quick recommendation of Jesús José for judge places them in the Domínguez camarilla along with the other nominees, López and Herrera, who had disavowed Cruz Chávez and the faithful. In fact, Jesús José Montoya later married a daughter of Reyes Domínguez.[12] Despite this connection, Montoya and Reyes Domínguez eventually had a falling-out for obscure reasons, and camarilla politics were reinvigorated, as turbulent as ever and decidedly unimpeded by primary family relations. (Remember that Reyes Domínguez was married to the sister of Cruz Chávez.)

The Faithful Respond

Except for one illuminating moment after the turn of the century, the surviving defenders of the faith at Tomochic all but disappear from official accounts, though this does not mean their voice was forever stilled. What brought them to light in 1897 was the issue of school attendance. Officialdom, we understand, frequently views education as a panacea (or cover-up) for social ills, and the case of Tomochic was no different, especially because authorities continued to portray the martyred participants as well as their survivors as "indios" and "fanáticos," or better said, superstitious heathens who lacked the schooling of the modern world. Governor Ahumada thought (or at least he made the statement) that the entire tragedy might have been averted had the villagers been formally (meaning "properly") educated in public schools as fostered (but hardly paid for) by the regime. One of his major priorities in the aftermath of the struggle, therefore, was to insure that a primary school was reestablished in the village—"reestablished" because we might recall that the French expatriate Santiago Simonet had sought to provide public education in the pueblo prior to the disturbances. Once hostilities erupted, Simonet had hovered around at a nearby rancho until the final assault, but then we lose track of him.

On the eve of the outbreak of hostilities, however, we did catch a brief glimpse of his successor, Jesús Armenta, apparently lured there by his in-law, Reyes Domínguez, to regenerate public education. Now, in 1895, Armenta returned as village teacher and soon noted that attendance was off, down to no more than half of those required by state law to take instruction. In January 1897 he filed a report with the jefe político listing school-age boys by those who did and did not attend. Among the names of those who did, we find Domínguez, López, and Ledesma, scions of families who had chosen not to participate in the troubles, as well as Calderón and Rodríguez, who did. But among those listed as truants we spot Cruz Chávez, now sixteen years old, Manuel Chávez, fourteen, and Carlos Medrano, about ten, all named for their fathers. Their widowed mothers may well have needed them for labor, as they claimed to Reyes Domínguez, but quite possibly the families were also making a statement about village affairs as they saw and experienced them; absenteeism is one way the less powerful protest against their superiors.[13]

Again the Camarillas

The following year, 1898, the governor received a complaint from several unidentified residents of Tomochic about the arbitrary actions of their village presidente, Reyes Domínguez, who had jailed the widows of the pious for failure to send their sons to school, despite their protests that they were poor and needed their children to work the fields. Naturally the presidente denied any such abuses and said he had rightfully fined the complainants one peso each for failure to insure that their children attend school. Still, the bombardment of charges against Domínguez and his camarilla continued. On one occasion at the home of Reyes Domínguez, schoolmaster Armenta had struck a pupil, José López, on the side of his head so forcefully with his hand that he drew blood. When the boy's mother protested, Domínguez had terrorized her, threatening to send her son to the army. (The lad must have been in his early teens, at most.) Moreover, Domínguez was supported in his contemptuous attitude and activities by his judicial and administrative associates, Bartolo Ledesma (back as judge despite his lack of legal qualifications), Francisco Ledesma (substitute judge), and Timoteo Ledesma (municipal treasurer). There we have the camarilla designated by name, the same ones we saw surrounding Domínguez even before the conflagration. Finally, the accusation surfaced in this multiple complaint that Reyes Domínguez had illegally taken land from Jesús José Montoya, which probably explains their fallout. So the alignment of competing groups in the pueblo had now become clear, as well as the simmering animosity that some survivors of the cataclysm continued to harbor for their tormentors.[14]

Throughout the next decade these forces grated and ground against one another. A sirviente of Reyes Domínguez complained that when he was sick, his amo had beaten him for failure to come to work. So the laborer, Ramos Hernández, had sought employment elsewhere in order to earn the pesos needed to buy his freedom. The jefe político looked into the matter, taking testimony from others who called Hernández "worthless," "prone to laziness, even robbery," but we do not know how he then disposed of the case.[15] A few years later Tarahumaras around Tomochic claimed that Montoya had fenced off for himself common land that belonged to them, and if he was up to par on that occasion, Domínguez must have sided eagerly with the natives. At any rate, in mid-1908 Montoya filed a formal complaint with the governor against his rival's machinations.[16]

While the outcome of this particular dispute is uncertain, we know who won the war. In 1900 Tomochic had 77 dwellings, more than two-thirds of them one-room homes and most of the rest only with two rooms. However, Montoya had a six-room house and Domínguez two dwellings, one of five rooms and the other of four. Each of them owned a liquor license, Domínguez likely in his sundries store and Montoya in the shop in his house. Selling liquor to the Tarahumaras still produced sizable revenue and even property if a native, through drink, could be driven into debt. While in these terms the difference between the pueblo's major competitors is not very great, tax records disclose a widening gap. They show that while Montoya paid taxes on 29 mules, cows, and mares, Domínguez paid on well more than 100, and that while Montoya had one piece of farmland, Domínguez had four and a commercial establishment (his store) to boot. Furthermore, the list states that Domínguez was being taxed for substantial urban property he owned, probably in Ciudad Guerrero. These indicators prove Reyes Domínguez to be the cacique—the boss—of Tomochic.[17]

And in 1906 we find confirmatory data in September's tax records.

Of an estimated nearly 100 heads of household in the community of 434 inhabitants, only eight were listed as paying taxes (testimony to the poverty of the place), and most of those monthly assessments are only one peso or less. Meanwhile, Vicente Montoya paid 1.70 pesos, a reasonable amount more than the others, but at 7 pesos Reyes Domínguez was assessed more than three times as much, and they both paid these taxes only on admitted holdings, which as a rule far underestimated real wealth. Domínguez's acknowledged taxable assets ran to 2,400 pesos, six to eight times that of Montoya. In sum, while Reyes Domínguez did not count among the Papigochic's upper crust, he had constructed a comfortable petty fiefdom for himself in Tomochic.[18]

No doubt about it, Reyes Domínguez (and his camarilla) ruled Tomochic from the troubled times (in a sense, even before them) until he departed in 1911 during renewed upheaval in the Papigochic as part of the Mexican Revolution. Whether these new convulsions had anything to do with his departure is not certain, but he died a decade later at age 64 in the relatively new community of San Juanito, a saw mill settlement further into the Sierra but not very far from Tomochic, where the lumbering industry had taken root and begun to prosper. His son Lisandro and much of his extended family stayed in Tomochic during the second decade of this century. Cesario Acosta became the pueblo's new presidente. As a teenager Cesario and an older brother had survived the final encounter at Tomochic in October 1892 because they were working at the mines around Jesús María at the time. However, they did not escape the tragedy, which claimed the lives of their father and younger brother. Finally, Jesús José Montoya and Lisandro Domínguez lived in the pueblo into the 1920s, but we have no hint of their relationship, either to one another or to pueblo politics.[19]

Utilizing the Tragedy of Tomochic

In the 1920s, their appetite for more land whetted by the promises of the recently ended great revolution, the people of Tomochic demanded additional acreage from their federal government and threatened to rebel if they did not get it. Their most immediate target was the immense Limantour tract which surrounded the pueblo. Recall that in the early 1890s it had been sold to an American agricultural conglomerate, the Cargill Lumber Company, which had vigorously exploited it for its timber even as rebellion raged within and around it. To state their case in 1921 the Tomochitecos recalled their past. Listen to how they addressed the country's new president, Alvaro Obregón, and you will hear the way they put the past to use:

> In the year 1888, [José Ives] Limantour was ceded a large amount of land owned by our fathers and grandparents. When Limantour took possession, our people fought. The government gave the struggle a religious tinge, but it [the rebellion] was over land. The only wealth in our area is the exploitation of forests and the cultivation of potatoes and corn. We are paid miserable salaries to cut wood. If latifundio continues [referring to the Cargill monopoly], it gravely prejudices us. Sooner or later, as latifundio continues, we or our children will rise again in arms to end latifundismo. We ask for justice.[20]

So history and memory, ever malleable, are reworked to fit new times. And in the irony of ironies, those who signed the belligerent petition dated September 30, 1921, were in the main the heirs, the sons and grandsons, of those who had ridiculed and rejected Cruz Chávez and his followers, the López, Domínguez, Ledesma, and Herrera families among them. Pedro López was, in fact, village presidente at the time.[21] These matters never end. Historical memory is destined to recall this grand drama, if only because its passionate themes are ageless and can be put to many uses.

18

Remembrance

THE TRAGEDY OF TOMOCHIC is part of a living past that both lies embedded in the present and foreshadows the future.[1] While the Porfirian government sought to erase the debacle as simply one vestige of a past to be spurned, others have seized on it as a warning against tyranny, an inspiration for freedom, and a celebration of the human spirit. Even as the embers of the destroyed pueblo turned to ash, a young army lieutenant named Heriberto Frías, himself a participant in the repression, was composing a heartrending novel about the affair, destined to become a classic in which he ennobled the humble defenders and condemned the ruthlessness of Porfirian justice, themes that soon flowed into the national consciousness and beyond. In succeeding editions of his *Tomochic*, first published in 1893, Frías not only polished his prose, but increasingly demonized Porfirio Díaz as some sort of fiendish puppeteer who had cleverly manipulated common soldiers to ignite the inferno at Tomochic.[2] At about the same time, Lauro Aguirre, the longtime friend of the Urrea family who even in exile continued to consort with Teresa, wrapped the happenings at Tomochic in his understanding of Spiritism and depicted the calamity as a necessary step in mankind's inevitable progression toward perfect communion with the Almighty: "In the march of civilization, in the moral and intellectual ascent of man, there are events so sublime and extraordinary that they seem to be outside of the slow, but always progressive march of man. . . . Heroic Tomochitecos! Your sacrifice has not been in vain. . . . You have been the precursors of a new era."[3]

Meanwhile the indefatigable Santana Pérez had seized the image of the martyred Tomochitecos to carry his own battle standard, and even Santa Teresa publicly identified her birthright with Tomochic: "The Tomochis are of the race of my father—for we are not Yaquis; they [the Yaquis] live far to the west of Tomochic—the Tomochis believed the troops of Porfirio Díaz were tyrants, and so they slew them."[4]

But Aguirre and Pérez were in a tiny minority. The truth is that in the early days following the cataclysm hardly anyone seemed to remember (or at least openly proclaim) the Tomochitecos as heroic warriors. Most thought of them as perhaps brave, but still raging savages, even though they knew that the martyrs of Tomochic had been hardworking mestizos like themselves. A most active ingredient in historical re-creation, imagination ran amok as anxious settlers in the Sierra spotted here, there, and everywhere dangerous and vengeful Tomochic "Indians" who had escaped the army's repression. Concerned Mormons feared attack by the unrepentant hostiles, called in comrades working at the fringes of their settlement outside Casas Grandes, and posted sentries in the mountains above their colonies. Further north witnesses identified Tomochitecos among the border raiders who assaulted key crossings like Nogales and Palomas.[5] We have noted that parents no doubt admonished youngsters to behave or the Tomochis would get them, and so we see memory creatively fashioned to fit all sorts of preoccupations.

Throughout the Papigochic and north into the United States, early recollection of Tomochic was no doubt nourished by that deeper layer of remembrance laid on the region by several centuries of Apache raids. Only in the 1880s had the Apaches finally been corralled, but for a long time after that the public mind conjured up fearsome Apaches who had left their reservations to commit dreadful crimes, and most authorities and teachers did less than they might have to dispel such misapprehensions. For officialdom, fear of Apaches was a handy tool for social management. Moreover, as the actual Apache threat lessened many people in the area simply shifted their notions of Apaches to Yaquis, and then Tomochi "Indians" also fell quite naturally into the same genre. These were valiant, ferocious Tomochis to be sure, but still superstitious savages bent on racist revenge. None of this approached reality, but still fit memories as desired and used.

As time passed, the memory of Tomochic flourished as needed. We have seen how in the 1920s the villagers themselves construed their past to demand more land of their government, and in doing so recalled the noble defense of the village by their predecessors.[6] In the decade of the 1930s, Chihuahua's preeminent historian, Francisco Almada, rendered his own version of the drama, *La Rebelion de Tomochi*, and while his laudable endeavor did not receive wide circulation, it certainly has structured local memory about the events—though cantina talk and history conferences may have refashioned the epic to reflect more current concerns.

Tomochic also spawned a moving corrido, one of those uniquely Mexican songs that commemorate all things from revolution to love affairs, both won and lost. We have left to us only an undated fragment of the corrido of Tomochic, so there is no certainty when it was written, only that it lionizes the Tomochic men and women as dauntless defenders of their land and homes against the overwhelming forces of the military.

> The government had the idea
> Of finishing with these Tomochis.
> But the dirty fight
> Cost it days and nights,
> Along with the Eleventh and Ninth Battalions.
>
> And Cruz Chávez told them.
> "We are not softies
> Brace yourselves, you raw recruits,
> For here it comes
> For the Eleventh and Ninth Battalions."
>
> How valiant are the Tomochis
> Willing to die on the line,
> Defying the tough machine gun,
> Defending their soil and their home.
>
> Teresita de Cabora, my love
> Resonates in the voice of Cruz,
> Sapping the will of the recruits
> To fight and die with honor.
>
> The women in the tower,
> What good shots they are.

The blood that runs in them
Is the blood of liberty.

The Tomochis are finished,
So are the recruits,
But the power of God lives.
Because He is the Supreme Good
The Eleventh and Ninth Batallions died.[7]

Broadening Appeal

During the restless 1960s both La Santa and the martyred faithful, costumed as national history lessons, appeared as part of a series of comic books and little magazines that carried the official imprimatur of the Office of the Secretary of Public Education. Sold inexpensively at street-corner newsstands, they were meant for wide circulation. Well designed and printed on quality paper, the comic book, *México: Historia de un pueblo: Tomochic* by Juan Manuel Aurrecoechea, had an initial press run of 50,000. The little magazines were labeled "Cuadernos mexicanos" (Mexican notebooks), to give them a veneer of approved educational material; the one on Teresa, by Mario Gill, had the additional title *La Doncella de Cabora*. No doubt the government aimed to mold and sanitize memory of these past events that resonated—or could be made to resonate—so clearly with opposition to the current regime's practices, including the strident demands by students and others for social justice for all Mexicans.

The point of these attractive publications was to vilify the Porfirian regime, to emphasize its tyranny and brutality, and in doing so to legitimize its overthrow by revolutionaries whose heirs now governed the state so well. On the heels of challenges to its authority, which late in the summer of 1968 culminated in the massacre at a plaza in downtown Mexico City where the country celebrates its cultural heritage, the government sought to brighten its image by darkening that of its predecessor. Those who shaped the publications methodically idealized the Tomochitecos and La Santa de Cabora, ascribing the origins of their struggle to property seizures by avaricious land companies, and with glee excoriated the Catholic Church while taking care to label Teresa a "mystic" and her Indian followers "pagans" and therefore "nothing like us." The writers and artists found formal schooling, that core symbol of progress and modernity, to be absent from the consciousness of Cruz Chávez and his enthusiastic bunch (as if they did not even recognize the value of education), and the authors painstakingly situated their subjects in a primitive life surrounded by virgin, untamed nature. Yes, they were fine shots with their rifles, but also profoundly religious people—superstitious pagans, in other words, and once again not like us. Then, as if these religious rustics needed other more modern and intelligent individuals to boost them toward a greater cause (they could not aspire to such noble ends on their own), the storytellers blended the dissent of Santa Teresa and the Tomochitecos through intermediaries—Heriberto Frías and Lauro Aguirre among them—into the Great Revolution of 1910 in whose legacy the government claimed to rule. In this way Teresa and the Tomochitecos became precursors to the revolution, bearing no resemblance to us today (up-to-date, educated, lawful), but nevertheless to be remembered (at a decent distance) for taking a stance against Porfirian despotism.[8]

As Mexican society seethed into the 1970s with Luis Echeverría as president, dramatists continued to rework Tomochic to suit their present-day concerns. As part of its endeavor to ease tensions, the government sponsored filmmaking and promoted a brief flourishing of Mexican cinema with a semblance—nothing more than that—of social bite meant to convey the notion of a new freedom of expression in the country. One such movie, which appeared in 1975 and was entitled *La Longitud de guerra,* reflected on Tomochic and Santa Teresa. It was made by Gonzalo Martínez Ortega, who had learned the lore of these events while growing up in Chihuahua, and he did much of the filming on site. (Indeed descendants of the packs of dogs he rounded up to gnaw at dead bodies after the climactic battle still roam the pueblo—wild and intimidating, at least to me.) The movie resembles a Hollywood television or B Western, with a heavy-set Cruz Chávez mounted on a magnificent white stallion and the charming children of Tomochic dancing without a care around their folkloric community, soon to be demolished by the army. Armed with their abiding faith in La Santa de Cabora and steeled by their skirmishing with Apaches, the Tomochitecos (in some ways resembling mythical Texans) fight to the death for their land and for justice (as an abstract of the class struggle the film-maker seemingly came to appreciate while learning his craft in the Soviet Union). These images have come to be the way that the people of Tomochic itself, many of whom had bit parts in the film, now re-member their past.[9] In fact, in the wake of the filming a new sundries store, owned and run by Sonorans, sprang up along the main road through town. The sign above the entrance proclaims the place "Farm-acia y Papelería Santa Terecita de Cabora"—the pharmacy and station-ery store named for a misspelled Santa Teresa.[10]

Today the disquiet in the souls of countless Mexicans is reflected in their troubled remembrance of Tomochic. For some, the defenders of their spiritual world are best recalled as tragic heroes fated to martyr-dom by the inevitable march of the progress promised by modernity; such a reach for glory has no hope of triumph.[11] Others are not so sure. They look around and see that despite centuries of rationalism, the po-liticization of religion, and the secularization of society, millions of their countrymen still confide in spirits and faith healers, still envision a forthcoming millennium and impatiently await its arrival, even more so as the year 2000 approaches.[12] They recall and rework their versions of Tomochic as reminders of the promise certain to be fulfilled. And still others, their vision clouded by "enlightenment," allay their apprehen-sions about this conviction by labeling it "superstition," but such pos-turing hardly diminishes the frightening magic embedded in all religions.

Teresa as Feminist

As was the case with Tomochic, the ferment of the 1960s also energized forces that soon reshaped Santa Teresa to meet their needs, in particu-lar among feminists and Mexican-Americans. Feminists today remem-ber Teresa as a precursor to their movement, as a woman who on her own became a dominating force in a man's world. The recent motion picture *Nobody's Girls: Women of the American Frontier* portrays her as a woman of the American West, proof that women of all ethnicities de-serve a leading role in whatever pageant we create about the pioneering and settlement of the American West. The screenplay of this movie tells us: "In every direction where the heart seeks its desire, women have gone. Most went because their men went, but others found in the unfinished society of the American West an opening for desire, where they could redefine themselves, take their lives in their own hands. Many of them failed. A few [such as Santa Teresa] succeeded, against the odds, and at a cost that cannot now be fully measured." And the movie concludes, on little evidence, that "La Santa de Cabora and the Yaqui Indians who died under her banner were to become legends of the Mexican Revolution."[13]

On the other hand, because Teresa was a Mexican who resided, performed her healings, and perhaps played politics on both sides of the border, Mexican-Americans have recalled her as one of their heroines. The authors of the book *La Chicana: Mexican-American Women* write that Teresa Urrea "remains a symbol of resistance to oppression for contemporary Chicanos. She is thereby a Chicana counterpart to La Virgen de Guadalupe, a symbol of warmth, succor, and hope for the poor, destitute, and exploited."[14] *El Grito* publications assert that Teresa lived and performed her healings in Aztlán, thus cementing Sonora and the U.S. Southwest to the mythical birthplace of the mighty Aztecs, and from the journal *Grito el Sol* we learn: "Yes, later, her followers brought flowers to the evangelist's grave. They claimed to hear voices and noises below the grave, begging them to dig her out. Others believed Teresa remained asleep in her coffin waiting to be dug out and ready again to help her fellow [Mexican-American] countrymen."[15]

While ratifying her claims to special powers and buoyed by Teresa's own vacillations about their origin, both feminists and Mexican-Americans have chosen to cloak Teresa in a secular garb that more resembles their own. They remember her as a fearsome fighter for social justice, but seem to be reluctant to recall the spirituality that pervaded her life.

La Santa Recalled

At the same time, people everywhere appear to be hungry for a personal experience with a higher being, and as we approach a new millennium, there is a heightened expectation in many places of a promised coming, not only among Christians in the United States, but among much of mankind.[16] In this mood of our times, then, it should come as no surprise that Santa Teresa is now being recalled in these terms. The place is Clifton, Arizona, where she died. The time quite recently, on Saturday, April 9, 1994, when a multitude celebrated the First Annual Santa Teresa Day. Now how did all of this come about?[17]

In the spring of 1993 Robin D. Gilliam, the curator of History and Interpretation (itself a marvelous juxtaposition) at the museum in Silver City, New Mexico, less than two hours by automobile southeast of Clifton, was preparing an exhibit of fin-de-siècle photographs when he came across the picture of a beautiful young woman, perhaps in her twenties, dressed in an elegant long gown of the period. No one in Silver City could identify her, but the photo carried the date 1901 and the signature of O. A. Risdon, one of the region's best-known photographers, who had spent much of his life in Clifton. Gilliam forwarded the picture to Clifton's weekly newspaper, *The Copper Era*, where it appeared on March 31 with the title: "Mystery lady's identity sought" and the accompanying query: "Take a good look at the photograph. Does it resemble anyone the reader would know? Any clues?"[18]

One of the directors of Clifton's historical society, Charles Spezia, saw the photo as an especially seductive image of the city's past. Born and raised in Clifton, Spezia had returned after retirement and now actively promotes regional lore both to attract tourists and to enhance community identity. He and two other members of the historical society board believed the picture to be that of Teresa Urrea (although Spezia now has his doubts), and on April 21 *The Copper Era* declared, "Mystery lady is identified." A niece of Teresa, María Aguirre, who still resides in Clifton, verified that a copy of the picture had once been the property of the Urrea family and later been given to a scholar who was writing a book about Teresita. But at that point the trail grows cold.[19] Other photographs of Teresa hardly resemble the "mystery lady," but no matter; La Santa de Cabora had reemerged in the public mind. Although local people remembered little of her, the void was soon filled by a newly mesmerized and peripatetic devotee.

Luis Pérez, a former journalism professor who resides in Silver City, where he promotes local tourism, had become intrigued by Santa Teresa since coming across her picture several years ago in the historical museum at Alamos, the former silver mining town not far from the old Urrea rancho at Cabora. Then, reading a recent novel about Santa

Teresa, *La Insolita historia de la Santa de Cabora,* he learned that she had died in Clifton. The fact that his family roots stretched back to a pueblo in the Sierra not very far from Tomochic, plus his instincts for journalism and tourism, led him to investigate Teresa's life with a truly ebullient passion. Pérez, who does not consider himself to be overly religious, traveled to Clifton to seek out Teresa's unmarked grave. Using period photographs of the landscape and later paintings based on these photos, he narrowed the search to the Ward's Canyon Cemetery. Still he could not pinpoint her grave. So he sat down in that graveyard, which sprawls across the countryside to ponder possibilities, and quite spontaneously a sweet aroma floated to his senses from a certain spot. He remembered that the faithful at Cabora had reported the sweet scent emanating from La Santa herself as she ministered to the sick, as well as from the moistened mixtures she used in her healings, and now a similar lovely fragrance surrounded him. In other words, Pérez had a spiritual experience that he insists led him to the exact location of Teresa's remains. He recounted as much to Clifton's City Council and suggested that a monument commemorating the woman's compassion and charity be erected at the site or at some prominent junction in town.

The Council took Pérez's suggestion under advisement the fall of 1993, but some townspeople, among them Walter Mares, a journalist and member of Greenlee County's Chamber of Commerce, actively pressed the case for Teresa. For him, remembering Teresa made good sense for Clifton beyond honoring La Santa's good works. First of all, the town, despite its charming setting along the sides of the deep, rocky gorge of the San Francisco River, found its population dwindling to only about 2,500 and had committed itself to historical restoration, both to preserve the locale's colorful past and to take advantage of tourism's enchantment with old mining sites. The city had recently inveigled the Southern Pacific Railroad into donating the old train station, which was then remodeled by the city as a picturesque period piece that now proudly houses the county's Chamber of Commerce.

Moreover, and perhaps much more important, from 1983 to 1986 Clifton had been polarized by a ferocious strike that gained international attention when Phelps Dodge, the multinational copper company, broke the local mine workers' union, long known for its cohesiveness and militancy. The conflict splintered the community and the union itself: company versus union, outsiders hired as "scab" replacements against local strikers, an older generation against a younger one, even down into families, parents against children, brothers and sisters divided. Townspeople said the place needed a miracle in order to regain its balance and sense of community.

Clifton's priest, Father Joseph Baker, knows that God grants miracles but senses no special relationship between Teresa and the Divine. Still, he is cautious in his consideration of God's will. He knows that remembrance of Teresa's capabilities to heal still exists in the local mind, even if muted, but wonders if her teachings in any way meshed with Catholic doctrine, or even if Teresa believed as a Catholic. When he came to his parish four years ago he had not even heard of Santa Teresa, though he had worked much of his religious life in the Tucson diocese that includes Clifton. Since then he has occasionally received an inquiry about La Santa, usually a request for some soil from her grave, and he responds by sending a few pinches of dirt in a plastic bag to the petitioners, some from as far away as Ohio and Hermosillo. The soil comes from the parish cemetery, where Father Baker and other Catholics believe Teresa to be buried, and in the parish house he keeps a bottleful of dirt handy to answer requests for the spiritual relic. He makes no judgments about the merits of the requests; he simply responds to those who feel the spiritual need for the soil. It is a wise priest who understands that popular religiosity frequently lacks doctrinal purity but still can be honored.

Even civic authorities, who planned Santa Teresa Day more as a secular happening than a spiritual revival, feared the power of official religion to turn the tables on their intentions. So they deliberately scheduled their event outside the Lenten season and in their announcements carefully limited to Yaqui Indians those people who had declared Teresa a saint. Charles Spezia, whose career was as a chemist, stated, "We're modern here; none of that superstitious stuff for us." And it is true that since the strike displaced many of the city's old-timers, the new blood in town tends to sport a modern, boastful rejection of formal religion. Still, many residents remain deeply spiritual in the embrace of Roman Catholicism, once dominant in the area, despite the sign on the main road through town that reads: "Welcome. First Southern Baptist Church on hill above Chevron station." And as the celebration of Santa Teresa approached, it became obvious that even those in Clifton who could not recall Teresa were anxious to meet her.

Saturday morning of the day devoted to Santa Teresa broke beautifully over Clifton, not a puff of white in the pastel blue sky. *The Copper Era* had headlined the event the previous Wednesday, but no one was sure who or how many might gather at the restored train depot to hear Luis Pérez recount the story of Teresa Urrea.[20] The promoters of the event need not have worried. Hundreds filled the lecture hall to overflowing: Hispanics and Anglos, longtime residents of the community and newcomers, some fifteen relatives of Teresa Urrea. Present in the crowd were strikers who had lost their jobs at Phelps Dodge; scabs who had replaced them; and plant managers and ex-union officials who had opposed each other. But few had even heard of a Santa Teresa until seeing the picture of the "mystery woman" in the newspaper. Some mentioned stories about Teresa passed on to them by their parents and grandparents, remembering her vaguely as a charitable person in Clifton's past, known for her healing powers. None revered her as a saint, and none seemed even to have thought of her grave site as a potential venue for personal piety.

But then with unrestrained enthusiasm and a good deal of personal emotion, Luis Pérez beautifully reconstructed the memory of Teresa Urrea for this very respectful, curious, perhaps even spiritually hungry audience. He refigured La Santa in both historical and contemporary likenesses, deliberately linking her presence to Sor Juana Inés de la Cruz, the rebellious, liberated nun of Mexico's colonial past, and to Mother Teresa of Calcutta. In explaining Teresa's mission and her qualities, he quoted from the Bible and from poets such as the nineteenth-century Englishman Leigh Hunt, noteworthy for his soft-spoken earnestness about human social values.

So Pérez chose to remember Teresa Urrea as not particularly religious—that is, as a member of no official church—but so loving of her fellow man that she experienced the grace of God. This was a vision that could embrace all those present at his talk and stopped well short of declaring her a "Santa" and arousing unwanted debate.

An exuberant Pérez also proclaimed her the winner of a beauty pageant in New York City, one which to my knowledge never took place. And he spoke of a cave above the rancho at Cabora where Teresa had meditated and scraped the soil that she used in her healings; nothing in the historical record indicates that Teresa utilized such a cave. Nonetheless, Pérez brought to the gathering in Clifton a salt shaker full of dirt from that cave and after his presentation offered a sprinkling to those who cared for one. Twenty or thirty people—one in a wheelchair, another with fearsome physical hurts, several with unrestrained tears streaming down their cheeks—requested a few grains of that soil, myself included, all for our own private reasons.

As the day of celebration slid into carnival—hot dogs, hamburgers, chilacas and menudo, inexpensive jewelry and pricey clay sculptures, drawings, paintings, and photographs by local artists, and finally a block dance featuring spirited norteño music—remembrance of Teresa put down new roots and sprouted new, quite lovely blossoms. Some declared her born in Clifton. Others exaggerated her charitable works, and even invented some new ones for her. These are people not particularly surprised by mentions of miracle cures, for they already possess an appreciation for the grace of God. Nor did the gathering in any way approach a clamorous religious revival. More properly, people seemed to drift into that state of comradeship and gentle exhilaration—that ambiguous, in-between sublime state of communality—in which hope is reborn and humanness, togetherness, and equality gather higher meaning. "I feel joy and self-esteem, and pride"—he meant of both place and people—explained Félix Vásquez, who has lived all of his 74 years in Clifton: "We are together again." Others regretted that Teresa had disappeared from their memory. "We had heard the name from our parents, but we never had come to know her. Now we do."

As a consequence of their needs and longings, and of these events, the people of Clifton have come to know Teresa, and they remember her as they see fit. The wife of a local bar owner paid $700 for an oil painting of Teresita to be prominently displayed in her home. The Urrea family has discovered and decorated La Santa's grave, laid a concrete slab at the spot identified by Luis Pérez, and surrounded it with a newly painted ornamental wrought-iron fence; whether the site is exact, or even approximately correct, does not matter in the slightest. As the climax to the celebration of Santa Teresa, a cortege of autos, headlights ablaze in the fading sunlight and their route cleared by local uniformed police, carried those dozens who especially wished to honor Teresa to the place proclaimed as her grave. Walter Mares, a recovering alcoholic, read to the gathering the passage for July first from a *Twenty-Four Hours a Day* book frequently read by those in Alcoholics Anonymous—words that for him best remembered Teresa: "Learn the lesson of trust and calm in the midst of the storms of life." He thinks she may heal tensions in Clifton, and even more among all humanity, and in this way Teresa serves the religious as well as the nonreligious in these contentious times.

Indeed, people are recalling La Santa as they wish, as best suits them, and reports of recent healings are already in circulation: in the summer of 1994 the image of Teresa was seen hovering over a woman who suffered crippling migraine headaches but who now is cured. Faith is already working its miracles. People are recalling their history as needed to ponder, revalidate, and critique their present; they are reformulating their past to consider and serve their contemporary anxieties and demands. If toward such ends some recall a resuscitated Teresa Urrea and find for her a niche in their lives, the wonderment of it only validates for us the mystery and magnificence of remembrance.

And yes, already some unidentified believer has left a rolled up message—probably a petition—carefully tied with a ribbon to the iron fence around the grave site. We may be certain there will soon be more.

Reference Matter

Notes

The following abbreviations are used in the notes; a complete listing of archives consulted can be found in the Selected Bibliography, pp. 389–403.

ADN   Archivo de la Secretaría de la Defensa Nacional (Mexico City). Sections: Históricos and Cancelados.

AEC   Archivo del Estado de Chihuahua, Palacio de Gobierno (Chihuahua City). Notarías, Archivo Histórico, Sección de Protocolos, Distrito de Guerrero.

AGG   Archivo Particular del Lic. Hector González y González (Guerrero, Chihuahua), Partes de los acontecimientos de Tomochic ocurridos la tarde del 7 de diciembre de 1891.

AGN   Archivo General de la Nación (Mexico City).

AHAD   Archivo Histórico del Arzobispado de Durango (Durango City).

AHES   Archivo Histórico del Estado de Sonora (Hermosillo).

AMCG   Archivo Municipal de Ciudad Guerrero (Guerrero, Chihuahua).

AMO   Archivo Municipal de Ocampo (Ocampo, Chihuahua).

APD   Archivo Porfirio Díaz, Universidad Iberoamericana (Mexico City).

BFO   British Foreign Office Embassy and Consular Archives (London). Correspondence: Series II, F. O. 204, vol. 207 (1889).

BSCEH   *Boletín de la Sociedad Chihuahuense de Estudios Históricos* (Chihuahua City).

CIDECH   Centro de Información del Estado de Chihuahua (Chihuahua City), Archivo Particular de Francisco Almada.

SRA   Archivo Histórico, Secretaría de la Reforma Agraria (Mexico City).

SRE   Archivo Histórico, Secretaría del Estado y Despacho de Relaciones Exteriores (Mexico City).

USDS   U.S. Department of State (Washington, D.C.). Consular Reports: Guaymas 1889–91; Nuevo Laredo 1871–1906.

USNA   U.S. National Archives (Washington, D.C.) Military Records Branch, Adjutant General's Office, Record Group 94.

Chapter 1

1. J. C. Chávez, *Peleando*, pp. 32, 35.

2. Ibid., p. 30.

3. I lived in the geographical area encompassed in this book during parts of the 1980s. A hand-drawn map of the pueblo at the time of the events under discussion appears in J. C. Chávez, *Peleando*, between pp. 72 and 73. Another hand-drawn map of the village may be found in APD, Leg. 17, Exp. 013266, Portilla to Joleury, 5 September 1892. A third map appears in W. C. Holden, *Teresita*, p. 157. The maps of Tomochic prepared for this book were drawn from these sources.

4. The present-day church stands on approximately the same site. Recent excavations there have uncovered remnants of the old structure destroyed by the combat of October 1892.

5. J. C. Chávez, *Peleando*, p. 31.

6. Ibid.

7. This concept is admirably illustrated in Christian, *Person and God*, pp. 114–87.

8. J. C. Chávez, *Peleando*, pp. 32–33.

9. AGG; Almada, *Rebelión de Tomochi*, p. 42.

10. J. C. Chávez, *Peleando*, p. 30.

11. Ibid.

12. AMCG, Leg. 1891, Exp. Comunicaciones con inferiores, Juan Ignacio Chávez, presidente, Tomochic, to Jefe Político, 1 December 1891; Exp. Comunicaciones con superiores, Silviano González, Jefe Político, Guerrero, to Gobernador, 3 December 1891. This invaluable archive was reorganized during the time this book was in preparation; therefore, some of the documents cited do not carry their new *legajo* and *expediente* numbers. However, dating throughout remains consistent with the present chronological organization of the archive, and all of the notes identify the correspondents. See also AGG; Almada, *Rebelión de Tomochi*, p. 42; and J. C. Chávez, *Peleando*, p. 30.

13. APD, Legs. 50–51, Exp. 006595–601, Lauro Carrillo, gobernador, Chihuahua, to Porfirio Díaz, 9 December 1891; Leg. 16, Exp. 015494–95, Rafael Pimentel, Chihuahua, to Díaz, 15 December 1891. J. C. Chávez, *Peleando*, pp. 13, 31.

14. J. C. Chávez, *Peleando*, p. 31.

15. Almada, *Rebelión de Tomochi*, p. 43; J. C. Chávez, *Peleando*, p. 32.

16. AGG; Chávez Calderón, *Defensa de Tomochi*, p. 18; J. C. Chávez, *Peleando*, p. 32.

17. AGG; J. C. Chávez, *Peleando*, p. 33.

18. J. C. Chávez, *Peleando*, p. 33.

19. Ibid.

20. AGG; Almada, *Rebelión de Tomochi*, p. 43; J. C. Chávez, *Peleando*, pp. 33–35.

21. J. C. Chávez, *Peleando*, p. 35.

22. Ibid., p. 36.

23. APD, Legs. 50–51, Exps. 006595–601, Carrillo to Díaz, 9 December 1891; Leg. 50, Exp. 006673–75, Telegrama, Carrillo to Díaz, 10 December 1891; Leg. 50, Exp. 006607, Ahumada to Díaz, 10 December 1891.

24. AGG; J. C. Chávez, *Peleando*, p. 36.

25. AGG.

26. AGG.

27. Almada, *Rebelión de Tomochi*, pp. 454–46.

28. AGG; Almada, *Rebelión de Tomochi*, pp. 46–47; J. C. Chávez, *Peleando*, pp. 58–59.

29. AGG; Almada, *Rebelión de Tomochi*, pp. 40–41, appendix 4, p. 153.

30. AMCG, Leg. 1891, Exp. Comunicaciones con inferiores, Ramón A. Sáenz to Jefe Político, 28 December 1891. See also J. C. Chávez, *Peleando*, p. 43; Almada, *Rebelión de Tomochi*, pp. 45, 50.

31. APD, Leg. 50, Exps. 006602–6, Rangel to Díaz, 9 December 1891; J. C. Chávez, *Peleando*, p. 37.

32. J. C. Chávez, *Peleando*, p. 42.

33. Ibid., p. 43.

34. APD, Leg. 50, Exp. 006722–26, Carrillo to Díaz, 11 December 1891.

Chapter 2

1. APD, Leg. 50, Exp. 12, Nos. 006764–68, Carrillo to Díaz, 12 December 1891.

2. For a stimulating if not always convincing attempt to categorize those individuals most likely to join millenarian movements see Barkun, *Disaster and the Millennium*, ch. 4.

3. Brondo Whitt, *Patriarcos*, pp. 144–46.

4. AMCG, Leg. 6, Exp. 72, Comunicaciones con inferiores (Reorganization by Santa Anna in 1854).

5. AMCG, Leg. 6, Exp. 69, Padrón general de Tomochi [1864]. *Padrones* are various kinds of census lists. This padrón covers the entire district of Guerrero.

6. AMCG, Leg. 6, Exp. 69, Padrón general de Tomochi [1864]; Leg. 22, Exp. 235, Padrón general de Tomochic [1890]. Parroquia de la Concepción (Ciudad Guerrero), Libro de bautismos, 16 enero de 1886, terminando el 10 de diciembre de 1888, p. 10.

7. Archivo de Protocolos, Palacio Municipal, Ciudad Guerrero, Protocolos del 9 de enero de 1886 al 31 de diciembre de 1886, No. 37.

8. AMCG, Leg. 6, Exp. Correspondencia, No. 106, Jesús José Chávez, presidente de Tomochic, to Jefe Político, 3 July 1858 and 19 October 1867.

9. For an excellent book on Tarahumara culture see Merrill, *Rarámuri Souls*.

10. AMCG, Leg. 7, Exp. 82, Comunicaciones con inferiores, Jesús José Chávez, presidente, Tomochic, to Jefe Político, 3 July 1858.

11. AMCG, Leg. 7, Exp. 82, Comunicaciones con inferiores, (Padre) Felipe de Jesús Silva, Tomochic, to Jefe Político, 10 February 1859.

12. AMCG, Leg. 7, Exp. 82, Comunicaciones con inferiores, Juan Domínguez, juzgado de Tomochic, to Jefe Político, 18 June 1857.

13. AMCG, Leg. 8, Exp. 91, Comunicaciones con inferiores, Carlos Medrano, juez de paz, Tomochic, to Jefe Político, 10 June 1862; Archivo de Protocolos, Cuidad Guerrero, Protocolos del 9 de enero de 1886 al 31 de diciembre de 1886, No. 37.

14. AMCG, Comunicaciones con inferiores, 1883, Julián Rodríguez, tesoro de la sección de Tomochic, to Jefe Político, 9 October 1883.

15. AMCG, Memoriales presentados en los años 1869, '72, '73, '81, '82, '83, '84, '85, '86, '87, Cruz Chávez, Tomochic, to Jefe Político, 17 May 1885.

16. AMCG, Leg. 6, Exp. 69; Leg. 22, Exp. 235 (1890), Estado de Chihuahua, Padrón de Tomochic.

17. Conclusion drawn from survey of documents in Archivo de Papigochic from 1821 to 1916. The only mention found for Cruz Chávez was AMGC, Leg. 24, Exp. 246, Juan Ignacio Chávez, presidente, Tomochic, to Jefe Político, 19 May 1891.

18. Archivo de Protocolos, Cuidad Guerrero, Protocolos del 9 de enero de 1886 al 31 de diciembre de 1886, No. 37; AMCG, Leg. 22, Exp. 235, Tomochic padrón for 1890.

19. AMCG, Leg. 20, Exp. 228, Comunicaciones con inferiores, Manuel Chávez, juzgado de paz, Tomochic, to Jefe Político, 2 January 1889.

20. Archivo Judicial de la Municipalidad de Guerrero, Palacio Municipal Guerrero City, Chihuahua. Juzgado Menor, Civiles, 1887–88, 13 October 1887.

21. For examples see AMCG, Comunicaciones con inferiores, Jesús María Bustillos, juez de estado civil, Namiquipa, to Jefe Político, 28 April 1875; and Leg. 16, Exp. 186, Jesús José Alderete, comisario, Basúchil, to Jefe Político, 6 April 1885.

22. Examples of disputes include Archivo Judicial de la Municipalidad de Guerrero, Juzgado Menor, Guerrero, Civiles, 8 June 1868 and 4 September 1887. AMCG, Leg. 8, Exp. 98, Comunicaciones con superiores, Governor, Chihuahua, to Jefe Político, 31 September and 19 October 1864; Leg. 10, Exp.

123, Comunicaciones con inferiores, Jesús B——, Namiquipa, to Jefe Político, 19 March 1871; Leg. 10, Exp. 122, Comunicaciones con superiores, Governor to Jefe Político, 6 January 1871; Leg. 11, Exp. 143, Martín Carraso, comisario, Tejolócachic, to Governor, 20 January 1876; Leg. 11, Exp. 143, Comunicaciones con inferiores, Manuel Terrazas, comisario, Hacienda de Providencia, to Jefe Político, 24 February 1876; Leg. 16, Exp. 186, Borrador de Comunicaciones con inferiores, 1885–86, 9 September 1885; Leg. 17, Exp. 203, Comunicaciones con inferiores, Atmo [Artemio] Rodríguez, Ramón Hernández, Jesús Lara, Cleto Lara, Valentín Banda, Santiago Montáñez to Jefe Político, 6 April 1888; Leg. 19, Exp. 219, María Martiniana Márquez, Guerrero, to Jefe Político, 25 July 1889.

23. AMCG, Leg. 8, Exp. 91, Comunicaciones con inferiores, Carlos Medrano, juez de paz, Tomochic, to Jefe Político, 10 June 1862; Memoriales presentadas en los años 1869–87, Carlos Medrano, Tomochic, to Jefe Político, 8 June 1887; Archivo de Protocolos, Guerrero, Protocolos del 9 de enero de 1886 al 31 de diciembre de 1886, No. 37.

24. AMCG, Leg. 11 Exp. 144, Comunicaciones con inferiores, 1 October 1877; Leg. 12, Exp. 147, Comunicaciones con inferiores, Dolores Mendías, comisario, Tomochic, to Jefe Político, 2 April 1887.

25. AMCG, Leg. 13, Exp. 158, Comunicaciones con inferiores, Cecilio Gallegos, comisario suplente, Tomochic, to Jefe Político, 31 August 1880.

26. AMCG, Leg. 14, Exp. 140, Comunicaciones con inferiores, Reyes Domínguez, comisario, Tomochic, to Jefe Político, 2 September 1882.

27. AMCG, Leg. 16, Exp. 191, Borrador, Jefe Político, 13 January 1886; Comunicaciones con inferiores, Cecilio Gallegos, comisario, Tomochic, to Jefe Político, 13 January 1885. Archivo Judicial de la Municipalidad de Guerrero, Juzgado Menor, Guerrero, Civiles, 1887–88, 4 November 1887; J. C. Chávez, *Peleando*, p. 68.

28. APD, Leg. 17, Exp. 000226; *El Diario del hogar*, 16 April 1890, p. 3; 31 May 1890, p. 2; 24 August 1890, p. 2; 15 September 1890, p. 3.

29. AMCG, Leg. 12, Exp. 149, Comunicaciones con inferiores, Dolores Mendías, Tomochic, to Jefe Político, 5 January 1878.

30. AMCG, Leg. 17, Exp. 203, Comunicaciones con inferiores, Jesús Medrano, presidente, Tomochic, to Jefe Político, 1 April 1888.

31. AMCG, Leg. 12, Exp. 148, Comunicaciones con inferiores, Pachera to Jefe Político, 33 May 1878.

32. AMCG, Leg. 12, Exp. 148, Comunicaciones con inferiores, Reyes Domínguez, comisario, Tomochic, to Jefe Político, 24 May 1878; Leg. 12, Exp. 149, Reyes Domínguez, junta menor de beneficia, Tomochic, to Jefe Político, 24 April 1878, 8 June 1878.

33. AMCG, Leg. 12, Exp. 150, Comunicaciones con inferiores, Reyes Domínguez, junta [menor] de beneficia, Tomochic, to Jefe Político, 2 May 1878;

Leg. 12, Exp. 148, Domínguez, comisario, to Jefe Político, 24 May 1878; Leg. 12, Exp. 149, Domínguez, junta menor de beneficia, to Jefe Político, 8 June 1878.

34. AMCG, Leg. 17, Exp. 203, Jefe Político to Ayuntamiento (Ciudad Guerrero), 26 January 1888; Comunicaciones con inferiores, José Dolores Rodríguez, comisario, Tomochic, to Jefe Político, 28 February 1888.

35. AMCG, Leg. 17, Exp. 203, Comunicaciones con inferiores, Jesús Medrano, presidente, Tomochic, to Jefe Político, 1 April 1888; Leg. 17, Exp. 203, Jefe Político to Ayuntamiento, 26 June 1888.

36. AMCG, Leg. 17, Exp. 203, Comunicaciones con inferiores, Jesús Medrano, presidente, Tomochic, to Ayuntamiento, 28 March 1888; Medrano to Jefe Político, 1 and 10 April, 1888.

37. AMCG, Leg. 17, Exp. 203, Comunicaciones con inferiores, Atmo [Artemio] Rodríguez, Ramón Hernández, Jesús Lara, Cleto Lara, Valentín Banda, Santiago Montáñez to Jefe Político, 6 April 1888; Jesús Medrano, presidente, Tomochic, to Jefe Político, 3 April 1888, and Santiago Simonet, Tomochic, to Ayuntamiento, 15 May 1888.

38. AMCG, Colección de comunicaciones con inferiores mes de junio de 1889, Jorge Ortiz to Jefe Político, 14 and 17 June, 1889.

39. J. C. Chávez, *Peleando*, pp. 63–70; *El Monitor republicano*, 2 November 1892, p. 1; AMCG, Leg. 30, Exp. 291; *El Paso Daily Times*, 9 September 1896; Almada, *Gobernadores*, p. 419; Almada, *Apuntes históricos*, p. 390.

40. AMCG, Comunicaciones con inferiores, telegramas oficiales, el año de 1891, Carlos Perlaz, Pinos Altos, to Jefe Político, 29 January 1891; Ramón Ochoa, Pinos Altos, to Jefe Político, 24 February 1891; G. A. Nieto, Chihuahua, to Jefe Político, 16 April 1891; Leg. 20, Exp. 227, Comunicaciones con inferiores, Miguel Prado, Pinos Altos, to Jefe Político, 15 April 1891; Leg. 23, Exp. 241, Copia de comunicaciones con inferiores, 27 June 1891 to 19 September 1891; Leg. 23, Exp. 243, Comunicaciones con superiores, Governor to Jefe Político, 6 and 21 February 1891; Comunicaciones con inferiores, septiembre de 1890–20 de febrero 1891, Libro 11, Circular 11, 28 January 1891; Colección de comunicaciones con inferiores, mes de marzo de 1892, Juez, juzgado de primera estancia del distrito de Rayón, to Jefe Político, 3 March 1892; Comunicaciones con superiores, Governor Lauro Carrillo to Jefe Político, 9 March 1891; Rafael Pimentel, Chihuahua, to Jefe Político, 25 June 1891. Almada, *Resumen*, pp. 346–49, *Revolución*, 1: 98, and *Rebelión de Tomochi*, pp. 30–32. Irrab, "Efemérides chihuahuenses," *BSCEH*, June 1939, p. 37; August 1939, p. 105.

41. Almada, *Resumen*, pp. 348–49, and *Rebelión de Tomochi*, p. 32.

42. APD, Leg. 50, Exp. 12, Nos. 006722–26, Carrillo to Díaz, 11 December 1891.

43. AGN, Colección Alfredo Robles Domínguez, vol. 7, Serie Manuel González Ramírez, vol. 3, folios 141–45.

44. AMCG, Comunicaciones con inferiores, junio de 1892, Informe de Silviano González a Gobernador, 1891; Luis Comadurán, presidente, Bachíniva, to Jefe Político, 3 June 1892. *El Diario del hogar*, 16 April 1890, p. 3. APD, Leg. 17, Exp. 3, Nos. 001400–403, Luis Torres to Porfirio Díaz, 14 June 1892; Leg. 25, Exp. 17, No. 012032, Luis Terrazas to Enrique Creel, 25 July 1893.

45. Archivo Histórico del Estado de Jalisco, Ramo de Gobernación, Leg. Seguridad pública, Exp. . . . la carestía del maíz, 16 July 1892, and Exp. Departamento de San Juan de los Lagos, 18 July 1892; Domecq, *La Insólita historia*, pp. 203–4; *Informes que los gobernadores*, p. 313 (Governor Lauro Carrillo to congress, 1891), p. 321 (Carrillo to congress, 1892).

46. For Catholic village processions, see Christian, *Local Religion*, pp. 46–47, 63–65, 119–20; Kselman, *Miracles and Prophecies*, pp. 29–30, 162.

47. Almada, *Rebelión de Tomochi*, pp. 40, 49, 153.

48. AMCG, Leg. 12, Exp. 147, Comunicaciones con superiores, Borrador de correspondenica con el supremo gobierno, 18 July 1877. The governor's response is dated 4 September 1877. Also, J. C. Chávez, *Peleando*, p. 57.

49. J. C. Chávez, *Peleando*, p. 57.

50. Tayna Luhrmann aptly discusses the so-called rationality debate among scholars in her study of witches' magic, *Persuasions*, esp. pp. 345–56.

51. Paso y Troncoso, *Guerras con tribus*, pp. 181–83; Cardoza y Aragón, *José Guadalupe Posada*, plate no. 29; Berdecio and Applebaum, *Posada's Prints*, pp. 85, 87.

52. *El Diario del hogar*, 10 February 1892, p. 2; Almada, *Rebelión de Tomochi*, pp. 37–38.

53. J. C. Chávez, *Peleando*, pp. 58–59. Zacarías Márquez Terrazas, a well-known historian of Chihuahua, is from the Papigochic and kindly furnished the background on El Chopeque; personal communication, 19 May 1993.

54. Almada, *Rebelión de Tomochi*, p. 48.

55. *El Monitor republicano*, 2 November 1892, p. 1; J. C. Chávez, *Peleando*, p. 56.

56. J. C. Chávez, *Peleando*, p. 56; *El Monitor republicano*, 2 November 1892, p. 1.

57. J. C. Chávez, *Peleando*, p. 56; *El Monitor republicano*, 2 November 1892, p. 1.

Chapter 3

1. *La Ilustración espírita*, June 1891, p. 51; February 1892, p. 280; March 1892, p. 316.

2. *La Ilustración espírita*, February 1892, p. 280; *El Paso Times*, 9 September 1896, p. 3; W. C. Holden, *Teresita*, pp. 103–5.

3. J. C. Chávez, *Peleando*, p. 56.

4. AMCG, Leg. 16, Exp. 158, Comunicaciones con inferiores, Cecilio Gallegos, comisario, Tomochic, to Jefe Político, 19 February 1885.

5. *El Monitor republicano,* 2 November 1892, p. 1.

6. Ibid.; J. C. Chávez, *Peleando,* pp. 56–57.

7. J. C. Chávez, *Peleando,* p. 57.

8. For a good overview of the campaigns accompanied by copies of primary documents, see Sheridan and Naylor, *Rarámuri,* esp. chs. 2, 4. See also Almada, *Resumen,* chs. 10, 13; Dunne, *Early Jesuit Missions* and *Pioneer Jesuits.*

9. Sheridan and Naylor, *Rarámuri,* p. 73.

10. Ibid.

11. Ibid., p. 37.

12. Interview with Father Luis G. Verplanken, longtime missionary among the Tarahumaras, 21 July 1980, at his mission center and hospital in Creel, Chihuahua.

13. For Glandorff, see Dunne, *Early Jesuit Missions,* pp. 206–20; and S. Terrazas, "Gran sabio."

14. SRA, Archivo Histórico, Terrenos Nacionales, Diversos, 1.322.1 (06), Leg. 2, Exp. 26, Limantour, José Ives, y su hermano Julio.

15. Tamarón y Romeral, *Demostración,* p. 145; *El Correo de Chihuahua,* 17 February 1899, pp. 1–2; AMCG, Leg. 2, Exp. 19, Comunicaciones con inferiores, Padrón de Tomochi . . . 1831.

16. AMCG, Leg. 2, Exp. 19, Comunicaciones con inferiores, Padrón de Tomochi . . . 1831.

17. AMCG, Colección de Comunicaciones de los Pueblos, 1871, Carlos Medrano, comandancia, Tomochic, to Jefe Político, 12 April 1871.

18. AMGC, Leg. 5, Exp. 68, Comunicaciones con inferiores, Padre Felipe de Jesús Silva, Tomochic, to Jefe Político, 1 April 1852, and Exp. 66, Silva to Jefe Político, 30 April 1853.

19. AHAD, Cartas, José de la Luz Corral, vicar, Chihuahua, to Bishop Vicente Salinas, 3 April 1891, 8 June 1892, and 12 May 1893. Also, AMCG, Leg. 26, Exp. 267, "Comunicaciones con inferiores," Juez 1º menor, Temósachic, to Jefe Político, 30 August 1890, and Leg. 23, Exp. 239, Cura [Julio Irigoyen to Jefe Político], n. d. [1893?]; Leg. 14, Exp. 170, Casa electoral to Jefe Político, 25 June 1882; "Comunicaciones con superiores," Telegramas oficiales, 1888 R[afael] Pimentel, Chihuahua, to Jefe Político, 8 May 1888; Leg. 9, Exp. 112, Governor to Jefe Político, 17 May 1869.

20. AMCG, Leg. 10, Exp. 129, Comunicaciones con inferiores, Ignacio Gallegos, comisario, Tomochic, to Jefe Político, 5 January 1873.

21. *Los Pastores,* p. 11. John G. Bourke renders his report of the play in "Miracle Play," pp. 89–95.

22. Bourke, "American Congo," p. 609. For a fine essay on Judas burnings see Beezley, *Judas,* pp. 89–124.

23. Remington, *Pony Tracks,* p. 158.

24. Bourke, "Popular Medicine," pp. 144–46, and "American Congo," p. 606.

25. The examples are from Bourke: "American Congo," pp. 590–610, "Popular Medicine," pp. 119–46, and "Diary," vols. 102–9, 7 March 1891–16 May 1892. For a splendid example of Bourke's ethnographic skills in recording the magic in everyday lives, see his entry for 24 November 1891. See also Hudson, *Healer of Los Olmos*, and Romano, "Don Pedrito Jaramillo."

26. See Berdecio and Applebaum, *Posada's Prints*, for examples, pp. 30–32, 42.

27. Lumholtz, *Unknown Mexico*, 1: 11–12.

28. AMCG, Leg. 25, Exp. 261, Comunicaciones con superiores, Governor to Jefe Político, 8 February 1892.

29. *El Monitor republicano*, 15 November 1892, p. 3.

30. Bourke, "Diary," vols. 102–9, entry for 24 November 1891.

31. *El Monitor republicano*, 15 November 1892, p. 3.

32. Ibid.

33. Concerning the "cuestión juarista" in the Sierra and environs, a long conversation in 1983 with the late Sra. Matilda Caraveo of Chihuahua City proved most stimulating and enlightening; she was born in 1890 in Morís, district of Rayón, Chihuahua. Her kindness and that of her family toward me is gratefully acknowledged.

The Reform itself has been the subject of many studies from varying perspectives. Useful places to start in English are Hale, *Mexican Liberalism* and *Transformation of Liberalism*; Sinkin, *Mexican Reform*. For the debate over the place of Indians in the new society, see Powell, "Mexican Intellectuals," pp. 19–36. For an example of how priests reacted to the pressures of the Reform in the Sierra, see Almada, *Apuntes históricos*, pp. 355–64.

34. *El Progreso*, 18 March 1896, p. 2.

35. AMCG, Leg. 7, Exp. 89, Comunicaciones con superiores, Governor to Jefe Político, 21 July 1862; Leg. 9, Exp. 112, Governor to Jefe Político, 13 October 1869; Leg. 41, Exp. 371, Governor to Jefe Político, 24 May 1899; Leg. 44, Exp. 397, Comunicaciones con inferiores, Lorenzo Merino, Bachíniva, to Jefe Político, 28 March 1858; Leg. 44, Exp. 397, Presidente, Cruces, to Jefe Político, 25 March 1901. AHAD, Impresos, Atad I, José I. Gallegos to all parishes, 21 January 1863.

36. AMCG, Leg. 7, Exp. 82, Comunicaciones con superiores, Governor to Jefe Político, 3 April 1858.

37. AMCG, Leg. 5, Exp. 68, Comunicaciones con inferiores, Padre Silva, Tomochic, to Jefe Político, 6 April 1863.

38. AMCG, Leg. 8, Exp. 93 and 94, Patricio Arreola, juez suplente, Tomochic, to Jefe Político, 27 March 1863 and n.d. [1863?]; Leg. 8, Exp. 94, Comunicaciones con inferiores, Lucio Mendoza, juez [de paz] suplente, Tomochic, to Jefe Político, 27 May 1863.

39. AHAD, Impresos, Atad I, José I. Gallegos, 27 May 1863.

40. AMCG, Leg. 20, Exp. 224, Comunicaciones con inferiores, Carlos Perla, presidente, Morís, to Jefe Político, 20 July 1889.

41. AGN, Bienes nacionalizados, 48-127/173, Luis Comadurán to Porfirio Díaz, 1884.

42. AMCG, Leg. 7, Exp. 89, Comunicaciones con superiories, Governor to Jefe Político, 21 July 1862; Leg. 10, Exp. 122, Governor to Jefe Político, 11 July 1871.

43. AMCG, Leg. 13, Exp. 13, Comunicaciones con inferiores, Vecinos de Tomochic to Jefe Político, 3 February 1880; Correspondencia oficial de las autoridades subalternas, año 1880, Cecilio Gallegos, comisario, Tomochic, to Jefe Político, 1 October 1880; Leg. 16. Exp. 186, Borrador de comunicaciones con inferiores, 1885–86, 2 December 1885.

44. AMCG, Comunicaciones con inferiores, Jesús María Ortiz, juzgado civil, Tomochic, to Jefe Político, 23 November 1888.

45. Three books by Michelet from the library of Reyes Domínguez have passed down through his family and in 1983 were loaned to me for review by Sra. Refugio Ledesma de Domínguez of Tomochic.

46. J. C. Chávez, *Peleando*, p. 57.

47. Almada, *Rebelión de Tomochi*, p. 48.

48. *El Monitor republicano*, 2 November 1892, p. 2.

49. Ibid.

50. Almada, *Rebelión de Tomochi*, p. 62. The Ortiz family was one of the oldest in Tomochic. José María Ortiz appears on the padrón of 1843, age 42, married with three children. Jesús María Ortiz is twenty years old and married to Encarnación Márquez, age sixteen, when they are recorded on the padrón of 1864. By the padrón of 1890, Jesús María is remarried, to María Encarnación Quesada and has six children. Jorge is twenty and married to María Gregoria Gómez; they live with their two young children on a small rancho outside of Tomochic proper. Household patterns in the village make it likely that Jesús María was the son of José María and Jorge the son of Jesús María, but this still remains to be proved.

51. O. de Rico, "Documentos," Lauro Carrillo to Porfirio Díaz, 13 December 1891, pp. 34–35.

52. J. C. Chávez, *Peleando*, p. 57.

Chapter 4

1. The notion of a village son of a bitch is borrowed from Migdal, *Peasants, Politics, and Revolution*, p. 138.

2. Brondo Whitt, *Patriarcos*, pp. 152–62.

3. AMCG, Leg. 6, Exp. 69, Padrón general de Tomochic, 1864; Leg. 22,

Exp. 235, Padrón general de Tomochic, 1890; Leg. 11, Exp. 41, Derecho de votar, Tomochic, 1875. Interviews with Ricardo Domínguez (formerly of Tomochic), 22–25 July 1980, Creel, Chihuahua, and with Antonio Tello, 27 July 1980, Tomochic.

4. AMCG, Leg. 6, Exp. 69, Padrón general de Tomochic, 1864. Age at marriage is calculated from the series of census reports, assuming the year of marriage to be one year before the birth of the first child.

5. AMCG, Leg. 6, Exp. 69, Padrón general de Tomochic, 1864; Leg. 22, Exp. 235, Padrón general de Tomochic, 1890. Configurations of households were drawn from padrones.

6. AMCG, Leg. 4, Exp. 40, Padrón general de Tomochic, 1843; Leg. 6, Exp. 69, Padrón general de Tomochic, 1864; Leg. 22, Exp. 235, Padrón general de Tomochic, 1890.

7. Case, *Thirty Years*, pp. 79–81; Flippin, *Sketches*, p. 292.

8. The description of dwellings is drawn from a variety of sources: Bartlett, *Personal Narrative*, 1: 412; Case, *Thirty Years*, pp. 39, 58–69, 79–81; Flippin, *Sketches*, pp. 291–93; Gregg, *Commerce of the Prairies*, pp. 144–46; Parker, *Mules, Mines and Me*, pp. 15–16. Also interviews with Tomochitecos Antonio Tello in 1980 and Refugio Rodríguez and Jesús Orozco in 1983. Pictures of dwellings and a map of the pueblo appear in J. C. Chávez, *Peleando*, p. 47 and between pp. 72–73.

In 1989 I visited Tomochic with Professor Robert Schmidt, a physical geographer from the University of Texas, El Paso, who specializes in the environment of arid areas, specifically Chihuahua. Professor Schmidt detailed geographical and environmental facets of the valley and placed them in cultural context. My appreciation goes to him, not least for reducing his technical expertise to layman's terms for me. For a land survey of Tomochic see SRA, Terrenos nacionales, Chihuahua, Exp. 25/442 (721.12), Amplificación de ejidos, Temochic [Tomochic], and Exp. 231/577, Plano del pueblo de Tomochic, 1925. For climate in the region see *Dirección general de geografía*; Archivo de la Comisión Agraria Mixta, Exp. Tomochi, No. 2240. For detailed maps of the region see U.S. Army Corps of Engineers, Army Map Service, photo survey, 1956–57, "Chihuahua." For a map of the region in 1890 see *Carta general de la república*.

The best sources for geographical, geological, and environmental data for Chihuahua during the nineteenth century are: Escudero, *Noticias estadísticas*, esp. pp. 15–19 and 105–6; and *Boletín de la Sociedad Mexicana* 5, esp. pp. 168–81. For a more contemporary description, see Almada, *Geografía*; Brand, "Historical Geography" and "Natural Landscape." Also helpful is Ponce de León, *Datos geográficos*.

9. Lumholtz, *Unknown Mexico*, 1: 123–27; Parker, *Mules, Mines and Me*, p. 15; Case, *Thirty Years*, pp. 65–69.

10. Parker, *Mules, Mines and Me*, p. 16.

11. AMCG, Telegramas oficiales, 1886–87, F. F. Maceyra, Chihuahua, to Jefe Político, 3 February 1886; Parker, *Mules, Mines and Me*, pp. 87, 94–95, 394–99; Shepherd, *Silver Magnet*, p. 235; and Flippin, *Sketches*, pp. 78, 400–405.

12. AMCG, Leg. 4, Exp. 40, Padrón general de Tomochic, 1843; Leg. 6, Exp. 69, Padrón general de Tomochic, 1864; Leg. 22, Exp. 235, Padrón general de Tomochic, 1890.

13. For protests in the area concerning ejido lands at the time of the Revolution, see Lloyd, *Proceso de modernización,* and "Rancheros and Rebellion," pp. 87–111; Nugent, *Spent Cartridges.*

14. The titles to these grants were commonly called *hijuelas,* a term still used in land litigation. Technically, one hijuela equaled 24 hectares, or nearly 60 acres, but the word came to mean properties of almost any size.

15. One of the better examples is the Hacienda de Providencia, nearly 35,000 acres, granted to Manuel de Herrera on 2 June 1865. See AEC, Registro de Propiedad, Sec. I, Libro 10, pp. 21–22. Providencia later became the core of William Randolph Hearst's extensive holdings in the region.

16. AMCG, Leg. 7, Exp. 85, Protocolos, Manuel Chávez.

17. SRA, Chihuahua, 1.29 (06), Leg. Diversos, Exp. 192.

18. The best information on the surveys of the region is in SRA, Terrenos Nacionales, Deslindes 1.71(06), various expedientes. See, for example, No. 8, which covers Guerrero District in 1898. See also, SRA Nacionales en compra, various expedientes; for example, see Exp. 112, which covers Pachera for 1898. An excellent map of the district in 1884 can be found in SRA, Mapoteca, No. 1879, Distrito de Guerrero. For examples of surveys in the colonial period, see Van Young, *Hacienda and Market,* pp. 322–24.

19. SRA, 1.29(06), Leg. Diversos, Exp. No. 192, plano del pueblo (1886).

20. AMCG, Leg. 15, Exp. 175, Comunicaciones con inferiores, Dolores Mendías, Comisario, Tomochic, to Jefe Político, 2 November 1876.

21. AMCG, Leg. 15, Exp. 175, Comunicaciones con inferiores, Reyes Domínguez, comisario, Tomochic, to Jefe Político, 23 August 1883; Reyes Domínguez to Jefe Político, 1 September 1883.

22. AMCG, Colección de comunicaciones con inferiores, año de 1883, Reyes Domínguez, comisario, Tomochic, to Jefe Político, 9 August 1883.

23. AMCG, Leg. 15, Exp. 179, Borrador de comunicaciones con inferiores, enero 1884 al 30 abril 1885, 25 April 1884.

24. AMCG, Leg. 16, Exp. 186, Comunicaciones con inferiores, Cecilio Gallegos, comisario, Tomochic, to Jefe Político, 31 July 1885.

25. AMCG, Copias de comunicaciones, Libro No. 10 con comunicaciones, 27 junio de 1890 al 19 septiembre de 1890, Santiago Francisfortes and Jesús Benito (indígenas, Tomochic) to Jefe Político [August, 1890]; Leg. 23, Exp. 23, Comunicaciones con inferiores, Jesús Lara, indígena, Tomochic, to Jefe Político, 10 August 1891; Colección de comunicaciones con inferiores, mes de agosto 1890, Juan Ignacio Chávez, presidente, Tomochic, to Jefe Político, 27 August 1890.

26. Measure taken from a map prepared by the U.S. Army Corps of Engineers Map Service, Photo Survey, 1956–57, Chihuahua.

27. For example, see AMCG, Colección de comunicaciones con inferiores, Jesús Medrano, presidente, Tomochic, to Jefe Político, 4 November 1889.

28. *Ley de clasificar*. A copy may be found in the CIDECH.

29. AMCG, Colección de comunicaciones de inferiores, mes de agosto 1890, Juan Ignacio Chávez, presidente, Tomochic, to Jefe Político, 29 August 1890. John Woodhouse Audubon, youngest son of the famous U.S. ornithologist, John James Audubon, who traveled the district in July 1849, noted the profusion of cattle around Tomochic; see his *Western Journal*, p. 117.

30. For this and the following paragraph, see sources of geographical and environmental data for Tomochic in note 8 to this chapter.

31. Flippin, *Sketches*, pp. 7–8. In the early 1890s Lumholtz found that most ploughs in the Sierra had iron shares; *Unknown Mexico*, 1: 121.

32. AMCG, Leg. 17, Exp. 203, Comunicaciones con inferiores, Ignacio Dolores Rodríguez, Tomochic, to Jefe Político, 17 March 1888; Jesús Medrano, presidente, Tomochic, to Jefe Político, 1 April 1888.

33. AMCG, Leg. 6, Exp. 76, Registro de la guardia nacional, Tomochic, 1856.

34. AMCG, Leg. 9, Exp. 106, Comunicaciones con inferiores, Sabino Ledesma, Tomochic, to Jefe Político, 16 June 1867; Jorge Ortiz, presidente, Tomochic, to Jefe Político, 30 May 1889; Leg. 24, Exp. 245, Juan Ignacio Chávez, presidente, Tomochic, to Jefe Político, 26 November 1891.

35. AMCG, Leg. 8, Exp. 94, Comunicaciones con inferiores, Lucio Mendoza, comisario, Tomochic, to Jefe Político, 12 November 1683; Leg. 11, Exp. 138, Jesús María Ortiz, comisario, Tomochic, to Jefe Político, 20 March 1874.

36. "Mines of Santa Eulalia," p. 862; Audubon, *Western Journal*, p. 134.

37. *Engineering and Mining Journal* 48 (6 July 1889): 15.

38. *Diario oficial*, 15 January 1887, pp. 2–3; *El Estado de Chihuahua*, 31 January 1891, p. 3; Irrab, "Efemérides chihuahuenses," *BSCEH* 2 (January–February 1940): 323; *Engineering and Mining Journal* 41 (30 January 1886): 79.

39. BFO, Correspondence, Series II, F.O. 204, Vol. 207, 1889; Thomas Ryan, U.S. Legation, to Denys, 23 August 1889.

40. AMO, Demarcación de la cabeza, Padrón general de la sección 1ª de Jesús María, 5 February 1891. Also, AMCG, Leg. 17, Exp. 204, Comunicaciones con inferiores, Manuel Gallegos, Tomochic, to Ayuntamiento, Guerrero, 15 May 1888; and Almada, *Rebelión de Tomochi*, p. 170.

41. AMCG, Leg. 6, Exp. 76, Registro de la guardia nacional, Tomochic, 1856.

42. AMO, Demarcación de la cabeza: padrón general de la sección 3ª de Jesús María, 5 February 1891; *El Correo de Chihuahua*, 24 January 1899, p. 1.

43. Three U.S. writers have left us fascinating, detailed reminiscences of their experiences in Sierra mining country during the latter part of the nine-

teenth century: Flippin, *Sketches*; Parker, *Mines, Mules, and Me*; Shepherd, *Silver Magnet*.

44. *La Idea Libre*, 24 June 1899, p. 1; *Engineering and Mining Journal*, 4 October 1884, p. 236; Flippin, *Sketches*, pp. 61–63, 66–68; Parker, *Mules, Mines and Me*, pp. 28, 33–34, 88. For information on wages: *Engineering and Mining Journal*, 23 July 1881, pp. 59–60, 18 May 1882, p. 248, and 12 April 1884, p. 282; *American Mining Journal*, 2 March 1867, 4 May 1867, p. 102, and 9 May 1868, p. 293; Flippin, *Sketches*, p. 63; BFO, Series II, F.O. 204, Vol. 207, 1889. Also, El Paso Public Library, Southwestern Collection, Mining File, Mexico, State of Chihuahua, District of Rayón, No. 46. For early mining, see Audubon, *Western Journal*, p. 121. The processing of mining ore is explained in Flippin, *Sketches*, pp. 71–75; Flippin describes the skill of workers in hiding ore on their persons on pp. 59–61.

45. *La Voz de Arteaga*, 20 September 1896, 25 October 1896, both p. 6.

46. AMCG, Leg. 30, Exp. 292, Producción, Tomás Enriquez, presidente, Santo Tomás, to Jefe Político, 4 August 1893; and Leg. 20, Exp. 221, Ayuntamiento, Guerrero, decree, 30 July 1889; Santleben, *Texas Pioneer*, pp. 104–5; Gregg, *Commerce of the Prairies*, pp. 167–71; *La Justicia*, 11 January 1873, p. 3; *La Voz de Arteaga*, 5 May, 28 June, 26 July, 9 August, 4 October, 1 November, 1896, all p. 6; *El Siglo XX*, 17 August 1905, p. 1; Almada, *Resumen*, p. 360; Parker, *Mules, Mines and Me*, pp. 4, 41; Lumholtz, *Unknown Mexico*, 1: 40, 120, 212–13; Flippin, *Sketches*, pp. 7–10, 64–65, 89–90, 245–53, 288–90, 324–30.

47. Almada, *Revolución*, pp. 94–95, and *Resumen*, pp. 329–31; Parker, *Mines, Mules and Me*, p. 182; Irrab, "Efemérides chihuahuenses," *BSCEH* (January–15 February 1940): 321; AMCG, Telegramas oficiales, año de 1889, Pinos Altos to Jefe Político, 9 and 10 July 1889. For concerns of business entrepreneurs about worker productivity in this period see Haber, *Industry and Underdevelopment*, pp. 34–35.

48. AMCG, Leg. 22, Exp. 235, Padrón general de Tomochic, 1890.

49. J. C. Chávez, *Peleando*, pp. 49–52.

50. Most wills that mention the occupation of the wife or widow carry the phrase. For example see AEC, Protocolos de Matachic, 15 October 1903 to 15 October 1936, No. 5, 16 April 1909 (reference to Sra. Beatriz Arvizo de Antillón, age 36).

51. AMCG, Memoriales presentados en los años 1869–87, Cruz Chávez, Tomochic, to Jefe Político, 17 May 1885.

52. For examples of women pleading for the release of their menfolk from the military, see AMCG, Leg. 22, Exp. 34, C. Jacobo Cortés, juez de letras, 12 May 1890; Leg. 38, Exp. 350, presidente de Pachera to Jefe Político, 22 June 1897. Javiera Acosta's case is in AMCG, Leg. 46, Exp. 409, Jefe Político, 22 August 1902; Leg. 14, Exp. 171, Comunicaciones con inferiores, Javiera Acosta, Guerrero, to Jefe Político, 20 September 1882.

53. AMCG, Leg. 9, Exp. 117, Comunicaciones con inferiores, María Concepción Salazar, Guerrero, to Jefe Político, 30 September 1870.

54. *El Siglo XX*, 8 June 1905, p. 2.

55. AMCG, Leg. 7, Exp. 82, Comunicaciones con superiores, Governor to Jefe Político, 5 April 1858.

56. AMCG, Leg. 12, Exp. 149, Comunicaciones con inferiores, Reyes Domínguez, comisario, Tomochic, to Jefe Político, 15 February 1878.

57. AMCG, Leg. 14, Exp. 170, Comunicaciones con inferiores, Santiago Simonet, preceptor, Pachera, to Jefe Político, 29 September 1882; Leg. 17, Exp. 203, Comunicaciones con inferiores [Padrón de estudiantes], Tomochic, 1887–88; Leg. 18, Exp. 205, Jesús María Ortiz, juzgado civil, Tomochic, to Jefe Político, 12 June 1888.

58. AMCG, Leg. 7, Exp. 86, Comunicaciones con inferiores, Bachíniva to Jefe Político, 3 June 1863; Leg. 14, Exp. 166, Libro de sesiones ordinarias y estraordinarias del ayuntamiento, 1882–83, Resumen general de las faltas de asistencia . . . año escolar 1882–83; Leg. 15, Exp. 173, Programa de los exámenes públicas, 13 September 1883; Leg. 15, Exp. 1777, Lista de los útiles que solicitan los directores de los establecimeintos de instrucción pública, 4 April 1884; and Comunicaciones con superiores, C. Hernández, Chihuahua, 15 March 1892. Also, *Ley reglamentaria*; and AMO, Sesiones del ayuntamiento, julio 1891–abril 1892.

59. For examples, see AMCG, Leg. 6, Exp. 77, Comunicaciones con inferiores, Sección municipal, Guerrero, to Jefe Político, 25 January 1856; Leg. 14, Exp. 164, Jesús J. Bustillos, presidente, Bachíniva, to Jefe Político, 11 November 1881; Leg. 15, Exp. 177, Gabriel Ordóñez, preceptor, Rosario, to Jefe Político, 29 April 1884; Leg. 23, Exp. 243 [padrón of citizens assessed for school], Namiquipa, 1891; Leg. 27, Exp. 271, A. Pérez, presidente, Temósachic, to Jefe Político, 5 and 8 December, 1892. Also, de la Peña, *Chihuahua económico*, 1: 166–69.

60. AMCG, Leg. 22, Exp. 233, Comunicaciones con superiores, Gobernador to Jefe Político, 14 August 1890; Leg. 27 Exp. 271, Comunicaciones con inferiores, Rafael Márquez Quesada, presidente, Santo Tomás, to Jefe Político, 16 December 1892; Leg. 46, Exp. 42, director de escuela, Basúchil, to Jefe Político, 31 January 1902.

61. For salaries, see *Revista de Chihuahua* 1 (September 1895): 252; AMCG, Leg. 29, Exp. 289, Comunicaciones con superiores, Sección general de instrucción pública, to Jefe Político, 3 October 1893; Leg. 19, Exp. 217, Comunicaciones con inferiores, Jesús J. Armenta, preceptor, Pachera, to Jefe Político, August 1889.

62. AMCG, Comunicaciones con inferiores, Jesús Medrano, presidente, Tomochic, to Jefe Político, 5 April 1889; and Santiago Simonet, preceptor, Tomochic, to Jefe Político, 12 August, 10 September, and 17 October 1890.

63. AMCG, Leg. 3, Exp. 36, Comunicaciones con inferiores, Contribuciones . . . , Tomochic, 1840.

64. AMCG, Leg. 9, Exp. 107, Comunicaciones con inferiores, Ciudadanos vecinos . . . , Tomochic, 12 December 1865.

65. AMCG, Comunicaciones con inferiores, Contribuciones, Los Castillos, 1880.

66. AMCG, Leg. 16, Exp. 194, Comunicaciones con inferiores, Lista de las cuotas . . . , Tomochic, 1887.

67. AMCG, Leg. 17, Exp. 203, Comunicaciones con inferiores, Ignacio Dolores Rodríguez, Tomochic, to Jefe Político, 17 March 1888; Jesús Medrano, presidente, Tomochic, to Jefe Político, 1 April 1888.

68. AMCG, Leg. 12, Exp. 152, Comunicaciones con inferiores, Reyes Domínguez, juez de estado civil, Tomochic, to Jefe Político, 22 March 1879.

69. AMCG, Leg. 14, Exp. 171, Comunicaciones con inferiores, Dolores Rodríguez, vecino, Tomochic, to Jefe Político, 24 August 1882; Cruz Chávez, vecino, Tomochic, to Jefe Político, 24 August 1882.

70. AMCG, Colección oficial de autoridades subalternos, año de 1880, Reyes Domínguez, comisario, Tomochic, to Jefe Político, 4 January 1880; Leg. 14, Exp. 165, Colección de comunicaciones con inferiores, Reyes Domínguez, Tomochic, to Jefe Político, 24 and 31 July, 1881; Colección de comunicaciones con inferiores, año de 1883, Reyes Domínguez, comisario, Tomochic, to Jefe Político, 8 August 1883.

71. AMCG, Leg. 6, Exp. 69, Padrón general de Tomochic, 1864; Leg. 22, Exp. 235, Padrón general de Tomochic, 1890.

72. AMCG, Leg. 20, Exp. 238, Comunicaciones con inferiores, Jesús María Ortiz, juzgado civil, Tomochic, to Jefe Político, 23 November 1888.

73. AMCG, Leg. 11, Exp. 141, Comunicaciones con inferiores, Jesús María Oritz, comisario, Tomochic, to Jefe Político, 11 March 1875; Domingo López, comisario, Tomochic, to Jefe Político, 5 January 1877; Leg. 14, Exp. 166, comisario de Tomochic to Jefe Político, 18 August 1882.

74. J. C. Chávez, *Peleando*, p. 57.

75. AMCG, Leg. 22, Exp. 234, Comunicaciones con inferiores, Reyes Orozco, presidente, Santo Tomás, to Jefe Político, 12 April 1890; Manuel Nava, tesorero, Santo Tomás, to Jefe Político, 17 April 1890.

76. AMCG, Leg. 22, Exp. 234, Comunicaciones con inferiores, Jesús Medrano, presidente, Tomochic, to Jefe Político, 22 February 1890; Carlos Medrano, tesorero, Tomochic, to Jefe Político, 21 May 1890.

77. Camarilla politics are explained in Camp, *Mexico's Leaders*, pp. 9–10, 18–20. My thanks to Professor Camp for further elaboration on the process.

78. AGN, Ramo Revolución; Colección Alfredo Robles Domínguez, Vol. 7 (Informe de Tomás Dozal y Hermosillo), pp. 141–45.

79. AMCG, Leg. 12, Exp. 151, Comunicaciones con inferiores, Reyes Domínguez, comisario, Tomochic, to Jefe Político, 22 March 1879.

80. AMCG, Leg. 15, Exp. 179, Borrador de comunicaciones con autoridades inferiores, enero de 1884 a 30 abril de 1885, 3 May 1885.

81. Examples include AMCG, Colección de comunicaciones con inferiores, año de 1883, Reyes Domínguez, comisario, Tomochic, to Jefe Político,

9 August, 31 August, and 5 September 1883; Año de 1890, Juan Ignacio Chávez, presidente, Tomochic, to Jefe Político, 6 December 1890; Leg. 23, Exp. 243, Comunicaciones con inferiores, Jesús Lara, indígena, to Jefe Político, 10 August 1891.

82. AMCG, Leg. 18, Exp. 208, Comunicaciones con inferiores, Juan Ignacio Chávez, Santo Tomás, to Jefe Político, 3 July 1888.

83. Almada calls Juan Ignacio a relative of Joaquín Chávez; *Rebelión de Tomochi*, p. 38.

84. AMCG, Colección de comunicaciones con inferiores, mes de febrero 1889, Juan Ignacio Chávez, Tomochic, to Jefe Político, 5 February 1889; Leg. 20, Exp. 228, Reyes Domínguez, Tomochic, to Jefe Político, 20 June 1889; and Juan Ignacio Chávez, Tomochic, to Jefe Político, 5 February 1889.

85. AMCG, Leg. 22, Exp. 235, Padrón general de Tomochic, 1890.

86. AMCG, Colección de comunicaciones con inferiores, mes de septiembre de 1889, Jesús Medrano, presidente, Tomochic, to Jefe Político, 10 September 1889.

87. AMCG, Leg. 22, Exp. 234, Comunicaciones con inferiores, Jesús Medrano, presidente, Tomochic, to Jefe Político, 3 May 1890.

88. AMCG, Colección de comunicaciones con inferiores, meses de julio-diciembre de 1890, Juan Ignacio Chávez, presidente, Tomochic, to Jefe Político, 8 July; 18, 27, 29 August; 15 September; 22 November 1890.

89. AMCG, Colección de comunicaciones con inferiores, meses de julio-noviembre y diciembre de 1890, Juan Ignacio Chávez, presidente, Tomochic, to Jefe Político, 4 October, 20 November, 6 December 1890.

90. AMCG, Leg. 24, Exp. 246, Comunicaciones con inferiores, Juan Ignacio Chávez, presidente, Tomochic, to Jefe Político, 19 May 1891.

Chapter 5

1. Naylor and Polzer, *Presidio and Militia*, p. 422; Dunne, *Early Jesuit Missions*, pp. 59–60.

2. Porras Muñoz, *Frontera*, pp. 193–94. A short sketch of Guajardo Fajardo's public life appears in Márquez Terrazas, *Chihuahuenses egregios*, 1: 55–56.

3. Naylor and Polzer, *Presidio and Militia*, pp. 385, 412 n. 11; Sheridan and Naylor, *Rarámuri*, pp. 21, 30 n. 16; Almada, *Diccionario . . . chihuahuenses*, p. 238.

4. Naylor and Polzer, *Presidio and Militia*, p. 429; Porras Muñoz, *Frontera*, p. 196; Dunne, *Early Jesuit Missions*, p. 79.

5. Porras Muñoz, *Frontera*, p. 196; Sheridan and Naylor, *Rarámuri*, p. 16.

6. Porras Muñoz, *Frontera*, p. 197.

7. Archivo Municipal de Hidalgo del Parral, microcopy, Reel No. 1649b

(minas, solares, y terrenos), frame no. 06696, Alonso Sánchez; frames 0671–72, José de Olivas; and frame 0673, Pascual de Nájera. Also, Porras Muñoz, *Frontera*, p. 198.

8. Naylor and Polzer, *Presidio and Militia*, pp. 386–87; and Porras Muñoz, *Frontera*, pp. 199–200.

9. Naylor and Polzer, *Presidio and Militia* pp. 387–89.

10. Porras Muñoz, *Frontera*, pp. 201–2. For Guajardo Fajardo's continuing strife with the Bishop of Durango, see Porras Muñoz, *Iglesia y estado*, pp. 44, 159, 403, 412, 417, 434–35, 440–45.

11. Sheridan and Naylor, *Rarámuri*, pp. 41–43.

12. Ibid., pp. 39, 43–44.

13. Ibid., pp. 43–45, 49–50, 57.

14. Ibid., pp. 59–64.

15. My gratitude to William Douglas, director of the Center for Basque Studies at the University of Nevada, Reno, for his insights into the Basque immigrants to northern Mexico in the seventeenth century.

16. Brondo Whitt, *Patriarcos*, pp. 31–46.

17. For typical local attitudes of Hispanics toward the natives, see AMCG, Leg. 11, Exp. 143, Comunicaciones con inferiores, Emerio García, juzgado suplente, Tutuaca, to Jefe Político, 14 July 1876.

18. For Basúchil, see AMCG, Leg. 8, Exp. 93, Comunicaciones con superiores, Governor to Jefe Político, 6 August 1863; Leg. 32, Exp. 11, Governor to Jefe Político, 28 September 1894; Leg. 65, Exp. 567, Cuestiones geográficas, 1908, Basúchil; Leg. 23, Exp. 243, Comunicaciones con inferiores, Antonia Oliva, Basúchil, to Jefe Político, 4 September 1891; Leg. 27, Exp. 275, Nota de propriedades rústicas, May 1892; Leg. 40, Exp. 369, enero–julio de 1900, manifiesta . . . , vecinos de Basúchil to Jefe Político, 23 February 1900. For Rancho Colorado, see AMCG, Leg. 27, Exp. 275, Nota de propriedades rústicas, Rancho Colorado, May, 1892.

19. For the survey, authorized to begin on 9 December 1882, see SRA, Terrenos Nacionales, deslindes, No. 1.71(06), Chihuahua, Leg. 9, Exp. 8, Compañía Valenzuela, Jesús, deslinde practicado [Guerrero District] . . . , [registered on] 13 July 1885. For an outline map of the survey, see SRA, Mapoteca, No. 1879, Chihuahua, Distrito de Guerrero, drawn by A. O. Wingo in 1884. Tomochic itself was surveyed in November 1885. For that survey, see SRA, Terrenos Nacionales, Leg. Diversos, Exp. 192, Plan de Pueblo (1886).

20. Land transactions for the late nineteenth century are documented in AEC. Other property records for the period are held in the tax offices of the municipal palace in Guerrero City.

21. The anthropologist William B. Griffen has done splendid work on the Apaches in Chihuahua; see his *Apaches at War and Peace* and *Utmost Good Faith*. My gratitude goes to Professor Griffen for sorting out local clichés concerning the Apaches used in nineteenth-century correspondence. The classic contem-

porary report on Apache depredations in Chihuahua is Escudero, *Noticias estadísticas*, chs. 8 and 9; see also his *Observaciones*. Further detail is provided by Conde, *Ensayo estadístico*.

22. SRE, Archivos Históricos, Exp. 2-1-1771, Invasión de Chihuahua, Juan M. Flores, Durango, to Secretaría del Estado y Despacho de Relaciones Exteriores, 4 November 1877. See also J. C. Chávez, "Clamor de los Papigochics," pp. 399–405. To back up their main presidio system, the Spaniards established militia posts in places like the Papigochic; see Depalo, "Establishment of the Nueva Vizcaya Militia," pp. 223–49. On Namiquipa as a presidio, consult Nugent, *Spent Cartridges*, pp. 44–46, 50; for Yepómera, see AMCG, Leg. 8, Exp. 104, Libro de borradores, 1865–66, and Leg. 65, Exp. 567, Cuestiones geográficos, 1908; on the government granting rifles, see AMCG, Leg. 7, Exp. 78, Comunicaciones con superiores, Governor to Jefe Político, 10 December 1856.

23. AMCG, Leg. 10, Exp. 122, Comunicaciones con superiores, Governor to Jefe Político, 31 March 1871. For examples of practices of the raiders, see AGN, Sección colonial, Vol. 248, Indios bárbaros (1839–47), pp. 356–419; *El Farral*, 2 June 1835, p. 1; *El Imparcial* (Chihuahua), April–May 1871; and for taking Indians captive to be ransomed, see *Semanario del estado*, 15 January 1881, p. 4.

24. The state government feared that militia troops financed to hunt Apaches might turn traitor and assist its political enemies. Bands headed by the likes of Santana Pérez deliberately blurred the line between government service and sedition. The governor did not even know that Pérez had assembled a large troop in the summer of 1883, purportedly to raid an Indian encampment in neighboring Sonora—not that such units could legally cross state lines. In this instance Pérez reported a major success against the natives (Apaches?): 457 killed and 313 taken prisoner. The governor faintly praised the mission but ordered no more such campaigns without his permission. See AMCG, Leg. 8, Exp. 93, Comunicaciones con superiores, José María Zuloaga (peace commissioner), Corralitos, to Governor, 22 May 1863. For complaints concerning American complicity with Apaches, see SRE, Exp. 2-1-1771, Invasión de Chihuahua; AGN, Gobernación, Justicia, Vol. 248, Indios bárbaros (1839–47), Periódicos, *Noticioso*, 1835, p. 40; *Semanario del estado*, 15 January 1881, p. 4; AMCG, Leg. 13, Exp. 159, Comunicaciones con superiores, Governor to Jefe Político, 28 February 1880 and Leg. 15, Exp. 173, Governor to Jefe Político, 31 July 1883. For policies regarding recaptured cattle, see AGN, Gobernación, Justicia, Indios bárbaros (1839–47), vol. 248, pp. 408–19. Also AMCG, Leg. 7, Exp. 78, Comunicaciones con superiores, Governor to Jefe Político, 23 June, 6 and 9 October 1856, and Circular, 25 November 1856; Leg. 7, Exp. 83, Goveror to Jefe Político, 14 October 1859; Leg. 10, Exp. 122, Governor to Jefe Político, 13 December 1871; Leg. 12, Exp. 127, Circular, Governor to Jefe Político, 11 April 1877; Leg. 13, Exp. 155, Primer libro de borradores del gobierno del

estado, 27 June 1879; Leg. 13, Exp. 159, Governor to Jefe Político, 4 March 1881. For examples of Papigochic reluctance to join militia units to fight Apaches, see AMCG, Leg. 3, Exp. 36, Comunicaciones con superiores, Vicente Antillón to Governor, 1840; Leg. 7, Exp. 78, Governor to Jefe Político, 6 October 1856; Leg. 9, Exp. 109, Comunicaciones con inferiores, José María Chacón to Jefe Político, 31 December 1868 and 31 January 1869; Leg. 9, Exp. 106, Miguel Almeydo, presidente, Bachíniva, to Jefe Político, 21 May 1867.

25. AMCG, Leg. 7, Exp. 81, Comunicaciones con superiores, Governor to Jefe Político, 10 July 1878. The government offered 2,000 pesos ($1,600 U.S.) for the scalp of the especially fearsome Victorio; see AMCG, Leg. 13, Exp. 159, Comunicaciones con superiores, Governor to Jefe Político, 24 August 1880. Payments for scalps were slightly delayed in 1856 due to a shortage of state funds; AMCG, Leg. 7, Exp.78, Comunicaciones con superiores, Governor to Jefe Político, 26 December 1856. In 1840 the state government contracted with an American scalp hunter, the notorious James Kirker, to lift Apache hair in Chihuahua; AGN, Gobernación, Justicia, Indios bárbaros (1839–47), Vol. 248, pp. 356–90. For the raiding patterns of the Apaches, see Smith, "Apache Plunder," pp. 20–42, and Griffen, *Utmost Good Faith*, p. 335. Scalp hunting is covered in Brandes and Smith, "Scalp Business," pp. 2–16, and in Smith, "Scalp Hunters" and "Scalp Hunt." For Victorio, consult J. C. Chávez, "Extinción," p. 405.

26. J. C. Chávez, "Clamor de los Papigochics," p. 405.

27. For Governor Luis Terrazas' solicitation of assistance from the Papigochic during the French Intervention, see AMCG, Leg. 8, Exp. 93, Comunicaciones con superiores, Circular, 20 November 1863. For differing viewpoints on the governor's stance vis-à-vis the French, see Almada, *Intervención francesa,* and Fuentes Mares, *Mexico se refugió.* The role of the Apachería in the formation of the worldview of the people of Papigochic is forcefully argued by Ana María Alonso in her theoretically provocative *Thread of Blood.*

For other comments on Norteño character, see Leon-Portilla, "Norteño Variety," pp. 77–114, and *Endangered Cultures,* esp. the essay "Beyond Mesoamerica: Norteño Cultural Pluralism in the Pre-Hispanic and Colonial Periods," pp. 155–86. See also Carr, "Peculiaridades." Jane-Dale Lloyd provides fascinating aspects of Norteño culture for the late nineteenth century in the district just north of the Papigochic in her *Proceso de modernización.*

28. AMCG, Leg. 8, Exp. 98, Comunicaciones con inferiores, S. A. Márquez, Santo Tomás, to Jefe Político, 14 December 1864.

29. AMCG, Leg. 13, Exp. 155, Comunicaciones con inferiores, Primer libro de borradores del estado, 1 January 1879; *Censo . . . Chihuahua,* pp. 162–63. For the Papigochic, see Bastián, *Disidentes,* pp. 124–26, 139, 255–56, 274–77, 292; and Baldwin, *Protestants,* esp. pp. 46–47, 74–77, 117–20. For Mariano Irigoyen, consult Bastián, "Jacobinismo," p. 41.

30. The Mexican movie director Gonzálo Martínez Ortega entitled his

1975 feature film about the religious movement at Tomochic *La Longitud de guerra*.

31. AMCG, Leg. 28, Exp. 278, Comunicaciones con inferiores, División territorial del estado, 22 May 1893. For an example of a competitive election in the Papigochic, consider the district election of 1885 for jefe político. Gabriel Casavantes won with 1,787 votes, followed by Simón Amaya (828), Daniel Rico (362), Silviano González (270), and six others who received more than 100 votes each. For Juez de Letras (district judge), Manuel Rubio won with 1,787 (same as Casavantes), followed by Juan Rubio (677); of the other twelve candidates, five received more than 100 votes each. Twenty-two individuals ran for *síndico*, and balloting for municipal council was also divided; see AMCG, Leg. 19, Exp. 189, Resumen de votos . . . 1885. For examples among many of challenged elections, see AMCG, Leg. 10, Exp. 129, Comunicaciones con superiores, Governor to Jefe Político, 26 March 1872; Leg. 15, Exp. 183, Governor to Jefe Político, 1 April 1884; Leg. 14, Exp. 166, Comunicaciones con inferiores, Libro de sesiones ordinarias y extraordinarias del ayuntamiento, 1882–83, 3 January 1884; Leg. 15, Exp. 177, Jesús Delgado, juez, Guerrero, to Jefe Político, 14 September 1884; Leg. 17, Exp. 200, Jesús María Trevizo, Mátachic, to Jefe Político, 13 January 1888.

32. AMCG, Legs. 8 and 9, Comunicaciones con inferiores, contain substantial documentation about these events. For examples, see Leg. 8, Exp. 98, Circular, 1865; Leg. 8, Exp. 99, Lista de los ciudadanos en quienes esta junta municipal, Bachíniva, 1864; Fermín Fierro, Bachíniva, to Jefe Político, 2 and 25 September 1864; and José Atenogenio Márquez, presidente, Santo Tomás, to Jefe Político, 5 October 1864; Leg. 8, Exp. 100, Colección de actas adección al supremo gobierno, 13 April 1864, and Lista que comprende a una compañía, 17 August 1865; Leg. 8, Exp. 101, Feliciano Enríquez, comandancia militar de la Coalición de los Pueblos, to Jefe Político, 14 April and 28 November 1865; J. Bustamante, Ranchos de Santiago, to Jefe Político, 25 March 1865; José Rafael Antillón y Treviso, Guerrero, to Presidente Municipal de Santo Tomás, 30 June 1866; Jefe Político to presidentes municipales de Temósachic y Santo Tomás, 13 November 1865; Circular de Gobernador Ojinaga, 7 August 1865; and Alvino Licano, presidente, Temeychi, to Jefe Político, 28 January 1865; Leg. 8, Exp. 104, Feliciano Enríquez, comandante de cantones de Guerrero, Proclamación, 11 February 1866; Leg. 9, Exp. 106, Juan Nepomuceno Vargas, Santo Tomás, to Jefe Político, 22 November 1867, and Manuel Lazo, Namiquipa, to Jefe Político, 17 May 1867. See also Almada, *Resumen*, pp. 278, 284–85; *Revista de Chihuahua* 1 (April 1895): 69–70; Irrab, "Efemérides chihuahuenses," *BSCEH* 1 (August 1938): 125.

33. Irrab, "Efemérides," *BSCEH* 1 (January 1939): 271 (April 1939): 384; Almada, *Resumen*, pp. 297–99; Wasserman, *Capitalists*, pp. 34–35.

34. These happenings are outlined in Almada, *Resumen*, pp. 306–10, and Wasserman, *Capitalists*, pp. 35–36. For examples of the activities of Santana

Pérez, see AMCG, Leg. 10, Exp. 128, Comunicaciones con inferiores, Jesús José Bencomo, juzgado de Yepómera, to Jefe Político, 2 July 1872; Leg. 11, Exp. 143, Borrador de correspondencia con superior gobierno del estado, año de 1876, 17 November 1876; Leg. 12, Exp. 147, Luis J. Comadurán to Jefe Político, 16 March 1877; Leg. 16, Exp. 199, Santana Pérez, Yepómera, to Jefe Político, 22 April 1886; Leg. 17, Exp. 196, Borrador de comunicaciones con inferiores, 23 June 1887; and Leg. 30, Exp. 239, Comunicaciones con superiores, Governor to Jefe Político, 6 April 1893.

35. Some of the best recent work on the jefe político has been done by Romana Falcon of El Colegio de México; see her "Desaparición" and "Jefes políticos." The tendency of such middle-level officals to oscillate between loyalties and duties to the state and to their local region has been noted for sheriffs in seventeenth-century English society by Wrightson, *English Society*, p. 226, and for Latin American caciques by Adams, *Energy and Structure*, p. 52.

36. For the major changes incorporated into the Constitution of 1887, see Almada, *Resumen*, pp. 343–44.

37. Brondo Whitt, *Patriarcos*, pp. 183–88; Almada, *Diccionario chihuahuenses*, pp. 231, 233, and *Gobernadores*, pp. 381–84; AMCG, Leg. 4, Exp. 40, Padrón de Tomochic, 1843; personal interview with Jaime González, nephew of Silviano, at his home in Ciudad Guerrero, 1983.

38. AMCG, Leg. 48, Exp. 425, Comunicaciones con inferiores, Contribuciones que pagarán para el ferrocarril, 1903.

39. Palacio Municipal, Guerrero City, Registro público de propriedad, vol. 1, 1 May 1884–3 May 1892, 18 June 1891; AMCG, Leg. 12, Exp. 153, Libro de borradores para el ayuntamiento, Guerrero, 1 January 1879; Leg. 17, Exp. 203, Patentes, 20 February 1888; Leg. 57, Exp. 513, Comunicaciones con superiores, Governor to Jefe Político, March and April 1906; Leg. 65, Exp. 567, Cuestiones geográficas, 1908. See also AEC, Protocolos de Guerrero, 1896, 15 de noviembre de 1894 á 18 de diciembre de 1897, pp. 248–54; and 12 mayo de 1909 á 13 mayo de 1916, No. 1, 11 agosto de 1911, pp. 222–23. And see Almada, *Gobernadores*, pp. 381–84.

40. AMCG, Leg. 12, Exp. 147, Comunicaciones con superiores, Governor to Jefe Político, 6 October 1877.

41. For Chávez as cacique, see Alonso, *Thread of Blood*, pp. 145, 165–67, and 258 n.13.

42. Brondo Whitt, *Partriarcos*, p. 147; Almada, *Rebelión de Tomochi*, p. 38; J. C. Chávez, "Peleando," (January 1943): 323, n. 2.

43. AEC, Protocolos de Guerrero, 1890, de enero 1890 á 31 julio de 1890, No. 20, pp. 51–52; Protocolos de Guerrero, 1905, No. 45, pp. 197–98; Protocolos de Guerrero, 1906–7, del 28 de abril de 1906 á 16 de agosto de 1907, No. 59, pp. 232–35. AMCG, Leg. 14, Exp. 171, Comunicaciones con inferiores, Memorias por jefe político, 1882–83, 26 May 1882; Correspondencia del mes de abril de 1889, Joaquín Chávez, juez de primera instancia, to Jefe Po-

lítico, 10 May, 8 and 13 December, 1888; 22 January, 9 and 11 April 1889; Leg. 9, Exp. 108, Tomás Dozal y Hermosillo, jefe político, to Joaquín Chávez, 18 November 1866.

44. Almada, *Apuntes históricos*, p. 298, and *Resumen*, p. 212; Flippen, *Sketches*, pp. 99–103; personal interview with Matilda Caraveo, Chihuahua City, 1983. See also *La Voz de Arteaga*, 11 October 1896, p. 5; SRA, Archivo histórico, Terrenos nacionales, Mapoteca, No. 2075 (Chihuahua), Plano geográfico de las lineas de correos ordinarios del estado de Chihuahua [1830?]; de la Peña, *Chihuahua económico*, 3: 106. AMCG, Leg. 7, Exp. 78, Comunicaciones con superiores, Secretaría [del gobierno] to Jefe Político, 6 October 1856; Leg. 14, Exp. 172, Governor to Jefe Político, 5 March 1883; Leg. 16, Exp. 185, Tomás McManus, junta directiva de los ferrocarriles de Chihuahua, 15 January 1885.

45. *La Idea libre*, 14 June 1899; record books of the Pinos Altos Gold and Silver Mining Company (hereafter cited as Pinos Altos record books), Book No. 3, 20 November; Book No. 39, December, 1906; Book No. 191, 18 February 1907; Books No. 299–300, 21 April 1907; Book No. 365, 9 May 1907. These and other company record books, not all in good condition, are now the property of Lic. Abelardo Pérez Campos, who resides in Chihuahua City and Pinos Altos. The books mainly contain copies of correspondence and telegrams sent by the superintendent at the mine to the company's representatives in Chihuahua City and elsewhere. My gratitude goes to Lic. Pérez Campos for allowing me to consult these books. See also AEC, Protocolos de 1890, 1 de agosto de 1890 al 28 de octubre de 1890, No. 49, 22 September 1890, pp. 25–26; Parker, *Mines, Mules and Me*, pp. 104–5, 186–87, n. 16. And see AMCG, Leg. 50, Exp. 448, Correspondencia del Jefe Político, Vecinos de San Isidro al H. Congreso del Estado, September 1904; Leg. 65, Exp. 567, Cuestiones geográficas, 1908.

46. Froebel, *Seven Year's Travel*, pp. 361–62; Lumholtz, *Unknown Mexico*, 1: 220, 449; AMCG, Telegramas oficiales, 1886–87, Armendáriz, oficial 1°, to Jefe Político, 29 April 1886. And see Girón, *Heraclio Bernal*. Also see Almada, *Apuntes históricos*, pp. 335, 339, 386–87. For more on banditry and smuggling in and around the Papigochic, see SRA, Terrenos nacionales, deslindes, 1.71(06), Chihuahua. AEC, Seccion judicial, Archivo histórico del Corte Supremo, Leg. 1880, Exp. Consignación de la depositaría municipal de este lugar contra Basilio Solís por contrabando; Exp. Contra Luciano de Haro por contrabando; Exp. Juicio seguido contra Ignacio Aragón por contrabando; *Diario oficial*, 7 January 1876, p. 4. AMCG, Leg. 50 Exp. 446, Telegramas oficiales de 1886–88, F. F. Maceyra, Chihuahua, to Jefe Político, 23 April 1886; Rafael Soto, Cusihuiriachic, to Jefe Político, 1 October 1886; Celso González, Chihuahua, to Jefe Político, 13 January 1888; Leg. 17, Exp. 204, Governor to Jefe Político, 17 October 1888; Leg. 19, Exp. 214, Borrador de comunicaciones, el 9 de enero a 22 de abril de 1888, Exp. Circular No. 18, 2 April 1888.

47. AMCG, Leg. 59, Exp. 533, Comunicaciones con superiores, 1903, Governor to Jefe Político, 17 August 1903.

48. AMCG, Leg. 59, Exp. 533, Comunicaciones con superiores, Governor to Jefe Político, 11 May 1907.

49. AMCG, Leg. 13, Exp. 159, Comunicaciones con superiores, Correspondencia del gobernador del estado, 1880, 26 April, 22 June, and 19 August, 1880.

50. AMCG, Comunicaciones con inferiores, 1888–89, Joaquín Chávez, juez del primer juzgado, to Jefe Político, 1 December 1888; 22 January, 3, 6, 9, 11 April, 10 May, 1889; Joaquín Chávez, recaudación de rentas, to Jefe Político, 31 December 1889. See also Palacio municipal (Guerrero City), Registro público de propiedad, Guerrero, Vol. 1, Mayo de 1884 a 3 de Mayo 1892, 19 April 1890; and Archivo del Juzgado menor, Guerrero, Civiles, 1861–67. For further examples see AEC, Protocolos de 1890, del 10 de enero al 31 de julio de 1890, No. 20, 4 June 1890, pp. 51–52; del 4 de noviembre de 1890 á 31 de diciembre de 1890, No. 64, 6 November 1890, pp. 3–4; de 1 de enero de 1893 a 5 de abril de 1909, No. 28, 12 November 1905, pp. 286–89; 31 de enero de 1905 al 24 de abril 1906, No. 15, 29 April 1905, pp. 60–67, and No. 45, 25 July 1905, pp. 197–98. See also SRA, Terrenos nacionales, Nacionales en compra, 1.232(06), Exp. 361, 18 February 1904; Terrenos nacionales, baldíos, Exp. 1217, Joaquín Chávez, 28 February 1908; 1.21(06), Enajenaciones, Exps. Nos. 358, 360, and 619. See also Pinos Altos record books, Book No. 3, No. 91, Superintendent to Joaquín Chávez, San Isidro, 5 January 1890; *El Estado de Chihuahua*, 8 and 22 November 1890, both p. 3; Almada, *Rebelión de Tomochi*, p. 22, and *Resumen*, pp. 317–18; Irrab, "Efemérides chihuahuenses," *BSCEH* 1 (August 1938): 130.

51. AMCG, Leg. 48, Exp. 425, Comunicaciones con inferiores, Contribuciones para pagar para el ferrocarril, 1903; Leg. 63, Exp. 558, Comunicaciones con superiores, Governor to Jefe Político, 28 March 1908.

52. AMCG, Leg. 9, Exp. 106, Comunicaciones con inferiores, Jesús José Chávez, Tomochic, to Jefe Político, 19 October 1867.

Chapter 6

1. The political swirl in Chihuahua surrounding Carrillo's reelection is well told and documented in Pozo Marrero, "Dos movimientos," pp. 1–45; see also APD, Leg. 16, Caja 34, 016587–90, Fito Arriola, Chihuahua, to Porfirio Díaz, 26 November 1891; and AMCG, Telegramas oficiales de 1891, Miguel Prado, Jesús María, to Jefe Político, 22 November 1891, and Procopio Olea, Pinos Altos, to Jefe Político, 30 November 1891. These events are summarized in Almada, *Gobernadores*, pp. 264–65, 408–15, and *Rebelión de Tomochi*, pp. 15–17; also Flores, *Chihuahua*, pp. 181–91. For details on the drought as it affected the Papigochic, see AMCG, Leg. 17, Exp. 203, Silviano González to Ayuntamiento, 26 January 1888; Leg. 27, Exp. 275, Comunicaciones con inferiores,

Luis Comadurán, presidente Bachíniva, to Jefe Político, 3 June 1892; Exp. 271, Comadurán to Jefe Político, 16 December 1892, and Ignacio Bencomo, presidente, Mátachic, to Jefe Político, 23 December 1892; Leg. 30, Exp. 293, José María Aragón, presidente, Mátachic, to Jefe Político, 29 June 1893, and Rafael Márquez Quesada, president, Santo Tomás, to Jefe Político, 30 June 1893; Leg. 24, Exp. 246, Comunicaciones con superiores, Governor to Jefe Político, 15 October 1891.

2. Almada, *Gobernadores*, pp. 264, 385–94, 408–10, and *Rebelión de Tomochi*, pp. 16–17.

3. Almada, *Gobernadores*, pp. 257–63; Wasserman, *Capitalists*, pp. 36–37.

4. Almada, *Gobernadores*, pp. 390–91.

5. *El Progreso*, 4 December 1895, p. 2; APD, Leg. 16, Caja 34, No. 016575, Ahumada to Díaz, 1 December 1891, and No. 016578, Ahumada to Díaz, 10 December 1891.

6. APD, Leg. 50–51, Caja 12, Exp. 6595–601, Telegram, Carrillo to Díaz, 9 December 1891.

7. APD, Leg. 50–51, Caja 12, Exp. 6595–601, Telegram, Carrillo to Díaz, 9 December 1891; Leg. 50, Caja 12, No. 006673–75, Carrillo to Díaz, 10 December 1892; and Folio III, No. 00007, Carrillo to Díaz, 11 December 1891. For labeling as practice see Scott, *Domination*, p. 55.

8. APD, Leg. 50–51, Caja 12, Exp. 6595–601, Telegram, Carrillo to Díaz, 9 December 1891.

9. APD, Leg. 16, Caja 34, No. 016578, Telegram, Ahumada to Díaz, 10 December 1891.

10. APD, Leg. 50, Caja 12, No. 006673–75, Carrillo to Díaz, 10 December 1891.

11. APD, Leg. 50, Caja 12, 006722–26, Carrillo to Díaz, 11 December 1891.

12. Bricker, *The Indian Christ*, p. 6. For use of this concept against the Yaqui Indians in 1886, see Rojas Rabiela, *Indio en la prensa*, 2: 160.

13. Hale, *Mexican Liberalism*, pp. 239–40.

14. At the constitutional convention in 1856 a deputy from the state of Oaxaca, José Antonio Gamboa, suggested widespread intermarriage and the mass immigration of whites, so that "the Indians would be absorbed into our race" and "the threat of being absorbed by the Indian race" would disappear. Moreover, the deputy had a mathematical formula in mind: "five million Indians, ten million whites"; quoted in Sinkin, *Mexican Reform*, p. 130.

15. Hale, *Mexican Liberalism*, p. 223.

16. Rabiela, *Indio en la prensa*, 2: 366.

17. *El Universal*, 6 June 1893, p. 2. Criminologists of the period studied photographs of arrested persons for supposed physical criminal characteristics. For typical photos, see Levine, *Images of History*, pp. 29–31.

18. For a succinct statement on the manner in which officially sanctioned religious belief can reinforce the subordination of ordinary people, see Pessar, "Masking the Politics," pp. 256–60.

19. Vanderwood, *Disorder and Progress*, p. 91.

20. Danker, "Banditi and the State," p. 101.

21. See Vanderwood, *Disorder and Progress*, p. 4. For the "them" versus "us" dichotomy in war, see Fussell, *Great War*, pp. 79–82.

22. For a full discussion of the ongoing Mexican legislative debate over laws of exception, see Cosío Villegas, *Historia moderna La República restaurada; La Vida política*, pp. 227–359. Article 29 of Mexico's 1857 constitution permits laws of exception.

23. Irrab, "Efemérides chihuahuenses," *BSCEH* 1, No. 11 (April 1939): 384. See also Almada, *Rebelión de Tomochi*, p. 47.

24. *El Diario del hogar*, 10 February 1892, p. 2.

25. *San Francisco Chronicle*, 31 January 1892, p. 13; AMCG, Comunicaciones con inferiores, enero de 1892, Lic. Manuel Rubio, juez de letras, Guerrero, to Jefe Político, 23 January 1892.

26. *El Diario del hogar*, 10 February 1893, p. 2.

Chapter 7

1. *Viva Zapata!*, Darryl F. Zanuck, producer; Elia Kazan, director; John Steinbeck, screenwriter, 20th-Century Fox, 1952.

2. Yeager, "Porfirian Commercial Propaganda," p. 232.

3. Vanderwood, *Disorder and Progress*, p. 134.

4. Ibid., pp. 67, 131–32.

5. Ibid., chs. 9, 10, and pp. 101–29.

6. Conger, "Díaz and Church Hierarchy," pp. 17, 26–51, 71–108, 160–92, 208–13, 242.

7. Ibid., pp. 166–69.

8. Ibid., pp. 26–51. See also Schmitt, "Catholic Adjustment," pp. 182–204, and "Díaz Conciliation," pp. 520–25, 531–32.

9. Beezley and MacLachlan, *El Gran Pueblo*, pp. 97–98.

10. Edmunds, Sheldon, and Inwards, *Reports*. The comments on pulque appear on p. 5.

11. The price is from Edmunds, Sheldon, and Inwards, *Reports*, pp. 45–46.

12. SRA, Archivo Histórico, Terrenos nacionales, 1.29(06), Chihuahua, Limantour; also Terrenos nacionales, Diversos, 1.322.1(06), Leg. 2, Exp. 26, Limantour, José Ives, y su hermano, Julio.

13. SRA, Archivo Histórico, Terrenos nacionales, Diversos, 1.322.1(06), Leg. 2, Exp. 26, Limantour, José Ives, y su hermano, Julio.

14. Garza still awaits the biography he deserves. The best treatment to date

is Garza Guajardo, *En Busca.* See also *New York Times,* 7 January 1892, p. 2; *St. Louis Republic,* 4 January, p. 1, 9 January, p. 2, 10 January, p. 13, and 12 January, p. 2, 1892; *El Paso Daily Herald,* 9 January 1892, p. 1. Also Cuthbertson, "Catarino Garza," p. 335; Navarro Burciaga, "Catarino Garza," pp. 59–96.

15. Saldivar, *Documentos,* p. 9; *Chicago Times,* 9 January 1892, p. 2; *San Francisco Chronicle,* 2 January 1892, p. 4.

16. *St. Louis Republic,* 5 and 18 January, both p. 1, and 21 January, p. 2, 1892; *New York Times,* 7 January 1892, p. 2. See also USDS, Consular Reports, Nuevo Laredo, 1871–1906, Despatches, June 4, 1891–June 30, 1893, No. 339, Consul Sutton to William F. Warton, assistant secretary of state, 13 November 1891.

17. *San Francisco Chronicle,* 6 and 14 January, 1892, both p. 2.

18. APD, Leg. 16, Caja 34, No. 016575, Ahumada to Díaz, 1 December 1891; Leg. 50, Caja 12, Nos. 007322–25, Carrillo to Díaz, 28 December 1891, and No. 0077349, Rangel to Díaz, 29 December 1891. *El Monitor republicano,* 15 December 1891, p. 3. See also Marrero, "Dos Movimientos," pp. 21–22.

19. AMCG, Leg. 23, Exp. 244, Borrador, Comunicaciones con inferiores, 22 de julio de 1891 a 23 de enero de 1892, 2 December 1891; Leg. 24, Exp. 245, Manuel Rubio, juez de letras, to Jefe Político, 25 November 1891; and Exp. 246, Gabriel Sáenz, agente especial, to Jefe Político, 28 December 1891.

20. *San Francisco Chronicle,* 15 January 1892, p. 2.

21. APD, Leg. 50, Caja 12, No. 006602–6, Rangel to Díaz, 9 December 1891.

22. APD, Leg. 50 Caja 12, No. 006601, Rangel to Díaz, 9 December 1891.

23. APD, Leg. 16, Caja 34, No. 016578, telegram, Ahumada to Díaz, 10 December 1891.

24. APD, Leg. 50, Caja 12, Nos. 006764–68, Carrillo to Díaz, 12 December 1891. AGG, "Partes." Authorities took the discarded cargo to the house of Juan Ignacio Chávez, Tomochic's presidente; see AHCG, Leg. 23, Exp. 244, "Comunicaciones con inferiores," Borrador, 22 julio de 1891 al 23 enero de 1892.

25. APD, Leg. 50, Caja 12, Nos. 006931–32, Carrillo to Díaz, 18 December 1891; AHES, Leg. 1891–92, Exp. Persecución; AMCG, Leg. 23, Exp. 243, Comunicaciones con inferiores, Governor to Jefe Político, 22 December 1891; Leg. 24, Exp. 246, Ramón Ochoa, presidente, Pinos Altos, to Jefe Político, [15 or 16] December 1891. See also J. C. Chávez, *Peleando,* p. 44, and Almada, *Rebelión de Tomochi,* p. 54.

26. AMCG, Leg. 23, Exp. 244, Comunicaciones con inferiores, Borrador, 22 julio de 1891 al 23 enero de 1892; Leg. 24, Exp. 246, Juan Ignacio Chávez, Tomochic, to Jefe Político, 16 December 1891; José de la Luz Ramírez, presidente, Tomósachic, to Jefe Político, 22 December 1891; Ramón A. Sáenz to Jefe Político, 25 December 1891; Rafael Márquez Quesada, presidente, Santo Tomás, to Jefe Político, 2 January 1892; Luis Paredes, Jefe Político of the Dis-

trict of Andrés del Río, to Jefe Político, 31 December 1891; Telegramas oficiales, Ramón G. Ochoa, Pinos Altos, to Jefe Político; Leg. 23, Exp. 243, Comunicaciones con superiores, Governor to Jefe Político, 29 December 1891. See also J. C. Chávez, *Peleando*, pp. 52, 72; Irrab, "Efemérides chihuahuenses," *BSCEH* 1 (April 1939): 384.

27. APD, Leg. 50, Caja 12, Nos. 006764–68, Carrillo to Díaz, 12 December 1891; AHES, Leg. 1891–92, Exp. Persecución.

28. AHES, Leg. 1891–92, Exp. Persecución; APD, Leg. 50, Caja 12, Nos. 006764–68, Carrillo to Díaz, 12 December 1891 and Nos. 006820–21, Izábal to Díaz, 14 December 1891; Pozo Marrero, "Dos Movimientos," Documentos, Díaz to Torres and Izábal, 14 December 1891, p. 39.

Chapter 8

1. APD, Leg. 17, Caja 1, No. 000262, Carrillo to Díaz, 2 January 1892.

2. *El Tiempo* (Las Cruces), 17 April 1890, p. 1; W. C. Holden, *Teresita*, chs. 8–10. Besides Holden's careful anthropological work, there is a substantial literature on Teresa Urrea, although much of it is polemical and of remarkably uneven quality; see Domecq, *La Insólita historia* (a praiseworthy novel) and "Teresa Urrea"; Gill, "Teresa Urrea"; Larralde, "Santa Teresa"; Macklin, "Folk Saints"; Macklin and Crumrine, "Three North Mexican Movements"; Putnam, "Teresa Urrea"; Ridgeway, "Saint or Nurse?"; Rodríguez and Rodríguez, "Teresa Urrea."

3. David Yetman, an environmental anthropolgist in the Southwest Center at the University of Arizona, has for some 30 years traveled, researched, and written about Sonora. He knows the Alamos district well and graciously provided most of the geographical and environmental details pertaining to Cabora. I thank him for his excellent, detailed letters of 24 April and 29 July 1993.

4. For examples among many descriptions, see W. C. Holden, *Teresita*, pp. 28–30, 49–51; *Arizona Daily Star*, 28 June 1892, p. 4; *La Ilustración espírita*, April 1891, p. 368, and March 1892, pp. 314–15; *La Opinión*, 28 February 1937, Pt. 2, p. 1; *El Monitor republicano*, 10 January 1890, p. 3; *San Francisco Examiner*, 27 July 1900, p. 7; *Tombstone Prospector*, 21 November 1895, p. 4.

5. USNA, Military Reference Branch, Record Group 94, "Santa Teresa," Adjutant General's Office, No. 34579.

6. *La Ilustración espírita*, September 1892, p. 139; W. C. Holden, *Teresita*, pp. 62–64.

7. W. C. Holden, *Teresita*, pp. 78–81.

8. *La Opinión*, 28 February 1937, Part 2, p. 1: W. C. Holden, *Teresita*, ch. 1. For the Tehuecos, see Sauer, *Aboriginal*, pp. 15–18. For Urreas, see González Dávila, *Diccionario de Sinaloa*, pp. 636–40.

9. W. C. Holden, *Teresita*, p. 10; *La Ilustración espírita*, January 1892, p. 256.

10. *La Ilustración espírita*, January 1892, p. 256; W. C. Holden, *Teresita*, ch. 1.

11. W. C. Holden, *Teresita*, ch. 2.

12. Personal correspondence, Yetman to Vanderwood, 24 April and 29 July 1993.

13. W. C. Holden, *Teresita*, pp. 22–23.

14. Ibid., pp. 24–26.

15. Ibid., ch. 3.

16. *La Ilustración espírita*, September 1892, p. 141; W. C. Holden, *Teresita*, pp. 43–46. Teresa's knowledge of local medicines, including hallucinogenics, is stressed in Larralde, "Santa Teresa," ch. 2.

17. *La Ilustración espírita*, January 1892, pp. 256–57; September 1892, pp. 138–39.

18. *La Ilustración espírita*, January 1892, p. 258 and September 1892, p. 138; W. C. Holden, *Teresita*, pp. 58, 68–72.

19. *Arizona Daily Gazette*, 10 February 1901, p. 5; Ridgway, "Saint or Nurse?" p. 1.

20. *La Ilustración espírita*, April 1891, p. 367; January 1892, p. 258; February 1892, p. 278. *El Monitor republicano*, 10 January 1890, p. 3.

21. *San Francisco Examiner*, 27 July 1900, p. 7; *La Ilustración espírita*, September 1892, p. 141.

22. *San Francisco Examiner*, 27 July 1900, p. 7; *La Ilustración espírita*, April 1892, p. 368.

23. *Graham County Bulletin*, 8 November 1895, p. 3; *The Copper Era*, 7 February 1901, p. 1.

24. *La Ilustración espírita*, February 1892, p. 279; September 1892, p. 139.

25. *La Ilustración espírita*, April 1891, p. 369; January 1892, p. 260; September 1892, p. 142.

26. *La Opinión*, 7 March 1937, Sec. 2, p. 1.

27. *El Monitor republicano*, 10 January 1890, p. 3.

28. Larralde, "Santa Teresa," pp. 13–21.

29. *La Ilustración espírita*, April 1891, p. 368; *El Tiempo* (Las Cruces), 17 April 1890, p. 1.

30. *La Ilustración espírita*, April 1891, p. 368.

31. *The Copper Era*, 7 February 1901, p. 1; *La Ilustración espírita*, April 1891, p. 367; W. C. Holden, *Teresita*, pp. 41–42.

32. The comments concerning the relationship between mystical experience and culture are based upon Lewis, *Ecstatic Religion*, p. 16. Michele Stephen of LaTrobe University in Melbourne, Australia, introduced me to the concept of "autonomous imagination." See her "Culture, the Self," and "Self, the Sacred Other."

33. *El Monitor republicano*, 10 January 1890, p. 3.

34. *San Francisco Chronicle*, 9 December 1900, p. 40; *San Francisco Call*,

9 September 1900, p. 40; *El Sábado* as quoted in *El Monitor republicano*, 10 January 1890, p. 3.

35. *El Tiempo* (Las Cruces), 17 April 1890, p. 1; *La Ilustración espírita*, September 1892, pp. 142–43; W. C. Holden, *Teresita*, pp. 81–82.

36. This aspect of La Salette and Lourdes is best analyzed in Kselman, *Miracles and Prophesies*.

37. SRE, Archivo histórico, Sección Siglo Diez y Nueve, Leg. María Teresa Urrea, Exp. III, Nos. 513-890-2 and 11-19-11. *El Diario del Hogar*, 23 October 1890, p. 2; 18 February 1892, p. 3.

38. *La Ilustración espírita*, January 1892, p. 257; February 1892, p. 280.

39. *La Ilustración espírita*, April 1891, pp. 367–68; January 1892, pp. 259–60; February 1892, pp. 279–80. W. C. Holden, *Teresita*, pp. 82–85.

40. *La Ilustración espírita*, September 1892, p. 140.

41. *La Ilustración espírita*, January 1892, p. 260; March 1892, p. 315.

42. On Spiritism in Mexico, see Finkler, "Social Consequences," pp. 627, 642; Macklin, "Santos folklóricos." Jean-Pierre Bastián places Mexican Spiritists, along with other such groups, in Porfirian perspective in "Una geografía política de la oposición al porfirismo de las sociedades de ideas al origen de la revolución de 1910," in Chávez and Grijalva, *Cincuenta años*, 2: 397–422. Much good scholarly work has been done on Spiritism in other parts of Latin America; see, for example, Hess, *Spiritists and Scientists*, and Warren, "Spiritism in Brazil." For a succinct overview of the origins and content of spiritism, see Kselman, *Death and the Afterlife*, pp. 143–62. My special gratitude goes to Anne Braude, Professor of Religious Studies at Carlton College, Northfield, Minnesota, who has studied and written well on spiritism, and patiently explained such belief to me in a series of phone conversations in the fall of 1993.

43. *La Ilustración espírita*, April 1891, pp. 366–69. The report is dated 9 January 1890.

44. *La Ilustración espírita*, February 1892, p. 281; March 1892, p. 314. The report from Boroyeca is dated 12 November 1891 and was carried in three installments in *La Ilustración espírita*, January–March, 1892.

45. *La Ilustración espírita*, March 1892, p. 314.

46. My discussion of the nature of the exchange between official and local religion is influenced by Krantz, *History from Below;* and Scott, *Domination* and *Weapons of the Weak*. Kselman notes the same process in *Miracles and Prophecies*, p. 4 and *passim*. An excellent study of the interaction is R. Gutiérrez, *When Jesus Came*. Professor Eric Van Young has done some of the best recent theoretical examination of the complex interrelationship (the so-called dialogue) between people in power and the popular masses. See, for example, his well-reasoned and stimulating critique of Scott in "The Cuautla Lazarus"; also "The State as Vampire."

47. Shepherd, *Silver Magnet*. Batopilas is the mining complex that Alexander "Boss" Shepherd, the famous Washington, D.C., politician, so success-

fully exploited from the late 1880s well into this century. Grant Shepherd is Alexander's son.

48. SRE, "Sobre Lauro Aguirre," No. 9-15-15, 1898; *El Paso Times*, 10 January 1925, p. 11; *La Opinión*, 21 March 1937, p. 1; *La Patria* (El Paso), 9 January 1925, p. 1; *La Oásis*, 15 August 1896, p. 1; *El Atalaya*, 9 June 1892, p. 2. See also Valadés, *Díaz contra Dios*, p. 21. Activities of the survey companies in Sonora and Chihuahua are aptly discussed by W. H. Holden, *Mexico and the Survey* (see pp. 97–102 for Hüller and p. 193 for the Alamos controversy). In 1901 Aguirre wrote and published through his own newspaper *Tomochic!* (its full title, *Tomochic! Rendición! Revoluciones recientes y futuras de México;—Papel y participación en ellas de—La Santa de Cabora, "La Juana de Arco" mexicana;—y de—"El presidente necesario;" "Héroes—Pilatos" moderno*), in which he utilized events surrounding Tomochic and Teresa to discuss Mexican politics in Spiritist terms. Although a political polemic, it still yields historical details not available elsewhere. Furthermore, it ardently renders (albeit in a rambling prose that challenges the reader's wits and concentration) a Spiritist view of the world in motion. For Aguirre's complaints about survey companies in Baja California and land disputes involving Tomás Urrea, see W. H. Holden, *Mexico and the Survey*, pp. 14, 21–22, 24.

49. Aguirre's report dated 28 July 1892 appears in *La Ilustración espírita*, September 1892, pp. 138–44.

50. *La Ilustración espírita*, September 1892, p. 141.

51. *San Francisco Bulletin*, 9 September 1900, p. 20.

52. *The Copper Era*, 7 February 1901, p. 1.

53. *San Francisco Call*, 9 September 1900, p. 40.

Chapter 9

1. *New York Journal*, 3 March 1901, p. 23.

2. *El Tiempo* (Las Cruces), 17 April 1890, p. 1.

3. USNA, Military Records Branch, RG 94, "Santa Teresa," AGO No. 34579.

4. *The Copper Era*, 7 February 1901, p. 1; for letters from Heaven during the nineteenth century, see Kselman, *Miracles and Prophesies*, p. 65.

5. *El Diario del hogar*, 9 April 1890, p. 1; *La Ilustración espírita*, 9 April 1890, p. 2, and Vol. 10 (1890–91), pp. 158–59.

6. Quoted in W. C. Holden, *Teresita*, p. 103. See also *El Tiempo* (Las Cruces), 17 April 1890, p. 1; *Arizona Daily Star*, 28 June 1892, p. 4.

7. *El Tiempo* (Las Cruces), 17 April 1890, p. 1.

8. *La Ilustración espírita*, April 1891, p. 369. For use of baptism in moving people from past religious allegiances to a new religious sect, see Fields, *Revival and Rebellion*, pp. 117–23.

9. *El Tiempo* (Las Cruces), 17 April 1890, p. 1; *La Ilustración espírita*, April 1891, p. 369.

10. For lampooning of priests, see lithographs of José Guadalupe Posada reprinted in various works, for example, Cardoza y Aragón, *Posada*, figures 81 and 82. On priests as parasites, see Parry and Block, *Money*, p. 88.

11. *El Monitor republicano*, 2 November 1892, p. 1. We should not generalize about the attitudes of priests toward prophets and visionaries. In *Visions of Moving Cruciifixes in Modern Spain*, William A. Christian, Jr., describes how different priests witnessing the same phenomena of moving crucifixes drew widely different conclusions about their meaning for parishioners.

12. This idea is most forcefully stated by Rigoberta Menchú in her moving autobiography, *I, Rigoberta Menchú*, p. 133.

13. *La Ilustración espírita*, September 1892, p. 138; Aguirre, *Tomochic!*, pp. 1–48 *passim*.

14. *The Copper Era*, 7 February 1901, p. 1. Parry and Block emphasize that besides money per se, other processes, such as the expansion of the external market into local affairs, help to dissolve traditional community ties; see *Money*, pp. 4–14.

15. *La Ilustración espírita*, April 1891, p. 369; *New York Journal*, 3 March 1901, p. 1.

16. Hess, *Spiritists and Scientists*, pp. 17–19; Finkler, "Social Consequences," p. 630.

17. AMCG, Leg. 6, Exp. 69, Padrón general de Tomochic, 1864.

18. Here my ideas were stimulated by the Polynesian studies of anthropologist Kenelm Burridge; see his *New Heaven*, pp. 41–46. For comparison, see the impact of money on the nineteenth-century French countryside elegantly related in Weber, *Peasants into Frenchmen*, pp. 33–40. Money in its diverse forms is considered in Neale, *Monies*. For provocative discussions about money and morality, see Parry and Block, *Money*.

19. W. C. Holden, *Teresita*, pp. 52–53.

20. *La Ilustración espírita*, June 1891, pp. 50–51.

21. Ibid., pp. 51–52.

22. For another Sonoran illustration of how diverse native groups come to worship the same "santo," see Griffith, *Beliefs and Holy Places*, pp. 60–61.

23. The primary source for these events is Paso y Troncoso, *Guerras con tribus*, pp. 181–82. These happenings are also discussed and analyzed in Macklin, "Folk Saints"; Macklin and Crumrine, "Three North Mexican Movements"; Spicer, "Contrasting Forms."

24. For Mayo flood myth, see Crumrine, *Mayo Indians*, pp. 139–41. Flooding had ravaged the area in 1868; see Hu-DeHart, *Yaqui Resistance*, p. 89.

25. *La Ilustración espírita*, September 1892, p. 138.

26. Ibid., pp. 182–83; Almada, *Rebelión de Tomochic*, pp. 69–71.

27. Crumrine, " 'La Tierra,' " 1144–45.

28. Giddings, *Yaqui Myths*, p. 109.

29. Painter, *With Good Heart*, pp. 106–7.

30. Ibid., p. 56.

31. *New York Journal*, 3 March 1901, p. 1.

32. APD, Leg. 17, Caja 1, No. 000331, General Marcos Carrillo to Porfirio Díaz, 21 December 1891. In this same document Díaz responded to General Carrillo that he had already contacted Governor Izábal "about the best way to work together to end the Yaqui problem," which indicates that the president had decided upon the "final solution": deportation of the natives to Yucatan, which began soon afterward. In a series of dispatches to the U.S. Department of State, the U.S. consul at Guaymas, Alexander Willard, detailed native resistance to the Mexican government's intentions to colonize the Yaqui and Mayo River valleys with large-scale commercial farmers; see USDS, Consular Reports, Mexico, Guaymas, Willard to W. F. Wharton, Assistant Secretary of State, No. 949, 21 October 1889; No. 984, 22 May 1890; No. 1022, 31 December 1890; and No. 1065, 31 December 1891. Hu-DeHart provides a good overview in *Yaqui Resistance*, pp. 118–33. Contention among the Yaquis over Cajeme's leadership is mentioned in Spicer, *Cycles of Conquest*, pp. 70–71.

33. William Merrill, my anthropologist friend at the Smithsonian Institution, is pondering the ways in which the Tarahumaras responded to colonizers and other outsiders; letter, Merrill to Vanderwood, 16 March 1993. Spicer concluded that the Yaquis and the Mayos accepted the discipline and agricultural development of Jesuit mission life in ways that the Tarahumaras did not. As a result, the former became more or less integrated into colonial patterns, while Tarahumaras remained separate and distinct. See Spicer, *Cycles of Conquest*, p. 58. More recently anthropologists and historians have challenged his thesis.

34. In *Teresita* W. C. Holden gives us an overview of La Santa's life after Cabora.

35. Bynum, " 'And Woman His Humanity,' " p. 258; Dezan, "Role of Women"; Mack, "Women as Prophets," p. 32; Nolan and Nolan, *Christian Pilgrimage*, pp. 287–89. For the Alice, the Lakwena, movement in Uganda, see Vanderwood, "Using the Present." That prophets are often women is mentioned in Burridge, *New Heaven*, pp. 41–42.

Chapter 10

1. The ambush at El Alamo is covered in the following: APD, Leg. 17, Caja 1, No. 000267, Carlos A. Díaz, prefect, Batacosa, to Governor, 26 December 1891, and Nos. 000330–31, General Marcos Carrillo to Porfirio Díaz, 3 January 1892; Caja 2, No. 000926, General Juan A. Hernández to Porfirio Díaz, 29 December 1891; Leg. 50, Caja 12, Nos. 007313–14, Rafael Izábal to Porfirio

Díaz, 28 December 1891. AHES, Leg. 1892, Exp. Persecuciones, Telegrama, Carlos A. Díaz, prefect, Alamos, to Governor 26 December 1891; Governor Lauro Carrillo, Chihuahua, to Governor Rafael Izábal, Sonora, 28 December 1891; Jesús G. Coronado, presidente, Sahuaripa, to Governor, 2 January 1892. Almada, *Rebelión de Tomochi*, pp. 54–55; W. C. Holden, *Teresita*, pp. 131–37; J. C. Chávez, *Peleando*, p. 81.

2. APD, Leg. 17, Caja 1, No. 000330, General Marcos Carrillo to Porfirio Díaz, 3 January 1892; AHES, Leg. 1892, Exp. Persecuciones, Jesús G. Coronado, presidente, Sahuaripa, to Governor, 2 January 1892.

3. AHES, Leg. 1892, Exp. Persecuciones, Governor Rafael Izábal to Governor Lauro Carrillo, 28 December 1892; Francisco Parada, Quiriego, to Governor, 28 December 1892 (Governor Izábal passed the Parada report on to Porfirio Díaz the same day: APD, Leg. 17, Caja 1, Nos. 000265–66). Also see APD, Leg. 17, Caja 1, No. 000330 General Marcos Carrillo to Porfirio Díaz, 3 January 1892.

4. APD, Leg. 17, Caja 1, No. 000330, General Marcos Carrillo to Porfirio Díaz, 3 January 1892; AHES, Leg. 1892, Exp. Persecuciones, Coronel Lorenzo Torres to Governor Rafael Izábal, 1 January 1892; Almada, *Rebelión de Tomochi*, p. 57; J. C. Chávez, *Peleando*, p. 81; Chávez Calderón, *Defensa de Tomochi*, p. 22; W. C. Holden, *Teresita*, p. 137.

5. *New York Times*, 16 February 1892, p. 5.

6. APD, Leg. 17, Caja 1, No. 000330, General Marcos Carrillo to Porifirio Díaz, 3 January 1892.

7. APD, Leg. 17, Caja 2, No. 0009927, Porfirio Díaz to General Juan A. Hernández, 29 December 1892.

8. AHES, Leg. 1892, Exp. Persecuciones, Jesús G. Coronado, presidente, Sahuaripa, to Governor, 2 January 1892. For death of Jesús José Chávez, see AHES, Leg. 1892, Exp. Persecuciones, Coronel Lorenzo Torres to Governor Rafael Izábal, 1 January 1892; APD, Leg. 17, Caja 1, No. 000330, General Marcos Carrillo to Porfirio Díaz, 3 January 1892; Almada, *Rebelión de Tomochi*, p. 57; J. C. Chávez, *Peleando*, p. 81; Chávez Calderón, *Defensa de Tomochi*, p. 22; W. C. Holden, *Teresita*, p. 137.

9. AHES, Leg. 1892, Exp. Persecuciones, Ramón A. Corral, Secretary of State, Sonora, to Francisco Parada, presidente, Quiriego, 26 December 1891; General Marcos Carrillo to Ramón Corral, 28 December 1891; Carlos A. Díaz, prefect, Alamos, to Ramón Corral, 28 December 1891, and to Governor, 3 January 1892; Governor Rafael Izábal to Governor Lauro Carrillo, 29 December 1892. APD, Leg. 50, Caja 12, Nos. 007313–14, Governor Rafael Izábal to Porfirio Díaz, 28 December 1891; No. 007427, Izábal to Díaz, 31 December 1891; Nos. 007428–29, Governor Lauro Carrillo to Porfirio Díaz, 31 December 1891. Also consult Almada, *Rebelión de Tomochi*, p. 57.

10. AHES, Leg. 1892, Exp. Persecuciones, Jesús G. Coronado, presidente, Sahuaripa, to Governor, 2 January 1892; Porfirio Díaz to [?], 3 January 1892.

11. AMCG, Leg. Comunicaciones con superiores, Exp. Telegramas, Governor Lauro Carrillo to Silviano González, 29 and 31 December 1891; APD, Leg. 17, Exp. 1, Nos. 000271–77, Governor Lauro Carrillo to Porfirio Díaz, 25 January 1892. For the pursuit, see AMCG, Leg. Comunicaciones con inferiores, Exp. Telegramas oficiales, 1892, Presidente, Jesús María, to Jefe Político, 22 January 1892; APD, Leg. 17, Caja 1, No. 000268, Governor Lauro Carrillo to Porfirio Díaz, 2 January 1892.

12. AMCG, Leg. Comunicaciones con inferiores, mes de enero 1892, Exp. Bartolo Ledesma, comisario, Tomochic, to Jefe Político, 25 January 1892.

13. AMCG, Leg. Comunicaciones con inferiores, mes de enero 1892, Exp. Reyes Domínguez, presidente, Tomochic, to Jefe Político, 29 enero 1892; Almada, *Rebelión de Tomochi*, p. 58 and appendix 10, pp. 165–70; AHES, Leg. 192, Exp. Persecuciones (list of Tomochitecos being pursued).

14. For bodily resurrection in religious belief, see McDannell and Lang, *Heaven*, pp. 12–13, 49–52.

15. AMCG, Leg. 27, Comunicaciones con inferiores, mes de enero 1892, Exp. 273, Reyes Domínguez, presidente, Tomochic, to Jefe Político, 29 January 1892, and mes de febrero, Reyes Domínguez to Jefe Político, 16 February 1892; Bartolo Ledesma to Jefe Político, 19 January 1892, and Juan Ignacio Chávez to Jefe Político, 2 and 7 January 1892. Also see Almada, *Rebelión de Tomochi*, pp. 54–57, and 64.

16. AMCG, Leg. 27, Comunicaciones con inferiores, mes de febrero 1892, Exp. 273, Reyes Domínguez, presidente, Tomochic, to Jefe Político, 16 February 1892.

17. Marrero, "Dos movimientos," pp. 109–127.

18. AMCG, Leg. Comunicaciones con superiores, Telegramas, 1892, Governor Lauro Carrillo to Jefe Político, 11 and 22 January and 7 February 1892.

19. The account of this meeting is based on the mediator's report: AGN, Archivo Histórico de la Revolución Mexicana, Series Manuel González Ramírez, Vol. 3, Folios 141–45.

20. APD, Leg. 17, Caja 1, No. 000262, Governor Lauro Carrillo to Porfirio Díaz, 8 January 1892.

21. APD, Leg. 17, Caja 4, Nos. 001687–88, Miguel Ahumada to Porfirio Díaz, 6 February 1892; Nos. 001917–22, Governor Lauro Carrillo to Porfirio Díaz, 9 February 1892; Leg. 51, Caja 3, No. 001759, Agustín Sanginés to Porfirio Díaz, 9 March 1892; No. 001761, Colonel Carrillo to Díaz, 9 March 1892; No. 001763, Colonel Carrillo to Díaz, 10 March 1892; Caja 4, Nos. 001881–82, telegrams to Porfiro Díaz in support of the Terrazas group, 14 March 1892; No. 001892, Carrillo to Díaz, 18 March 1892; Caja 5, No. 002507, Ahumada to Díaz, 1 April 1892; Rafael Pimentel to Porfirio Díaz, 2 April 1892; Nos. 002558–60, Carrillo to Díaz, 4 April 1892; No. 0025586, Carrillo to Díaz, 5 April 1892, Nos. 002587–88, Carrillo to Díaz, 6 April 1892; Caja 27, No.

013273, Petition of citizens of Chihuahua to block Carrillo's reelection, March 1892. Also see *El Tiempo* (Mexico City), 2 April 1892, p. 2.

22. APD, Leg. 51, Caja 7, No. 004043, Porfirio Díaz to Rafael Pimentel, 7 June 1892; Leg. 5, Caja 8, Nos. 004251–52, Miguel Ahumada to Porfirio Díaz, 16 June 1892; Caja 9, Nos. 004870–71, L. B. Caballero to Enrique Creel, 9 July 1892; Nos. 004950–56, Caballero to Creel, 10 July 1892; Leg. 17, Caja 5, No. 012031, Caballero Larriva, Batopilas, to Enrique Creel, 11 July 1892; Nos. 012032–34, Luis Terrazas to Enrique Creel, 25 July 1892.

23. AHAD, Leg. Cortes de 1892, Exp. No. 207, Padre Castelo, Uruachic, to Presbítero Luis Terrazas y Córdova, vicario, Chihuahua City, 24 August, and No. 222, 19 September 1892.

24. *El Monitor republicano*, 2 November 1892, p. 1.

25. AMCG, Leg. 25, Comunicaciones con superiores, mes de agosto 1862, Exp. 263, Governor to Jefe Político, 2 August 1892; Jefe Político to Governor, 22 and 28 July 1892; Almada, *Rebelión de Tomochi*, pp. 85–86.

26. APD, Leg. 51, Caja 11, No. 006236, Porfirio Díaz to General José María Rangel; Nos. 006237–38, Rangel to Díaz; No. 006245, Reyes Domínguez to Porfirio Díaz; No. 006280, Rafael Pimentel to Porfirio Díaz, all 18 August 1892. AMCG, Leg. Comunicaciones con superiores, mes de agosto de 1892, Jefe Político to Governor, 15 August 1892; Governor to Jefe Político, 23 August 1892. Almada, *Rebelión de Tomochi*, p. 86; appendix 5, pp. 155–56; appendix 6, pp. 157–58.

27. López-Portillo y Rojas, *Elevación*, pp. 217, 226–29.

28. *New York Times*, 16 February 1892, p. 5.

29. Pinos Altos Mining Company, Record Books, 1892, Nos. 1–5, 2 March; Nos. 27–30, 15 March; Nos. 194–95, 9 July; and Nos. 203–4, 17 July. AMCG, Leg. Comunicaciones con superiores, Jefe Político to Governor, 18 and 25 June 1892; Leg. Comunicaciones con inferiores, Exp. Luis Comadurán, Bachíniva, to Jefe Político, 3 June 1892; Leg. 23, Comunicaciones con superiores, Exp. 243, Governor to Jefe Político, 25 December 1891; Exp. 244, Borrador, Comunicaciones con inferiores, 22 julio de 1891 a 23 enero de 1892, entry for 21 January 1892. Also consult APD, Leg. 17, Caja 25, Nos. 012032–35, Luis Terrazas to Enrique Creel, 25 July 1892. See also *La Voz de México*, 2 July 1892, p. 2; *La Patria* (Mexico City), 30 October 1892, p. 2; Almada, *Rebelión de Tomochi*, pp. 52, 86–87.

30. AMCG, Leg. 27, Comunicaciones con inferiores, abril de 1892, Exp. 274, Manuel Rubio, juez de letras, Guerrero, to Jefe Político, 23 April, 6 and 7 May, 1892. Also see Almada, *Rebelión de Tomochi*, p. 67.

31. AMCG, Leg. Comunicaciones con inferiores, julio de 1892, Exp. Constancia a petición de parte (sworn statement of Juan de la Cruz, accompanied by Padre Julio Irigoyen) to judicial notary, J. Orozco, signed by Padre Irigoyen, 26 July 1892.

32. AMCG, Leg. Comunicaciones con inferiores, Leg. Ramón G. Ochoa,

Pinos Altos, to Jefe Político, 30 July 1892; Leg. Comunicaciones con superiores, Exp. Rafael Pimentel to Jefe Político, 30 August 1892. Also, *El Monitor republicano,* 25 October 1892, p. 2; Almada, *Rebelión de Tomochi,* pp. 87, 90–93; J. C. Chávez, *Peleando,* pp. 104–6.

Chapter 11

1. Dávila, *Sonora,* p. 272; APD, Leg. 51, Caja 5, Nos. 003482–83, Governor Rafael Izábal to Porfirio Díaz, 18 May 1892.

2. Paso y Troncoso, *Guerras con tribus,* p. 203.

3. APD, Leg. 51, Caja 5, Nos. 003482–83, Governor Rafael Izábal to Porfirio Díaz, 18 May 1892; Paso y Troncoso, *Guerras con tribus,* pp. 198–99; Almada, *Rebelión de Tomochi,* pp. 71–75.

4. Paso y Troncoso, *Guerras con tribus,* p. 197.

5. Ibid., pp. 196–97; APD, Leg. 51, Caja 5, Nos. 003514–15, General Abraham Bandala to Porfirio Díaz, 20 May 1892.

6. Paso y Troncoso, *Guerras con tribus,* pp. 196–99.

7. APD, Leg. 51, Caja 5, Nos. 003514–15, General Abraham Bandala to Porfirio Díaz, 20 May 1892; No. 003593, Bandala to Díaz, 24 May 1892; Caja 7 [no number], Porfirio Díaz to Governor Rafael Izábal, 26 May 1892.

8. APD, Leg. 51, Caja 5, Nos. 003511–13, Governor Rafael Izábal to Porfirio Díaz, 20 May 1892.

9. APD, Leg. 51, Caja 5, Nos. 003511–13, Governor Rafael Izábal to Porfirio Díaz, 20 May 1892; Nos. 003516–18, General Abraham Bandala to Porfirio Díaz, 20 May 1892. Paso y Troncoso, *Guerras con tribus,* pp. 198–99.

10. APD, Leg. 51, Caja 5, Nos. 003516–18, General Abraham Bandala to Porfirio Díaz, 20 May 1892.

11. *La Ilustración espírita,* 1 December 1892, pp. 82–83.

12. *Arizona Daily Gazette,* 10 November 1901, p. 5; *The Copper Era,* 7 February 1901, p. 1.

13. *La Ilustración espírita,* 1 December 1892, pp. 81–82.

14. *New York Times,* 16 June 1892, p. 1.

15. *Arizona Daily Star,* 28 June 1892, p. 4.

16. APD, Leg. 51, Caja 7, No. 003796, Governor Rafael Izábal to Porfirio Díaz, 2 June 1892.

17. *New York Times,* 29 June 1892, p. 10. For Teresa's reception, see *Arizona Daily Citizen,* 4 June 1892, p. 1; SRE, Leg. María Teresa Urrea, Exp. III, Nos. 5313-890-2 and 11-19-11, pp. 9–14; APD, Leg. 17, Caja 24, No. 011526, Governor Rafael Izábal to Porfirio Díaz, 25 June 1892; *La Ilustración espírita,* 1 December 1892, p. 81.

18. I have excerpted the poem for brevity's sake. For the complete poem, see Valadés, *Díaz contra Dios,* pp. 34–36. For the Yaquis gaining weapons,

see SRE, Leg. María Teresa Urrea, Exp. III, Nos. 513-890-2 and 11-19-11, pp. 9–14.

19. A wonderful Hispanic lady who asked to remain anonymous, a folk healer in the region of Corpus Christi, Texas, recently told me of her vision of Joan of Arc, who appeared outside her home on a great white horse, sword raised in hand, at a time when the seer was experiencing some difficult personal problems. Soon after the vision her predicament was resolved, her faith intensified, and she learned that she had (had been granted) healing powers. I sincerely thank this woman for sharing her mystical experiences with me as well as the spiritual beliefs that accompany her faith healing. She is a very gentle and sympathetic teacher.

20. *Phoenix Weekly Herald*, 30 June 1892, p. 3; *La Opinión*, 21 March 1937, Part 21, p. 1; *Arizona Daily Star*, 24 June 1892, p. 1.

21. *Arizona Daily Citizen*, 9 June 1892, p. 1; SRE, Leg. María Teresa Urrea, Exp. III, No. 11-19-11; *Arizona Daily Star*, 28 June 1892, p. 4, and 6 July 1892, p. 4; *La Ilustración espírita*, 1 December 1892, p. 112; Valadés, *Díaz contra Dios*, p. 27.

22. *La Ilustración espírita*, 1 December 1892, p. 111; *Arizona Daily Star*, 28 July 1892, p. 4.

23. SRE, Leg. María Teresa Urrea, Exp. III, Nos. 513-890-2 and 11-19-11, pp. 9–14.

24. Pimería Alta Historical Society, Historical Archive, File: "Teresa Urrea" (newspaper clippings and other materials).

25. The exchange is in APD, Leg. 51, Caja 11, No. 006236, Porfirio Díaz to General José María Rangel, 18 August 1892; Nos. 006237–38, Rangel to Díaz, 18 August 1892; Nos. 006239–40, Rangel to Díaz, 20 August 1892. An interesting historical footnote: the "bandit Garza" was on his way, via Florida to join a revolution in Colombia.

Chapter 12

1. APD, Leg. 51, Caja 12, Nos. 006999–7013, José María Rangel to Porfirio Díaz, 6 September 1892; J. C. Chávez, *Peleando*, p. 83.

2. APD, Leg. 51, Caja 12, Nos. 006803–10, Rafael Pimentel to Porfirio Díaz, 4 September 1892; Nos. 006999–7013, José María Rangel to Porfirio Díaz, 6 September 1892; Nos. 007016–24, José María Avalos to Porfirio Díaz, 6 September 1892, J. C. Chávez, *Peleando*, p. 85; Almada, *Rebelión de Tomochi*, p. 88.

3. APD, Leg. 51, Caja 12, Nos. 006722–31, Rafael Pimentel to Porfirio Díaz, 3 September 1892; Nos. 006803–10, Rafael Pimentel to Porfirio Díaz, 4 September 1892; Nos. 006999–7013, José María Rangel to Porfirio Díaz, 6 September 1892. J. C. Chávez, *Peleando*, pp. 85–86.

4. APD, Leg. 51, Caja 12, No. 006715, José María Avalos to Porfirio Díaz; Nos. 006720–21, Miguel Ahumada to Porfirio Díaz; Nos. 006722–731, Rafael Pimentel to Porfirio Díaz, all 3 September 1892; No. 006882, Ahumada to Díaz, 5 September 1892.

5. *New York Times*, 12 September 1892, p. 5; Almada, *Rebelión de Tomochi*, p. 90.

6. AMCG, Leg. 1892, Exp. Telegramas oficiales, José María Avalos to Jefe Político, 3 September 1892; APD, Leg. 51, Caja 11, Nos. 006541–49, José María Rangel to Porfirio Díaz, 30 August 1892; *El Monitor republicano*, 2 November 1892, p. 1.

7. AMCG, Leg. 25, Exp. 263, Comunicaciones con superiores, José María Rangel to Gobernador, and Comunicaciones con inferiores, José María Rangel to Jefe Político, both 29 August 1892; APD, Leg. 51, Caja 11, Nos. 006537–38, Rafael Pimentel to Porfirio Díaz, and Nos. 006541–49, José María Rangel to Porfirio Díaz, both 30 August 1892.

8. For strength of army forces confronting Tomochic in September 1892, see APD, Leg. 51, Caja 11, Nos. 006354–61, José María Rangel to Porfirio Díaz, 23 August 1892, and Nos. 006363–64, Abraham Bandala to Porfiro Díaz, 26 August 1892; Caja 12, Nos. 006999–7013, José María Rangel to Porfirio Díaz; Nos. 007016–7024, José María Avalos to Porfirio Díaz, both 6 September 1892. Almada sets the number of defenders at 68; *Rebelión de Tomochi*, pp. 87–88. Pimentel underestimated their number at 33; APD, Leg. 51, Caja 11, Rafael Pimentel to Porfirio Díaz, 25 August 1892.

9. ADN, Archivo de Cancelados, exps. [by surnames]: Márquez, Rosendo; Bandala, Abraham; Cruz, Felipe; Hernández, Juan A. See also entries under these names in *Diccionario porrúa*: Bandala, 1: 296; Rangel, 3: 2413; Torres, 3: 2979. Aspects of Carlos Pacheco's career are mentioned in *Boletín militar* 1 (4 November 1892): 1–3. Hernández is covered in E. Gutiérrez, *Rasgos biográficos*. There is data on Rangel in Ortiz Figueroa, "El Papel de la fuerza rural." Captain Francisco Castro's career is summarized in J. C. Chávez, *Peleando*, pp. 12–14. *Peleando* also has scattered biographical material on all of the generals involved at Tomochic, as does Almada's *Rebelión de Tomochi*.

10. Cosío Villegas, *Historia moderna*, 6: 97–98.

11. APD, Leg. 51, Caja 14, No. 007822, José María Rangel to Porfirio Díaz, 1 October 1892.

12. The best study to date on the professionalization of the Porfirian army and its use in politics is Alexius, "Army and Politics." As an example of the official curriculum for student officers at the Colegio Militar, see *Fragmentos del reglamento*.

13. Alexius, "Army and Politics," pp. 26–97.

14. APD, Leg. 51, Caja 10, Nos. 005587–88, Rafael Pimentel to Porfirio Díaz, 26 July 1892.

15. Alexius, "Army and Politics," pp. 52–67, 90–92. For cases of solicita-

tions for judicial relief stemming from the Papigochic, see AMCG, Leg. 16, Exp. 185, Comunicaciones con superiores, Governor to Jefe Político, 15 April 1885; Leg. 36, Exp. 332, Comunicaciones con inferiores, Mes de octubre-noviembre 1896, Militar [Military Command] en Chihuahua to Jefe Político, 26 October 1896.

16. APD, Leg. 51, Caja 10, No. 005669, Rafael Pimentel to Porfirio Díaz, 29 July 1892.

17. AMGC, Leg. 14, Exp. 166, Libro de secciones ordinarias y extraordinarias, 1882–83, entry for 21 August 1883; Leg. 19, Exp. 217, Circular No. 133.

18. AMCG, Leg. 18, Exp. 207, Comunicaciones con inferiores, José A. Blanco, presidente, Santo Tomás, to Jefe Político, 18 July 1888; Benedicto Acosta, presidente, Temósachic, to Jefe Político, 20 July 1888; Juan N. Bencomo, presidente, Mátachic, to Jefe Político, 21 July 1888; Luis J. Hernández, jefe de policía, Pinos Altos, to Jefe Político, 27 July 1888.

19. Alexius, "Army and Politics," pp. 103–15.

20. *Boletín militar* 1 (10 June 1885): 1.

21. For example, see Argueta, *One Day*, pp. 35–36, 98.

22. *Boletín militar* 1 (8 January 1886): 4–5, (2 October 1886): 7.

23. *Boletín militar* 1 (8 January 1886): 4–5.

24. Argueta, *One Day*, p. 98.

25. *Boletín militar* 1 (10 June 1885): 2.

26. J. C. Chávez, *Peleando*, p. 71.

27. Alexius, "Army and Politics," pp. 14–25, 93–103.

28. The characteristics of weaponry mentioned in this book were provided by David T. Farrelly of San Diego, California, a specialist on the history of guns, who owns a remarkable personal collection of these weapons as well as a formidable library which he uses to study and document them. I am indebted to him for his patience and thoroughness in explaining to me details down to the length of firing pins and the last particle of powder in a bullet. As a young man I served in the U.S. Army during the Korean War and fired some weapons in training but do not remember much of those days.

For weapons used at Tomochic see APD, Leg. 51, Caja 12, No. 006879, Rafael Pimentel to Porfirio Díaz, 5 September 1892; Caja 13, Nos. 007255–56, Abraham Bandala to Porfirio Díaz, 11 September 1892; Leg. 52, Caja 4, Nos. 002107–8, José María Rangel to Porfirio Díaz, 14 April 1893. Also consult Almada, *Rebelión de Tomochi*, pp. 96–97; J. C. Chávez, *Peleando*, p. 32; Chávez Calderón, *Defensa de Tomochi*, pp. 36, 41–42; AMCG, Leg. 1892, Exp. Comunicaciones con inferiores, mes de septiembre 1892, Francisco Ponce de León, Jefe de Seguridad Pública de Chihuahua, to Jefe Político, 18 September 1892.

29. APD, Leg. 51, Caja 11, Nos. 006237–38, José María Rangel to Porfirio Díaz, 18 August 1892; No. 006399, Porfirio Díaz to Abraham Bandala, 24 August 1892; No. 006428, Rafael Pimentel to Porfirio Díaz; Nos. 006429–32,

José María Rangel to Porfirio Díaz; No. 006420, Porfirio Díaz to José María Rangel, all 25 August 1892.

30. APD, Leg. 51, Caja 12, No. 006715, José María Avalos to Porfirio Díaz, 3 September 1892; Nos. 006792–93, José María Rangel to Porfirio Díaz, 4 September 1892; Leg. 17, Caja 27, No. 013266, Dimasio Portilla, Guerrero City, to Luis N. Jileury, Chihuahua City, 5 September 1892. Also see Almada, *Rebelión de Tomochi*, pp. 88–89; J. C. Chávez, *Peleando*, pp. 86–87.

31. APD, Leg. 51, Caja 12, Nos. 006803–10, Rafael Pimentel to Porfirio Díaz, 4 September 1892; Leg. 17, Caja 27, No. 013266, Dimasio Portilla, Guerrero City, to Luis N. Jileury, Chihuahua City, 5 September 1892. Also consult Chávez Calderón, *Defensa de Tomochi*, pp. 26–27; J. C. Chávez, *Peleando*, p. 85; Almada, *Rebelión de Tomochi*, pp. 88–90.

32. APD, Leg. 17, Caja 27, No. 0013266, Dimasio Portilla, Guerrero City, to Luis N. Jileury, Chihuahua City, 5 September 1892; Caja 29, No. 014471, Santana Pérez to Guillermo Urrutia, 24 September 1892; Leg. 51, Caja 12, Nos. 006800–6801, Rafael Pimentel to Porfirio Díaz, 4 September 1892; Nos. 0006868–75, José María Avalos to Porfirio Díaz, 5 September 1892. AMCG, Leg. 1892, Exp. Telegramas oficiales, Rafael Pimentel to Jefe Político, 3 September 1892. Also see J. C. Chávez, *Peleando*, pp. 100–102; and *La Voz de México*, 22 November 1892, p. 3.

33. APD, Leg. 51, Caja 12, Nos. 006891–96, Rafael Pimentel to Porfirio Díaz, 5 September 1892.

34. APD, Leg. 51, Caja 12, Nos. 0066792–93, José María Rangel to Porfirio Díaz, 4 September 1892.

35. APD, Leg. 51, Caja 12, Nos. 007103–4, José María Rangel to Porfirio Díaz, and No. 007101, Felipe Cruz to Porfirio Díaz, both 7 September 1892; Caja 13, Nos. 007697–7700, Rafael Pimentel to Porfirio Díaz, 27 September 1892. J. C. Chávez, *Peleando*, pp. 106–8.

36. AMCG, Leg. 26, Exp. 268, Comunicaciones con inferiores, Ignacio Bencomo, presidente, Mátachic, to Jefe Político, 26 September 1892; Atenogenes Mendoza, presidente, Temeychic, to Jefe Político, and Rafael Márquez Quesada, presidente, Santo Tomás to Jefe Político, both 27 September 1892.

37. AMCG, Leg. 27, Exp. 275, Comunicaciones con inferiores, 16 agosto 1892 a 2 enero 1893, entry for 28 September 1892; Leg. 26, Exp. 265, Nicolás Coronado y Arméndez, presidente, San Isidro, to Jefe Político, 27 September 1892; Leg. 1892, Exp. Mes de septiembre 1892, Pascual Orozco, Tomás Orozco, Victor Solís, Agustín Molinar, all of San Isidro, to Jefe Político, 27 September 1892.

38. APD, Leg. 51, Caja 12, No. 006733, Abraham Bandala to Porfirio Díaz, 3 September 1892; No. 007180, Abraham Bandala to Porfirio Díaz, 10 September 1892; Nos. 0077109–10, Rafael Pimentel to Porfirio Díaz, 7 September 1892; Caja 13, Nos. 007255–56, Abraham Bandala to Porfirio Díaz, 11 September 1892; J. C. Chávez, *Peleando*, p. 104.

39. APD, Leg. 51, Caja 13, Nos. 0007265–68, Felipe Cruz to Porfirio Díaz, 12 September 1890.

40. APD, Leg. 51, Caja 12, Nos. 006885–88, José María Rangel to Porfirio Díaz, 5 September 1892; Leg. 51, Caja 13, No. 007344, José María Rangel to Porfirio Díaz, 14 September 1892; No. 007385, Felipe Cruz to Porfirio Díaz, 18 September 1892; No. 07534, Felipe Cruz to Porfirio Díaz, 21 September 1892.

41. APD, Leg. 51, Caja 14, No. 007822, José María Rangel to Porfirio Díaz, 1 October 1892.

42. APD, Leg. 51, Caja 12, No. 007015, Miguel Ahumada to Porfirio Díaz, 6 September 1892.

43. APD, Leg. 51, Caja 13, No. 007448, Felipe Cruz to Porfirio Díaz, 19 September 1892.

44. APD, Leg. 51, Caja 13, Nos. 007762–64, Rafael Pimentel to Porfirio Díaz, 29 September 1892.

Chapter 13

1. *El Monitor republicano*, 9 November 1892, p. 1.

2. J. C. Chávez, *Peleando*, pp. 95–96.

3. Almada, *Rebelión de Tomochi*, p. 109. One newspaper later reported that five of the prisoners, three federal soldiers and two national guardsmen, joined the Tomochitecos, but the entire account of the troubles in the village is so distorted that it lacks credibility; see *El Imparcial* (Guaymas), 16 November 1892. No other documentation mentions that five men switched sides.

4. *El Monitor republicano*, 1 November 1892, p. 1, and 15 November 1892, p. 3; Gill, "Teresa Urrea," p. 635.

5. Chávez Calderón, *Defensa de Tomochi*, pp. 27, 31; *El Monitor republicano*, 15 November 1892, p. 3.

6. AMCG, Leg. Telegramas oficiales de 1892, Exp. General Juan A. Hernández to Jefe Político, 17 October 1892; Gill, "Teresa Urrea," p. 635; *El Monitor republicano*, 9 November 1892, p. 1, and 15 November 1892, p. 3.

7. Almada, *Rebelión de Tomochi*, p. 109.

8. J. C. Chávez, *Peleando*, p. 86.

9. APD, Leg. 51, Caja 13, Nos. 007263–64 and 007375, Felipe Cruz to Porfirio Díaz, both 12 September 1892.

10. Lumholtz, *Unknown Mexico*, 1: 132.

11. AMCG, Leg. 23, Exp. 244, Borrador de comunicaciones con inferiores, 22 de julio de 1892 al 23 de enero de 1893, entries for 4 and 12 November 1892; Leg. 25, Exp. 261, Comunicaciones con inferiores, Jesús José Escudero to District Judge, Chihuahua City, 12 December 1891; Leg. 26, Exp. 268, David Ramos, presidente, Bocoyna, to Jefe Político, 25 September 1892, and Tomás

Ramos, San Isidro, to Jefe Político, 26 September 1892; Leg. 27, Exp. 273, Comunicaciones con inferiores, José D. González, presidente, Bocoyna, to Jefe Político, 22 February 1892; Sasturno Beltrán, presidente, Bachíniva, to Jefe Político, 13 May 1892; Leg. 25, Comunicacions con superiores, Exp. 263, Governor to Jefe Político, 10 October 1892. And see Almada, *Rebelión de Tomochi*, pp. 93–94.

12. Chávez Calderón, *Defensa de Tomochi*, pp. 33–34; McDannell and Lang, *Heaven*, p. 13.

13. AMCG, Leg. 26, Exp. 268, Comunicaciones con inferiores, Sóstenes Beltrán, presidente, Pachera, to Jefe Político, 2 and 15 September 1892; Borrador de 16 de agosto de 1892 a 3 de enero de 1893, mes de septiembre de 1892, entry for 31 October; Tomás Ramos, San Isidro, to Jefe Político, 25 September 1892.

14. AHAD, Leg. Cartas de 1892, Exp. Luis Terrazas y Córdoba, vicar, Chihuahua City, to José Vicente Salinas, bishop of Durango, 16 and 20 September 1892; Padre Manuel Castelo to José Vicente Salinas, 24 August 1892; Padre Manuel Castelo to Luis Terrazas y Córdoba, 24 August and 19 September, 1892. The correspondence between Cruz Chavez and Padre Castelo is printed in *El Monitor republicano*, 2 November 1892, p. 1.

15. APD, Leg. 51, Caja 13, No. 007616, Rafael Pimentel to Porfirio Díaz, 24 September 1892; Nos. 007725–26, Felipe Cruz to Porfirio Díaz, 28 September 1892; Caja 14, No. 007828, Felipe Cruz to Porifio Díaz, 28 September 1892. See also AMCG, Leg. 27, Exp. 276, "Libro de comunicaciones con inferiores, 16 de agosto de 1892 a 3 de enero de 1893," entry for Domingo Herrera; Leg. Telegramas oficiales de 1892, Exp. Ramón G. Ochoa, Pinos Altos, to Jefe Político, and Francisco Castro to Jefe Político, both 30 July 1892; Rafael Pimentel to Jefe Político, 30 August 1892. Gill, "Teresa Urrea," p. 631; Almada, *Rebelión de Tomochi*, pp. 87, 90–93; Almada, *Resumen*, p. 352; Chavez, *Peleando*, pp. 105–6; Irrab, "Efemérides chihuahuenses," *BSCEH* 1 (December 1938): 230 and (January 1939): 269–274; *El Monitor republicano*, 25 October 1892, p. 3.

Chapter 14

1. APD, Leg. 51, Caja 13, Nos. 007697–700, Rafael Pimentel to Porfirio Díaz, and No. 007701, Felipe Cruz to Porfirio Díaz, both 27 September 1892; J. C. Chávez, *Peleando*, pp. 106–8; Almada, *Rebelión de Tomochi*, p. 93.

2. APD, Leg. 51, Caja 13, Nos. 007723–724, Rafael Pimentel to Porfirio Díaz, 28 September 1892.

3. Irrab, "Efemérides chihuahuenses," *BSCEH* 2 (September 1939): 147; *La Opinión*, 28 March 1937, Sec. 2, p. 2; J. C. Chávez, *Peleando*, pp. 106–8; Almada, *Rebelión de Tomochi*, p. 93.

4. J. C. Chávez, *Peleando*, p. 108.

5. APD, Leg. 51, Caja 14, No. 007898, Porfirio Díaz to José María Rangel, 1 October 1892; Almada, *Rebelión de Tomochi*, p. 93.

6. APD, Leg. 51, Caja 13, No. 0077718, Felipe Cruz to Porfirio Díaz, 28 September 1892, and No. 007759, 29 September 1892; Nos. 0007766–67, Rafael Pimentel to Porfirio Díaz, 29 September 1892; Caja 14, Nos. 007859–60, Rosendo Márquez to Porfirio Díaz, 3 October 1892.

7. APD, Leg. 17, Caja 32, No. 015876, Rosendo Márquez to Porfirio Díaz, 10 October 1892.

8. APD, Leg. 51, Caja 14, No. 007934, Rosendo Márquez to Porfirio Díaz, 6 October 1892; Leg. 17, Caja 32, No. 015876, Rosendo Márquez to Porfirio Díaz, 10 October 1892.

9. APD, Leg. 17, Caja 32, No. 015879, Rosendo Márquez to Porfirio Díaz, 17 October 1892.

10. APD, Leg. 17, Caja 32, No. 015879, Rosendo Márquez to Porfirio Díaz, 17 October 1892; Leg. 51, Caja 14, No. 008092, Miguel Ahumada to Porfirio Díaz, 18 October 1892. AMCG, Leg. Borrador de libro de comunicaciones con inferiores, 16 de agosto de 1892 a 3 de enero de 1893, Jefe Político to Presidente Municipal de Temósachic, 17 October 1892; J. C. Chávez, *Peleando*, p. 109.

11. APD, Leg. 17, Caja 32, No. 015879, Rosendo Márquez to Porfirio Díaz, 17 October 1892; *La Voz de México*, 20 October 1892, p. 3.

12. For details on troop strength, see APD, Leg. 17, Caja 32, No. 015879, Rosendo Márquez to Porfirio Díaz, 17 October 1892; Pinos Altos Record Books, No. 1892, A. Echevarría, superintendent, to secretary, Pinos Altos Bullion Company, London, 10 October 1892; *La Opinión*, 4 April 1937, Sec. 2, p. 1; Almada, *Rebelión de Tomochi*, pp. 95, 109–10; J. C. Chávez, *Peleando*, pp. 104, 110–11.

13. J. C. Chávez, *Peleando*, pp. 110, 117.

14. AHES, Leg. 1892, Exp. Tomochic, Ejército Nacional Columna Expedicionaria, Colonel [Lorenzo] Torres to General [Abraham] Bandala, 2 November 1892. This detailed document chronicles the October battle at Tomochic day by day.

15. APD, Leg. 17, Caja 32, No. 015879, Rosendo Márquez to Porfirio Díaz, 17 October 1892; Leg. 51, Caja 14, Nos. 008154–60, Rosendo Márquez to Porfirio Díaz, 22 October 1892; Leg. 17, Caja 35, No. 017413, Rosendo Márquez to Porfirio Díaz, 6 November 1892. AMCG, Leg. Telegramas oficiales, 1892, Exp. Jefe Político to Governor, 25 October 1892. AHES, Leg. 1892, Exp. Tomochic, Ejército Nacional Columna Expedicionaria, Colonel [Lorenzo Torres] to General [Abraham] Bandala, 2 November 1892. Also see Almada, *Rebelión de Tomochi*, pp. 96–97; Chávez Calderón, *Defensa de Tomochi*, pp. 35–41; J. C. Chávez, *Peleando*, pp. 110–18.

16. For siege tactics, see Duffy, *Siege Warfare*.

17. APD, Leg. 17, Caja 35, No. 017417, Rosendo Márquez to Porfirio Díaz, and Leg. 51, Caja 14, No. 008190, Miguel Ahumada to Porfirio Díaz, both 24 October 1892; Almada, *Rebelión de Tomochi*, p. 99.

18. APD, Leg. 17, Caja 35, No. 017417, Rosendo Márquez to Porfirio Díaz, 24 October 1892; AMCG, Leg. 1892, Exp. Colección de comunicaciones con superiores, mes de noviembre de 1892, Military Zone Commander to Governor, 2 November 1892.

19. APD, Leg. 17, Caja 35, No. 017417, Rosendo Márquez to Porfirio Díaz, 24 October 1892.

20. AHES, Leg. 1892, Exp. Tomochic, Ejército Nacional, Columna expedicionaria, Colonel [Lorenzo] Torres to General [Abraham] Bandala, 2 November 1892; Frías, *Tomochic*, pp. 85, 89–90, 106; Almada, *Rebelión de Tomochi*, pp. 100–101.

21. Almada, *Rebelión de Tomochi*, p. 93; J. C. Chávez, *Peleando*, p. 121; Irrab, "Efemérides chihuahuenses," *BSCEH* 1 (June 1939): 269.

22. Frías, *Tomochic*, p. 86. I thank my Chihuahuense friend Adrián Ortiz Martínez, a native of San Francisco del Oro, for introducing me to typical Norteño food like that consumed by soldiers at the turn of the century.

23. AHES, Leg. 1892, Exp. Tomochic, Ejército Nacional, Columna, expedicionaria, Colonel [Lorenzo] Torres a General [Abraham] Bandala, 2 November 1892; J. C. Chávez, *Peleando*, p. 118; Frías, *Tomochic*, p. 93; Almada, *Rebelión de Tomochi*, pp. 99–100.

24. Almada, *Rebelión de Tomochi*, pp. 101–3.

25. AHES, Leg. 1892, Exp. Tomochic, Ejército Nacional, Columna expedicionaria, Colonel [Lorenzo] Torres a General [Abraham] Bandala, 2 November 1892; Frías, *Tomochic*, p. 113; J. C. Chávez, *Peleando*, p. 122; Almada, *Rebelión de Tomochi*, pp. 100–103.

26. AHES, Leg. 1892, Exp. Tomochic, Ejército Nacional, Columna expedicionaria, Colonel [Lorenzo] Torres a General [Abraham] Bandala, 2 November 1892; Frías, *Tomochic*, p. 117; J. C. Chávez, *Peleando*, pp. 124–26; Chávez Calderón, *Defensa de Tomochi*, p. 48; Almada, *Rebelión de Tomochi*, pp. 102–3.

27. J. C. Chávez, *Peleando*, p. 123; Frías, *Tomochic*, p. 125; Chávez Calderón, *Defensa de Tomochi*, pp. 46–48; Almada, *Rebelión de Tomochi*, pp. 103–4.

28. Almada, *Rebelión de Tomochi*, p. 105.

29. AHES, Leg. 1892, Exp. Tomochic, Ejército Nacional, Columna expedicionaria, Colonel [Lorenzo] Torres to General [Abraham] Bandala, 2 November 1892; J. C. Chávez, *Peleando*, pp. 125–26; Frías, *Tomochic*, pp. 128–29; Almada, *Rebelión de Tomochi*, pp. 104–5; Chávez Calderón, *Defensa de Tomochi*, pp. 49–50.

30. AMCG, Leg. 1892, Exp. Colección de comunicaciones, mes de octubre 1892, Report of Rangel from Tomochic [to his superiores], 29 October 1892; J. C. Chávez, *Peleando*, p. 135.

Chapter 15

1. Almada, *Rebelión de Tomochi*, p. 98; Gill, "Teresa Urrea," p. 640.

2. APD, Leg. 51, Caja 15, No. 008915, Miguel Ahumada to Porfirio Díaz, 5 December 1892; AMCG Leg. Cartas de 1892, Exp. No. 312, Luis Terrazas y Córdova to Jesús Vicente Salinas, 7 and 21 December 1892.

3. AMCG, Leg. 25. Exp. 263, Comunicaciones con superiores, Rosendo Márquez to Jefe Político, 9 and 10 November 1892; Governor to Jefe Político, and Cirilio Hernández, secretaría del gobierno, to Jefe Político, both 14 November 1892.

4. APD, Leg. 17. Caja 35, No. 017413, Rosendo Márquez to Porfirio Díaz, 6 November 1892.

5. APD, Leg. 17, Caja 35, No. 017418, Porfirio Díaz to Rosendo Márquez, [?] November 1892.

6. *El Paso Daily Times*, 27 October 1892, p. 7, reprinted in *Arizona Weekly Citizen*, 5 November 1892, p. 1; *La Voz de México*, 13 and 17 November 1892, both p. 3; *El Tiempo* (Mexico City), 28 October and 6 December, both 1892, p. 2. The series of lengthy articles appeared in both *El Monitor republicano* and *El Diario del hogar* during November 1892.

7. APD, Leg. 17 Caja 36, Nos. 017737–38, José María Rangel to Porfirio Díaz, 17 November 1892; *El Tiempo* (Mexico City), 28 October 1892, p. 2 and 6, 17 December 1892, both p. 3; *La Voz de México*, 23 November 1892, p. 3; Almada, *Rebelión de Tomochi*, p. 108.

8. APD, Leg. 17, Caja 34, Nos. 016801–2, Abraham Bandala to Porfirio Díaz, 7 November 1892; *El Tiempo* (Mexico City), 28 October 1892, p. 2.

9. APD, Leg. 717, Caja 34, No. 016703, Circular to Jefe Político de Guerrero from Governor Miguel Ahumada, 3 November 1892. AMCG, Leg. 25, Exp. 254, Comunicaciones con inferiores, el 16 de agosto de 1892 a 3 de enero de 1893, Circular No. 114, Jefe Político to all presidentes municipales, 27 October 1892, and Borrador: libro de comunicaciones con inferiores, 16 de agosto de 1892 a 3 de enero de 1893, Circular No. 117, Jefe Político to all municipalities, 31 October 1892; Leg. 27, Exp. 269, Comunicaciones con inferiores, Guadalupe Quijada, presidente, Temósachic, to Jefe Político, 2 November 1892.

10. AMCG, Leg. 27, Exp. 269, Comunicaciones con inferiores, Ramón A. Sáenz, presidente, Rosario, to Jefe Político, 4 November 1892; Sóstenes Beltrán, presidente, Pachera, to Jefe Político, 5 November 1892. *New York Times*, 28 December 1892, p. 1.

11. APD, Leg. 7, Caja 34, No. 016703, Miguel Ahumada to Porfirio Díaz, 3 November 1892; No. 016704, Miguel Ahumada to Porfirio Díaz, 10 November 1892; Leg 51, Caja 14, No. 008288, Miguel Ahumada to Porfirio Díaz, 31 October 1892; Nos. 0088303–5, Miguel Ahumada to Porfirio Díaz, 1 November 1892; Caja 15, No. 008461, Miguel Ahumada to Porfirio Díaz, 10 November

1892. AMCG, Leg. 27, Exp. 269, Comunicaciones con superiores, Proclamation of Governor Miguel Ahumada to District of Guerrero, 3 November 1892.

12. For Tosánachic, see AMCG, Leg. 25, Exp. 263, Comunicaciones con superiores, Rosendo Márquez to Jefe Político, 25 October 1892; Cirilio Hernández, secretaría del Gobierno, to Jefe Político, 12 December 1892; Leg. 27. Exp. 269, Comunicaciones con inferiores, Estimio Quintana, presidente, Tosánachic, to Jefe Político, 16 December 1892; Borrador: libro de comunicaciones con inferiores, 16 de agosto de 1892 a 3 de enero de 1892, No. 2109, 14 and 25 October 1892; Libro de comunicaciones al gobernador, 4 de enero a 23 de mayo de 1893, entry for 23 February 1893; Leg. 30, Exp. 291, Miguel del Río, presidente, Tosánachic, to Jefe Político, 11 October 1892. Also APD, Leg. 17, Caja 35, No. 017408, Rosendo Márquez to Porfirio Díaz, 17 November 1892; Leg. 51, Caja 14, Nos. 008341–42, Miguel Ahumada to Porfirio Díaz, 3 November 1892; Caja 15, Nos. 008553–54, Miguel Ahumada to Porfirio Díaz, 17 November 1892. Also *El Diario del hogar*, 9 November 1892, p. 2; and Almada, *Rebelión de Tomochi*, p. 113. For Yepómera and Anaya, see AMCG, Leg. 27, Exp. 269, Comunicaciones con inferiores, Guadalupe Quijada, presidente, Temósachic, to Jefe Político, 1 November 1892; Leg. 1889, Exp. Mes de Octubre de 1889, Citizens of Yepómera to Jefe Político, 18 September 1889; Exp. Borrador: libro de comunicaciones con inferiores, 16 de agosto de 1892 a 3 de junio de 1893, No. 2100, Jefe Político to presidente, Temósachic, 17 October 1892; No. 2162, Jefe Político to presidente, Temósachic, 6 November 1892; Leg. Telegramas oficiales, año de 1889, [Governor] to Jefe Político, 23 August 1889; M. Gaytán to Governor, 24 August 1889; Leg. 25, Exp. 264, Comunicaciones con superiores, Governor to Jefe Político, 7 November 1892. Also APD, Leg. 51, Caja 15, No. 008458, Miguel Ahumada to Porfirio Díaz, 10 November 1892; Irrab, "Efemérides chihuahenses," *BSCEH* 2 (June 1939): 32; Almada, *Rebelión de Tomochi*, pp. 112–14; *El Imparcial* (Guaymas), 21 November 1892, p. 2.

13. AMCG, Leg. 28, Exp. 280, Comunicaciones con inferiores, Manuel Córdoba, presidente, Namiquipa, to Jefe Político, 2 April 1892; Leg. 27, Exp. 269, Guadalupe Quijada, presidente, Temósachic, to Jefe Político, 2 November 1892; Ignacio Bencomo, presidente, Mátachic, to Jefe Político, 3 November 1892; Manuel Córdoba, presidente, Namiquipa, to Jefe Político, 5 November 1892; Leg. 1893, Exp. Mes de mayo 1893, José María Varela, presidente, Yepómera, to Jefe Político, 12 May 1893. APD, Leg. 51, Caja 14, No. 008357, Miguel Ahumada to Porfirio Díaz, 4 November 1892; Leg. 17, Caja 35, 017413, Rosendo Márquez to Porfirio Díaz, 6 November 1892; Leg. 52, Caja 4, Nos. 001864–68, Miguel Ahumada to Porfirio Díaz, 6 November 1892, and No. 001998, Miguel Ahumada to Porfirio Díaz, 11 April 1893. Almada, *Rebelión de Tomochi*, pp. 117–22.

14. APD, Leg. 51, Caja 4, Nos. 0001993–96, Miguel Ahumada to Porfirio Díaz, 11 April 1893.

15. McDannell and Lang, *Heaven*, pp. 12–13.

16. APD, Leg. 52, Caja 4, No. 001917, Miguel Ahumada to Porfirio Díaz, 8 April 1893. AMCG, Leg. 1893, Exp. Colección de comunicaciones de inferiores de abril de 1893, Manuel Sorriva, comandante, Rancho Colorado, to Jefe Político, 5 April 1893; Exp. Mes de mayo 1893, José María Serrán, juzgado menor, Temósachic, to Jefe Político, 3 May 1893.

17. The battle at Santo Tomás is best documented through the correspondence between Porifiro Díaz, his generals, and Governor Ahumada in APD, Leg. 52, Cajas 4–8. Also consult AMCG, Leg. 27, Exp. 276, Libro de comunicaciones, 6 de abril a 25 de mayo de 1893, entries for 24 and 26 April, 1893, and Leg. 28, Exp. 280, Comunicaciones con superiores, Juan A. Hernández to Jefe Político, 16 April 1893. Also see *El Imparcial* (Guaymas), 17 May 1893, p. 1. For overviews, see Almada, *Rebelión de Tomochi*, pp. 122–23 and 190–93, and Irrab, "Efemérides chihuahenses," *BSCEH* 2 (October 1939): 190–93, and 2 (November 1939): 221. Also Pinos Altos Record Books, 1893, Document nos. 28–30, 27 April 1893.

18. APD, Leg. 52, Caja 5, Nos. 002841–43, Juan A. Hernández to Porfirio Díaz, 6 May 1893; Caja 6, Nos. 003047–49, Rafael García Martínez to Porfirio Díaz, 10 May 1893; No. 003051, Juan A. Hernández to Porfirio Díaz, 10 May 1893; Caja 8, Nos. 004243–44, Miguel Ahumada to Porfirio Díaz, 3 July 1893; No. 003572, Juan A. Hernández to Porfirio Díaz, 29 May 1893; Caja 7, No. 003995, Juan A. Hernández to Porfirio Díaz, 21 June 1893. AMCG, Leg. 1893, Exp. Comunicaciones con inferiores, mes de agosto, 1893, Presidente, Cocomórochic to Jefe Político, [?] August 1893; Almada, *Rebelión de Tomochi*, pp. 111, 125, 131–32.

19. AMCG, Leg. 28, Exp. 279, Comunicaciones con inferiores, José María Serrano, juez menor, Temósachic, to Jefe Político, 13 February 1893; *El Imparcial* (Guaymas), 28 March and 17 April 1893.

20. APD, Leg. 52, Caja 6, Nos. 003457–59, Juan A. Hernández to Porfirio Díaz, 24 May 1893; Caja 7, Nos. 003725–27, Juan A. Hernández to Porfirio Díaz, 3 June 1893; No. 004120, Miguel Ahumada to Porfirio Díaz, 27 June 1893. AMCG, Leg. 27, Exp. 276, Libro de comunicaciones a gobernador, 4 de enero de 1893 a 23 de mayo de 1894, entry for 2 May 1893; Leg. 28, Exp. 278, Comunicaciones con inferiores, General Pablo Yañez, Mátachic, to Jefe Político, 1 May 1893.

21. SRE, Archivo Histórico, nineteenth-century file, Exp. No. 9-15-14, Extradiciones. APD, Leg. 52, Caja 6, Nos. 003149–52, Juan A. Hernández to Porfirio Díaz, 12 May 1893; Caja 8, Nos. 004243–44, Juan A. Hernández to Porfirio Díaz, 3 July 1893; Caja 19, Nos. 011101–2, Juan A. Hernández to Porfirio Díaz, 21 November 1892, AMCG, Leg. 29, Exp. 290, Comunicaciones con inferiores, Presidente, Tosánachic, to Jefe Político, 23 November 1893 and 3 January 1894; Leg. 30, Exp. 292, Francisco Reynoso, capitán, seguridad

pública, to Jefe Político, 1 July 1893; Leg. 32, Exp. 313, Juan Ruiz, presidente, Temósachic, to Jefe Político, 12 January 1894. Also see Almada, *Rebelión de Tomochi*, pp. 124, 130–31, 135. The Pérez decree is reprinted in González Ramírez, *Fuentes*, 5: 33–39.

22. *New York Times*, 17 August 1895, p. 9; APD, Leg. 52, Cajas 4 and 5, Nos. 002400–401, Rafael García Ramírez, jefe político, Ciudad Júarez, to Porfirio Díaz, 22 April 1893.

23. *New York Times*, 17 August 1895, p. 9. The best U.S. file on Ochoa is USNA, Military Records Branch, Adjutant General's Office, Record Group 94, File Nos. 1339, 4943, 34579, and 43798.

24. AMCG, Leg. 31, Exp. 303, Comunicaciones con inferiores, José Ruiz, president, Temósachic, to Jefe Político, 13 July 1894; Leg. 32, Exp. 314, Juez, Guerrero, to Jefe Político, 18 June 1894; Exp. 311, Comunicaciones con superiores, Circular No. 107, 27 February 1894; Exp. 310, Governor to Jefe Político, 15 January 1894. *El Progreso*, 29 February 1896, p. 1; Almada, *Rebelión de Tomochi*, pp. 133–34. Also consult Almada, *Memoria de la administración*, pp. 32, 58.

25. AMCG, Leg. 32, Exp. 310, Comunicaciones con superiores, Governor to Jefe Político, [various dates] May, and 12 April; Exps. 310 and 311, Governor to Jefe Político, 26 July; Exp. 311, Governor to Jefe Político, 24 September, all 1894; Leg. 1893, Exp. Comunicaciones con inferiores, mes de febrero 1893, Abelado Pérez, presidente, Temósachic, to Jefe Político, 9 February 1893; Leg. 31, Exp. 304, vecinos, Santo Tomás, to Jefe Político, 17 July 1894; *El Progreso*, 29 February 1896, p. 1. Once he accepted the amnesty of 1894, Santana Pérez steered clear of politics and died on 19 December 1911 at his home in Yepómera; see Almada, *Rebelión de Tomochi*, p. 135.

Chapter 16

1. For Nogales at the turn of the century, see Ready, *Open Range*, pp. 43–57, and Peck, "In Memory of Man." My thanks to the director of the Pimería Alta Historical Society, Ms. Susan Spader, and her staff for sending me materials on Nogales.

2. *The Tombstone Prospector*, 7 November 1895, p. 4; *Arizona Daily Star*, 17 June and 6 July 1892, both p. 4; *Phoenix Weekly Herald*, 23 June 1892, p. 4.

3. *San Francisco Call*, 9 September 1900, p. 40; *El Paso Daily Herald*, 11 September 1896, p. 1; *San Francisco Chronicle*, 13 August 1896, p. 1; *Arizona Silver Belt*, 27 August 1896, p. 2; *Arizona Daily Citizen*, 22 December 1906, p. 5; Pimería Alta Historical Society, Historical Archive, File on Teresa Urrea. For Yaqui displacement, see Hu-DeHart, *Yaqui Resistance*, p. 124; Spicer, *Yaquis*, pp. 158–61.

4. *El Paso Daily Times*, 16 August, 1895, p. 1; *Brownsville Daily Herald*, 29

March and 26 April, 1895, both p. 1; USNA, Military Records Branch, RG 94, "Santa Teresa," No. 34574, El Paso newspaper clipping, dated March [1895 or 1896?].

5. *Brownsville Daily Herald*, 29 March and 26 April, 1895, both p. 1; *El Paso Daily Times*, 16 August 1896, p. 1.

6. *Brownsville Daily Herald*, 26 April 1895, p. 1.

7. *El Paso Herald*, 11 September 1896, p. 1; *Graham County Republican*, 8 November 1896, p. 3; *The Tombstone Reporter*, 21 November 1895, p. 1. USNA, Military Reference Branch, RG 94, "Santa Teresa," No. 34574, Brigadier General Frank Wheaton, zone commander, to AGO, Washington, D.C., 14 March 1896 with newspaper clippings from *Denver Times*, 10 March 1896, p. 1, and *Denver Republican*, 11 March 1896, p. 1; also RG 94, "Victor Ochoa," No. 4943, Matías Romero, Mexican ambassador, to Walter Q. Gresham, Secretary of State, 19 March 1894.

8. USNA, Military Records Branch, RG 94, "Santa Teresa," No. 34574, Brigadier General Frank Wheaton, zone commander, to AGO, Washington, D.C., 14 March 1896, newspaper clippings from *Denver Times*, 10 March 1896, p. 1, and *Denver Republican*, 11 March 1896, p. 1.

9. USNA, Military Records Branch, RG 94, "Santa Teresa," No. 34574, Brigadier General Frank Wheaton, zone commander, to AGO, Washington, D.C., 14 March 1896; newspaper clippings, *Denver Times*, 10 March 1896, p. 1, *Denver Republican*, 11 March 1896, p. 1.

10. USNA, Military Records Branch, RG 94, "Santa Teresa," No. 34574, Brigadier General Frank Wheaton, zone commander, to AGO, Washington, D.C., 14 March 1896; newspaper clipping, *Denver Republican*, 11 March 1896, p. 1.

11. USNA, Military Records Branch, RG 94, "Santa Teresa," No. 34574, Brigadier General Frank Wheaton, zone commander, to AGO, Washington, D.C., 14 March 1896; newspaper clipping, *Denver Republican*, 11 March 1896, p. 1.

12. SRE, Archivo Histórico, nineteenth-century file, Exp. 9-15-4, Extradiciones, 23 July 1897; *Graham County Bulletin*, 26 June 1896, p. 1; *Rocky Mountain News*, 15 August 1896, p. 1.

13. Escobosa Gámez, "Asalto," pp. 27–35; *Arizona Daily Star*, 13 and 14 August 1896, both p. 1; *Denver Evening Post*, 13 August 1896, p. 2; *Arizona Silver Belt*, 20 August 1896, p. 2; *San Francisco Chronicle*, 13 August 1896, p. 1; *El Paso Daily Times*, 14 August 1896, p. 3; "They Raided," pp. 52–57; Peck, "In Memory of Man," pp. 373–75. Also mentioned in W. C. Holden, *Teresita*, pp. 169–70; SRE, Archivo Histórico, nineteenth-century File, Exp. III, 513-890-2 and 11-19-11, María Teresa Urrea.

14. In addition to the references cited in note 13 to this chapter, see *El Paso Daily Times*, 23 August 1896, p. 3; *Arizona Daily Citizen*, 14 August 1896, p. 4.

15. In addition to the references cited in note 13 to this chapter, see *El Paso*

Daily Times, 13 August 1896, p. 4, 14 August 1896, p. 4; *Arizona Daily Star*, 14 August 1896, p. 1; *New York Herald*, 14 August 1896, p. 9.

16. *Arizona Daily Citizen*, 12 August 1896, p. 1; *El Paso Daily Times*, 14 August 1896, p. 3; *Rocky Mountain News*, 13 August 1896, p. 7, 14 August 1896, p. 1, 18 August 1896, p. 1; *Arizona Silver Belt*, 27 August 1896, p. 2; *La Oásis*, 15 and 22 August, 1896, both p. 1; *New York Herald*, 13 August 1896, p. 12; Willson, "Deluded Yaquis," pp. 22–23; *Denver Evening Post*, 13 August 1896, p. 2.

17. *El Paso Daily Times*, 13 August 1896, p. 3, 14 August 1896, p. 3; *El Paso Daily Herald*, 11 September 1896, p. 1; *Denver Evening Post*, 13 August 1896, p. 2.

18. *El Paso Daily Herald*, 11 September 1896, p. 1.

19. *Rocky Mountain News*, 15 August 1896, p. 4.

20. SRE, Archivo Histórico, nineteenth-century file, Exp. 9-15-14, Extradiciones, 23 July 1897; *Brownsville Daily Herald*, 7 September 1896, p. 4; *El Paso Daily Times*, 10 September 1896, p. 3; USNA, Military Reference Branch, RG 94, Teresa Urrea, No. 43798, Louis M. Buford, U.S. consul, Paso del Norte, to W. W. Rockhill, Assistant Secretary of State, 9 September 1896; Victor Ochoa, No. 4943, Richard Olney, attorney general, to Secretary of State, 8 March 1894.

21. *New York Herald*, 17 August 1896, p. 1; *Chicago Tribune*, 13 August 1896, p. 1; 15 August 1896, p. 3.

22. USNA, Military Records Division, RG 94, "Santa Teresa," AGO No. 34579, undated El Paso newspaper clipping [1896?]; *Arizona Daily Gazette*, 20 August 1899, p. 5; *El Paso Daily Herald*, 29 June 1899, p. 6; *El Paso Daily Times*, 14 August 1896, p. 3. See also Valadés, *Díaz contra Dios*, pp. 99–100.

23. *New York Journal*, 3 March 1901, p. 23; *Arizona Range News*, 4 July 1900, p. 2; *San Francisco Examiner*, 27 July 1900, p. 7; SRE, Archivo Histórico, nineteenth-century file, Exp. No. 9-15-14, Extradiciones; Exp. III, 513-890-2 and 11-19-11, María Teresa Urrea; "They Raided," p. 56; *The Copper Era*, 7 February 1901, p. 1; *Arizona Bulletin*, 27 July 1900, p. 1; *Arizona Range News*, 4 July 1900, p. 2; *Arizona Daily Gazette*, 10 February 1901, p. 5; *Tucson Daily Star*, 23 April 1903, p. 2; *St. John's Herald*, 18 May 1901, p. 2; Ridgeway, "Saint or Nurse?" pp. 22–23; W. C. Holden, *Teresita*, pp. 172–73.

24. *Copper Era*, 23 August 1900, p. 4; *New York Journal*, 3 March 1901, p. 23; Ridgeway, "Saint or Nurse?" p. 23; W. C. Holden, *Teresita*, pp. 178–80; Larralde, "Santa Teresa," p. 85; *San Francisco Bulletin*, 9 September 1900, p. 20; *San Francisco Chronicle*, 9 September 1900, p. 5, 13 September 1900, p. 9, and 23 September 1900, p. 10; *San Francisco Call*, 9 September 1900, p. 40, 21 September 1901, p. 4, and 23 September 1901, p. 13; *San Francisco Examiner*, 9 September 1900, p. 23; *The World*, 3 March 1901, p. 11, and 10 March 1901, p. 8; *Arizona Daily Citizen*, 22 December 1906, p. 5.

25. *The Copper Era*, 7 February 1900, [p. 2?].

26. *Los Angeles Daily Times*, 15 December 1902, p. 5; *Ventura Weekly Free Press*, 28 August 1903, p. 5.

27. *Los Angeles Daily Times*, 27 August 1903, p. 6.

28. Ventura County (California) Superior Court Records, File No. 3024, Theresa [sic] Rodríguez versus Guadalupe Rodríguez, 2 October 1903; *San Jose Daily Mercury*, 21 August 1900, p. 3; *Los Angeles Record*, 17 December 1902, p. 1, 27 August 1903, p. 5; *Ventura Weekly Free Press*, 28 August 1903, p. 5, 29 January 1904, p. 8; *Los Angeles Daily Times*, 27 August 1903, p. 6; *Los Angeles Express*, 27 August 1903, p. 3; W. C. Holden, *Teresita*, pp. 180, 183-96; Domecq, "Teresa Urrea," p. 167; Rodríguez and Rodríguez, "Teresa Urrea," p. 197. See *The Copper Era*, 25 September 1902, p. 3; 9 October 1902, p. 2; 13 November 1902, p. 2; 25 December 1902, p. 4; 18 January 1906, p. 2; the 25 September 1902 article reported that Tomás Urrea left an estate worth $200,000 (presumably his land in Sonora) to his wife in Alamos and $2,000 in gold coin to his "friend" (common-law wife), Gabriela, of Clifton.

29. *The Copper Era*, 18 January 1906, p. 2.

30. *The Arizona Daily Citizen*, 22 December 1906, p. 5.

31. *Arizona Silver Belt*, 27 August 1896, p. 1. For a representation of Teresa as bourgeoise, see Larralde, "Santa Teresa," p. 90. Her will listed the following assets: house ($3,000), diamond ring ($100), gold watch and chain ($65). Her only creditor was the funeral home to which her estate owed $125 for the casket and $63 for the rental of 21 horses. In 1907, the sale of three rings, a new trunk, and a sewing machine that had belonged to her brought $141 to the estate. The heirs were her daughters, Laura and Magdalena. Graham County, Recorder's Office, Probate Division, No. 407, "Teresa Urrea," 18 January 1910.

Chapter 17

1. *El Diario del hogar*, 30 November 1892, p. 2.

2. AMCG, Leg. 25, Exp. 264, Comunicaciones con superiores, Rosendo Márquez to Jefe Político, 8 and 21 November 1892; C[irilio] Hernández [Governor] to Jefe Político, 10 and 21 November 1892; Comunicaciones con inferiores, Rafael Quezada, presidente, Santo Tomás, to Jefe Político, 18 November 1892.

3. AMCG, Leg. 25, Exp. 264, Comunicaciones con superiores, C[irilio] Hernández [Governor] to Jefe Político, 17 and 21 November 1892; Jefe Político to Governor, 8 December 1892; Leg. 26, Exp. 265, Governor to Jefe Político, 12 December 1892; Leg. 27, Exp. 270, Comunicaciones con inferiores, José de la Luz Córdoba to Jefe Político, 14 and 28 November 1892.

4. AMCG, Leg. 27, Exp. 270, Comunicaciones con inferiores, José de la Luz Córdova to Jefe Político, 14, 15, 19, and 22 November 1892.

5. AMCG, Leg. 27, Exp. 276, Comunicaciones con inferiores, José de la Luz Córdova to Jefe Político, 16 November 1892; Libro de comunicaciones con inferiores, 16 de agosto de 1892 a 3 de enero de 1893, entry for 16 November 1892.

6. AMCG, Leg. 27, Exp. 270, Comunicaciones con inferiores, José de la Luz Córdova to Jefe Político, 14 November 1892; Leg. 22, Exp. 234, Borrador de ocurrencias de 1890 a 1893, entry for 31 December 1892; Almada, *Rebelión de Tomochi*, pp. 115–16.

7. AMCG, Leg. 27, Exp. 270, Comunicaciones con inferiores, José de la Luz Córdova to Jefe Político, 22 November 1892; J. González, presidente, Rancho Colorado, to Jefe Político, 12 November 1892; Pascual Escárcega, presidente, Guadalupe, to Jefe Político, 12 November 1892; Libro de comunicaciones con inferiores, 26 de agosto de 1892 a enero de 1893, Circular No. 112, 31 de octubre de 1893, Jefe Político to all municipalities; Leg. 25, Exp. 264, Governor to Jefe Político, 10, 14, and 22 November 1892; Telegramas oficiales, Miguel Ahumada to Jefe Político, 4, 8, and 9 November 1892. Also, APD, Leg. 51, Caja 14, Nos. 008397–99, Miguel Ahumada to Porfirio Díaz, 7 November 1892; Leg. 52, Caja 8, No. 004510, Juan Hernández to Porfirio Díaz, 28 July 1893. See also Almada, *Rebelión de Tomochi*, pp. 114–15.

8. AMCG, Leg. 27, Exp. 271, Comunicaciones con inferiores, Reyes Domínguez to Jefe Político, 8 December 1892.

9. AMCG, Leg. 27, Exp. 271, Comunicaciones con inferiores, Reyes Domínguez to Jefe Político, 8 and 25 December 1892; 25 and 28 May, 1, 3, and 22 August, 20 September, 10, 19, and 20 October, all 1893; Cirilio Domínguez to Jefe Político, 24 May, 31 September, 3 and 24 December, all 1893.

10. AMCG, Leg. 27, Exp. 271, Comunicaciones con inferiores, Reyes Domínguez to Jefe Político, 8 December 1892; Cirilio Domínguez, acting presidente, Tomochic, to Jefe Político, 24 December 1892; Leg. 27, Exp. 276, Libro de comunicaciones, 16 de agosto de 1892 a 3 de enero de 1893, entries for 16 November 1892 and 30 January 1893; Comunicaciones con superiores, Governor to Jefe Político, 17 December 1892. See also Archivo de la Comisión Agraria Mixta (Chihuahua City), Leg. 23/577, Exp. No. 23:442 (721.1), Ejidos, Dotación, Tomochic.

11. AMCG, Leg. 28, Exp. 278, Bartolo Ledesma, juez de paz, Tomochic, to Jefe Político, 10 May and 5 September 1893; Nicolás López, juez suplente, to Jefe Político, 11 September 1893.

12. AMCG, Leg. 42, Exp. 380, Padrón general . . . de Tomochic.

13. AMCG, Leg 35, Exp. 331, Colección de comunicaciones de enero a octubre de 1895, Presidente, Tomochic, to Jefe Político, 30 July 1895; Comunicaciones con superiores, Governor to Jefe Político, 17 May 1895; Leg. 38, Exp. 50, Comunicaciones con inferiores, Jesús J. Armenta to Jefe Político, 29 January 1897. For Ahumada on schools as panacea, see APD, Leg. 17, Caja 34, No. 016708, Miguel Ahumada to Porfirio Díaz, 23 November 1892.

14. AMCG, Leg. 39, Exp. 362, Comunicaciones con superiores, Governor to Jefe Político, 17 June 1898.

15. AMCG, Leg. 42, Exp. 380, Correspondencia, Ramos Hernández, Tomochic, to Jefe Político, 28 September 1900.

16. AMCG, Leg. 62, Exp. 554, Comunicaciones con superiores, Governor to Jefe Político, 1 July and 17 September 1908.

17. AMCG, Leg. 42, Exp. 380, Correspondencia, Lista de casas, Tomochic, 26 April 1900; Leg. 43, Exp. 388, Colección de manifestaciones hechas a la junta calificadora, C[iudad] Guerrero, Tomo I, 1900, Tomochic; Leg. 49, Exp. 436, Comunicaciones con inferiores, July 1903, Lista de personas que tiene expendio de licores, 10 July 1903.

18. AMCG, Leg. 43, Exp. 388, Colección de manifestaciones hechas a la junta calificadora, [Distrito de] Guerrero, Tomo I, 1900; Leg. 49, Exp. 443b, Comunicaciones diversos, Noticia . . . impuestos, 1906, Lisandro Domínguez, presidente, Tomochic, to Jefe Político, 8 September 1906.

19. AMCG, Leg. 74, Exp. 616, Correspondencia, Cesario Acosta, presidente, Tomochic, to Jefe Político, 27 October 1911; Almada, *Rebelión de Tomochi*, p. 115.

20. SRA, Terrenos Nacionales, 1.322.1(06), Leg. 2, Exp. 26, Baldios, Limantour, Jose Ives, y su hermano, Julio. After the Revolution and well into the 1940s, Cargill vigorously battled to defend his holdings through the Mexican judicial system but parcel by parcel finally lost them all. Cargill's loss was Tomochic's gain. For grants of land to Tomochic after the 1920s, see SRA, Archivo General, Legs. 233/442 and 231/577, Exp. No. 23/442, Dotación de ejidos, Tomochic; and Archivo de la Comisión Agraria Mixta (Chihuahua City), Leg. 23/577, Exp. 23:442 (721.1), Ejidos, Dotación, Tomochic, "Petición al Presidente Adolfo López Mateos," 31 January 1960. For the Limantour litigation, see SRA, Terrenos nacionales, 1.322.1 (06) [Chihuahua], Leg. 2, Exp. 26, "Limantour, José Ives, y su hermano, Julio."

21. SRA, Terrenos Nacionales, 1.322.1 (06) [Chihuahua], Leg. 2, Exp. 26, Baldíos, Tomochic.

Chapter 18

1. This concept of remembrance is elucidated in Rappaport, *Politics of Memory*. See also her *Cumbe Reborn*. For broad approaches to the subject, see Johnson et al., *Making Histories*, Part 6, "Popular Memory," pp. 205–52.

2. Frías, *Tomochic*. Saborit, *Los Doblados de Tomóchic*, argues forcefully that Frías did not write the famous book at all; instead it was the work of journalist Joaquín Clausell, a friend of Frías, who first published the story in installments in his newspaper *El Demócrata*.

3. Aguirre, *Tomochic!*, p. 4.

4. *Arizona Daily Gazette*, 20 August 1899, p. 8.

5. Hardy, "Mormon Colonies," pp. 129–30; *Deseret Weekly*, 22 July 1893, p. 129, and 28 April 1894, p. 573; *El Paso Daily Times*, 14 August 1896, p. 3.

6. SRA, Terrenos Nacionales, 1.322.1 (06), Leg. 2, Exp. 26, Baldíos, Limantour

7. J. C. Chávez, *Peleando*, pp. 141–42. Unfortuantely, corridos do not translate well into any other language.

8. See Aurrecoechea, *Mexico:* . . . *Tomochic*, and Gill, *Cuadernos:* . . . *La Doncella.*

9. *La Longitud de guerra* is critiqued in Ayala Blanco, *Condicion del cine mexicano*, pp. 182–86.

10. A special debt of gratitude is owed Lic. Zacarías Márquez Terrazas, former *cronista* of the City of Chihuahua who now is employed in the education and culture office of the Chihuahua state government. At my behest, Professor Márquez Terrazas traveled to Tomochic, took pictures of the "Teresita" shop and surroundings and taped conversations with various residents of the pueblo in order to bring my earlier findings up to date.

11. Carlos Martínez Assad, "Regreso a Tomochic," *Nexos* (June 1991): 69–76.

12. Carlos Monsiváis, "Aproximaciones y reintegros de los milenarismos desautorizados," *El Financiero*, 2 March 1989, p. 76.

13. Screenplay, *Nobody's Girls: Women of the American Frontier*, p. 2, film written, produced, and directed by Mirra Bank Brockman, released 1995.

14. Mirandé and Enríquez, *Chicana*, p. 86.

15. Larralde, "Chicana Saint," p. 101. The Aztlán perspective is from Rodríguez and Rodríguez, "Teresa Urrea," p. 48.

16. Professor Thomas Langham, chair of sociology of Our Lady of the Lake University, San Antonio, provided me with many sketches of visionary experiences reported in U.S. magazines and newspapers over the past year or so. For examples, see the weeping Madonna in Virginia in *U.S. News and World Report*, 29 March 1993, pp. 46–55; the visions outside of Atlanta in *Charlotte Observer*, 18 July 1993, pp. 5–6. Monsignor Lawrence Baird, director of the Diocese of Orange, California, provided information on recent apparitions in the United States.

17. I spent several days in Clifton in early April 1994 and attended the Santa Teresa Day celebration on April 9. I conducted numerous interviews in person and by telephone with the principals involved before, during, and after the event. For their generous cooperation I am very thankful to Walter Mares, president of the Greenlee County Chamber of Commerce; Lynn Ruger, immediate past president of the Greenlee County Historical Society; Charles Spezia, board director of the Society; Father Joseph Baker of Sacred Heart Roman Catholic Church; Father Cornelius McGrenra of Holy Cross Catholic Church (Morensi); Fred McAnich, former pastor of Sacred Heart, now with the Arizona Historical Society; Dan Brosnan, archivist at the Roman Catholic Diocese of Tucson; and Luis Pérez, who is writing a book about Teresa Urrea.

Christine Marín, curator/archivist at the Chicano Research Collection, Arizona State University, Tempe, Arizona, cheerfully and expeditiously provided information on the history of Clifton. Finally, my appreciation goes to María Aguirre (niece of Teresa Urrea); Al Fernández, who for many years published a marvelous column about local history in the Clifton newspaper; Cruz Pérez; Amy McCuller (a relative of the Van Orders, who were close friends of Teresa); Harriet Sweeting, and Dolores and Félix Vásquez, all longtime residents of Clifton who are brimming with remembrance. Their generosity allowed me to bring this book to closure.

18. *The Copper Era*, 31 March 1994, p. 3.

19. *The Copper Era*, 21 April 1994, p. 3. María Aguirre states that the picture was once in the possession of a Urrea family member who gave it to William Curry Holden for his book, *Teresita*. There are fine drawings in Holden's book, but no photographs. The materials he used in preparing the book are now in the Holden Collection at Texas Tech University, Lubbock, Texas, but to date this particular photo has not been discovered in the collection.

20. *The Copper Era*, 7 April 1994, p. 1.

Selected Bibliography

Archival Sources

Archivo de la Comisión Agraria Mixta, Chihuahua City.

Archivo del Estado de Chihuahua, Palacio de Gobierno, Chihuahua City. Notarías, Archivo Histórico, Sección Protocolos, Distrito de Guerrero.

Archivo del Estado de Chihuahua, Palacio de Gobierno, Chihuahua City. Sección Judicial, Archivo Histórico del Corte Supremo.

Archivo de la Secretaría de la Defensa Nacional, Mexico City.

Archivo General de la Nación, Mexico City. Sections: Bienes Nacionalizados, Colonial, Justicia, Gobernación, and Colección Alfredo Robles Domínguez.

Archivo Histórico del Arzobispado de Durango, Durango City.

Archivo Histórico del Estado de Durango, Durango City.

Archivo Histórico del Estado de Jalisco, Guadalajara.

Archivo Histórico del Estado de Sonora, Hermosillo.

Archivo Histórico, Secretaría del Estado y Despacho de Relaciones Exteriores, Mexico City.

Archivo Histórico, Secretaría de la Reforma Agraria, Mexico City.

Archivo Judicial de la Municipalidad de Guerrero, Palacio Municipal, Guerrero City, Chihuahua. Juzgado Menor.

Archivo Municipal de Ciudad Guerrero, Guerrero City.

Archivo Municipal de Hidalgo del Parral, Biblioteca Franklin, Parral, Chihuahua.

Archivo Municipal de Ocampo, Ocampo, Chihuahua.

Archivo Particular del Lic. Hector González y González, Guerrero City.

Archivo Particular del Dr. Rubén Osorio, Chihuahua City.

Archivo Particular del Lic. Abelardo Pérez Campos, Chihuahua City.

Archivo Porfirio Díaz, Universidad Iberoamericana, Mexico City.

Archivo de Protocolos, Palacio Municipal, Guerrero City.

Archivo de la Secretaría de la Defensa Nacional, Mexico City. Sections: Históricos and Cancelados.

Bancroft Collection, University of California, Berkeley.

British Foreign Office, Embassy and Consular Archives, London. Correspondence: Series II, F. O. 204, vol. 207 (1889).

Centro de Información del Estado de Chihuahua, Chihuahua City. Archivo Particular de Francisco Almada.

El Paso Public Library, El Paso, Tex.

Graham County Recorder's Office, Safford, Ariz.

Pimería Alta Historical Society, Nogales, Ariz.

U.S. Army Corps of Engineers, Washington, D.C. Army Map Service, photo survey, 1956–57, Chihuahua.

U.S. Department of State, Washington, D.C. Consular Reports: Guaymas 1889–91; Nuevo Laredo 1871–1906.

U.S. National Archives, Washington, D.C. Military Records Branch, Adjutant General's Office, Record Group 94.

Ventura County Superior Court Records, Ventura, Calif.

Newspapers and Periodicals

American Mining Journal, 1867–68.

Arizona Bulletin (Solomonville, Ariz.), 1900.

Arizona Daily Citizen (Tucson), 1892 and 1896.

Arizona Daily Gazette (Phoenix), 1899 and 1901.

Arizona Daily Star (Tucson), 1892 and 1896.

Arizona Range News [Phoenix?], 1900.

Arizona Silver Belt (Globe, Ariz.), 1892 and 1896.

Arizona Weekly Citizen (Tucson), 1892.

El Atalaya (Nogales, Ariz.), 1892.

Boletín de la Sociedad Chihuahuense de Estudios Históricos, 1938–43.

Boletín de la Sociedad Mexicanade Geografía y Estadística, vol. 5. Mexico City: Imprenta de G. Torres, 1857.

Boletín militar (Mexico City), 1885–92.

Brownsville Daily Herald, 1895 and 1896.

Chicago Times, 1892.

Chicago Tribune, 1896.

The Copper Era (Clifton, Ariz.), 1900–1906 and 1993–94.

El Correo de Chihuahua, 1899.

Denver Evening Post, 1896.

Denver Republican, 1896.

Deseret Weekly (Salt Lake City), 1893–94.

El Diario del hogar (Mexico City), 1890–93.

Diario oficial (Chihuahua), 1887.

El Paso Daily Herald, 1892–99.

El Paso Daily Times, 1892–96 and 1925.

Engineering and Mining Journal, 1881–89.

El Estado de Chihuahua, 1890–91.

El Farral (Chihuahua), 1835.

Graham County Bulletin (Safford, Ariz.), 1895–96.
Graham County Republican [Solomonville, Ariz.?], 1896.
La Idea Libre (Chihuahua), 1899–1901.
La Ilustración espirita (Mexico City), 1890–92.
El Imparcial (Chihuahua), 1871.
El Imparcial (Guaymas), 1891–92.
La Justica (Chihuahua), 1873.
Los Angeles Daily Times, 1903.
Los Angeles Express, 1903.
Los Angeles Record, 1902–3.
Los Angeles Times, 1896, 1902, and 1904.
El Monitor republicano (Mexico City), 1890–92.
New York Herald, 1896.
New York Journal, 1901.
New York Times, 1892–94.
La Oásis (Nogales, Ariz.), 1892 and 1896.
La Opinión (Los Angeles), 1937.
La Patria (El Paso), 1925.
La Patria (Mexico City), 1892.
Phoenix Weekly Herald, 1892.
El Progreso (Chihuahua), 1895–96.
Revista de Chihuahua, 1895.
Rocky Mountain News (Denver), 1896.
San Francisco Bulletin, 1900.
San Francisco Call, 1896, 1900, and 1901.
San Francisco Chronicle, 1892, 1896, and 1900.
San Francisco Examiner, 1896 and 1900.
San Jose Daily Mercury, 1900.
Semanario del estado (Chihuahua), 1875, 1876, and 1881.
El Siglo XX (Chihuahua), 1905.
St. John's Herald (St. John's, Ariz.), 1901.
St. Louis Republic, 1892.
El Tiempo (Las Cruces, N.M.), 1890–92.
El Tiempo (Mexico City), 1892.
The Tombstone Prospector, 1895.
The Tombstone Reporter, 1895.
Tucson Daily Star, 1903.
El Universal (Mexico City), 1893.
Ventura Weekly Free Press (Ventura, Calif.), 1903–4.
La Voz de Arteaga (Chínipas), 1896.
La Voz de México (Mexico City), 1892.
The World (New York), 1901.

General Sources

Adams, Richard N. *Energy and Structure: A Theory of Social Power.* Austin: University of Texas Press, 1975.

Aguirre, Lauro. *Tomochic! Rendición! Revoluciones recientes y futuras de México— Papel y participación en las de— "La Santa de Cabora," "Juana de Arco" mexicana;—y de— "El presidente necessario;" "Héroes—Pilatos" moderno.* El Paso: Imprenta de "El Progresita," 1901.

Alexius, Robert M. "The Army and Politics in Porfirian Mexico." Ph.D diss., University of Texas at Austin, 1976.

Almada, Francisco R. "Los Apaches." *Boletín de la Sociedad Chihuahuense de Estudios Históricos* 2 (2 June 1939): 5–15.

——. *Apuntes históricos de la región de Chínipas.* Chihuahua: n.p., 1937.

——. *Diccionario de historia, geografía y biografía chihuahuenses.* Juárez: Impresa de Juárez, 1968.

——. *Geografía del estado de Chihuahua.* Chihuahua: Impresa Ruiz Sandoval, 1945.

——. *Gobernadores del estado de Chihuahua.* Chihuahua: Centro Librero "La Prensa," 1980.

——. *La Intervención francesa y el imperio en el estado de Chihuahua.* Chihuahua: Ediciones Universidad Autónoma de Chihuahua, 1972.

——. *La Rebelión de Tomochi.* Chihuahua: Talleres Linotipográficos del Gobierno del Estado, 1938.

——. *Resumen de la historia del estado de Chihuahua.* Mexico City: Libros Mexicanos, 1955.

——. *La Revolución en el estado de Chihuahua.* 2 vols. Chihuahua: Biblioteca del Instituto Nacional de Estudios Históricos de la Revolución Mexicana, 1964.

Alonso, Ana María. *Thread of Blood: Colonialism, Revolution, and Gender on Mexico's Northern Frontier.* Tucson: University of Arizona Press, 1995.

Argueta, Manlio. *One Day of Life.* New York: Vintage, 1983.

Audubon, John Woodhouse. *Audubon's Western Journal, 1849–1850.* Tucson: University of Arizona Press, 1984.

Aurrecoechea, Juan Manuel. *México—Historia de un pueblo: Tomochic.* Mexico City: SEP [Secretaría de Educación Pública]/Editorial Nueva Imagen, 1981.

Ayala Blanco, Jorge. *La Condición del cine mexicano (1973–1985).* Mexico City: Editorial Posada, 1986.

Baldwin, Deborah J. *Protestants and the Mexican Revolution: Missionaries, Ministers, and Social Change.* Urbana: University of Illinois Press, 1990.

Barkun, Michael. *Disaster and the Millennium.* New Haven: Yale University Press, 1974.

Bartlett, John Russell. *Personal Narrative of Explorations and Incidents in Texas,*

New Mexico, California, Sonora, and Chihuahua, 1850–1853. 2 vols. Chicago: Rio Grande Press Inc., 1965.

Bastián, Jean-Pierre. *Los Disidentes: Sociedades protestantes y revolución en México, 1872–1911.* Mexico City: Fondo de Cultura Económica, Colegio de México, 1989.

——. "Jacobinismo y ruptura revolucionaria durante el porfiriato." *Mexican Studies/Estudios Mexicanos* 7 (Winter 1991): 29–46.

Beezley, William H. *Judas at the Jockey Club and Other Episodes in Porfirian Mexico.* Lincoln: University of Nebraska Press, 1987.

Beezley, William H., and Colin M. MacLachlan. *El Gran Pueblo: A History of the Mexican Experience.* Fairlawn, N.J.: Prentice-Hall, 1994.

Berdecio, Roberto, and Stanley Applebaum, eds. *Posada's Popular Mexican Prints.* New York: Dover Publications Inc., 1972.

Bourke, John G. "The American Congo." *Scribner's Magazine* 15 (May 1894): 590–610.

——. "Diary of John Gregory Bourke, 20 November 1872–4 March 1895." Microfilm, 10 rolls (124 vols). Ann Arbor, Mich.: Bell and Howell, 1967.

——. "The Miracle Play of the Rio Grande." *Journal of American Folk-Lore* 6 (April–June 1893): 89–95.

——. "Popular Medicine, Customs, and Superstitions of the Rio Grande." *Journal of American Folk-Lore* 7 (April–June 1894): 119–46.

Brand, Donald D. "Historical Geography of Northwestern Chihuahua." Ph.D. diss., University of California, Berkeley, 1933.

——. "The Natural Landscape of Northwestern Chihuahua." *University of New Mexico Bulletin,* n.s. 316 (1937).

Brandes, Ray, and Ralph A. Smith. "The Scalp Business on the Border, 1837–1850." *Smoke Signal* (Fall 1962).

Bricker, Victoria Reifler. *The Indian Christ, the Indian King: The Historical Substrate of Maya Myth and Ritual.* Austin: University of Texas Press, 1981.

Brondo Whitt, E. *Los Patriarcos del Papigochi.* Guerrero: n.p., 1941.

Burridge, Kenelm. *New Heaven, New Earth: A Study of Millenarian Activities.* New York: Schocken Books, 1969.

Bynum, Carolyn Walker. " '. . . And Woman His Humanity': Female Imagery in the Religious Writing of the Late Middle Ages." In *Gender and Religion: On the Complexity of Symbols,* ed. Carolyn Walker Bynum, Steven Harrell, and Paul Richman. Boston: Beacon Press, 1986.

Camp, Roderic A. *Mexico's Leaders: Their Education and Recruitment.* Tucson: University of Arizona Press, 1979.

Cardoza y Aragón, Luis. *José Guadalupe Posada.* Mexico City: Universidad Nacional Autónoma de México, 1963.

Carr, Barry. "Las Peculiaridades del norte mexicano, 1880–1927; Ensayo de interpretación." *Historia mexicana* 3 (January–March 1973): 320–46.

Carta general de la república mexicana formada en el Ministro de Fomento con los datos mas recientes por disposición del Secretario del Ramo, General Carlos Pacheco. Mexico City: Tipográfica del Gobierno, 1890.

Case, Alden Buell. *Thirty Years with the Mexicans: In Peace and Revolution.* New York: Fleming H. Revell, 1917.

Censo y división territorial del estado de Chihuahua. Mexico City: Oficina Tipográfica de la Secretaría de Fomento, 1904.

Chávez, Alicia Hernández, and Manuel Mino Grijalva, coordinators. *Cincuenta años de historia en México: En el cincuentenario del Centro de Estudios Históricos.* 2 vols. Mexico City: El Colegio de México, 1991.

Chávez, Juan Carlos. "Clamor de los Papigochics del siglo xvii por los constantes ataques de los apaches." *Boletín de la Sociedad Chihuahuense de Estudios Históricos.* 1 (15 April 1939): 399–405.

——. "Extinción de los Apaches—Victorio." *Boletín de la Sociedad Chihuahuense de Estudios Históricos* 1 (April 1939): 336–40.

——. *Peleando en Tomochi.* Ciudad Juárez: Imprenta Moderna, 1955.

——. "Peleando en Tomochi." *Boletín de la Sociedad Chihuahuense de Estudios Históricos* 4 (20 January 1943): 314–29; (20 February 1943): 355–71; (20 March 1943): 398–416; (20 April 1943): 437–57; (20 May 1943): 480–504.

Chávez Calderón, Plácido. *La defensa de Tomochi.* Mexico City: Editorial Jus, 1964.

Christian, Jr., William A. *Local Religion in Sixteenth-Century Spain.* Princeton, N.J.: Princeton University Press, 1981.

——. *Person and God in a Spanish Valley.* Princeton, N.J.: Princeton University Press, 1972.

——. *Visions of Moving Crucifixes in Modern Spain.* Princeton, N.J.: Princeton University Press, 1992.

Cockroft, James D. *Intellectual Precursors of the Mexican Revolution, 1900–1913.* Austin: Institute of Latin American Studies, University of Texas, Austin, 1968.

Conde, Pedro García. *Ensayo estadístico sobre el estado de Chihuahua.* Chihuahua: Imprenta del gobierno a cargo de Cayetano Ramos, 1842.

Conger, Robert O. "Porfirio Díaz and the Church Heirarchy, 1876–1911." Ph.D. diss., University of New Mexico, 1985.

Cosío Villegas, Daniel, ed. *Historia moderna de México.* 6 vols. Mexico City: Editorial Hermes, 1955–1970.

Crumrine, N. Ross. *The Mayo Indians of Sonora: A People Who Refuse to Die.* Tucson: University of Arizona Press, 1977.

——. " 'La Tierra te devorará': Un análisis estructural de los mitos de los indígenas mayo." *America Indígena* 3 (1973): 1119–50.

Cuthburtson, Gilbert M. "Catarino Garza and the Garza War." *Texana* 12 (1974): 335–48.

Daniels, Ted. *Millennialism: An International Bibliography.* New York: Garland Publishing, 1992.

Danker, Uwe. "Banditi and the State: Robbers and the Authorities in the Holy Roman Empire in the Late Seventeenth and Early Eighteenth Centuries." In *The German Underworld: Deviants and Outcasts in German History*, ed. Richard J. Evans. London: Routledge, 1991.

Dávila, F. T. *Sonora: Histórico y descriptivo*. Nogales, Ariz.: Tipografía de R. Bernal, 1894.

de la Peña, Moisés T. *Chihuahua económico*. 3 vols. Mexico City: Talleres gráficos de Adrián Morales, 1943.

Depalo, Jr., William A. "The Establishment of the Nueva Vizcaya Militia During the Administration of Theodore de Croix, 1776–1783." *New Mexico Historical Review* 38 (July 1973): 223–49.

Dezan, Suzanne. "The Role of Women in Religious Riots During the French Revolution." *Eighteenth Century Studies* 22 (Spring 1989): 451–68.

Diccionario porrúa: Historia, biografía, y geografía de México. 3 vols. Mexico City: Ediciones Porrúa, 1986.

Direción general de geografía y meteorología; Servicio Meteorológico Nacional, normales, climatológicas, período 1941–1970. Mexico City: 1976.

Domecq de Rodríguez, Brianda. *La Insólita historia de La Santa de Cabora*. Mexico City: Plantea, 1990.

———. "Teresa Urrea: La Santa de Cabora." In *Temas sonorenses: A través de los simposios de historia*. Hermosillo: Gobierno del Estado de Sonora, 1984.

Duffy, Christopher. *Siege Warfare*. 2 vols. London: Routledge and Kegan, 1979–84.

Dunne, Peter Masten. *Early Jesuit Missions in the Tarahumara*. Berkeley: University of California Press, 1948.

———. *Pioneer Jesuits in Northern Mexico*. Los Angeles: University of California Press, 1944.

Edmunds, James, John Prince Sheldon, and Richard Inwards. *Reports Upon the Degollado Territory, State of Chihuahua, Mexico*. London: n.p., 1890.

Escobosa Gámez, Gilberto. "Asalto a la villa de Nogales." *Memoria del xii simposio de historia y antropología de Sonora*. Hemosillo: Gobierno del Estado de Sonora, 1987.

Escudero, José Agustín. *Noticias estadísticas del estado de Chihuahua*. Mexico City: Juan Ojeda, 1834.

———. *Observaciones sobre el estado actual del departamento de Chihuahua y los medios de ponerlo a cubierto de las incursiones de los bárbaros*. Mexico City: Juan Ojeda, 1839.

Falcón, Romana. "La Desaparición de jefes políticos en Coahuila: Una paradoja porfirista." *Historia mexicana* 37 (January–March 1988): 423–67.

———. "Jefes políticos y rebeliones campesinas: Uso y abuso del poder en el estado de México." In *Patterns of Contention in Mexican History*, ed. Jaime Rodríguez. Wilmington, Del.: Scholarly Resources, 1992.

Fields, Karen E. "Charismatic Religion as Popular Protest: The Ordinary and the Extraordinary in Social Movements." *Theory and Society* 11 (1982): 321–61.

———. *Revival and Rebellion in Colonial Africa: Revisions to the Theory of Indirect Rule*. Princeton, N.J.: Princeton University Press, 1985.

Finkler, Kaja. "The Social Consequences of Wellness: A View of Healing Outcomes from the Micro and Macro Perspectives." *International Journal of Health Services* 16 (1986): 627–42.

Flippin, J. R. *Sketches from the Mountains of Mexico*. Cincinnati: Standard Publishing Co., 1889.

Flores, Enrique González. *Chihuahua de la Independencia a la Revolución*. Mexico City: Ediciones Botas, 1949.

Fragmentos del reglamento del Colegio Militar. Mexico City: Imprenta de J. F. Jens, 1895.

Frías, Heriberto. *Tomochic*. Mexico City: Editorial Porrua, 1968.

Frobel, Julius. *Seven Years' Travel in Central America, Northern Mexico, and the Far West of the United States*. London: R. Bentley, 1859.

Fuentes Mares, José. *. . . Y México se refugió en el desierto: Luis Terrazas, Su historia y destino*. Mexico City: Editorial Jus, 1954.

Fussel, Paul. *The Great War and Modern Memory*. New York: Oxford University Press, 1975.

Garza Guajardo, Celso. *En Busca de Catarino Garza, 1859–1895*. Monterrey: Centro de Información de Historia Regional, Universidad Autónoma de Nuevo León, 1989.

Giddings, Ruth Warner. *Yaqui Myths and Legends*. Tucson: University of Arizona Press, 1959.

Gill, Mario. *Cuadernos mexicanos: La Doncella de Cabora*. Mexico City: SEP [Secretaría de Educación Pública]/Conasupo, [1973?].

———. "Teresa Urrea, la santa de Cabora." *Historia mexicana* 6 (April–June 1957): 626–44.

Girón, Nicole. *Heraclio Bernal: Bandolero, cacique o precursor de la Revolución?* Mexico City: Instituto de Antropología e Historia, 1976.

González Dávila, Amado. *Diccionario geografía, histórico, biográfico, estadístico del estado de Sinaloa*. Culiacán: n.p., 1959.

González Ramírez, M., director. *Fuentes para la historia de la revolución mexicana*. 5 vols. Mexico City: Fondo de la Cultura Económica, 1954–59.

Gregg, Josiah. *Commerce of the Prairies*. Ed. Max L. Morehead. Norman: University of Oklahoma Press, 1954.

Griffen, William B. *Apaches at War and Peace: The Janos Presidio, 1750–1858*. Tucson: University of Arizona Press, 1988.

———. *Utmost Good Faith: Patterns of Apache-Mexican Hostilities in Northern Chihuahua Border Warfare, 1821–1843*. Tucson: University of Arizona Press, 1989.

Griffith, James S. *Beliefs and Holy Places: A Spiritual Geography of the Pimería Alta.* Tucson: University of Arizona Press, 1992.

Gutiérrez, Eugenio. *Rasgos biográficos del general de brigada Juan A. Hernández, jefe de la octava zona militar.* Oaxaca: Imprenta de Julián A. Soto, 1909.

Gutiérrez, Ramón A. *When Jesus Came, the Corn Mothers Went Away: Marriage, Sexuality, and Power in New Mexico, 1500–1846.* Stanford, Calif.: Stanford University Press, 1991.

Haber, Stephen H. *Industry and Underdevelopment: The Industrialization of Mexico.* Stanford. Calif.: Stanford University Press, 1989.

Hale, Charles A. *Mexican Liberalism in the Age of Mora, 1821–1853.* New Haven: Yale University Press, 1968.

——. *The Transformation of Liberalism in Late Nineteenth-Century Mexico.* Princeton, N.J.: Princeton University Press, 1989.

Hardy, Blaine Carmon. "The Mormon Colonies of Northern Mexico: A History, 1885–1912." Ph.D. diss., Wayne State University, 1963.

Hess, David J. *Spiritists and Scientists: Ideology, Spiritism, and Brazilian Culture.* University Park: Pennsylvania State University Press, 1991.

Holden, William Curry. *Teresita.* Owings Mills, Md.: Stemmer House, 1978.

Holden, William H. *Mexico and the Survey of Public Lands: The Management of Modernization, 1876–1911.* DeKalb: Northern Illinois University Press, 1994.

Hu-DeHart, Evelyn. *Yaqui Resistance and Survival: The Struggle for Land and Autonomy, 1821–1910.* Madison: University of Wisconsin Press, 1984.

Hudson, William M. *The Healer of Los Olmos and Other Mexican Lore.* Dallas: Southern Methodist University Press, 1951.

Illades Aguiar, Lilián. *La Rebelión de Tomóchic.* Mexico City: Instituto Nacional de Antropología y Historia, 1993.

Informes que los gobernadores del estado de Chihuahua han presentado ante el Congreso del mismo, desde el año 1849 hasta el de 1906. Chihuahua: Imprenta del Gobierno, 1910.

Irrab, Noel. "Efemérides chihuahuenses." *Boletín de la Sociedad Chihuahuense de Estudios Históricos* (1938–40).

Johnson, Richard, Gregor Mclennan, Bill Schwartz, and David Sutton, eds. *Making Histories: Studies in History-Writing and Politics.* Minneapolis: University of Minnesota Press, 1982.

Krantz, Frederick, ed. *History from Below: Studies in Popular Protest and Popular Ideology.* Oxford: Basil Blackwell, 1988.

Kselman, Thomas A. *Death and the Afterlife in Modern France.* Princeton, N.J.: Princeton University Press, 1993.

——. *Miracles and Prophecies in Nineteenth-Century France.* New Brunswick, N.J.: Rutgers University Press, 1983.

Larralde, Carlos. "Santa Teresa, a Chicana Mystic." In *Grito el Sol*. Berkeley, Calif.: Tonatiuh International, 1978.

León-Portilla, Miguel. *Endangered Cultures*. Trans. Julie Goodson-Laws. Dallas: Southern Methodist University Press, 1990.

——. "The Norteño Variety of Mexican Culture: An Ethnohistorical Approach." In *Plural Society in the Southwest*, ed. Edward H. Spicer and Raymond H. Thompson. New York: Interbook, 1972.

Levine, Robert M. *Images of History: Nineteenth- and Early Twentieth-Century Latin American Photographs*. Durham, N.C.: Duke University Press, 1989.

——. *Vale of Tears: Revisiting the Canudos Massacre in Northeastern Brazil, 1893–1897*. Berkeley: University of California Press, 1992.

Lewis, I. M. *Ecstatic Religion: An Anthropological Study of Spirit Possession and Shamanism*. Harmondsworth, U.K.: Penguin Books, 1971.

Ley de clasificar, juzgar, y sentenciar el delito de abigeato. Chihuahua: Imprenta del Gobierno, 1880.

Ley reglamentaria de la instrucción pública del estado. Chihuahua: Imprenta del Gobierno, 1890.

Lloyd, Jane-Dale. *El Proceso de modernización del noroeste de Chihuahua, 1880–1910*. Mexico City: Universidad Iberoamericana, 1987.

——. "Rancheros and Rebellion: The Case of Northwestern Chihuahua." In *Rural Revolt in Mexico and U.S. Intervention*, ed. Daniel Nugent. La Jolla.: University of California, San Diego, 1988.

López-Portillo y Rojas, José. *Elevación y caída de Porfirio Díaz*. Mexico City: Librería Español, 1921.

Luhrmann, Tayna M. *Persuasions of the Witch's Craft: Ritual Magic in Contemporary England*. Cambridge, Mass.: Harvard University Press, 1989.

Lumholz, Carl. *Unknown Mexico: A Record of Five Years Exploration among the Tribes of the Western Sierra Madre*. 2 vols. Glorieta, N.M.: Rio Grande Press, 1973.

McDannell, Colleen, and Bernhard Lang. *Heaven: A History*. New Haven: Yale University Press, 1988.

Mack, Phyllis. "Women as Prophets During the English Civil War." *Feminist Studies* 8 (Spring 1982): 19–45.

Macklin, Barbara June. "Folk Saints, Healers, and Spiritist Cults in Northern Mexico." *Revista Interamericana Review* 3 (Winter 1974): 351–67.

——. "Santos folklóricos, curanderismo y cultos espiritistas en México: Elección divina y social." *Anuario indigenista* 34 (December 1974): 195–214.

Macklin, Barbara June, and Ross Crumrine. "Three North Mexican Folk Saint Movements." *Comparative Studies in Society and History* 15 (January 1973): 89–105.

Márquez Terrazas, Zacarías. *Chihuahuenses egregios*. 2 vols. Chihuahua: Editorial Camino, 1985.

Memoria de la administración pública del estado de Chihuahua . . . Col. Miguel Ahumada. Chihuahua: Imprenta del Gobierno, 1896.

Menchú, Rigoberta. *I, Rigoberta Menchú: An Indian Woman in Guatemala*. London: Verso, 1983.

Merrill, William L. *Rarámuri Souls: Knowledge and Social Process in Northern Mexico*. Washington, D.C.: Smithsonian Institution Press, 1988.

Migdal, Joel S. *Peasants, Politics, and Revolution: Pressures Toward Political and Social Change in the New World*. Princeton, N.J.: Princeton University Press, 1974.

"The Mines of Santa Eulalia." *Harper's New Monthly Magazine* 35 (November 1867): 681–702.

Mirandé, Alfredo, and Evangelina Enríquez. *La Chicana: Mexican-American Women*. Chicago: University of Chicago Press, 1979.

Navarro Burciaga, José Luis. "Catarino Garza, periodista opositar a Porfirio Díaz en Tamaulipas." In *Porfirio Díaz frente al descontento popular regional, (1891–1893)*, ed. Friedrich Katz; Jane-Dale Lloyd, coordinator. Mexico City: Universidad Iberoamericana, 1986.

Naylor, Thomas H., and Charles W. Polzer, eds. *The Presidio and the Militia in Northern New Spain, 1570–1700*. Tucson: University of Arizona Press, 1986.

Neale, Walter C. *Monies in Societies*. San Francisco: Chandler and Sharp Publishers, 1976.

Nolan, Mary Lee, and Sidney Nolan. *Christian Pilgrimage in Modern Western Europe*. Chapel Hill: University of North Carolina Press, 1989.

Normales climatológicas: Período 1941–1970. Mexico City: Servicio Meteorológico Nacional, Dirección General de Geografía y Meteorología, 1976.

Nueva colección de leyes del estado formado por la comisión al efecto con arreglo de decreto de enero de 1868 . . . . Chihuahua: Imprenta del Gobierno, 1868.

Nugent, Daniel. *Spent Cartridges of Revolution: An Anthropological History of Namiquipa, Chihuahua*. Chicago: University of Chicago Press, 1993.

O. de Rico, Ursula [pseudonym for Rubén Osorio]. "Documentos para la historia de Tomochic." Manuscripts, 1994.

Ortiz Figueroa, Jesús. "El Papel de la fuerza rural en la política del porfiriato, 1880–1888." Paper presented at the Annual Conference of the Pacific Coast Council on Latin American Studies, Mexicali, Mexico, 20 October 1988.

Osorio, Rubén. *Tomóchic en llamas*. Mexico City: Consejo Nacional para la Cultura y las Artes, 1995.

Painter, Muriel Thayer. *With Good Heart: Yaqui Beliefs and Ceremonies in a Pascua Village*. Tucson: University of Arizona Press, 1986.

Parker, Morris B. *Mules, Mines and Me, 1895–1932*. Tucson: University of Arizona Press, 1979.

Parry, Jonathan, and Maurice Block, eds. *Money and Morality of Exchange*. Cambridge, Eng.: Cambridge University Press, 1989.

Paso y Troncoso, Francisco P. *Las Guerras con las tribus Yaqui y Mayo.* Mexico: Instituto Nacional Indigenista, 1977.

——. *Relaciones del Siglo XVII relativas a Chihuahua: Sorocahui y otros pueblos. M.s. encontrados y coleccionados por F. del Paso y Troncoso en los archivos de la Real Academia de Historia de Madrid y del Archivo de Indias de Sevilla,* ed. Vargas Rea. Mexico City: Biblioteca de Historiadores Mexicanos, 1950.

Los Pastores: A Mexican Play of the Nativity. Trans. M. R. Cole. Boston: For American Folk-Lore Society by Houghton-Mifflin, 1907.

Peck, A. M. "In Memory of Man." Manuscript, Pimería Alta Historical Society Library (Nogales, Ariz.).

Pessar, Patricia R. "Masking the Politics of Religion: The Case of Brazilian Millenarianism." *Journal of Latin American Lore* 7 (Winter 1981): 255–77.

Ponce de León, José María. "Los Antiguos minerales o reales de minas, el mineral de Uruáchic." *Revista Chihuahuense* (30 April 1909): 1–3.

——. *Datos geográficos y estadísticas del estado de Chihuahua.* Chihuahua: Imprenta del Gobierno, 1907.

Porras Muñoz, Guillermo. *La Frontera con los indios de Nueva Vizcaya en el siglo XVII.* Mexico City: Fomento Cultural de Banamex, 1980.

——. *Iglesia y estado en Nueva Vizcaya (1562–1821).* Mexico City: Universidad Nacional Autónoma de México, 1980.

Pozo Marrero, Acalia. "Dos Movimientos populares en el noroeste de Chihuahua: Tomochic y La Ascención, 1891–1892." M.A. thesis, Universidad Iberoamericana, 1991.

Powell, T. G. "Mexican Intellectuals and the Indian Question, 1876–1911." *Hispanic American Historical Review* 38 (February 1968): 19–36.

Putnam, Frank Bishop. "Teresa Urrea, 'The Santa de Cabora.'" *Southern California Quarterly* 45 (September 1963): 245–64.

Raat, Dirk W. *Revoltosos: Mexico's Rebels in the United States, 1903–1923.* College Station: Texas A & M University Press, 1981.

Rappaport, Joanne. *Cumbe Reborn: An Andean Ethnography of History.* Chicago: Chicago University Press, 1994.

——. *The Politics of Memory: Native Historical Interpretation in the Colombian Highlands.* Cambridge, Eng.: Cambridge University Press, 1994.

Ready, Alma. *Open Range and Hidden Silver.* Nogales, Ariz.: Alto Press, 1973.

Reglamento para el ejercicio y maniobras de la infantería. 2 vols. Mexico City: Secretaría de Guerra y Marina, Talleres de E. M. General de Ejército, 1914.

Remington, Frederick. *Pony Tracks.* New York: Harper and Brothers Publishers, 1899.

Ridgeway, William R. "Saint or Nurse? Arizona Historian Relates Poignant Story of Beauteous Teresa Urrea." *Arizona Days and Ways (Arizona Republic* magazine section), 27 September 1953, pp. 17–20.

Rodríguez, Richard, and Gloria L. Rodríguez. "Teresa Urrea: Her Life as It

Affected the Mexican-U.S. Frontier." *Voices: Readings from "El Grito,"* *1967–1973.* Berkeley: Quinto Sol.

Rojas Rabiela, T., coordinator, and J. L. Ramos, J. Chávez, A. Escobar, C. Sheridan, and R. Tranquilo. *El indio en la prensa nacional mexicana del siglo xix: Catálogo de noticias.* 3 vols. Mexico City: Centro de Investigacions y Estudios Superiores en Antropología Social, Universidad Autónoma de México, Cuadernos de la Casa Chata, No. 137, Secretaría de Educación Pública, 1987.

Romano, Octavio. "Don Pedrito Jaramillo, the Emergence of a Mexican-American Folk Saint." Ph.D. diss., University of California, Berkeley, 1964.

Saborit, Antonio. *Los Doblados de Tomóchic: Un episodio de historia y literatura.* Mexico City: Cal y Arena, 1994.

Saldivar, Gabriel. *Documentos de la rebelión de Catarino E. Garza en la frontera de Tamaulipas y sur de Texas, 1891–1892.* Mexico City: n.p., 1943.

Santleben, August. *A Texas Pioneer: Early Staging and Overland Freighting Days in the Frontiers of Texas and Mexico.* New York: Neale Publishing, 1910.

Sauer, Carl O. *Aboriginal Population of Northwestern Mexico.* Ibero-Americana Series, no. 10. Berkeley: University of California Press, 1935.

Schmitt, Karl M. "Catholic Adjustment to the Secular State: The Case of Mexico, 1867–1911." *Catholic Historical Review* 48 (July 1962): 182–204.

———. "The Díaz Conciliation Policy on State and Local Levels, 1876–1911." *Hispanic American Historical Review* 15 (November 1960): 513–32.

Scott, James C. *Domination and the Arts of Resistance.* New Haven: Yale University Press, 1990.

———. *Weapons of the Weak: Everyday Forms of Peasant Resistance.* New Haven: Yale University Press, 1985.

Shepherd, Grant. *The Silver Magnet: Fifty Years in a Mexican Silver Mine.* New York: E. P. Dutton and Co., Inc., 1938.

Sheridan, Thomas E., and Thomas A. Naylor, eds. *Rarámuri: A Tarahumara Colonial Document, 1607–1791.* Flagstaff, Ariz.: Northland Press, 1979.

Sinkin, Richard N. *The Mexican Reform, 1855–1876: A Study in Liberal Nation-Building.* Austin, Tex.: Institute of Latin American Studies, 1979.

Smith, Ralph A. "Apache Plunder Trails Southward, 1831–1840." *New Mexico Historical Review* 37 (January 1962): 20–42.

———. "The Scalp Hunters in the Borderlands, 1835–1850." *Arizona and the West* 6 (Spring 1964): 5–22.

———. "The Scalp Hunt in Chihuahua." *New Mexico Historical Review* 40 (April 1965): 116–40.

Spicer, Edward H. "Contrasting Forms of Nativism Among the Mayos and Yaquis of Sonora, Mexico." In *The Social Anthropology of Latin America: Essays in Honor of Ralph Leon Beals,* ed. Walter Goldschmidt and Harry Hoijer. Los Angeles: Latin American Center, University of California, Los Angeles, 1970.

———. *Cycles of Conquest: The Impact of Spain, Mexico, and the United States on the Indians of the Southwest, 1533–1960*. Tucson: University of Arizona Press, 1962.

———. *The Yaquis: A Cultural History*. Tucson: University of Arizona Press, 1980.

Stephen, Michele, "Culture, the Self, and the Autonomous Image." Paper presented at the meeting of the American Anthropological Association, Philadelphia, 1986.

———. "Self, the Sacred Other, and Autonomous Imagination." In *The Religious Imagination in New Guinea*, ed. Gilbert Herdt and Michele Stephen. New Brunswick, N.J.: Rutgers University Press, 1989.

Tamarón y Romeral, Pedro. *Demostración del vastísimo obispado de la Nueva Vizcaya—1765*. Ed. Vito Alessio Robles. Mexico City: José Porrúa e Hijos, 1937.

Terrazas, Silvestre. "El Gran Sabio y santo Padre Glandorff en Chihuahua." *Boletín de la Sociedad Chihuahuense de Estudios Históricos* 2 (July 1940): 375–77; 3 (October–December 1940): 408–11.

———. "Mineral que produce mas de 80 milliones en oro." *Boletín de la Sociedad Chihuahuense de Estudios Históricos* 2 (15 October 1939): 200–202ff.

"They Raided Nogales: Santa Teresa and the Mexican Insurrection of 1896." *True West*, March 1989, pp. 52–57.

Valadés, José C. *Porfirio Díaz contra el gran poder de Dios: Las Rebeliones de Tomochic y Temósachic*. Mexico City: Ediciones Leega Júcar, 1985.

Vanderwood, Paul J. *Disorder and Progress: Bandits, Police, and Mexican Development*. Wilmington, Del.: Scholarly Resources, 1992.

———. "Using the Present to Study the Past: Religious Movements in Mexico and Uganda a Century Apart." *Mexican Studies/Estudios mexicanos* 10 (Winter 1994): 99–134.

Van Young, Eric. "Agustín Marroquín: The Sociopath as Rebel." In *The Human Tradition in Latin America: The Nineteenth Century*, ed. Judith Ewell and William H. Beezley. Wilmington, Del.: Scholarly Resources, 1989.

———. "The Cuautla Lazarus: Double Subjectives in Reading Texts on Popular Collective Action." *Colonial Latin American Review* 2 (1993): 3–26.

———. *Hacienda and Market in Eighteenth-Century Mexico: The Rural Economy of the Guadalajara Region, 1675–1820*. Berkeley: University of California Press, 1981.

———. "The Other Rebellion: Popular Violence and Ideology in Mexico, 1810–1816." Manuscript in preparation.

———. "Millennium on the Northern Marches: The Mad Messiah of Durango and Popular Rebellion in Mexico, 1800–1805." *Comparative Studies in Society and History* 28 (1986): 385–413.

——. " 'The Raw and the Cooked': Popular and Elite Ideology in Mexico, 1800–1821." In *The Middle Period in Latin American History: Values and Attitudes in the Eighteenth and Nineteenth Centuries*, ed. Mark D. Szuchman. Boulder, Colo.: Lynne Rienner Publishers, 1989.

——. "The State as Vampire: Hegemonic and Popular Culture in Mexico, 1600–1900." In *Rituals of Rule, Rituals of Resistance: Public Celebration and Popular Culture in Mexico*, ed. William H. Beezley, Cheryl E. Martin, and William E. French. Wilmington, Del.: Scholarly Resources Press, 1994.

——, ed. *Mexico's Regions: Comparative History and Development*. La Jolla: Center for U.S.-Mexican Studies, University of California, San Diego, 1992.

Vargas Valdez, Jesús, ed. *Tomóchic: La revolución adelantada: Resistencia y lucha de un pueblo de Chihuahua contra el sistema porfirista (1891–1892)*. 2 vols. Juarez: Universidad Autónoma de Ciudad Juárez, 1994.

Vinson, Mark C. "Vanished Clifton/Morensi: An Architect's Perspective." *Journal of Arizona History* 33 (Summer 1992): 183–206.

Warren, Donald, Jr. "Spiritism in Brazil." *Journal of Inter-American Affairs* 10 (July 1968): 393–405.

Wasserman, Mark. *Capitalists, Caciques, and Revolution: The Native Elite and Foreign Enterprise in Chihuahua, Mexico, 1854–1911*. Chapel Hill: University of North Carolina Press, 1984.

——. *Persistent Oligarchs: Elites and Politics in Chihuahua, Mexico, 1910–1940*. Durham, N.C.: Duke University Press, 1993.

Weber, Eugen. *Peasants into Frenchmen: The Modernization of Rural France, 1870–1914*. Stanford, Calif.: Stanford University Press, 1976.

Willson, Roscoe G. "Deluded Yaquis Invade Town Under Order of Witch." *Arizona Days and Ways* (*Arizona Republic* magazine section) 10 March 1957, pp. 22–23.

Woodbridge, Bradford. "Santa Teresa." *Overland Monthly* (October 1896): 422–27.

Wrightson, Keith. *English Society, 1580–1680*. New Brunswick, N.J.: Rutgers University Press, 1982.

Yeager, Gene. "Porfirian Commercial Propaganda: Mexico in World Expositions." *The Americas* 34 (October 1977): 230–43.

Index

In this index an "f" after a number indicates a separate reference on the next page, and an "ff" indicates separate references on the next two pages. A continuous discussion over two or more pages is indicated by a span of page numbers, e.g., "57–59." *Passim* is used for a cluster of references in close but not consecutive sequence.

Library of Congress Cataloging-in-Publication Data

Vanderwood, Paul J.
    The power of God against the guns of government : religious upheaval
in Mexico at the turn of the nineteenth century / Paul J. Vanderwood.
        p.   cm.
    Includes bibliographical references and index.
    ISBN 0-8047-3038-5 (alk. paper). — ISBN 0-8047-3039-3 (pbk. :
alk. paper)
        1. Tomochic (Mexico)—Church history—19th century.   2. Tomochic
(Mexico)—Religion.   3. Church and state—Mexico—Tomochic.
4. Tomochic (Mexico)—History—19th century.   5. Government,
Resistance to—Mexico—Tomochic—History—19th century.   6. Urrea,
Teresa.   I. Title.
    BR615.T65V36   1998
    972'.16—dc21   97-32506

This book is printed on acid-free, recycled paper.

Original printing 1998